Microsoft

D0897421

Step by Step

Microsoft®
Project
Version 2002

Microsoft Office Family Member

Carl Chatfield, PMP
Timothy Johnson, MCP

PUBLISHED BY
Microsoft Press
A Division of Microsoft Corporation
One Microsoft Way
Redmond, Washington 98052-6399

Library of Congress Cataloging-in-Publication Data
Chatfield, Carl S., 1964-
   Microsoft Project Version 2002 Step by Step / Carl Chatfield, Timothy Johnson.
      p. cm.
   Includes index.
   ISBN 0-7356-1301-X
   1. Microsoft Project 2000--Handbooks, manuals, etc. 2. Project
management--Computer programs--Handbooks, manuals, etc. I. Johnson, Timothy,
1962-. II. Title.

   HD69.P75 C466 2002
   658.4'04'02855369--dc21   2002141576

Printed and bound in the United States of America.

5 6 7 8 9   QWT   7 6 5 4 3

Distributed in Canada by H.B. Fenn and Company Ltd.

A CIP catalogue record for this book is available from the British Library.

Microsoft Press books are available through booksellers and distributors worldwide. For further information about international editions, contact your local Microsoft Corporation office or contact Microsoft Press International directly at fax (425) 936-7329. Visit our Web site at www.microsoft.com/mspress. Send comments to *mspinput@microsoft.com*.

Acquisitions Editor: Kong Cheung
Project Editor: Jenny Moss Benson

Body Part No. X08-06243

Contents

3: Setting Up Resources   42

4: Assigning Resources to Tasks   56

5: Formatting and Printing Your Plan   70

6: Tracking Progress on Tasks   88

Part 2   Managing a Complex Project

7: Fine-Tuning Task Details   102

8: Fine-Tuning Resource and Assignment Details   130

9: Fine-Tuning the Project Plan   146

Part 3   Special Subjects

Part 4   Appendices

What's New in Microsoft Project 2002

You'll notice some changes as soon as you start Microsoft Project 2002. The toolbars and menu bar have a new look, and there's a new Project Guide assistance system on the left side of your screen. But the features that are new or greatly improved in this version of Microsoft Project go beyond just changes in appearance. Some changes won't be apparent to you until you start using the program.

To help you quickly identify features that are new or greatly enhanced with this version, this book uses the icon in the margin whenever those features are discussed or shown. If you want to learn about only the new features of the program, you can skim through the book, completing only those topics that show this icon.

The following table lists the new features that you might be interested in, as well as the chapters in which those features are discussed.

To learn how to	Using this new feature	See
Find information in the Microsoft Project online Help	Ask A Question box	Chapter 1, page 7
Use task panes for common activities such as opening files	Task pane	Chapter 1, page 7
Get wizard-like assistance in performing common tasks	Project Guide	Chapter 1, page 9
Change the results of some common actions in Microsoft Project	Smart Tags	Chapter 4, page 64
Save up to 11 sets of baseline data in a single project plan	Multiple baselines	Chapter 6, page 91
Adjust the upper, middle, and lower tiers of the timescale	Three-tiered timescale	Chapter 9, page 151
Include row and column totals when printing usage views	Row and column totals	Chapter 9, page 163
Export structured data from Microsoft Project to a different format	Export Wizard	Chapter 12, page 211
Control how completed and uncompleted segments of a task are scheduled around the status date	Reschedule around status date	Chapter 14, page 255

To learn how to	Using this new feature	See
See related earned value indicators on their own tables	Schedule and Cost Earned Value Tables	Chapter 19, page 339
Use additional earned value schedule indicators	SV%, SPI	Chapter 19, page 340
Use additional earned value cost indicators	CV%, CPI, EAC, TCPI	Chapter 19, page 342
Enter whatever percent complete value you want for tasks when doing earned value analysis	Physical percent complete	Chapter 19, page 343

Tip

To see a more complete list of new and improved features in Microsoft Project, type **What's new?** into the **Ask A Question** box in the upper right corner of the Microsoft Project window.

Getting Help

Every effort has been made to ensure the accuracy of this book and the contents of its CD-ROM. If you do run into problems, please contact the appropriate source for help and assistance:

Getting Help with This Book and Its CD-ROM

If your question or issue concerns the content of this book or its companion CD-ROM, please first search the online Microsoft Knowledge Base, which provides support information for known errors in or corrections to this book, at the following Web site:

http://www.microsoft.com/mspress/support/search.asp

If you do not find your answer at the online Knowledge Base, send your comments or questions to Microsoft Press Technical Support at:

mspinput@microsoft.com

Getting Help with Microsoft Project 2002

If your question is about a Microsoft software product, including Microsoft Project, and not about the content of this Microsoft Press book, please search the Microsoft Knowledge Base at:

http://support.microsoft.com/directory

In the United States, Microsoft software product support issues not covered by the Microsoft Knowledge Base are addressed by Microsoft Product Support Services. The Microsoft software support options available from Microsoft Product Support Services are listed at:

http://support.microsoft.com/directory

Outside the United States, for support information specific to your location, please refer to the Worldwide Support menu on the Microsoft Product Support Services Web site for the site specific to your country:

http://support.microsoft.com/directory

Tip

You can also type your question into the **Ask A Question** box in the upper right corner of the Microsoft Project window to search Microsoft Project online Help.

Using the Book's CD-ROM

The CD-ROM inside the back cover of this book contains all the practice files you'll use as you work through the exercises in the book. By using practice files, you won't waste time creating sample project plans—instead, you can jump right in and concentrate on learning how to use Microsoft Project 2002.

Important

This book also contains a trial version of the Microsoft Project 2002 Standard software. This software is fully functional, but it expires 60 days after you install it. You can use it to complete the chapters in this book if you want. However, you should not install the trial version if you have already installed the full version of either Microsoft Project 2002 Standard or Professional edition.

System Requirements

The chapters in this book were written with the assumption that you can run Microsoft Project Standard at a minimum, and the following system requirements apply to Microsoft Project Standard. You can also complete the chapters of this book using Microsoft Project Professional, or either Standard or Professional edition with Microsoft Project Server. Microsoft Project Professional and Microsoft Project Server have different system requirements than Microsoft Project Standard.

To use this book, you will need:

Computer/Processor

Computer with a Pentium 133-megahertz (MHz) or higher processor

Memory

RAM requirements depend on the operating system used:

- Windows 98 or Windows 98 Second Edition
  24 MB of RAM plus an additional 32 MB of RAM for Microsoft Project

- Windows Me, or Microsoft Windows NT 4.0
  32 MB of RAM for the operating system plus an additional 32 MB of RAM for Microsoft Project

- Windows 2000
  64 MB of RAM for the operating system plus an additional 32 MB of RAM for Microsoft Project

- Windows XP
  128 MB of RAM for the operating system plus an additional 32 MB of RAM for Microsoft Project

Hard Disk

Hard disk space requirements will vary depending on configuration; custom installation choices may require more or less hard disk space.

- 105 MB of available hard disk space is required for the typical installation of Microsoft Project, with 70 MB on the hard disk where the operating system is installed.

- 55 MB for typical installation on a system with Office XP installed. 310 MB for a full installation on system without Office XP installed. Users without Windows XP, Windows 2000, Windows Me, Office XP, Office 2000 SR-1, or Microsoft Project 2000 will require an extra 50 MB of hard disk space for System Files Update.

Operating System

Microsoft Windows 98, Windows 98 Second Edition, Windows Millennium Edition (Windows Me), Windows NT 4.0 with Service Pack 6 or later, Windows 2000, or Windows XP or later operating system

Drive

CD-ROM drive

Display

Super VGA (800 × 600) or higher-resolution monitor with 256 colors

Peripherals

Microsoft Mouse, Microsoft IntelliMouse, or compatible pointing device

Software Requirement

Microsoft Internet Explorer 5.01 or later (Internet Explorer 5.5 or later recommended)

Installing the Practice Files

You need to install the practice files on your hard disk before you use them in the chapters' exercises. Follow these steps to prepare the CD's files for your use:

1 Insert the CD-ROM into the CD-ROM drive of your computer.

A starting menu appears.

Important

If the starting menu does not appear, start Windows Explorer. In the left pane, locate the icon for your CD-ROM and click this icon. In the right pane, double-click the file named *StartCd*.

2 Click Install Practice Files.

3 Click OK in the initial message box to open the Select Options box.

4 If you want to install the practice files to a location other than the default folder (C:\ProjectSBS), click the Change Folder button, select the new drive and path, and then click OK.

5 Click the Continue button to install the practice files.

6 After the practice files have been installed, click OK.

Within the installation folder (C:\ProjectSBS) are subfolders for each chapter.

7 Remove the CD-ROM from the CD-ROM drive, and return it to the envelope at the back of the book.

Using the Practice Files

Each chapter's introduction lists the files that are needed for that chapter and explains any file preparation that you need to take care of before you start working through the chapter.

Chapter	Folder	Files
1	Chapter 1 Getting Started	(no practice file)
2	Chapter 2 Simple Tasks	Wingtip Toys Commercial 2a
3	Chapter 3 Simple Resources	Wingtip Toys Commercial 3a
4	Chapter 4 Simple Assignments	Wingtip Toys Commercial 4a
5	Chapter 5 Simple Formatting	Wingtip Toys Commercial 5a, Logo
6	Chapter 6 Simple Tracking	Wingtip Toys Commercial 6a
7	Chapter 7 Complex Tasks	Short Film Project 7a
8	Chapter 8 Complex Resources and Assignments	Short Film Project 8a
9	Chapter 9 Complex Plan	Short Film Project 9a
10	Chapter 10 Complex Formatting	Short Film Project 10a
11	Chapter 11 Printing	Short Film Project 11a
12	Chapter 12 Publishing Online	Short Film Project 12a
13	Chapter 13 Sharing	Short Film Project 13a, Letter to Client, Sample Task List
14	Chapter 14 Complex Tracking	Short Film Project 14a, Short Film Project 14b, Short Film Project 14c, Short Film Project 14d
15	Chapter 15 Reporting Status	Short Film Project 15a
16	Chapter 16 Getting Back on Track	Short Film Project 16a
17	Chapter 17 Advanced Formatting	Parnell Film 17a
18	Chapter 18 Customizing	Parnell Aerospace Promo 18a, Wingtip Toys Commercial 18b
19	Chapter 19 Earned Value	Short Film Project 19a
20	Chapter 20 Consolidating	Wingtip Toys Commercial 20a, Parnell Aerospace Promo 20b

Uninstalling the Practice Files

After you finish working through this book, you should uninstall the practice files to free up hard disk space:

1 On the Windows taskbar, click the Start button, and then click Control Panel (if you're using Windows XP), or point to Settings, and then click Control Panel (if you're using Windows 2000).

2 Double-click the Add or Remove Programs icon.

3 Click Project SBS Practice, and then click Change/Remove.

4 Click Yes when the confirmation dialog box appears.

Important

If you need additional help installing or uninstalling the practice files, please see the section "Getting Help" earlier in this book. Microsoft's product support does not provide support for this book, the CD-ROM, or the evaluation software.

Installing the Evaluation Software

This book's CD-ROM contains a 60-day trial version of Microsoft Project 2002 Standard.

Tip

The trial included on this CD is in English. To find information about Microsoft Project 2002 trial availability in your country or region, visit the Microsoft Office Sites Worldwide Web page: *http://www.microsoft.com/office/worldwide.htm*

Instructions for Installation

1 Insert the CD-ROM into the CD-ROM drive of your computer.

A starting menu appears.

2 Close any Windows programs that are running

3 Click Install Microsoft Project Trial

The installation wizard will walk you through the setup.

Conventions and Features

You can save time when you use this book by understanding how the Step by Step series shows special instructions, keys to press, buttons to click, and so on.

Convention	Meaning
1 **2**	Numbered steps guide you through hands-on exercises in each topic.
●	A round bullet indicates an exercise that has only one step.
FileName 	Practice files that you'll need to use in a chapter are shown above the CD icon.
new in **Project** 2002	This icon indicates a new or greatly improved feature in this version of Microsoft Project.
Tip	This section provides a helpful hint or shortcut that makes working through a task easier.
Important	This section points out information that you need to know to complete the procedure.
Save 	The first time a button is referenced in a topic, a picture of the button appears in the margin area with a label.
Bold type	Text that you are supposed to type appears in bold type in the procedures.
Bold italic type	Terms that are explained in the glossary at the end of the book are shown in blue bold italic type within the chapter.

Managing a Simple Project

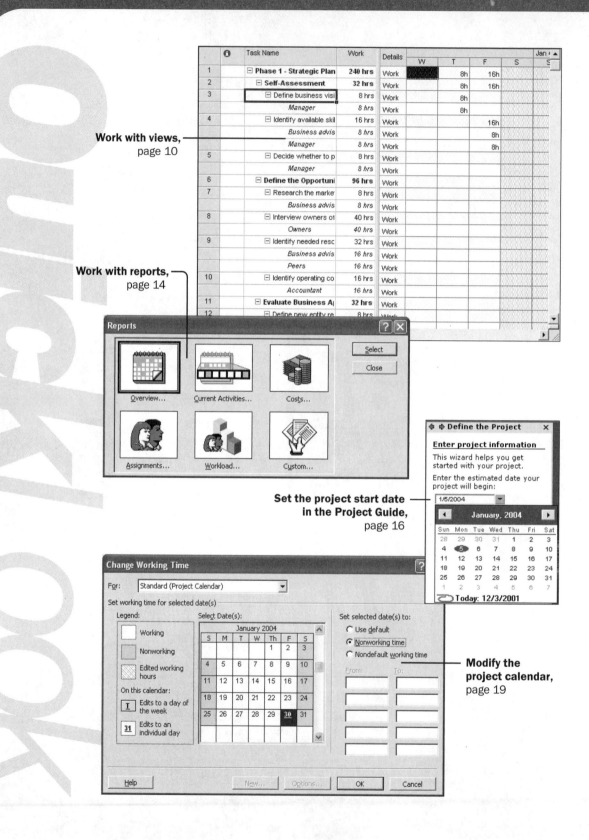

Work with views,
page 10

Work with reports,
page 14

**Set the project start date
in the Project Guide,**
page 16

**Modify the
project calendar,**
page 19

Chapter 1
Getting Started with Microsoft Project

After completing this chapter, you will be able to:

✔ **Understand the family of Microsoft Project 2002 products.**

✔ **Understand what a good project management tool can help you do.**

✔ **Start Microsoft Project and identify the major parts of the Microsoft Project window.**

✔ **Use views to work with project plan details in different ways.**

✔ **Use reports to print project plan details.**

✔ **Create a project plan and enter a project start date.**

✔ **Set the working and nonworking time for a project.**

✔ **Enter a project plan's properties.**

Project management is a broadly practiced art and science. If you're reading this book, there's a good chance that either you're seriously involved in project management, or you want to be.

At its heart, project management is a toolbox of skills and tools that help you predict and control the outcomes of endeavors your organization undertakes. Your organization might do other work apart from projects. *Projects* (such as a film project) are distinct from *ongoing operations* (such as payroll services) in that projects are temporary endeavors undertaken to create some sort of unique deliverable or end result. With a good project management system in place, you should be able to answer such questions as:

■ What *tasks* must be done to produce the *deliverable* of the project?

■ Who will complete these tasks?

■ What's the best way to communicate project details to people who have an interest in the project?

■ When should each task be performed?

■ How much will it cost?

■ What if some tasks are not completed as scheduled?

Good project management does not guarantee the success of every project, but poor project management usually guarantees failure.

Microsoft Project should be one of the most frequently used tools in your project management toolbox. This book explains how to use Microsoft Project to build project plans complete with tasks and resources, use the extensive formatting features in Microsoft Project to organize and format the project plan details, track actual work against the plan, and take corrective action when things get off track.

Tip

If you are new to project management, stop right here and read Appendix B, "A Short Course in Project Management," before proceeding with this chapter. It won't take you long, and it will help you properly assess and organize your specific project scheduling needs and build solid plans in Microsoft Project.

The exercises in this book revolve around a fictitious film production company, Southridge Video and Film Productions. Chances are you don't work for a film production company, but you probably have seen a TV commercial or film recently. Each is its own project; some in fact are fairly complex projects involving hundreds of resources and aggressive *deadlines*. We think you'll be able to recognize many of the scheduling problems Southridge Video encounters, and apply the solutions to your own scheduling needs.

This chapter walks you through the Microsoft Project interface and presents the steps necessary to create a new project plan in Microsoft Project.

Tip

To follow along with the exercises in this book, you need to install the practice files from the companion CD. (You cannot just copy the files.) You will find instructions for installing the files in the "Using the Book's CD-ROM" section at the beginning of the book.

Managing Your Projects with Microsoft Project

The best project management tool in the world can never replace your good judgment. However, the tool can and should help you accomplish the following:

- Track all the information you gather about the work, duration, and resource requirements for your project.
- Visualize and present your project plan in standard, well-defined formats.
- Schedule tasks and resources consistently and effectively.
- Exchange project information with Microsoft Office applications.
- Communicate with resources and other stakeholders while you, the project manager, retain ultimate control of the project.
- Manage projects using a program that looks and feels like other desktop productivity applications.

The Microsoft Project 2002 family encompasses a broad range of products, including the following:

- Microsoft Project 2002 Standard edition, a Microsoft Windows–based desktop application for project management. The Standard edition has several new project management features and interface improvements and is the direct upgrade of Microsoft Project 2000. The Standard edition also enables you to collaborate with others through Microsoft Project 2002 Server.

- Microsoft Project 2002 Professional edition, a Windows-based desktop application that includes the full feature set of the Standard edition, plus additional project team planning and communications features—especially when used with Microsoft Project 2002 Server.

- Microsoft Project 2002 Server, an intranet-based solution that enables enterprise-level (with Microsoft Project Professional) or workgroup-level (with Microsoft Project Standard) project collaboration, timesheet reporting, and status reporting.

- Microsoft Project 2002 Web Access, the Internet Explorer–based interface for working with Microsoft Project Server.

Tip

To learn more about the new features in Microsoft Project 2002 and the differences between the Standard and Professional editions, type **What's new?** into the Ask A Question box in the upper right corner of the Microsoft Project window.

This book focuses mainly on the feature set of Microsoft Project Standard edition, the entry-level desktop project management tool. Everything you can do in the Standard edition you can also do in the Professional edition. You can complete the exercises in this book with either the Standard or Professional edition, and they do not require access to Microsoft Project Server.

Tip

To learn more about Microsoft Project 2002 Professional edition and Microsoft Project 2002 Server, see Appendix A, "Introducing Microsoft Project Server." Throughout the book you'll also see tips about Standard edition features that are enhanced in the Professional edition. All of the Microsoft Project illustrations you see in this book are from Microsoft Project Standard edition. If you are running Microsoft Project Professional, you will see a few differences in the interface.

What Can a Scheduling Engine Do for You?

Many projects are not managed with a real scheduling tool such as Microsoft Project, but they should be. It's common to see task and resource lists from spreadsheet programs such as Microsoft Excel, or even nicely formatted Gantt charts from drawing programs such as Microsoft Visio. One big advantage Microsoft Project has over such applications is that it includes a scheduling engine—a computational brain that can handle issues such as ripple effects when task 1 in a 100-task sequence changes its start date. This scheduling engine can also account for nonworking time such as weekends when calculating a task's start and finish dates. Applications such as Excel and Visio might have a place in your project management toolbox, but to be really successful you'll need a scheduling engine such as Microsoft Project.

Starting Microsoft Project

Microsoft Project is a member of the Microsoft Office family of desktop programs, so much of what you see in Microsoft Project is similar to what you see in Microsoft Word, Microsoft Excel, and Microsoft Access. For example, Microsoft Project's menu bar and toolbars are similar in organization, if not in content, to other Office applications.

In this exercise, you'll start Microsoft Project, create a file based on a *template* (a file containing some initial data that you can use as a starting point for a new project plan), and see the major areas of the default Microsoft Project interface:

1 On the Windows taskbar, click the Start button.

The Start menu appears.

2 On the Start menu, point to All Programs (in Microsoft Windows XP) or Programs (in previous versions of Windows), and then click Microsoft Project.

Microsoft Project appears. Your screen should look similar to the following illustration:

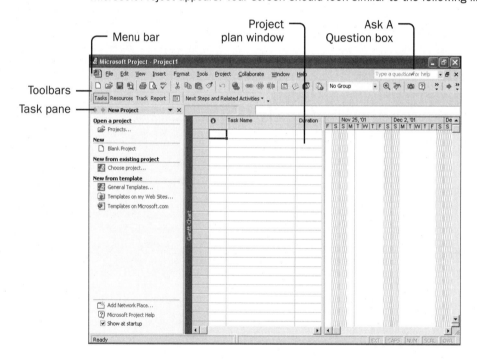

Important

Toolbar Options

Depending on the screen resolution you have set on your computer and which toolbar buttons you use most often, it's possible that not every button on every toolbar will appear on your Microsoft Project toolbars. If a button mentioned in this book doesn't appear on a toolbar, click the Toolbar Options down arrow on that toolbar to display the rest of the available buttons.

If you've used Office applications, or if you're upgrading from a previous version of Microsoft Project, you'll be familiar with many of the major interface elements in the Microsoft Project window. Let's walk through them:

■ The main menu bar enables you to give instructions to Microsoft Project.

■ Toolbars provide quick access to the most common tasks; most toolbar buttons correspond to a menu bar command. Like other Office family applications, Microsoft Project customizes the menus and toolbars for you, based on how frequently you use specific commands or toolbar buttons. The most frequently used commands and buttons will remain visible on the menus and toolbars, whereas the commands and buttons you don't use will be temporarily hidden.

■ The project plan window contains a view of the active project plan. (We'll refer to the types of documents Microsoft Project works with as *project plans*, not documents or schedules.) The name of the active view appears on the left edge of the view— in this case, the Gantt Chart view is displayed.

Ask A Question

new in
Project
2002

■ The Ask A Question box enables you to quickly search Microsoft Project's online Help for instructions on performing common activities in Microsoft Project. Just type in a question and press Enter. Throughout this book we'll suggest questions you can enter into this box to learn more about specific features. The Ask A Question box replaces the Office Assistant (the cartoonlike character such as Clippit), which is turned off by default in Microsoft Project 2002. However, if you enable the Office Assistant in any Office family application, such as Word, Visio, or Microsoft Project, it will appear in all of the Office family applications.

Task pane

new in
Project
2002

■ The New Project task pane in Microsoft Project is similar to the task panes you might see in the Microsoft Office XP applications. It is a convenient list of recently opened files as well as another means of creating new files. In addition to this task pane, Microsoft Project includes the Project Guide, which is discussed below.

Next you will view the templates included with Microsoft Project and create a project plan based on one of them.

3 In the New Project task pane, under New From Template, click the General Templates link.

The Templates dialog box appears.

4 Click the Project Templates tab.

Your screen should look similar to the illustration shown on the following page.

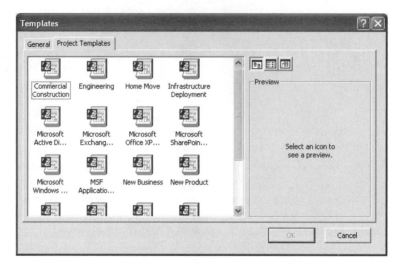

All the templates listed have been developed by project management professionals specifically for Microsoft Project.

5 Click New Business, and then click OK.

Important

Depending on how Microsoft Project was installed on your computer, the templates included with Microsoft Project might be installed at this point. This "install on first use" setting is one of the setup choices for optional components included with Microsoft Project. If you have never seen the templates included with Microsoft Project before, spend some time browsing through them. You might find one that matches an upcoming project for which you'd like to develop a full plan. Starting with a predefined template can save you a lot of effort.

Microsoft Project creates a project plan based on the New Business template, closes the New Project task pane, and displays the Tasks activity list in the Project Guide. Your screen should look similar to the following illustration:

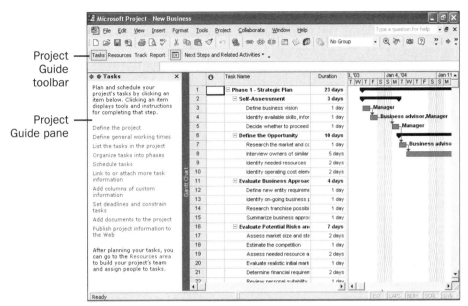

Project Guide toolbar

Project Guide pane

Project Guide
new in
Project
2002

The Project Guide is a wizardlike interface you can use when creating or fine-tuning a project plan. In later chapters you will use the Project Guide to perform many common activities relating to tasks, resources, and assignments. You can view all activities in the Project Guide through the Project Guide toolbar. This toolbar is divided into the most common subject areas of Microsoft Project (Tasks, Resources, Track, and Report). You can also view the entire Project Guide activity *outline* by clicking the Next Steps And Related Activities button.

For the next few exercises in this chapter, you will use the sample data provided by the template to identify the major parts of the Microsoft Project interface.

Exploring Views

The working space in Microsoft Project is called a *view*. Microsoft Project contains dozens of views, but you normally work with just one view (sometimes two) at a time. You use views to enter, edit, analyze, and display your project information. The default view, the one you see when Microsoft Project starts, is the *Gantt Chart view* shown on the next page.

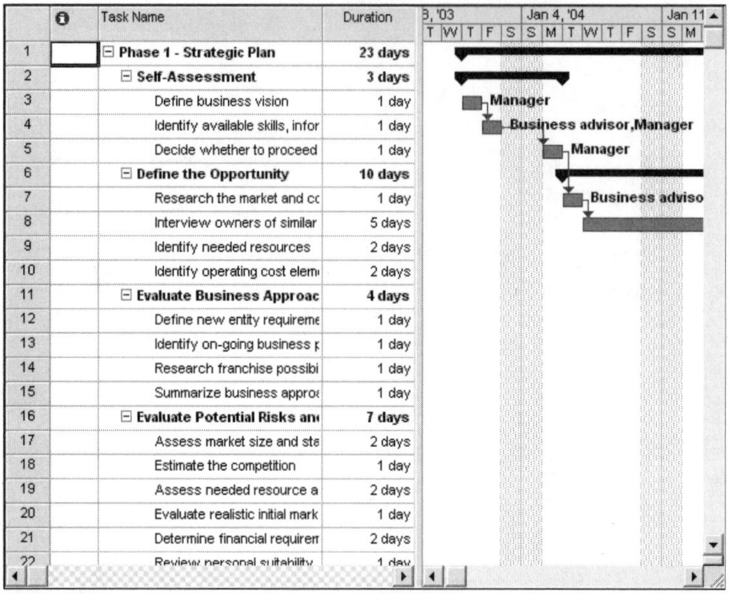

	ⓘ	Task Name	Duration	3, '03	Jan 4, '04	Jan 11
				T W T F S	S M T W T F S	S M
1		⊟ Phase 1 - Strategic Plan	23 days			
2		⊟ Self-Assessment	3 days			
3		Define business vision	1 day	Manager		
4		Identify available skills, infor	1 day	Business advisor,Manager		
5		Decide whether to proceed	1 day	Manager		
6		⊟ Define the Opportunity	10 days			
7		Research the market and co	1 day	Business adviso		
8		Interview owners of similar	5 days			
9		Identify needed resources	2 days			
10		Identify operating cost elem	2 days			
11		⊟ Evaluate Business Approac	4 days			
12		Define new entity requireme	1 day			
13		Identify on-going business p	1 day			
14		Research franchise possibi	1 day			
15		Summarize business appro	1 day			
16		⊟ Evaluate Potential Risks an	7 days			
17		Assess market size and sta	2 days			
18		Estimate the competition	1 day			
19		Assess needed resource a	2 days			
20		Evaluate realistic initial mark	1 day			
21		Determine financial requirem	2 days			
22		Review personal suitability	1 day			

In general, views focus on either task or resource details. The Gantt Chart view, for example, lists task details in a table on the left side of the view and graphically represents each task as a bar in the chart on the right side of the view. The Gantt Chart view is a common way to represent a project plan, especially when presenting it to others. It is also useful for entering and fine-tuning task details and for analyzing your project.

In this exercise, you'll start at the Gantt Chart view and then switch to other views that highlight different aspects of a project plan. Finally, you'll explore combination views that let you focus in on specific project details more easily:

1 On the View menu, click Resource Sheet.

The Resource Sheet view replaces the Gantt Chart view. The Project Guide is updated to display a list of activities specific to resources:

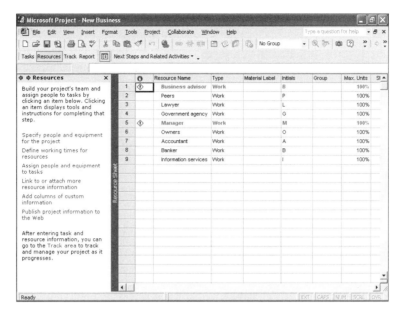

The Resource Sheet view displays details about resources in a row-and-column format (called a *table*), with one resource per row. This view is called a sheet view. There is one other sheet view, the Task Sheet view, which lists the task details. Note that Resource Sheet view doesn't tell you anything about the tasks to which resources might be assigned. To see that type of information, you'll switch to a different view.

2   On the View menu, click Task Usage.

The Task Usage view replaces the Resource Sheet view, and the Project Guide is updated again.

This usage view groups resources according to tasks to which they're assigned. Another usage view, the Resource Usage view, flips this around to display all the tasks assigned to each resource. Usage views also show you work assignments per resource on a timescale such as daily or weekly.

3   In the table portion of the view on the left, click the name of Task 3, *Define business vision.*

Go To
Selected Task

4   On the Standard toolbar, click the Go To Selected Task button.

The timescale side of the view scrolls to show you the scheduled work values for this task, shown on the following page.

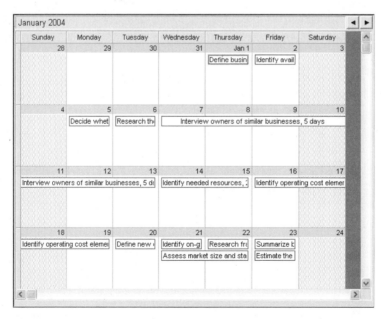

	ⓘ	Task Name	Work	Details	W	T	F	S	Jan ◢ S
1		⊟ Phase 1 - Strategic Plan	**240 hrs**	Work	▬▬▬	8h	16h		
2		⊟ Self-Assessment	**32 hrs**	Work		8h	16h		
3		⊟ Define business visi	8 hrs	Work		8h			
		Manager	*8 hrs*	Work		8h			
4		⊟ Identify available skil	16 hrs	Work			16h		
		Business advis	*8 hrs*	Work			8h		
		Manager	*8 hrs*	Work			8h		
5		⊟ Decide whether to p	8 hrs	Work					
		Manager	*8 hrs*	Work					
6		⊟ **Define the Opportuni**	**96 hrs**	Work					
7		⊟ Research the marke	8 hrs	Work					
		Business advis	*8 hrs*	Work					
8		⊟ Interview owners of	40 hrs	Work					
		Owners	*40 hrs*	Work					
9		⊟ Identify needed resc	32 hrs	Work					
		Business advis	*16 hrs*	Work					
		Peers	*16 hrs*	Work					
10		⊟ Identify operating co	16 hrs	Work					
		Accountant	*16 hrs*	Work					
11		⊟ **Evaluate Business A**	**32 hrs**	Work					
12		⊟ Define new entity re	8 hrs	Work					
		Manager	*8 hrs*	*Work*					

A usage view is a fairly sophisticated way of viewing project details. Next you'll switch to a simpler view.

5 On the View menu, click Calendar.

The Calendar view appears:

January 2004						◄ ►
Sunday	**Monday**	**Tuesday**	**Wednesday**	**Thursday**	**Friday**	**Saturday**
28	29	30	31	Jan 1 Define busin	2 Identify avail	3
4	5 Decide whet	6 Research th	7 Interview owners of similar businesses, 5 days	8	9	10
11 Interview owners of similar businesses, 5 d	12	13	14 Identify needed resources,	15	16 Identify operating cost elemer	17
18 Identify operating cost elemer	19 Define new	20 Identify on-g Assess market size and sta	21 Research fr	22 Summarize Estimate the	23	24

This simple month-at-a-glance view lacks the table structure, timescale, or chart elements you've seen in previous views. Task names appear on the days they're scheduled to start, and if a task's duration is longer than one day, its name will span multiple days.

Another common view used in project management is the Network Diagram. You'll look at this next.

6 On the View menu, click Network Diagram.

The Network Diagram view appears. Use the scroll bars to view different parts of the Network Diagram view:

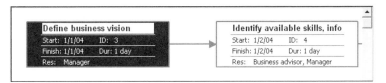

This view focuses on task relationships. Each box or node in the Network Diagram displays details about a task, and lines between boxes indicate task relationships. Like the Calendar view, the Network Diagram view lacks a table structure; the entire view is a chart.

To conclude this exercise, you'll look at combination views. These **split** the project plan window into two panes, each pane containing a different view. The views are synchronized, so selecting a specific task or resource in one view causes the other view to display details about that task or resource.

7 On the View menu, click More Views.

The More Views dialog box appears. This dialog box lists all the predefined views available in Microsoft Project.

8 In the Views box, click Task Entry, and then click the Apply button.

The Task Entry view appears:

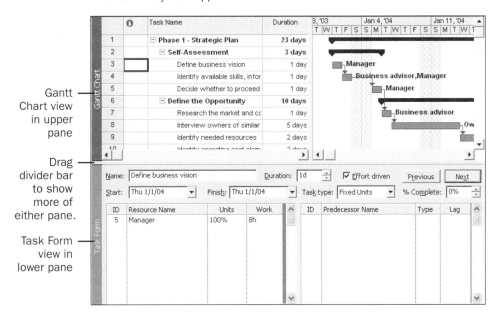

Gantt Chart view in upper pane

Drag divider bar to show more of either pane.

Task Form view in lower pane

Tip

Depending on your screen resolution, you might need to close the Project Guide to see the full width of this view. To do this, click the Close button in the upper right corner of the Project Guide. You can also make the Project Guide pane narrower by dragging its right edge to the left.

This view is a predefined split-screen or combination view, with the Gantt chart in the upper pane and the Task form in the lower pane. A form is the final element of a view you'll see in this chapter. A form displays details about the selected task or resource, much like a dialog box. You can enter, change, or review these details in the form.

9 In the Gantt Chart portion of the view, if the selection is not on task 3, *Define business vision*, click that task's name.

The details about task 3 appear in the Task Form portion of the view.

10 In the Gantt Chart portion of the view, click the name of task 4, *Identify available skills, information, and support*.

The details about task 4 appear in the Task Form.

Tip

Besides using the predefined combination views, you can display two views of your choice by clicking Split on the Window menu. After the Microsoft Project window is split into two panes, click in the upper or lower pane, and then choose the view you want to appear there. To return to a single view, on the Window menu, click Remove Split.

It is important to understand that in all these views, as well as all the other views in Microsoft Project, you are looking at different aspects of the same set of details about a single project plan. Even a simple project plan can contain too much data to display all at once. You can use views to help you focus in on the specific details you want.

In later exercises you'll do more with views to further focus in on the most relevant project details.

Exploring Reports

Reports are predefined formats intended for printing Microsoft Project data. Unlike views, which you can either print or work with on the screen, reports are designed to be printed. You don't enter data directly into a report. Microsoft Project includes several predefined task and resource reports you can manipulate to get the information you want.

In this exercise, you view a report in the Print Preview window:

1 On the View menu, click Reports.

The Reports dialog box appears, showing the six broad categories of reports available in Microsoft Project.

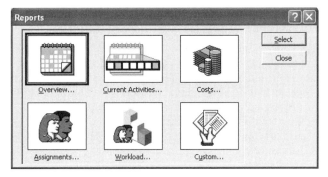

2   Click Custom, and then click the Select button.

The Custom Reports dialog box appears, listing all predefined reports in Microsoft Project and any custom reports that have been added.

3   In the Reports list, click Task, and then click the Preview button.

Microsoft Project displays the Task report in the Print Preview window. Your screen should look similar to the following illustration:

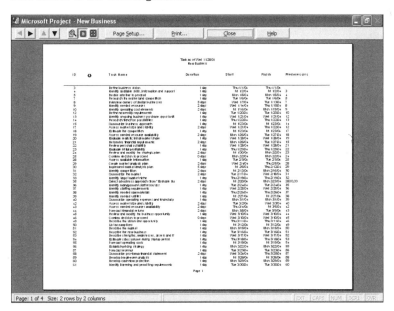

This report is a complete list of project tasks (except for summary tasks), similar to what you'd see in the *Entry table* of the Gantt Chart view. If you want to zoom in, move the mouse pointer (shaped like a magnifying glass) to a portion of the report, and click. Click again to toggle back to the full page preview.

4   On the Print Preview toolbar, click the Close button.

The Print Preview window closes, and the Custom Reports dialog box reappears.

5 In the Custom Reports dialog box, click the Close button.

6 Click the Close button again to close the Reports dialog box.

Troubleshooting

We've frequently seen Microsoft Project users go to a lot of trouble to customize the Gantt Chart view to include specific information they want in the format they want. Before you do that, check the predefined views (for online work or printing) or reports (for printing). There's a good chance the Microsoft Project designers have anticipated your needs and provided a predefined solution for you. For more information, type **All about printing and reporting** into the Ask A Question box.

To conclude this exercise, you'll close the file you've been using to explore views and reports.

7 On the File menu, click Close to close the New Business plan. When prompted to save changes, click the No button.

Creating a New Project Plan

Now that you've had a brief look at the major parts of the Microsoft Project interface, you are ready to create the project plan you will use throughout this book.

A project plan is essentially a model you construct of some aspects of the real project you anticipate—what you think will happen, or what you want to happen (it's usually best if these are not too different). This model focuses on some but not all aspects of the real project—tasks, resources, time frames, and possibly their associated costs.

Tip

Depending on your needs and the information to which you have access, the project plan might not deal with other important aspects of the real project. Many large projects, for example, are carried out in organizations that have a formal change management process. Before a major change to the scope of a project is allowed, it must first be evaluated and approved by the people managing and implementing the project. This is an important project management activity, but not something done directly within Microsoft Project.

In this exercise, you create a new plan using the Project Guide:

1 On the File menu, click the New command.

The New Project task pane appears.

2 Under New, click the Blank Project link.

Microsoft Project creates a new project, and the New Project task pane is replaced by the Tasks pane of the Project Guide:

Click here to see the full outline of
activities supported by the Project Guide.

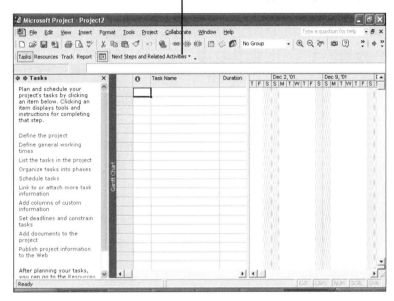

Take a moment to look over the Tasks pane. This pane contains links to several activities, all focused on tasks. (You'll see other types of activities in later chapters.) If you want to see where you are in the sequence of activities in the Project Guide, just click the Next Steps And Related Activities button on the Project Guide toolbar. The name of the current activity appears checked. Each activity in the Project Guide consists of a series of numbered steps. Each step appears in its own pane, like pages in a book.

3 In the Tasks pane, click the Define The Project link.

The Define The Project pane appears.

4 In the Date box, click the down arrow.

A small monthly calendar appears. By default, Microsoft Project uses the current date as the project start date. However, in this exercise, you change the project start date to January 5, 2004.

5 Click the left or right arrow until January 2004 is displayed.

6 Click 5, as shown on the next page.

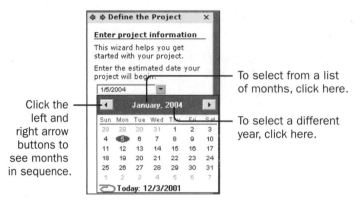

Click the left and right arrow buttons to see months in sequence.

To select from a list of months, click here.

To select a different year, click here.

Tip

You use this type of calendar in several places in Microsoft Project. Here is a handy shortcut for quickly picking a date with the calendar: Click the name of the month to display a short-cut menu of all months, and then select the month you want. Next click the year to display up and down arrows, and then type or select the year you want.

7 At the bottom of the pane, click the Save And Go To Step 2 link.

The second pane appears. This pane gives you the option of using the collaboration features supported by Microsoft Project Server. To learn more about Microsoft Project Server, see Appendix A, "Introducing Microsoft Project Server."

8 Under Collaborate On Your Project, select the No option, and then click the Save And Go To Step 3 link.

The Save Your Project pane appears.

Save

9 On the Standard toolbar, click the Save button. You can also click the Save link or button in the pane.

Because this project plan has not previously been saved, the Save As dialog box appears.

10 Locate the Chapter 1 Getting Started folder in the Project SBS folder on your hard disk.

11 In the File Name box, type **Wingtip Toys Commercial 1**.

12 Click the Save button to close the Save As dialog box.

Microsoft Project saves the project plan as Wingtip Toys Commercial 1.

Tip

You can instruct Microsoft Project to automatically save the active project plan at predefined intervals, such as every 10 minutes. On the Tools menu, click Options. In the Options dialog box, click the Save tab, select the Save Every check box, and then specify the time interval you want.

13 At the bottom of the pane, click the Save And Go To Step 4 link.

The final page of the Define The Project pane appears.

14 At the bottom of the pane, click the Save And Finish link.

The top-level Tasks pane appears again. You've completed the Define The Project activity.

Setting Nonworking Days

This exercise introduces *calendars*, the primary means by which you control when tasks and resources can be scheduled for work in Microsoft Project. In later chapters you will work with other types of calendars; in this chapter you will work only with the *project calendar*.

The project calendar defines the general working and nonworking time for tasks. Think of the project calendar as your organization's normal working times. This might be, for example, Monday through Friday, 8 A.M. through 5 P.M. with an hour off for lunch. Your organization or specific resources might have exceptions to this normal working time, such as holidays or vacation. In a later chapter you'll address resource vacations, but here you'll address a holiday in the project calendar:

1 In the Tasks pane, click the Define General Working Times link.

The Project Working Times pane appears. Your screen should look similar to the following illustration:

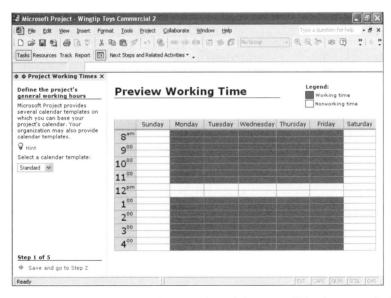

Notice the Preview Working Time portion of the pane. This shows you (in blue) the times at which Microsoft Project can schedule tasks and resources and (in yellow) when it cannot, based on the settings in the project calendar.

Tip

Click the Hint link in the Project Working Times pane. The hint appears in place, without navigating away from the pane. Click it again to collapse it. You will see many such hints throughout the Project Guide.

2 In the Select A Calendar Template box, click the down arrow.

The list that appears contains the three *base calendars* included with Microsoft Project. These are as follows:

- Standard: the traditional working day, Monday through Friday from 8 A.M. to 5 P.M., with an hour off for lunch.

- 24 Hours: has no nonworking time.

- Night Shift: covers a "graveyard" shift schedule of Monday night through Saturday morning, 11 P.M. to 8 A.M., with a one-hour break.

Just one of the base calendars serves as the project calendar. For this project you'll use the Standard base calendar as the project calendar, so leave it selected.

Tip

To learn more about calendars, type **All about calendars** into the Ask A Question box in the upper right corner of the Microsoft Project window.

3 At the bottom of the pane, click the Save And Go To Step 2 link.

The second pane appears. This pane gives you the option of changing the project calendar's working time for a specific day of every week. For example, you could choose to end the workday every Wednesday at 3 P.M. instead of 5 P.M. For this project, however, you'll use the default work week.

4 At the bottom of the pane, click the Save And Go To Step 3 link.

The third pane appears. Here you'll specify some specific nonworking days for the project calendar.

5 Click the Change Working Time link in the pane.

The Project Guide displays the Change Working Time dialog box. This is the same dialog box you would see if you clicked the Change Working Time command on the Tools menu.

6 In the calendar below the Select Date(s) label, scroll up or down to January 2004. You know that the entire staff will be at a morale event January 30, and no work should be scheduled that day.

7 Select the date January 30.

8 Under Set Selected Date(s) To, click Nonworking Time:

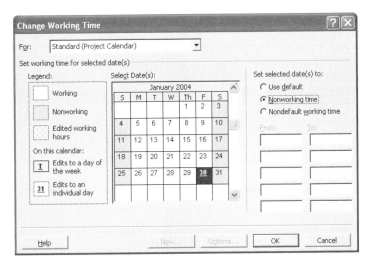

This date is now nonworking time for the project. In the dialog box, the date appears underlined, and it is formatted gray to indicate nonworking time.

9 Click OK to close the Change Working Time dialog box.

10 To verify the change to the project calendar, scroll the chart portion of the Gantt Chart view (the portion on the right) to the right until Friday, January 30, is visible. Like the weekends, January 30 is formatted gray to indicate nonworking time:

Friday, January 30 is a nonworking day
and is formatted in gray (as are weekends)
in the Gantt Chart

ⓘ	Task Name	Duration	Jan 25, '04							Feb 1, '04							Feb
			F	S	S	M	T	W	T	F	S	S	M	T	W	T	F	S	S	M

11 At the bottom of the pane, click the Save And Go To Step 4 link.

Take a moment to read the text in the Define Time Units pane, because this is a common source of confusion among Microsoft Project users. Because you did not change the default working times for the project calendar, you should not change these time units.

12 At the bottom of the pane, click the Save And Go To Step 5 link.

The final pane of the Project Working Times activity appears.

13 At the bottom of the pane, click the Save And Finish link.

The top-level Tasks pane appears again. You've completed the Define General Working Times activity.

Entering Project Properties

Like other programs in the Office family, Microsoft Project keeps track of several file properties. Some of these properties are statistics, such as how many times the file has been revised. Other properties include information you might want to record about a project plan, such as the project manager's name or keywords to support a file search. Microsoft Project also uses properties in page headers and footers when printing.

In this exercise, you enter some properties that you will use later when printing project information and for other purposes:

1   On the File menu, click Properties.

The Properties dialog box appears.

2   Click the Summary tab.

3   In the Subject box, type **Video Production Schedule**.

4   In the Author box, type your name.

5   In the Manager box, type your name, type your manager's name, or leave the box blank.

6   In the Company box, type **Southridge Video**.

7   Select the Save Preview Picture check box:

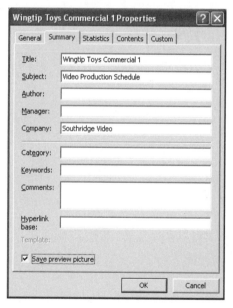

8   Click OK to close the dialog box.

"A Database That Knows About Time"

The project plans you create in Microsoft Project are files that have many things in common with database files, like those you might work with in Microsoft Access. If you were to peek inside a Microsoft Project Plan (MPP) file, you'd find it has much in common with a database file format. Data is stored in a set of tables, and relationships connect information in different tables. In fact it's not uncommon for Microsoft Project users in large organizations to save project plans in a database format, sometimes to a central database on a network server.

What Microsoft Project provides that a regular database application can't, however, is the active scheduling engine mentioned earlier. One Microsoft Project expert we know describes it as "a database that knows about time."

Chapter Wrap-Up

This chapter covered how to create a project plan.

If you are going on to other chapters:

Save

1   On the Standard toolbar, click the Save button to save changes made to Wingtip Toys Commercial project plan.

2   On the File menu, click Close.

If you aren't continuing to other chapters:

1   On the Standard toolbar, click the Save button to save changes made to Wingtip Toys Commercial project plan.

2   To quit Microsoft Project for now, on the File menu, click Exit.

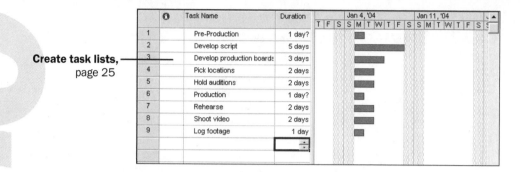

Create task lists,
page 25

Create summary tasks,
page 32

Link tasks to create dependencies,
page 35

Add notes and hyperlinks to the Web,
page 38

Chapter 2
Creating a Task List

After completing this chapter, you will be able to:

✔ **Enter task information.**

✔ **Estimate and enter how long each task should last.**

✔ **Create a milestone to track an important event.**

✔ **Organize tasks into phases.**

✔ **Create task relationships by linking tasks.**

✔ **Record task details in notes and insert a hyperlink to content on the World Wide Web.**

✔ **Check a project plan's overall duration.**

In this chapter, you will work with *tasks*. You will focus mainly on creating and arranging tasks in the right sequence and with the right durations.

Wingtip Toys
Commercial 2a

This chapter uses the practice file Wingtip Toys Commercial 2a. This file contains the project start date and properties you entered in Chapter 1, "Getting Started with Microsoft Project." For details about installing the practice files, see "Using the Book's CD-ROM" at the beginning of this book.

Entering Tasks

Tasks are the most basic building blocks of any project—tasks represent the *work* to be done to accomplish the goals of the project. Tasks describe project work in terms of sequence, duration, and *resource* requirements. Later in this chapter, you will work with two special types of tasks: summary tasks (which summarize or "roll up" the durations, costs, and so on of subtasks) and milestones (which indicate a significant event in the life of a project).

In this exercise, you enter the first tasks required in the video project:

1 If Microsoft Project is not already open, start it now.

Open

2 On the Standard toolbar, click the Open button.

The Open dialog box appears.

3 Navigate to the Chapter 2 Simple Tasks folder, and double-click the Wingtip Toys Commercial 2a file.

4 On the File menu, click Save As.

The Save As dialog box appears.

5 In the File Name box, type **Wingtip Toys Commercial 2**, and then click Save.

6 If the Tasks pane is not already displayed in the Project Guide, on the Project Guide toolbar, click Tasks.

7 In the Tasks pane, click the List The Tasks In The Project link.

The List Tasks pane appears. Take a moment to read the information in the pane. Later you'll use this pane to create a milestone task.

8 Click the cell directly below the Task Name column heading.

9 Type **Pre-Production**, and then press Enter.

10 Select the name of the new Task 1, *Pre-Production*.

Go To
Selected Task

11 On the Standard toolbar, click the Go To Selected Task button.

The chart side of the view scrolls to show you the Gantt bar for this task.

Your screen should look similar to the following illustration:

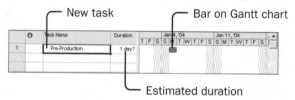

The task you entered is given a unique ID number. Each task has a unique ID number, but it does not necessarily represent the order in which tasks occur.

Microsoft Project assigns a duration of one day to the new task, and the question mark indicates that this is an estimated duration. A corresponding task bar of one day's length appears in the Gantt chart. By default the task start date is the same as the project start date.

12 Enter the following task names below the *Pre-Production* task name, pressing Enter after each task name:

Develop script

Develop production boards

Pick locations

Hold auditions

Production

Rehearse

Shoot video

Log footage

Your screen should look similar to the following illustration:

		Task Name	Duration	Jan 4, '04	Jan 11, '04
	O			T F S S M T W T F S	S M T W T F S
1		Pre-Production	1 day?	■	
2		Develop script	1 day?	■	
3		Develop production boards	1 day?	■	
4		Pick locations	1 day?	■	
5		Hold auditions	1 day?	■	
6		Production	1 day?	■	
7		Rehearse	1 day?	■	
8		Shoot video	1 day?	■	
9		Log footage	1 day?	■	

Tip

In addition to typing task information directly into Microsoft Project, you can develop task lists in other applications and then import them into Microsoft Project. For example, Microsoft Project 2002 installs a Microsoft Excel template named Microsoft Project Task List Import Template, which you or others can complete and then import into Microsoft Project with the proper structure. In Excel, this template appears on the Spreadsheet Solutions tab of the Templates dialog box. You can also import your Microsoft Outlook task list into a project plan. In Microsoft Project, click Import Outlook Tasks on the Tools menu.

Project Management Focus: Defining the Right Tasks for the Right Deliverable

Every project has an ultimate goal or intent: the reason that the project was started. This is called the project *deliverable*. This deliverable is usually a product, such as a TV commercial, or a service or event, such as a software training session. Defining the right tasks to create the right deliverable is an essential skill for a project manager. The task lists you create in Microsoft Project should describe all the work required, and only the work required, to complete the project successfully.

In developing your task lists, you might find it helpful to distinguish product scope from project scope. *Product scope* describes the quality, features, and functions of the deliverable of the project. In the scenario used in Part 1 of this book, for example, the deliverable is a TV commercial, and the product scope might include its length, subject, and audience. *Project scope*, on the other hand, describes the work required to deliver such a product or service. In our scenario, the project scope includes detailed tasks relating to the creation of a TV commercial, such as holding auditions, shooting the video, editing it, and so on.

Estimating Durations

A task's *duration* is the amount of time you expect it will take to complete the task. Microsoft Project can work with task durations that range from minutes to months. Depending on the scope of your project, you'll probably want to work with task durations on the scale of hours, days, and weeks.

For example, a project might have a *project calendar* with working time defined as 8 A.M. through 5 P.M. with an hour off for lunch Monday through Friday, leaving nonworking time defined as evenings and weekends. If you estimate that a task will take 16 hours of working time, you could enter its duration as **2d** to schedule work over two eight-hour workdays. You should then expect that starting the task at 8 A.M. on a Friday means that it wouldn't be completed until 5 P.M. on the following Monday. No work would be scheduled over the weekend, because Saturday and Sunday have been defined as nonworking time.

Tip

You determine the overall duration of a project by calculating the difference between the earliest start date and the latest finish date of the tasks that compose it. The project duration is also affected by other factors, such as task relationships, which are discussed in the topic "Linking Tasks," later in this chapter. Because Microsoft Project distinguishes between working and nonworking time, a task's duration doesn't necessarily correlate to elapsed time.

When working in Microsoft Project, you can use abbreviations for durations:

If you enter this abbreviation	It appears like this	And means
m	min	minute
h	hr	hour
d	day	day
w	wk	week
mo	mon	month

Tip

You can schedule tasks to occur during working and nonworking time. To do this, assign an *elapsed duration* to a task. You enter elapsed duration by preceding the duration abbreviation with an e. For example, type **3ed** to indicate three elapsed days. You might use an elapsed duration for a task that you don't directly control, but that nonetheless is critical to your project. For instance, you might have the tasks *Pour foundation concrete* and *Remove foundation forms* in a construction project. If so, you might also want a task called *Wait for concrete to cure*, because you don't want to remove the forms until the concrete has cured. The task *Wait for concrete to cure* should have an elapsed duration, because the concrete will cure over a contiguous range of days, whether they are working or nonworking days. If the concrete takes 48 hours to cure, you can enter the duration for that task as **2ed**, schedule the task to start on Friday at 9 A.M., and expect it to be complete by Sunday at 9 A.M. In most cases, however, you'll work with nonelapsed durations in Microsoft Project.

Microsoft Project uses standard values for minutes and hours for durations: one minute equals 60 seconds and one hour equals 60 minutes. However, you can define nonstandard durations for days, weeks, and months for your project. To do this, on the Tools menu, click the Options command, and in the Options dialog box, click the Calendar tab, illustrated here:

With a setting of eight hours per day, entering a two-day task duration is the same as entering 16 hours.

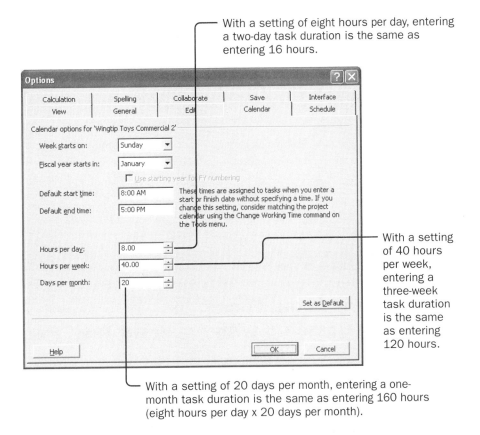

With a setting of 40 hours per week, entering a three-week task duration is the same as entering 120 hours.

With a setting of 20 days per month, entering a one-month task duration is the same as entering 160 hours (eight hours per day x 20 days per month).

The exercises in this chapter use the default values: 8 hours per day, 40 hours per week, and 20 days per month.

Tip

Although it's beyond the scope of this book, Program Evaluation and Review Technique (PERT) analysis can be a useful tool for estimating task durations. For more information, type **Estimate task durations by using PERT analysis** into the Ask A Question box in the upper right corner of the Microsoft Project window.

In this exercise, you enter durations for the tasks you've created. When you created those tasks, Microsoft Project entered an estimated duration of one day for each. (The question mark in the Duration field indicates that the duration is an explicit estimate, although really you should consider all task durations to be estimates until the task is completed.) To enter durations:

1 Click the cell below the Duration column heading for Task 2, *Develop script*.

The Duration field for task 2 is selected.

2 Type **5d**, and then press Enter.

The value 5 *days* appears in the Duration field.

3 Enter the following durations for the remaining tasks:

Task ID	Task name	Duration
3	Develop production boards	**3d**
4	Pick locations	**2d**
5	Hold auditions	**2d**
6	Production	(Press Enter to skip this task for now)
7	Rehearse	**2d**
8	Shoot video	**2d**
9	Log footage	**1d**

Project Management Focus:
How Do You Come Up with Accurate Task Durations?

You should consider two general rules when estimating task durations:

■ Project duration often correlates to task duration; long projects tend to have tasks with longer durations than short projects.

■ If you track progress against your project plan (described in Chapter 6, "Tracking Progress on Tasks," and in Part 2, "Managing a Complex Project"), you need to think about the level of detail you want to apply to your project's tasks. If you have a multi-year project, for example, it might not be practical or even possible to track tasks that are measured in minutes or hours. In general, you should measure task durations at the lowest level of detail or control you care about, but no lower.

For the projects you work on in this book, the durations are supplied for you. For your real-world projects, you will often have to estimate task durations. Good sources of task duration estimates include:

■ Historical information from previous, similar projects.

■ Estimates from the people who will complete the tasks.

■ The expert judgment of people who have managed similar projects.

■ Professional or industry organizations related to projects similar to yours.

For complex projects, you probably would combine these and other sources to estimate task durations. Because inaccurate task duration estimates are a major source of *risk* in any project, making good estimates is well worth the effort.

Your screen should look similar to the following illustration:

	❶	Task Name	Duration	Jan 4, '04	Jan 11, '04
1		Pre-Production	1 day?		
2		Develop script	5 days		
3		Develop production boards	3 days		
4		Pick locations	2 days		
5		Hold auditions	2 days		
6		Production	1 day?		
7		Rehearse	2 days		
8		Shoot video	2 days		
9		Log footage	1 day		

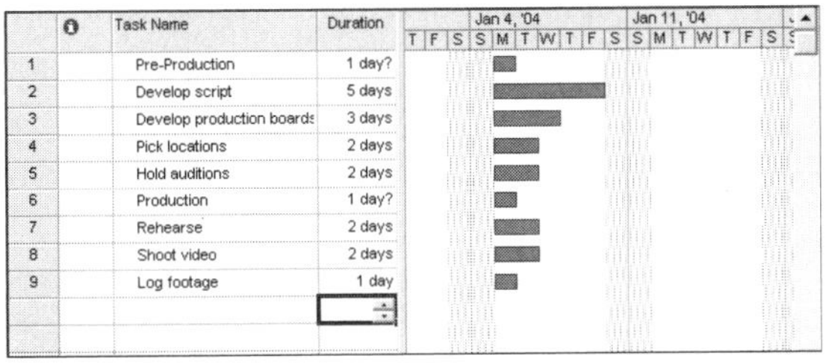

Entering a Milestone

In addition to tracking tasks to be completed, you might want to track an important event for your project, such as when the pre-production phase of the project will end. To do this, you will create a *milestone*.

Milestones are significant events that are either reached within the project (completion of a phase of work, for example) or imposed upon the project (a deadline by which to apply for funding, for example). Because the milestone itself doesn't normally include any work, milestones are represented as tasks with zero duration.

In this exercise, you create a milestone:

1 Click the name of Task 6, *Production*.

2 On the Insert menu, click New Task.

Microsoft Project inserts a row for a new task and renumbers the subsequent tasks.

3 Type **Pre-Production complete!**, and then press the Right Arrow key to move to the Duration field.

4 Either type **0d** in the Duration field, or in the List Tasks window select the Make Selected Task A Milestone option.

The milestone is added to your plan. Your screen should look similar to the following illustration:

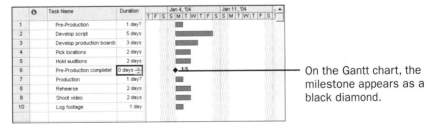

On the Gantt chart, the milestone appears as a black diamond.

5 At the bottom of the Enter Tasks pane, click the Done link.

The Tasks pane appears.

Tip

You can also mark a task of any duration as a milestone. Double-click the task name to display the Task Information dialog box, and then click the Advanced tab. Select the Mark Task As Milestone option.

Organizing Tasks into Phases

It is helpful to organize groups of closely related tasks into *phases*. Seeing phases of tasks helps you and anyone else reviewing a project plan to think in terms of major work items and detailed work items. For example, it is common to divide a film or video project into major phases of work such as pre-production, production, and post-production. You create phases by indenting and outdenting tasks. You can also collapse a task list into phases, much as you can work with an outline in Microsoft Word. In Microsoft Project, phases are represented by *summary tasks*.

A summary task behaves differently from other tasks. You can't edit its duration, start date, or other calculated values directly, because this information is derived or "rolled up" from the detail tasks, called subtasks. Summary tasks are useful for getting information about phases of project work.

Project Management Focus:
Top-Down and Bottom-Up Planning

The two most common approaches to developing tasks and phases are top-down and bottom-up planning.

Top-down planning identifies major phases or products of the project before filling in the tasks required to complete those phases. Complex projects can have several layers of phases. This approach works from general to specific.

Bottom-up planning identifies as many of the bottom-level detailed tasks as possible before organizing them into logical groups, called phases or summary tasks. This approach works from specific to general.

Creating accurate tasks and phases for most complex projects requires a combination of top-down and bottom-up planning. For some project work, you will already know the low-level tasks; for others, you might initially know only the broader project goals.

Microsoft Project Web Access, the browser-based interface for Microsoft Project Server, enables bottom-up planning by allowing resources to create new, detailed tasks that can be added below broad summary tasks in Microsoft Project. For more information about Microsoft Project Server, see Appendix A, "Introducing Microsoft Project Server."

In this exercise, you create two summary tasks by indenting tasks:

1 In the Tasks pane, click the Organize Tasks Into Phases link.

The Organize Tasks pane appears.

2 Select the names of tasks 2 through 6. Your screen should look similar to the following illustration:

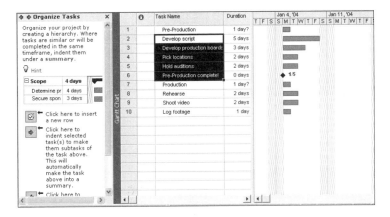

Indent Tasks

3 In the Organize Tasks pane, click the Indent Tasks button. (You can also click this button on the Formatting toolbar.)

Task 1 becomes a summary task, and a summary task bar for it appears in the Gantt chart. The summary task name is also formatted in bold type. Your screen should look similar to the following illustration:

Summary task ⎯⎯⎯⎯⎯⎯⎯ Summary task bar in the Gantt Chart

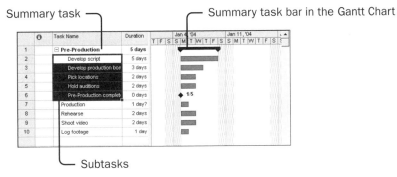

⎣⎯ Subtasks

4 Next select the names of tasks 8 through 10.

5 In the Organize Tasks pane, click the Indent Tasks button.

Task 7 becomes a summary task, and a summary task bar for it appears in the Gantt chart. Your screen should look similar to the following illustration:

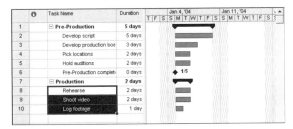

6 At the bottom of the Organize Tasks pane, click the Done link.

The Tasks pane appears.

Tip

If your organization uses a work breakdown structure (WBS) process in the project-planning phase, you may find it helpful to view WBS codes in Microsoft Project. For information about using WBS codes with Microsoft Project, type **View WBS codes** into the Ask A Question box in the upper right corner of the Microsoft Project window.

Linking Tasks

Projects require tasks to be done in a specific order. For example, the task of filming a scene must be completed before the task of editing the filmed scene can occur. These two tasks have a finish-to-start *relationship* (also called a link or a dependency), which has two aspects:

■ The second task must occur after the first task; this is a *sequence*.

■ The second task can occur only if the first task is completed; this is a *dependency*.

In Microsoft Project, the first task ("film the scene") is called the *predecessor* because it precedes tasks that depend on it. The second task ("Edit the filmed scene") is called the *successor* because it succeeds tasks on which it is dependent. Any task can be a predecessor for one or more successor tasks. Likewise, any task can be a successor to one or more predecessor tasks.

This might sound complicated, but it turns out tasks can have one of only four types of task relationships:

This task relationship	Means	Looks like this in the Gantt chart	Example
Finish-to-start (FS)	The finish date of the predecessor task determines the start date of the successor task.		A film scene must be shot before it can be edited.
Start-to-start (SS)	The start date of the predecessor task determines the start date of the successor task.		Reviewing a script and developing the script breakdown and schedule are closely related, and they should occur simultaneously.
Finish-to-finish (FF)	The finish date of the predecessor task determines the finish date of the successor task.		Tasks that require specific equipment must end when the equipment rental ends.
Start-to-finish (SF)	The start date of the predecessor task determines finish date of the successor task.		The time when the editing lab becomes available determines when a pre-editing task must end. (This type of relationship is rarely used.)

Tip

Representing task relationships and handling changes to scheduled start and finish dates is one area where using a scheduling engine like Microsoft Project really pays off. For example, you can change task durations or add or remove tasks from a chain of linked tasks, and Microsoft Project will reschedule tasks accordingly.

Task relationships appear in several ways in Microsoft Project. For example:

- In the Gantt Chart and Network Diagram views, task relationships appear as the lines connecting tasks.

- In tables, such as the Entry table, task ID numbers of predecessor tasks appear in the Predecessor fields of successor tasks.

You create task relationships by creating *links* between tasks. Currently, all the tasks in the project plan are scheduled to start on the same day—the project start date. In this exercise, you use different methods to create links between several tasks, creating finish-to-start relationships:

1 In the Tasks pane, click Schedule Tasks.

The Schedule Tasks pane appears. First you'll create a finish-to-start dependency between two tasks.

2 Select the names of tasks 2 and 3. Your screen should look similar to the following illustration:

⊕ ⊕ Schedule Tasks	X		🛈	Task Name	Duration	Jan 4, '04	Jan 11, '04
						T F S S M T W T F S S M T W T F S
Often a task's start or finish depends on the start or finish of another task. You can schedule these dependent tasks by linking them.		1		⊟ Pre-Production	5 days		
		2		Develop script	5 days		
		3		Develop production boa	3 days		
🖓 Hint		4		Pick locations	2 days		
		5		Hold auditions	2 days		
Link dependent tasks		6		Pre-Production complet	0 days	◆ 1/5	
On the right, select the tasks that you want to link:		7		⊟ Production	2 days		
		8		Rehearse	2 days		
Click here to to create a finish to start link.		9		Shoot video	2 days		
		10		Log footage	1 day		
Click here to create a start to start link.							
Click here to create a finish to finish link.							
Click to break the link for the selected tasks.							
Done							
⑦ More Information							

Finish-to-Start Link

3 In the Schedule Tasks pane, click the Finish-To-Start Link button.

Tip

To create a finish-to-start dependency, you can also click the Link Tasks button on the Standard toolbar.

Tasks 2 and 3 are linked with a finish-to-start relationship. Note that Microsoft Project changed the start date of Task 3 to the next working day following the completion of Task 2 (skipping over the weekend), and the duration of the Pre-Production summary task grew correspondingly. Your screen should look similar to the following illustration:

Link line ——— ——— Nonworking time

	0	Task Name	Duration	Jan 4, '04	Jan 11, '04
1		⊟ Pre-Production	**8 days**		
2		Develop script	5 days		
3		Develop production boa	3 days		
4		Pick locations	2 days		
5		Hold auditions	2 days		
6		Pre-Production complet:	0 days	◆ 1/5	
7		⊟ Production	**2 days**		
8		Rehearse	2 days		
9		Shoot video	2 days		
10		Log footage	1 day		

Tip

To unlink tasks, select the tasks you want to unlink, and then click the Unlink Tasks button on the Standard toolbar. If you unlink a single task that is part of a chain of linked tasks with finish-to-start relationships, Microsoft Project reestablishes links between the remaining tasks.

Next you will link several tasks at once.

4 Select the names of tasks 3 through 6.

5 In the Schedule Tasks pane, click the Finish-To-Start Link button.

Tasks 3 through 6 are linked with a finish-to-start relationship. Your screen should look similar to the following illustration:

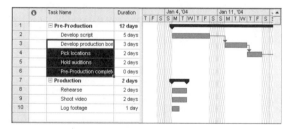

Next you will link two tasks in another way. You will make task 8 the predecessor of task 9.

6 Select the name of task 9.

7 On the Standard toolbar, click the Task Information button.

The Task Information dialog box appears.

8 Click the Predecessors tab.

9 Click the empty cell below the Task Name column heading, and then click the down arrow that appears.

10 In the Task Name list, click Rehearse, and press Enter. Your screen should look similar to the following illustration:

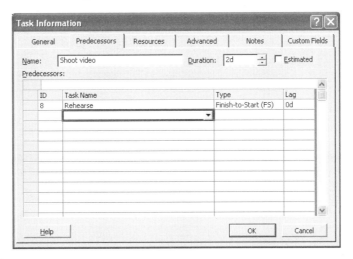

11 Click OK to close the Task Information dialog box.

Tasks 8 and 9 are linked with a finish-to-start relationship.

To wrap up this exercise, you'll link the remaining production tasks and then link the two summary tasks.

12 Select the names of tasks 9 and 10.

13 In the Schedule Tasks pane, click the Finish-To-Start Link button.

Tip

When working with summary tasks, you can either link summary tasks directly, or link the latest task in the first phase with the earliest task in the second phase. The scheduling end result is the same either way, but it's preferable to link the summary tasks to better reflect the sequential nature of the two phases. Under no circumstances, however, can you link a summary task to one if its own subtasks. Doing so would create a circular scheduling problem, so Microsoft Project doesn't allow it.

14 Now select the name of task 1, and while holding down the Ctrl key, select the name of task 7. This is how you make a nonadjacent selection in a table in Microsoft Project.

15 In the Schedule Tasks pane, click the Finish-To-Start Link button to link the two summary tasks.

16 Scroll the chart portion of the Gantt Chart view to the right until the second phase of the project plan is visible.

Your screen should look similar to the following illustration:

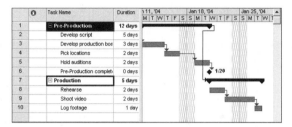

17 Click Done in the Schedule Tasks pane.

Tip

You can also create a finish-to-start relationship between tasks right in the Gantt chart. Point to the task bar of the predecessor task until the pointer changes to a four-pointed star. Then drag the mouse pointer up or down to the task bar of the successor task.

Documenting Tasks

You can record additional information about a task in a ***note***. For example, you might have detailed descriptions of a task and still want to keep the task's name succinct. You can add such details to a task note. That way, the information resides in the Microsoft Project file and can be easily viewed or printed.

There are three types of notes: task notes, resource notes, and assignment notes. You enter and review task notes on the Notes tab in the Task Information dialog box. (You can open the Task Information dialog box by clicking the Task Information command on the Project menu.) Notes in Microsoft Project support a wide range of text formatting options; you can even link to or store graphic images and other types of files in notes.

Hyperlinks enable you to connect a specific task to additional information that resides outside of the project plan—such as another file, a specific location in a file, a page on the World Wide Web, or a page on an intranet.

In this exercise, you enter task notes and hyperlinks to document important information about some tasks:

1 In the Tasks pane, click the Link To Or Attach More Task Information link.

The Add Information pane appears. Take a moment to read the information in the pane.

2 Select the name of Task 4, Pick locations.

3 In the Add Information pane, click the Add A Note link.

Tip

Task Notes

You can also click the Task Notes button on the Standard toolbar.

Microsoft Project displays the Task Information dialog box with the Notes tab visible.

4 In the Notes box, type **Includes exterior street scene and indoor studio scenes.**, and click OK.

A note icon appears in the Indicators column.

5 Point to the note icon:

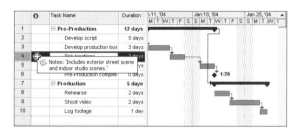

The note appears in a *ScreenTip*. For notes that are too long to appear in a ScreenTip, you can double-click the note icon to display the full text of the note.

To conclude this exercise, you create a hyperlink.

6 Select the name of Task 5, *Hold auditions*.

7 In the Add Information pane, click the Add A Hyperlink link.

Tip

Insert Hyperlink

You can also click the Insert Hyperlink button on the Standard toolbar.

The Insert Hyperlink dialog box appears.

8 In the Text To Display box, type **Check recent agent postings**.

9 In the Address box, type **http://www.southridgevideo.com**, and click OK.

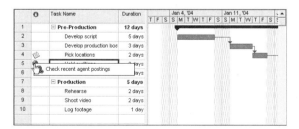

A hyperlink icon appears in the Indicators column. Pointing to the icon displays the descriptive text you typed above. Clicking the icon opens the Web page in your browser.

10 Click Done in the Add Information pane.

Checking the Plan's Duration

At this point, you might want to know how long the project is expected to take. You haven't directly entered a total project duration or finish date, but Microsoft Project has calculated these values, based on individual task durations and task relationships. An easy way to see the project's scheduled finish date is via the Project Information dialog box.

In this exercise, you see the current total duration and scheduled finish date of the project, based on the task durations and relationships you've entered:

1 On the Project menu, click Project Information.

The Project Information dialog box appears. Note the Finish date: 1/27/04.

You can't edit the finish date directly because this project is set to be scheduled from the start date. Microsoft Project calculates the project's finish date based on the total number of working days required to complete the tasks, starting at the project's start date.

Next let's look at the duration information in more detail.

2 Click the Statistics button.

The Project Statistics dialog box appears:

Project Statistics for 'Wingtip Toys Commercial 2'			
	Start		Finish
Current		Mon 1/5/04	Tue 1/27/04
Baseline		NA	NA
Actual		NA	NA
Variance		0d	0d

	Duration	Work	Cost
Current	17d	0h	$0.00
Baseline	0d?	0h	$0.00
Actual	0d	0h	$0.00
Remaining	17d	0h	$0.00

Percent complete:
Duration: 0%   Work: 0%

Close

You don't need to pay attention to all these numbers yet, but the current finish date and the current duration are worth noting. The duration is the number of working days in the project calendar between the project's start date and finish date.

You can visually verify these numbers on the Gantt chart.

3 Click the Close button to close the Project Statistics dialog box.

4 Click the Close button in the upper right corner of the Project Guide pane to close the Project Guide.

Next you will look at the complete project by changing the timescale in the Gantt Chart view.

5 On the View menu, click Zoom.

The Zoom dialog box appears.

6 Click Entire Project, and then click OK.

The entire project appears on the screen. Your screen should look similar to the following illustration:

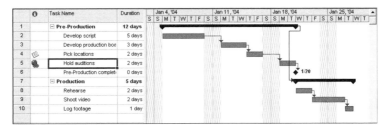

You can see the project's overall duration in the Gantt Chart view.

Tip

Zoom In
ZoomOut

You can also click the Zoom In and Zoom Out buttons to change the timescale of the Gantt Chart view.

Chapter Wrap-Up

This chapter covered how to create a task list.

If you are going on to other chapters:

Save

1 On the Standard toolbar, click the Save button to save changes made to Wingtip Toys Commercial 2.

2 On the File menu, click Close to close the project plan.

If you aren't continuing to other chapters:

1 On the Standard toolbar, click the Save button to save changes made to Wingtip Toys Commercial 2.

2 To quit Microsoft Project for now, on the File menu, click Exit.

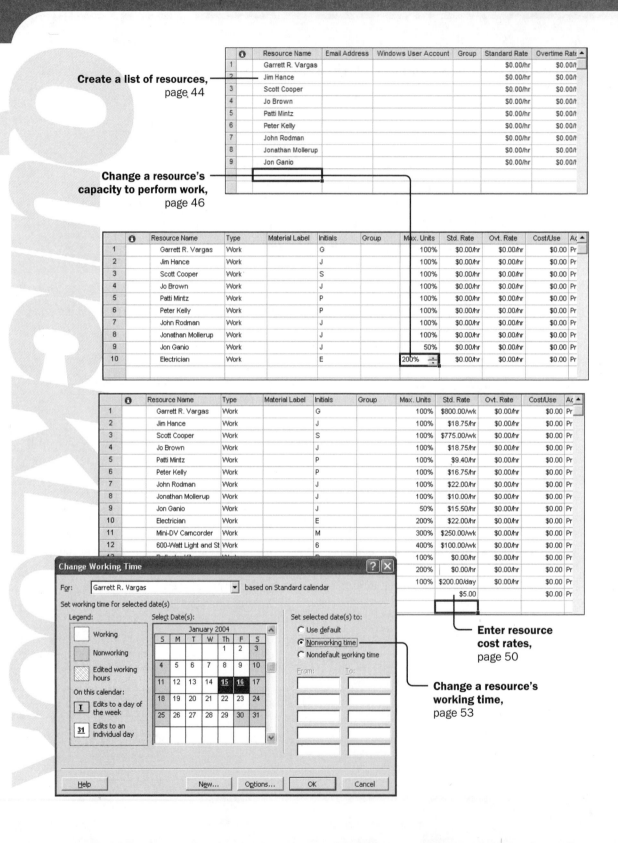

Create a list of resources, page 44

Change a resource's capacity to perform work, page 46

Enter resource cost rates, page 50

Change a resource's working time, page 53

Chapter 3
Setting Up Resources

After completing this chapter, you will be able to:

✔ **Set up basic resource information for the people who work on projects.**

✔ **Enter basic resource information for the equipment that will be used in projects.**

✔ **Enter basic resource information for the materials that will be consumed as the project progresses.**

✔ **Set up cost information for resources.**

✔ **Change a resource's availability for work.**

✔ **Record additional information about a resource in a note.**

Resources are the people, equipment, and material needed to complete the tasks in a project. Microsoft Project focuses on two aspects of resources: their availability and their costs. Availability determines when specific resources can work on tasks and how much work they can do, and costs refer to how much money will be required to pay for those resources.

In this chapter, you will set up the resources you need to complete the TV commercial project. Effective resource management is one of the most powerful advantages of using Microsoft Project over task-focused planning tools, such as paper-based organizers. You do not need to set up resources and assign them to tasks in Microsoft Project; however, without this information, you might have less control over who does what work, when, and at what cost. Setting up resource information in Microsoft Project takes a little effort, but the time is well spent if your project is primarily driven by time or cost *constraints*. (And nearly all complex projects are driven by one, if not both, of these factors.)

Wingtip Toys Commercial 3a

This chapter uses the practice file Wingtip Toys Commercial 3a. If you completed Chapter 2, "Creating a Task List," you might recognize this task list. For details about installing the practice files, see "Using the Book's CD-ROM" at the beginning of this book.

Setting Up People Resources

Microsoft Project works with two types of resources: work resources and material resources. *Work resources* are the people and equipment that do the work of the project. You will learn about material resources later in this chapter.

Some examples of work resources are listed in the table on the following page.

Work resource	Example
Individual people identified by name	Jon Ganio; Jim Hance
Individual people identified by job title or function	Director; camera operator
Groups of people who have common skills (When assigning such interchangeable resources to a task, you do not care who the individual resource is, as long as the resource has the right skills.)	Electricians; carpenters; extras
Equipment	Video camera; 600-watt light

Equipment resources don't need to be portable; a fixed location or piece of machinery (for example, a video editing studio) can also be considered equipment.

All projects require some people resources, and some projects require only people resources. Microsoft Project can help you make smarter decisions about how to manage work resources and monitor financial costs.

Tip

Microsoft Project Server provides substantial, enterprise-level resource management capabilities, such as skills-based resource assignments and a centralized enterprise resource pool. For more information, see Appendix A, "Introducing Microsoft Project Server."

In this exercise, you set up resource information for several people resources:

1   If Microsoft Project is not already open, start it now.

Open

2   On the Standard toolbar, click the Open button.

The Open dialog box appears.

3   Navigate to the Chapter 3 Simple Resources folder, and double-click the Wingtip Toys Commercial 3a file.

4   On the File menu, click Save As.

The Save As dialog box appears.

5   In the File Name box, type **Wingtip Toys Commercial 3**, and then click Save.

6   On the Project Guide toolbar, click Resources.

7   In the Resources pane, click the Specify People And Equipment For The Project link.

The Specify Resources pane appears, and the Project Guide: Simple Resource Sheet view replaces the Gantt Chart view.

8   Select the Enter Resources Manually option.

Tip

For your own projects, if your resource information resides in the right source on your network, such as a Microsoft Exchange address book or Active Directory, you can quickly import the resource information into Microsoft Project. This saves you the effort of retyping the information and reduces the chance of making a data-entry error.

9 In the Simple Resource Sheet view, click the cell directly below the Resource Name column heading.

10 Type **Garrett R. Vargas**, and press Enter.

Microsoft Project creates a new resource.

11 Widen the Resource Name column by moving the mouse pointer to the vertical divider line between the Resource Name and Email Address columns and double-clicking. Your screen should look like the following illustration:

Here is resource information you've entered.

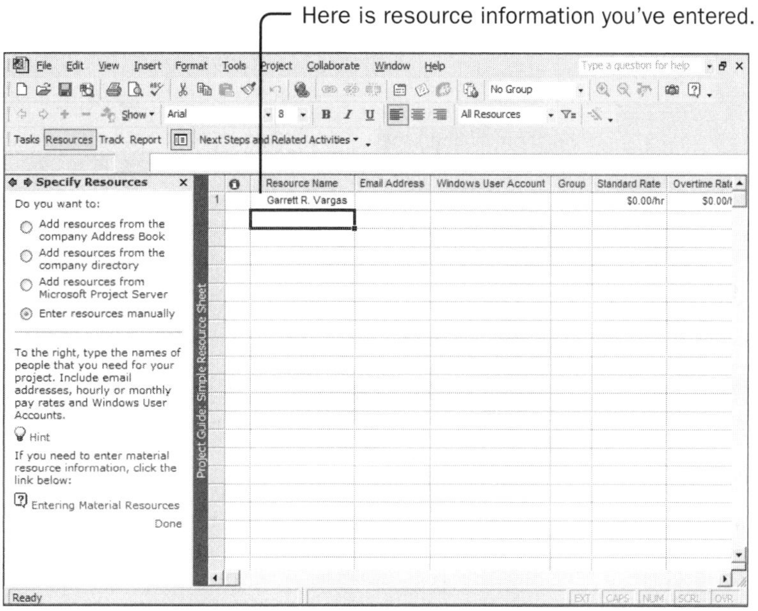

12 Enter the remaining resource information into the Simple Resource Sheet:

- Jim Hance
- Scott Cooper
- Jo Brown
- Patti Mintz

- Peter Kelly
- John Rodman
- Jonathan Mollerup
- Jon Ganio

Your screen should look similar to the following illustration:

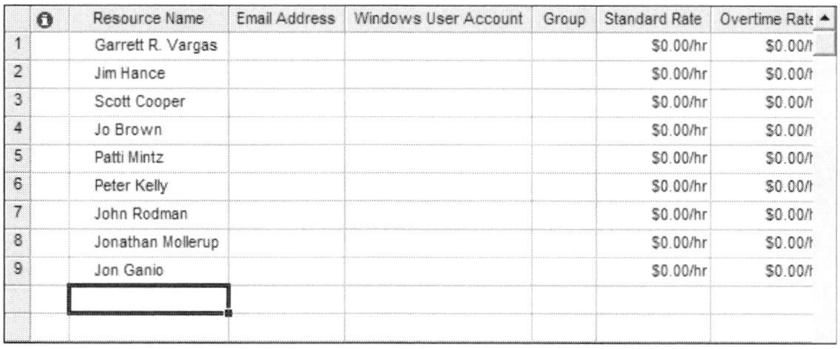

	🛈	Resource Name	Email Address	Windows User Account	Group	Standard Rate	Overtime Rate
1		Garrett R. Vargas				$0.00/hr	$0.00/h
2		Jim Hance				$0.00/hr	$0.00/h
3		Scott Cooper				$0.00/hr	$0.00/h
4		Jo Brown				$0.00/hr	$0.00/h
5		Patti Mintz				$0.00/hr	$0.00/h
6		Peter Kelly				$0.00/hr	$0.00/h
7		John Rodman				$0.00/hr	$0.00/h
8		Jonathan Mollerup				$0.00/hr	$0.00/h
9		Jon Ganio				$0.00/hr	$0.00/h

13 Click the Close button in the upper right corner of the Project Guide pane to close the Project Guide.

You can also have a resource that represents multiple people. Next you will switch to a different view to set up such a resource.

14 On the View menu, click Resource Sheet.

The Resource Sheet view appears. This sheet contains more resource-related fields than the Simple Resource Sheet does.

15 In the Resource Name field below the last resource, type **Electrician**, and then press Tab.

16 In the Type field, make sure that Work is selected, and then press Tab several times to move to the Max. Units field.

The Max. Units field represents the maximum capacity of a resource to accomplish any task. Specifying that a resource such as Garrett R. Vargas, for example, has 100 percent maximum units means that 100 percent of Garrett's time is available to work on the tasks to which you assign him. Microsoft Project will alert you if you assign Garrett to more tasks than he can accomplish at 100 percent maximum units (or, in other words, if Garrett becomes *overallocated*).

17 In the Max. Units field for the electrician, type or select **200%**, and then press Tab.

Tip

When you click a numeric field, up and down arrows appear. You can click these to display the number you want, or just type the number in the field.

The resource named Electrician does not represent a single person; instead, it represents a category of interchangeable people called electricians. Because the Electrician resource has a maximum units setting of 200 percent, you can plan on two electricians being available to work full time every workday. At this point in the planning phase, you do not know exactly who these electricians will be, and that's OK. You can still proceed with more general planning.

Now you'll update the maximum units value for Jon Ganio to indicate that he works half time.

18 Click the Max. Units field for Jon Ganio, type or select **50%**, and then press Enter.

Your screen should look similar to the following illustration:

	❶	Resource Name	Type	Material Label	Initials	Group	Max. Units	Std. Rate	Ovt. Rate	Cost/Use	Ac ▲
1		Garrett R. Vargas	Work		G	.	100%	$0.00/hr	$0.00/hr	$0.00	Pr
2		Jim Hance	Work		J		100%	$0.00/hr	$0.00/hr	$0.00	Pr
3		Scott Cooper	Work		S		100%	$0.00/hr	$0.00/hr	$0.00	Pr
4		Jo Brown	Work		J		100%	$0.00/hr	$0.00/hr	$0.00	Pr
5		Patti Mintz	Work		P		100%	$0.00/hr	$0.00/hr	$0.00	Pr
6		Peter Kelly	Work		P		100%	$0.00/hr	$0.00/hr	$0.00	Pr
7		John Rodman	Work		J		100%	$0.00/hr	$0.00/hr	$0.00	Pr
8		Jonathan Mollerup	Work		J		100%	$0.00/hr	$0.00/hr	$0.00	Pr
9		Jon Ganio	Work		J		50%	$0.00/hr	$0.00/hr	$0.00	Pr
10		Electrician	Work		E		200%	$0.00/hr	$0.00/hr	$0.00	Pr

When you create a new resource, Microsoft Project assigns it 100% max. units by default. You change the resource's max. units here.

Tip

If you prefer, you can enter maximum units as partial or whole numbers (for example, .5, 1, 2) rather than as percentages (50%, 100%, or 200%). To use this format, on the Tools menu, click Options, and then click the Schedule tab. In the Show Assignment Units As A box, click Decimal.

What Is the Best Way to Enter Resource Names?

In Microsoft Project, resource names can refer to specific people (for example, Jon Ganio or Jim Hance) or to specific job titles (for example, Camera Operator or Actor). Use whatever makes the most sense for your needs and for those who will see the project plan information you publish. The important questions are *Who will see these resource names?* and *How will they identify the resources?* The resource names you choose will appear both in Microsoft Project and in information published from Microsoft Project. For example, in the default Gantt Chart view, the name of the resource, as you enter it in the Resource Name field, appears next to the bars of the tasks to which that resource is assigned.

A resource might be somebody already on staff or a position to be filled later. If you have not yet filled all the resource positions required, you might not have real people's names yet. In that case, use placeholder names or job titles when setting up resources in Microsoft Project.

Setting Up Equipment Resources

You set up people and equipment resources exactly the same way in Microsoft Project. However, you should be aware of important differences in how you can schedule these two types of resources. For example, most people resources have a working day of no more than 12 hours, but equipment resources might work around the clock. Moreover, people resources might be flexible in the tasks they can perform, but equipment resources tend to be more specialized. For example, a director of photography for a film or video project might also act as a camera operator in a pinch, but a video camera cannot replace an editing studio.

You do not need to track every piece of equipment that will be used in your project, but you might want to set up equipment resources when:

■ Multiple teams or people might need a piece of equipment to do different tasks simultaneously, and the equipment might be overbooked.

■ You want to plan and track costs associated with the equipment.

In this exercise, you enter information about equipment resources in the Resource Information dialog box:

1 In the Resource Sheet, click the next empty cell in the Resource Name column.

Resource Information

2 On the Standard toolbar, click the Resource Information button.

The Resource Information dialog box appears.

Tip

You can also double-click a resource name or an empty cell in the Resource Name column to display the Resource Information dialog box.

3 Click the General tab if it is not already displayed.

In the upper portion of the General tab, you might recognize the fields you saw in the Resource Sheet view. As with many types of information in Microsoft Project, you can usually work in at least two ways: a table or a dialog box.

4 In the Resource Name field, type **Mini-DV Camcorder**.

5 In the Type field, click Work.

Your screen should look similar to the following illustration:

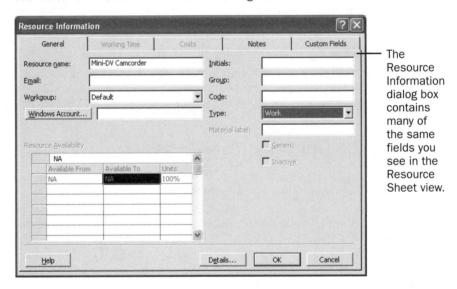

The Resource Information dialog box contains many of the same fields you see in the Resource Sheet view.

Tip

The Resource Information dialog box contains a button labeled Details. If you have an e-mail program that complies with the Messaging Application Programming Interface (MAPI) and the program is installed on the same computer as Microsoft Project, you can click Details to see contact information about the selected resource. MAPI-compliant programs include Microsoft Outlook and Microsoft Exchange.

6 Click OK to close the Resource Information dialog box and return to the Resource Sheet.

The Max. Units field shows 100% for this resource; next you will change this.

Tip

When creating a resource in the Resource Information dialog box, you cannot enter a Max. Units value. However, you can edit this value in the dialog box, as well as in the Resource Sheet, after you create the resource.

7 In the Max. Units field for the Mini-DV Camcorder, type or click **300%** and press Tab.

This means that you plan to have three camcorders available every workday.

8 Enter the following information about equipment resources directly in the Resource Sheet or in the Resource Information dialog box, whichever you prefer. In either case, make sure Work is selected in the Type field.

Resource name	Max. Units
600-Watt Light and Stand	400%
Reflector Kit	100%
Camera Boom	200%
Editing Lab	100%

Your screen should look similar to the following illustration:

	ⓘ	Resource Name	Type	Material Label	Initials	Group	Max. Units	Std. Rate	Ovt. Rate	Cost/Use	Ac
1		Garrett R. Vargas	Work		G		100%	$0.00/hr	$0.00/hr	$0.00	Pr
2		Jim Hance	Work		J		100%	$0.00/hr	$0.00/hr	$0.00	Pr
3		Scott Cooper	Work		S		100%	$0.00/hr	$0.00/hr	$0.00	Pr
4		Jo Brown	Work		J		100%	$0.00/hr	$0.00/hr	$0.00	Pr
5		Patti Mintz	Work		P		100%	$0.00/hr	$0.00/hr	$0.00	Pr
6		Peter Kelly	Work		P		100%	$0.00/hr	$0.00/hr	$0.00	Pr
7		John Rodman	Work		J		100%	$0.00/hr	$0.00/hr	$0.00	Pr
8		Jonathan Mollerup	Work		J		100%	$0.00/hr	$0.00/hr	$0.00	Pr
9		Jon Ganio	Work		J		50%	$0.00/hr	$0.00/hr	$0.00	Pr
10		Electrician	Work		E		200%	$0.00/hr	$0.00/hr	$0.00	Pr
11		Mini-DV Camcorder	Work		M		300%	$0.00/hr	$0.00/hr	$0.00	Pr
12		600-Watt Light and St	Work		6		400%	$0.00/hr	$0.00/hr	$0.00	Pr
13		Reflector Kit	Work		R		100%	$0.00/hr	$0.00/hr	$0.00	Pr
14		Camera Boom	Work		C		200%	$0.00/hr	$0.00/hr	$0.00	Pr
15		Editing Lab	Work		E		100%	$0.00/hr	$0.00/hr	$0.00	Pr

Setting Up Material Resources

Material resources are consumables that you use up as the project proceeds. On a construction project, material resources might include nails, lumber, and concrete. On your project, video tape is the consumable resource that interests you most. You work with material resources in Microsoft Project mainly to track the rate of consumption and the associated cost. Although Microsoft Project is not a complete system for tracking inventory, it can help you stay better informed about how quickly you are consuming your material resources.

Comparing Work and Material Resources

Following are some ways material resources are similar to and different from work resources.

For both material and work resources, you can edit and *contour* resource *assignments*, set up multiple pay rates, specify different pay rates to apply at different times, and share resources through a *resource pool*. (You will work with these subjects in later chapters.) In addition, cost calculations for material resources work just about the same way as they do for work resources.

Unlike work resources, however, material resources do not use overtime cost rates, resource calendars, or maximum units.

In this exercise, you enter information about a material resource:

1 In the Resource Sheet, click the next empty cell in the Resource Name column.

2 Type **Video Tape** and press Tab.

3 In the Type field, click Material, and press Tab.

4 In the Material Label field, type **30-min. cassette** and press Enter.

You will use 30-minute cassettes as the unit of measure to track video tape consumption during the project. Your screen should look similar to the following illustration:

	ⓘ	Resource Name	Type	Material Label	Initials	Group	Max. Units	Std. Rate	Ovt. Rate	Cost/Use	Ac ▲
1		Garrett R. Vargas	Work		G		100%	$0.00/hr	$0.00/hr	$0.00	Pr
2		Jim Hance	Work		J		100%	$0.00/hr	$0.00/hr	$0.00	Pr
3		Scott Cooper	Work		S		100%	$0.00/hr	$0.00/hr	$0.00	Pr
4		Jo Brown	Work		J		100%	$0.00/hr	$0.00/hr	$0.00	Pr
5		Patti Mintz	Work		P		100%	$0.00/hr	$0.00/hr	$0.00	Pr
6		Peter Kelly	Work		P		100%	$0.00/hr	$0.00/hr	$0.00	Pr
7		John Rodman	Work		J		100%	$0.00/hr	$0.00/hr	$0.00	Pr
8		Jonathan Mollerup	Work		J		100%	$0.00/hr	$0.00/hr	$0.00	Pr
9		Jon Ganio	Work		J		50%	$0.00/hr	$0.00/hr	$0.00	Pr
10		Electrician	Work		E		200%	$0.00/hr	$0.00/hr	$0.00	Pr
11		Mini-DV Camcorder	Work		M		300%	$0.00/hr	$0.00/hr	$0.00	Pr
12		600-Watt Light and St	Work		6		400%	$0.00/hr	$0.00/hr	$0.00	Pr
13		Reflector Kit	Work		R		100%	$0.00/hr	$0.00/hr	$0.00	Pr
14		Camera Boom	Work		C		200%	$0.00/hr	$0.00/hr	$0.00	Pr
15		Editing Lab	Work		E		100%	$0.00/hr	$0.00/hr	$0.00	Pr
16		Video Tape	Material	30-min. cassette	V			$0.00		$0.00	Pr

Here is the material resource you entered.

The Material Label field only applies to material resources.

Entering Resource Pay Rates

Almost all projects have some financial aspect, and cost drives the scope of many projects. Tracking and managing cost information allows the project manager to answer such important questions as:

■ What is the expected total cost of the project, based on our task duration and resource estimates?

■ Are we using expensive resources to do work that less expensive resources could do?

■ How much money will a specific type of resource or task cost over the life of the project?

■ Are we spending money at a rate that we can sustain for the planned duration of the project?

For the TV commercial project, you have been entrusted with pay rate information for all people resources used in the project. In the information below, note that the fees for the camcorders, the lights, and the editing lab are rental fees. Because the Southridge Video company already owns the reflector kit and camera booms, you will not bill yourself for them.

In this exercise, you enter cost information for each resource:

1 In the Resource Sheet, click the Std. Rate field for Resource 1, *Garrett R. Vargas*.

2 Type **800/w** and press Enter.

Garrett's standard weekly rate of $800 per week appears in the Std. Rate column.

3 In the Std. Rate field for Resource 2, Jim Hance, type **18.75/h**, and press Enter.

Jim's standard hourly rate appears in the Std. Rate column. Your screen should look similar to the following illustration:

	ⓘ	Resource Name	Type	Material Label	Initials	Group	Max. Units	Std. Rate	Ovt. Rate	Cost/Use	Ac ▲
1		Garrett R. Vargas	Work		G		100%	$800.00/wk	$0.00/hr	$0.00	Pr
2		Jim Hance	Work		J		100%	$18.75/hr	$0.00/hr	$0.00	Pr
3		Scott Cooper	Work		S		100%	$0.00/hr	$0.00/hr	$0.00	Pr

4 Enter the following standard pay rates for the given resources:

Resource name	Standard rate	Resource name	Standard rate
Scott Cooper	**775/w**	Electrician	**22/h**
Jo Brown	**18.75/h**	Mini-DV Camcorder	**250/w**
Patti Mintz	**9.40/h**	600-Watt Light and Stand	**100/w**
Peter Kelly	**16.75/h**	Reflector Kit	**0/h**
John Rodman	**22/h**	Camera Boom	**0/h**
Jonathan Mollerup	**10/h**	Editing Lab	**200/d**
Jon Ganio	**15.50/h**	Video Tape	**5**

Your screen should look similar to the following illustration:

	ⓘ	Resource Name	Type	Material Label	Initials	Group	Max. Units	Std. Rate	Ovt. Rate	Cost/Use	Ac ▲
1		Garrett R. Vargas	Work		G		100%	$800.00/wk	$0.00/hr	$0.00	Pr
2		Jim Hance	Work		J		100%	$18.75/hr	$0.00/hr	$0.00	Pr
3		Scott Cooper	Work		S		100%	$775.00/wk	$0.00/hr	$0.00	Pr
4		Jo Brown	Work		J		100%	$18.75/hr	$0.00/hr	$0.00	Pr
5		Patti Mintz	Work		P		100%	$9.40/hr	$0.00/hr	$0.00	Pr
6		Peter Kelly	Work		P		100%	$16.75/hr	$0.00/hr	$0.00	Pr
7		John Rodman	Work		J		100%	$22.00/hr	$0.00/hr	$0.00	Pr
8		Jonathan Mollerup	Work		J		100%	$10.00/hr	$0.00/hr	$0.00	Pr
9		Jon Ganio	Work		J		50%	$15.50/hr	$0.00/hr	$0.00	Pr
10		Electrician	Work		E		200%	$22.00/hr	$0.00/hr	$0.00	Pr
11		Mini-DV Camcorder	Work		M		300%	$250.00/wk	$0.00/hr	$0.00	Pr
12		600-Watt Light and St	Work		6		400%	$100.00/wk	$0.00/hr	$0.00	Pr
13		Reflector Kit	Work		R		100%	$0.00/hr	$0.00/hr	$0.00	Pr
14		Camera Boom	Work		C		200%	$0.00/hr	$0.00/hr	$0.00	Pr
15		Editing Lab	Work		E		100%	$200.00/day	$0.00/hr	$0.00	Pr
16		Video Tape	Material	30-min. cassett	V			$5.00		$0.00	Pr

Note that you don't enter a rate (hourly, daily, or weekly) for the video tape's cost. For material resources, the standard rate value is per unit of consumption—in our case, 30-minute cassettes.

Project Management Focus: Getting Resource Cost Information

Work and material resources account for the majority of costs in many projects. To take full advantage of the extensive cost management features in Microsoft Project, the project manager should know the costs associated with each work and material resource. For people resources, it might be difficult to get such information. In many organizations, only senior management and human resource specialists know the pay rates of all resources working on a project, and they might consider this information confidential. Depending on your organizational policies and project priorities, you might not be able to track resource pay rates. If you cannot track this information, your effectiveness as a project manager might be reduced, and the *sponsors* of your projects should understand this.

Adjusting Working Time for Individual Resources

Microsoft Project uses different types of calendars for different purposes. In this exercise, we will focus on the *resource calendar*. A resource calendar controls the working and nonworking times of a resource. Microsoft Project uses resource calendars to determine when work for a specific resource can be scheduled. Resource calendars apply only to work resources (people and equipment) and not to material resources.

When you initially create resources in a project plan, Microsoft Project creates a resource calendar for each resource. The initial working time settings for resource calendars exactly match those of the *Standard base calendar*. (This is a calendar built into Microsoft Project that accommodates an 8 A.M. to 5 P.M., Monday through Friday work schedule.) If all the working times of your resource match the working time of the Standard base calendar, you do not need to edit any resource calendars. However, chances are that some of your resources will need exceptions to the working time in the Standard base calendar—such as:

- A flex-time work schedule
- Vacation time
- Other times when a resource is not available to work on the project, such as time spent training or attending a conference

Any changes you make to the Standard base calendar are automatically reflected in all resource calendars that are based on the Standard base calendar. Any specific changes you have made to the working time of a resource are not changed, however.

Tip

If you have a resource who is available to work on your project only part-time, you might be tempted to set the working time of the resource in your project to reflect a part-time schedule—for example, 8 A.M. to 12 P.M. daily. However, a better approach would be to adjust the availability of the resource as recorded in the Max. Units field to 50%. Changing the unit availability of the resource keeps the focus on the capacity of the resource to work on the project, rather than on the specific times of the day when that work might occur. You set the maximum units for a resource in the Resource Sheet view, which you display by clicking Resource Sheet on the View menu. For more information about resource units, see "Setting Up People Resources," earlier in this chapter.

In this exercise, you specify the working and nonworking times for individual work resources:

1 On the Tools menu, click Change Working Time.

The Change Working Time dialog box appears.

2 In the For box, click Garrett R. Vargas.

Garrett R. Vargas's resource calendar appears in the Change Working Time dialog box. Garrett, the producer of the TV commercial, has told you he will not be available to work on Thursday and Friday, January 15 and 16.

3 In the calendar below the Select Date(s) label, drag the vertical scroll bar or click the up or down arrow buttons until January 2004 appears.

4 Select the dates January 15 and 16.

Tip

To quickly select this date range, drag from 15 through 16.

5 Under Set Selected Date(s) To, click Nonworking Time.

Your screen should look similar to the following illustration:

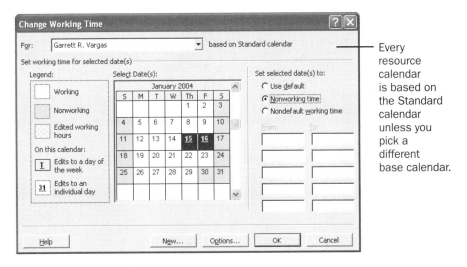

Every resource calendar is based on the Standard calendar unless you pick a different base calendar.

Microsoft Project will not schedule work for Garrett on these dates.

Tip

If your team uses the calendar module in Microsoft Outlook and Microsoft Project Web Access, resources can automatically report to you times they are not available to work on project activities. These times are based on calendar items marked as busy or out of office in Outlook. Once the times are reported, you can easily update the resource's working time in the project plan without retyping anything. For more information, see Appendix A, "Introducing Microsoft Project Server."

To conclude this exercise, you will set up a "4 by 10" work schedule (that is, 4 days per week, 10 hours per day) for a resource.

6 In the For box, click John Rodman.

7 When prompted to save the resource calendar changes you made for Garrett, click Yes.

8 Select the Monday through Thursday column headings.

Tip

To quickly select the Monday through Thursday column headings, drag from the M through the Th.

Although you can see only one month at a time in the dialog box, selecting a column heading for a day of the week selects every occurrence of that day—past, present, and future.

9 In the lower To box, click 5:00 PM and replace it with **7:00 PM**.

10 Click the Friday column heading.

11 Under Set Selected Date(s) To, click Nonworking Time.

Now Microsoft Project can schedule work for John as late as 7 P.M. every Monday through Thursday, but it will not schedule work for him on Fridays.

12 Click OK to close the Change Working Time dialog box.

Because you have not yet assigned these resources to tasks, you don't see the scheduling effect of their nonworking time settings. You will in Chapter 4, "Assigning Resources to Tasks."

Tip

If you find that you must edit several resource calendars in a similar way (to handle a night shift, for example), it may be easier to assign a different base calendar to a resource or collection of resources. This is more efficient than editing individual calendars, and it allows you to make project-wide adjustments to a single base calendar if needed.

For example, if your project includes a day shift and a night shift, you can apply the *Night Shift* base calendar to those resources who work the night shift. You change a resource's base calendar in Step 2 of the Resource Working Times Project Guide, or in the Base Calendar box on the Working Time tab of the Resource Information dialog box. You can open this dialog box by clicking Resource Information on the Project menu when in a resource view. For collections of resources, you can do this directly in the Base Calendar column on the Entry table in the Resource Sheet view.

Documenting Resources

You might recall from Chapter 2, "Creating a Task List," that you can record any additional information that you want about a task, resource, or assignment in a *note*. For example, if a resource is not available to work on a specific date range, it is a good idea to record why in a note. That way, the note resides in the project plan and can be easily viewed or printed.

In this exercise, you enter resource notes to document why a resource is not available to work on certain dates:

1   In the Resource Name column, click the name of Resource 1, Garrett R. Vargas.

Resource
Notes

2   On the Standard toolbar, click the Resource Notes button.

Microsoft Project displays the Resource Information dialog box with the Notes tab visible.

3   In the Notes box, type **Garrett attending West Coast film festival January 15 and 16; unavailable to work on project.** Then click OK.

A note icon appears in the Indicators column.

4   Point to the note icon:

	ⓘ	Resource Name	Type	Material Label	Initials	Group	Max. Units	Std. Rate	Ovt. Rate	Cost/Use	Ac ▲
1		Garrett R. Vargas	Work		G		100%	$800.00/wk	$0.00/hr	$0.00	Pr
2		Notes: 'Garrett attending West Coast film festival January 15 and 16; unavailable to work on project.'			J		100%	$18.75/hr	$0.00/hr	$0.00	Pr
3					S		100%	$775.00/wk	$0.00/hr	$0.00	Pr
4		Jo Brown	Work		J		100%	$18.75/hr	$0.00/hr	$0.00	Pr

The note appears in a ScreenTip. For notes that are too long to appear in a ScreenTip, you can double-click the note icon to display the full text of the note.

Chapter Wrap-Up

This chapter covered how to set up basic information about work and material resources.

If you are going on to other chapters:

Save

1   On the Standard toolbar, click the Save button to save changes made to Wingtip Toys Commercial 3.

2   On the File menu, click Close to close the project plan.

If you aren't continuing to other chapters:

1   On the Standard toolbar, click the Save button to save changes made to Wingtip Toys Commercial 3.

2   To quit Microsoft Project for now, on the File menu, click Exit.

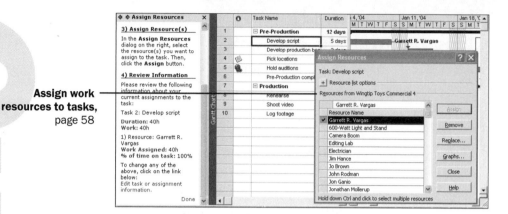

Assign work resources to tasks, page 58

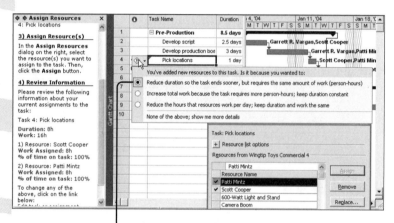

Control how effort-driven scheduling affects task durations, page 63

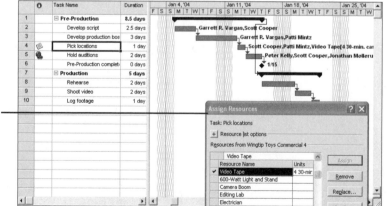

Assign material resources to tasks, page 67

Chapter 4
Assigning Resources to Tasks

After completing this chapter, you will be able to:

✔ **Assign resources to tasks.**

✔ **Control how Microsoft Project schedules additional assignments.**

✔ **Assign material resources to tasks.**

If you completed Chapter 2, "Creating a Task List," and Chapter 3, "Setting Up Resources," you have already created *tasks* and *resources*. Now you are ready to assign resources to tasks. An *assignment* is the matching of a resource to a task to do *work*. From the perspective of tasks, you might call the process of assigning a resource a task assignment; from the perspective of resources, you might call it a resource assignment. It is the same thing either way: a task plus a resource equals an assignment.

You do not have to assign resources to tasks in Microsoft Project; you could work with just tasks. But there are several good reasons to assign resources in your project plan. If you assign resources to tasks, you can answer questions such as:

■ Who should be working on what tasks and when?

■ Do you have the right number of resources to do the scope of work your project requires?

■ Are you expecting a resource to work on a task at a time when that resource will not be available to work (for example, when the resource will be on vacation)?

■ Have you assigned a resource to so many tasks that you have exceeded the capacity of the resource to work—in other words, have you *overallocated* the resource?

In this chapter, you assign resources to tasks. You assign work resources (people and equipment) and material resources to tasks, and you see where resource assignments should affect task duration and where they should not.

Wingtip Toys
Commercial 4a

This chapter uses the practice file Wingtip Toys Commercial 4a. This file contains the resource list you entered in Chapter 3. For details about installing the practice files, see "Using the Book's CD-ROM" at the beginning of this book.

Assigning Resources to Tasks

Assigning a resource to a task enables you to track the progress of the resource's work on the task. If you enter cost information, Microsoft Project also calculates resource and task costs for you.

You might recall from Chapter 3 that the capacity of a resource to work is measured in *units* and recorded in the Max. Units field. Unless you specify otherwise, Microsoft Project assigns 100 percent of the units for the resource to the task—that is, Microsoft Project assumes that all the resource's work time can be allotted to the task. If the resource has less than 100 percent maximum units, Microsoft Project assigns the resource's maximum units value.

In this exercise, you make the initial resource assignments to tasks in the project plan:

1   If Microsoft Project is not already open, start it now.

Open

2   On the Standard toolbar, click the Open button.

The Open dialog box appears.

3   Navigate to the Chapter 4 Simple Assignments folder, and double-click the Wingtip Toys Commercial 4a file.

4   On the File menu, click Save As.

The Save As dialog box appears.

5   In the File Name box, type **Wingtip Toys Commercial 4**, and then click the Save button.

6   On the Project Guide toolbar, click Resources.

7   In the Resources pane, click the Assign People And Equipment To Tasks link.

The Assign Resources Project Guide pane and the Gantt Chart view appear.

8   In the Assign Resources Project Guide pane, click the Assign Resources link.

The Assign Resources dialog box appears. In it you see resource names you entered in Chapter 3. If the Assign Resources dialog box obscures the Task Name column, drag the dialog box to the lower right corner of the screen. Your screen should look similar to the following illustration:

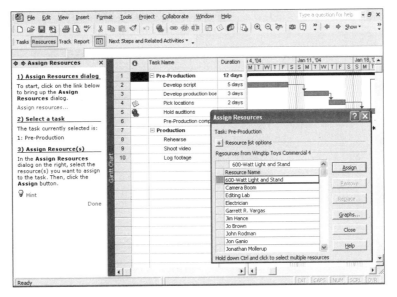

Tip

When you display the Assign Resources dialog box from the Project Guide, you see a slightly simplified version of the dialog box. You'll see the more complete version of it later in this chapter.

9   In the Task Name column, click Task 2, *Develop Script*.

10 In the Resource Name column in the Assign Resources dialog box, click Garrett R. Vargas, and then click the Assign button.

   A check mark appears next to Garrett's name, indicating that you have assigned him to the task of developing the script.

Tip

Except for assigned resources, which appear at the top of the list, resources are sorted alphabetically in the Assign Resources dialog box.

11 If necessary, scroll the Assign Resources pane down to see the information under step 4, *Review Information*. Your screen should look similar to the illustration shown on the following page.

The names of assigned resources
appear next to the Gantt bars.

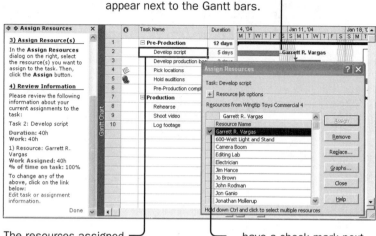

The resources assigned
to the selected task...

...have a check mark next
to their names in the Assign
Resources dialog box.

Here you can see the essential scheduling values for this task: *duration*, *work*, and assignment *units* (units are reported here as % of time on task). In the next exercise, you will look at these values more closely to understand the basic scheduling logic that Microsoft Project follows.

Next you assign two resources simultaneously to a task.

12 In the Task Name column, click the name of Task 3, Develop Production Boards.

13 In the Assign Resources dialog box, click Garrett R. Vargas, hold down the Ctrl key, click Patti Mintz, and then click the Assign button.

Check marks appear next to Garrett's and Patti's names, indicating that you have assigned both to Task 3.

Tip

You can also assign one or more resources to a task by using the mouse. First, select one resource in the Assign Resources dialog box. To select multiple resources, hold down Ctrl, and click the additional resource names. Point to the column to the left of the resource name. When the mouse pointer changes to a resource icon, drag the resource icon to the task name in the Task Name column.

To conclude this exercise, you will make initial resource assignments for remaining pre-production tasks.

14 In the Task Name column, click the name of Task 4, *Pick Locations*.

15 In the Assign Resources dialog box, click Scott Cooper, and then click the Assign button.

A check mark appears next to Scott's name, indicating that you have assigned him to Task 4.

Tip

To remove or unassign a resource from the selected task, in the Assign Resources dialog box, click the resource name, and then click the Remove button.

16 In the Task Name column, click the name of Task 5, *Hold Auditions*.

17 In the Assign Resources dialog box, click Peter Kelly, hold down the Ctrl key, click Scott Cooper, and then click the Assign button.

Check marks appear next to Peter's and Scott's names, indicating that you have assigned both to Task 5. Your screen should look similar to the following illustration:

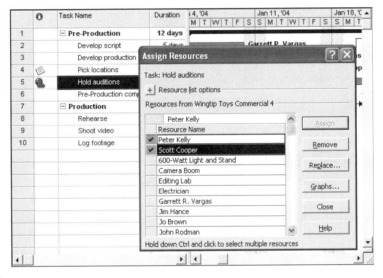

Tip

In Part 2 you will work more with assignments, but if you want to read more about assignments now, type **All about assignments** into the Ask A Question box in the upper right corner of the Microsoft Project window.

The Scheduling Formula: Duration, Units, and Work

After you create a task but before you assign a resource to it, the task has duration but no work associated with it. Why no work? Work represents the amount of effort a resource or resources will spend to complete a task. For example, if you have one person working full-time, the amount of time measured as work is the same as the amount of time measured as duration. In general, the amount of work will match the duration unless you assign more than one resource to a task or the one resource you assign is not working full-time.

Microsoft Project calculates work using what is sometimes called the *scheduling formula*:

Duration × Units = Work

Let's look at a specific example. The duration of Task 2 is five days. For our TV commercial project, five days equals 40 hours. When you assigned Garrett R. Vargas to Task 2, Microsoft Project applied 100 percent of Garrett's working time to this task. The scheduling formula for Task 2 looks like this:

40 hours task duration × 100% assignment units = 40 hours work

In other words, with Garrett assigned to Task 2 at 100 percent units, the task should require 40 hours of work.

Here's a more complex example. You assigned two resources, each at 100 percent assignment units, to Task 5. The scheduling formula for Task 5 looks like this:

16 hours task duration × 200% assignment units = 32 hours work

The 32 hours of work is the sum of Peter's 16 hours of work plus Scott's 16 hours of work. In other words, both resources will work on the task in parallel.

Assigning Additional Resources to a Task

Now you will assign additional resources to some of the pre-production tasks to see the effect on the overall duration of the tasks. By default, Microsoft Project uses a scheduling method called *effort-driven scheduling*. This means that the task's initial work value remains constant, regardless of the number of additional resources you assign. The most visible effect of effort-driven scheduling is that as you assign additional resources to a task, that task's duration decreases. Microsoft Project applies effort-driven scheduling only when you assign resources to or remove resources from tasks.

As you saw previously, you define the amount of work a task represents when you initially assign a resource or resources to it. If you later add resources to that task, the amount of work for the task does not change, but the task's duration decreases. Conversely, you might initially assign more than one resource to a task and later remove one of those resources from the task. If you do this with effort-driven scheduling on, the amount of work for the task stays constant. The duration, or time it takes the remaining resource to complete that task, increases.

Tip

By default, effort-driven scheduling is enabled for all tasks you create in Microsoft Project. To change the default setting for all new tasks in a project plan, on the Tools menu, click Options, and in the Options dialog box, click the Schedule tab. Select or clear the New Tasks Are Effort-Driven check box. To control effort-driven scheduling for a specific task or tasks, first select the task or tasks. Then on the Project menu, click Task Information, and on the Advanced tab of the Task Information dialog box, select or clear the Effort Driven check box.

In this exercise, you assign additional resources to tasks and see how this affects task durations:

1 In the Gantt Chart view, click the name of Task 2, *Develop Script*.

Currently, Garrett R. Vargas is assigned to this task. A quick check of the scheduling formula looks like this:

40 hours (the same as 5 days) task duration × 100% of Garrett's assignment units = 40 hours work.

If you want, you can scroll the Assign Resources pane down to see these values. Next you will assign a second resource to the task.

2 In the Resource Name column in the Assign Resources dialog box, click Scott Cooper, and click the Assign button.

Scott Cooper is assigned to Task 2. Your screen should look similar to the following illustration:

The duration of this task decreases as additional resources are assigned to it.

The name of the selected task also appears here.

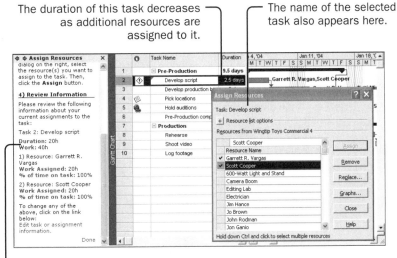

The 40 hours total task work is divided between the two assigned resources.

As you can see in the Gantt Chart view, Microsoft Project reduced the duration of Task 2 from 5 days to 2.5 days.

The total work required is still 40 hours, as it was when only Garrett was assigned to the task, but now the work is distributed evenly between Garrett and Scott. This shows how effort-driven scheduling works. If, after an initial assignment, you add resources to a task, the total work remains constant but is distributed among the assigned resources. Further, the task's duration decreases accordingly.

The scheduling formula now looks like this:

20 hours (the same as 2.5 days) task duration × 200% assignment units = 40 hours work

The 200 percent assignment units is the sum of Garrett's 100 percent plus Scott's 100 percent, and the 40 work hours is the sum of Garrett's 20 hours plus Scott's 20 hours.

The other important effect of reducing the duration of Task 2 is that the start dates of all successor tasks changed as well. In Chapter 2, you created finish-to-start task relationships for these tasks. In this example, you see the benefit of creating task relationships rather than entering fixed start and finish dates. Microsoft Project adjusts the start dates of successor tasks that do not have a constraint, such as a fixed start date or finish date.

Next you assign multiple resources to other tasks, using a Smart Tag to control how Microsoft Project schedules the work on the tasks.

3 In the Gantt Chart view, click the name of Task 4, *Pick Locations*.

Currently, only Scott Cooper is assigned to this two-day task. You'd like to assign an additional resource and reduce the task's duration to one day.

4 In the Resource Name column, click Patti Mintz, and then click the Assign button.

Patti Mintz is also assigned to Task 4.

Smart Tag
Indicator

Smart tag
new in
Project
2002

Note the Smart Tag indicator that appears next to the name of Task 4. Until you perform another action, you can use the Smart Tag to choose how you want Microsoft Project to handle the additional resource assignment.

5 Click the Smart Tag Actions button.

Look over the options in the list that appears. Your screen should look like the following illustration:

Clicking the Smart Tag Actions button displays a list of options, but it is available only until you perform another action in Microsoft Project.

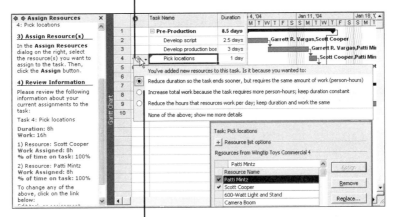

In the Actions list, the selected option describes the result of your most recent action; if this is not the result you want, pick another option.

These options let you choose the scheduling result you want, should it differ from the effort-driven scheduling result. You can adjust the task's duration, the resource's work, or the assignment units.

For this task, you want the additional resource assignment to reduce the task's duration. Because this is the default setting in the Smart Tag Actions list, you don't need to make any changes.

6   Click the Smart Tag Actions button again to close the list.

Tip

You will see other Smart Tags while using Microsoft Project. They generally appear when you might otherwise ask yourself, "Hmm, why did Microsoft Project just do that?" (For example, when a task's duration changes after you assign an additional resource.) The Smart Tag Actions list gives you the chance to change how Microsoft Project responds to your actions.

To conclude this exercise, you will assign additional resources to a task and change how Microsoft Project schedules the work on the task.

7   In the Gantt Chart view, click the name of Task 5, *Hold Auditions*.

8 In the Resource Name column of the Assign Resources dialog box, click Jonathan Mollerup, hold down the Ctrl key, click Patti Mintz, and then click the Assign button.

Microsoft Project assigns Jonathan and Patti to the task. Because effort-driven scheduling is on for this task, Microsoft Project reduces the duration of the task and adjusts the start dates of all successor tasks. Your screen should look similar to the following illustration:

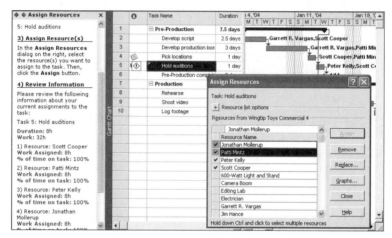

However, this time you do not want the additional resource assignments to change the task's duration. Jonathan and Patti will perform additional work on the task, beyond the scope of the task's previous work, which was assigned to Peter and Scott.

9 Click the Smart Tag Actions button.

10 In the Smart Tag Actions list, select the option Increase Total Work Because The Task Requires More Person-Hours; Keep Duration Constant.

Microsoft Project changes the task's duration back to two days and adjusts the start dates of all successor tasks. The additional resources get the same work values that the initially assigned resources had, so the total work on the task increases. Your screen should look similar to the following illustration:

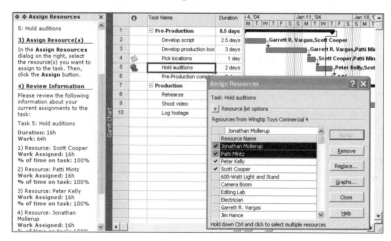

Tip

If you initially assign two resources to a task with a duration of three days (the same as 24 hours), Microsoft Project schedules each resource to work 24 hours, for a total of 48 hours of work on the task. However, you might initially assign one resource to a task with a duration of 24 hours and later add a second resource. In this case, effort-driven scheduling will cause Microsoft Project to schedule each resource to work 12 hours in parallel, for a total of 24 hours of work on the task. Remember that effort-driven scheduling adjusts task duration only if you add or delete resources from a task.

Project Management Focus: When Should Effort-Driven Scheduling Apply?

You should think through the extent to which effort-driven scheduling should apply to the tasks in your projects. For example, if one resource should take 10 hours to complete a task, could 10 resources complete the task in one hour? How about 20 resources in 30 minutes? Probably not; the resources would likely get in each other's way and require additional coordination to complete the task. If the task is very complicated, it might require significant ramp-up time before a resource could contribute fully. Overall productivity might even decrease if you assign more resources to the task.

No single rule exists about when you should apply effort-driven scheduling and when you should not. As the project manager, you should analyze the nature of the work required for each task in your project and use your best judgment.

Assigning Material Resources to Tasks

In Chapter 3, you created the material resource named *Video Tape*. In our TV commercial project, we are interested in tracking the use of video cassettes and their cost. When assigning a material resource, you can handle consumptions and cost in one of two ways:

- Assign a fixed-unit quantity of the material resource to the task. Microsoft Project will multiply the unit cost of this resource by the number of units assigned to determine the total cost. (You'll use this method in the following exercise.)

- Assign a variable-rate quantity of the material resource to the task. Microsoft Project will adjust the quantity and cost of the resource as the task's duration changes. (You'll use this method in Chapter 9, "Fine-Tuning the Project Plan.")

In this exercise, you assign the material resource *Video Tape* to a task and enter a fixed-unit quantity of consumption. You will also work with the more complete version of the Assign Resources dialog box:

1 In the Assign Resources dialog box, click the Close button.

2 Click the Close button in the upper right corner of the Project Guide to close the Project Guide pane.

Assign
Resources

3   On the Standard toolbar, click the Assign Resources button.

The Assign Resources dialog box appears. Unlike the version of this dialog box you saw using the Project Guide, this version includes the Units column. "Units" here refers to assignment units.

Tip

If you are using Microsoft Project Professional, you also see the R/D (request or demand) column in the Assign Resources dialog box. This relates to setting a priority for a resource assignment when using a Microsoft Project Server feature called resource substitution. For more information about Microsoft Project Server, see Appendix A, "Introducing Microsoft Project Server."

4   In the Task Name column, click the name of Task 4, *Pick Locations*.

You plan to use up to four tapes while picking locations.

5   In the Assign Resources dialog box, select the Units field for the Video Tape resource.

6   Type **4**, and then click the Assign button.

Microsoft Project assigns the video tape to the task. Your screen should look like the following illustration:

When you assign a material resource to a task, its
label value appears in the Units column...

	❶	Task Name	Duration	Jan 4, '04	Jan 11, '04	Jan 18, 04	Jan 25, '04
1		⊟ Pre-Production	8.5 days				
2		Develop script	2.5 days	Garrett R. Vargas,Scott Cooper			
3		Develop production boa	3 days	Garrett R. Vargas,Patti Mintz			
4		Pick locations	1 day	Scott Cooper,Patti Mintz,Video Tape[4 30-min. cas			
5		Hold auditions	2 days	Peter Kelly,Scott Cooper,Jonathan Molleru			
6		Pre-Production complet	0 days	1/15			
7		⊟ Production	5 days				
8		Rehearse	2 days				
9		Shoot video	2 days				
10		Log footage	1 day				

Assign Resources

Task: Pick locations

[+] Resource list options

Resources from Wingtip Toys Commercie 4

Video Tape		
Resource Name	Units	
✔ Video Tape	4 30-mir	Assign
600-Watt Light and Stand		Remove
Camera Boom		
Editing Lab		Replace...
Electrician		

...and next to the Gantt bar to which it is assigned.

Because video tape is a material resource, it cannot do work. Therefore, assigning a material resource does not affect the duration of a task.

Chapter Wrap-Up

This chapter covered how to assign resources to tasks and manage the scheduling results.

If you are going on to other chapters:

Save

1 On the Standard toolbar, click the Save button to save changes made to Wingtip Toys Commercial 4.

2 On the File menu, click Close to close the project plan.

If you aren't continuing to other chapters:

1 On the Standard toolbar, click the Save button to save changes made to Wingtip Toys Commercial 4.

2 To quit Microsoft Project for now, on the File menu, click Exit.

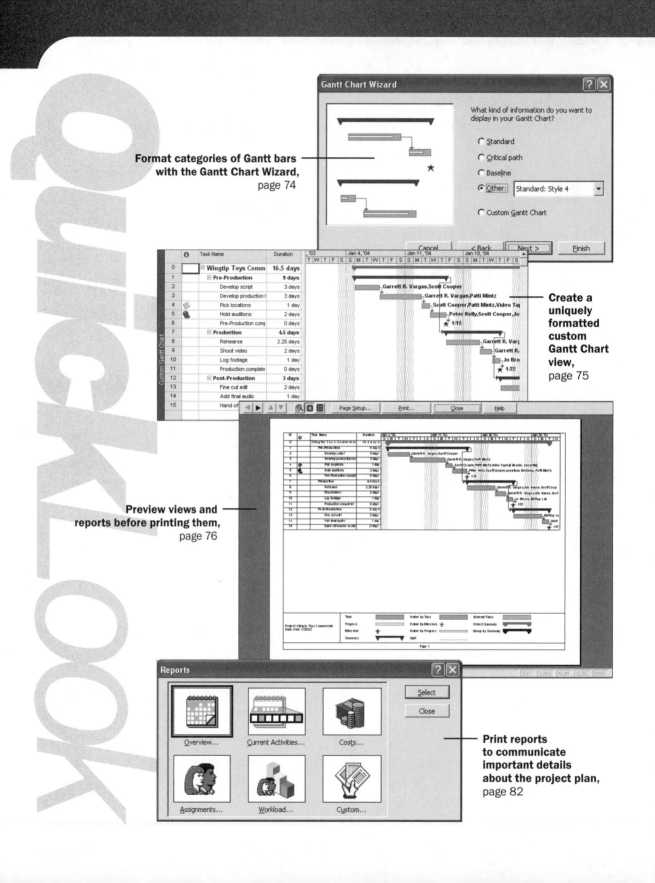

Format categories of Gantt bars with the Gantt Chart Wizard, page 74

Create a uniquely formatted custom Gantt Chart view, page 75

Preview views and reports before printing them, page 76

Print reports to communicate important details about the project plan, page 82

Chapter 5
Formatting and Printing Your Plan

After completing this chapter, you will be able to:

✔ Customize a chart and preview the way it will look when printed.

✔ Draw on the chart portion of a Gantt Chart view.

✔ Change the formatting of text in a project plan.

✔ Edit and print reports.

In this chapter, you use some of the formatting features in Microsoft Project to change the way your data appears, and then you preview the results in the Print Preview window. As you might recall from Chapter 1, "Getting Started with Microsoft Project," a Microsoft Project plan is really a database of information, not unlike a Microsoft Access database file. You don't normally see all the data in a project plan at one time, as you could with, say, a Microsoft Word document. Instead, you focus on the aspect of the plan that you're currently interested in. *Views* and *reports* are the most common ways to see or print a project plan's data. In both cases (especially with views), you can substantially format the data to meet your needs.

The primary way Microsoft Project represents tasks graphically is as bars on the chart portion of a Gantt Chart view. These are called Gantt bars. On a Gantt chart, tasks, summary tasks, and milestones all appear as Gantt bars, and each type of bar has its own format. Whenever you work with Gantt bars, keep in mind that they represent tasks in a project plan.

Tip

This chapter introduces you to some of the simpler view and report formatting features in Microsoft Project. You'll find quite a bit more material about formatting, printing, and publishing your project plans in Chapters 10, 11, 12, and 17. To find more information about available views and reports in Microsoft Project's online Help, type **All about printing and reporting** into the Ask A Question box in the upper right corner of the Microsoft Project window.

Wingtip Toys Commercial 5a

This chapter uses the practice file Wingtip Toys Commercial 5a. This file contains the tasks, resources, and assignments you created in previous chapters, plus additional details to complete the project plan. For details about installing the practice files, see "Using the Book's CD-ROM" at the beginning of this book.

Creating a Custom Gantt Chart View

For many people, a Gantt chart is synonymous with a project plan. In Microsoft Project, the default view is the Gantt Chart view. You are likely to spend a lot of your time in Microsoft Project in this view.

The Gantt Chart view consists of two parts: a *table* on the left and a *timescaled* bar chart on the right. The bars on the chart graphically represent the tasks in the table in terms of start and finish dates, duration, and status (for example, whether work on the task has started or not). Other elements on the chart, such as link lines, represent *relationships* between tasks. The Gantt chart is a popular and widely understood representation of project information throughout the project management world.

Tip

By default, Microsoft Project displays the Gantt Chart view when you start it. However, you can change this to display any view you want at startup. On the Tools menu, click Options. In the Options dialog box, click the View tab. In the Default View box, click the view you want. The next time you start Microsoft Project, that view will appear.

The default formatting applied to the Gantt Chart view works well for onscreen viewing, sharing with other programs, and printing. However, you can change the formatting of just about any element on the Gantt chart. In this exercise, we will focus on Gantt bars.

There are three distinct ways to format Gantt bars:

■ Format whole categories of Gantt bars in the Bar Styles dialog box, which you can open by clicking the Bar Styles command on the Format menu. In this case, the formatting changes you make to a type of Gantt bar (a *summary task*, for example) apply to all such Gantt bars in the Gantt chart.

■ Format whole categories of Gantt bars using the Gantt Chart Wizard, which you can start by clicking the Gantt Chart Wizard command on the Format menu. This wizard contains a series of pages in which you select formatting options for the most-used Gantt bars on the Gantt chart. Use the Gantt Chart Wizard to step you through some of the formatting actions that you can perform in the Bar Styles dialog box.

■ Format individual Gantt bars directly. The formatting changes you make have no effect on other bars in the Gantt chart. You can double-click a Gantt bar on the Gantt chart to see its formatting options.

In this exercise, you create a custom Gantt chart and apply predefined formatting to it with the Gantt Chart Wizard. You then preview the results for printing:

1 If Microsoft Project is not already open, start it now.

Open

2 On the Standard toolbar, click the Open button.

The Open dialog box appears.

3 Navigate to the Chapter 5 Simple Formatting folder, and double-click the Wingtip Toys Commercial 5a file.

4 On the File menu, click Save As.

The Save As dialog box appears.

5 In the File Name box, type **Wingtip Toys Commercial 5**, and then click the Save button.

Next you will display the *project summary task* to see the top-level or rolled-up details of the project. Microsoft Project automatically generates the project summary task but doesn't display it by default.

6 On the Tools menu, click Options.

7 In the Options dialog box, click the View tab.

8 Under the Outline Options For label, select the Show Project Summary Task check box, and then click the OK button.

Microsoft Project displays the project summary task at the top of the Gantt Chart view. You might see pound signs (##) in the project summary task's duration field. If so, complete steps 9 and 10.

9 Drag the vertical divider bar between the table and chart to the right until you can see the right edge of the Duration column.

10 Double-click the right edge of the Duration column, in the column heading.

Tip

You can also double-click anywhere in a column heading, and in the Column Definition dialog box that appears, click the Best Fit button.

The Duration column widens to show the widest value in the column. In this case, that value is the duration for the project summary task. Your screen should look similar to the following illustration:

Double-click the right edge of a column heading to widen that column.

Drag the divider bar to show more or less of the table and chart portions of the Gantt Chart view.

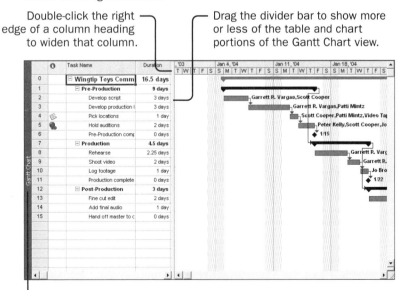

The name of the active view appears here.

Next you will create a copy of the Gantt Chart view so that the formatting changes you make won't affect the original Gantt Chart view.

11 On the View menu, click More Views.

The More Views dialog box appears, with the current view (the Gantt Chart view) selected.

12 Click the Copy button.

The View Definition dialog box appears.

13 In the Name field, type **Custom Gantt Chart**, and then click the OK button.

The View Definition dialog box closes. The Custom Gantt Chart view appears and is selected in the More Views dialog box.

14 In the More Views dialog box, click the Apply button.

At this point, the Custom Gantt Chart view is an exact copy of the original Gantt Chart view, so the two views look alike. Note, however, that the view title on the left edge of the view is updated.

Next you will use the Gantt Chart Wizard to format the Gantt bars and milestones in the chart portion of the Custom Gantt Chart view.

15 On the Format menu, click Gantt Chart Wizard.

The welcome page of the Gantt Chart Wizard appears. Your screen should look similar to the following illustration:

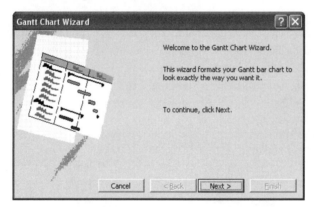

Tip

You can also start the Gantt Chart Wizard, and several other formatting features, using the items in the Report pane of the Project Guide.

16 Click Next.

The next screen of the Gantt Chart Wizard appears.

17 Click the Other button, and in the drop-down list next to the Other option, click Standard: Style 4.

Your screen should look similar to the following illustration:

The preview shows you the formatting options you choose on the right.

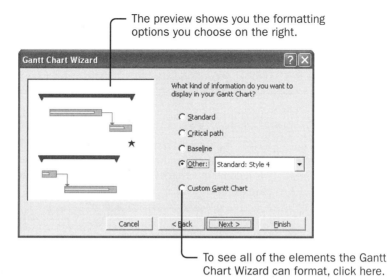

To see all of the elements the Gantt Chart Wizard can format, click here.

Tip

If you want to see the other built-in Gantt chart formats available in the wizard, click them in the Other box to see the preview on the left side of the wizard's window. When you are done, make sure that Standard Style 4 is selected.

18 This is the only selection you'll make in the Gantt Chart Wizard for now, so click the Finish button.

The final page of the Gantt Chart Wizard appears.

19 Click the Format It button, and then click the Exit Wizard button.

The Gantt Chart Wizard applies the Standard Style 4 formatting to the Custom Gantt Chart view and then closes. Your screen should look similar to the following illustration:

The reformatted Gantt bars (summary, task, and milestone) appear in the chart portion of the view.

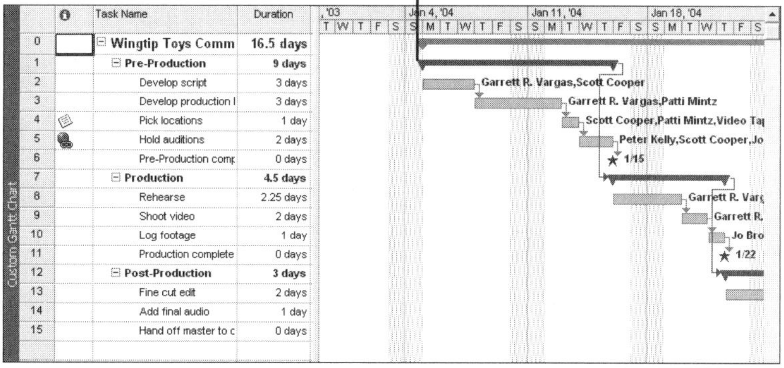

Here you can see the effects of the Standard Style 4 formatting applied to the project plan. Note that none of the data in the project plan has changed; only the way it is formatted has changed. These formatting changes affect only the Custom Gantt Chart view; all the other views in Microsoft Project are unaffected.

To conclude this exercise, you will preview the Custom Gantt Chart view. What you see on the screen closely approximates what you'd see on the printed page, and you'll verify this now.

20 On the File menu, click Print Preview.

Microsoft Project displays the Custom Gantt Chart view in the Print Preview window. You will do more work in the Print Preview window later in this chapter and in chapter 11, "Printing Project Information." Your screen should look similar to the following illustration:

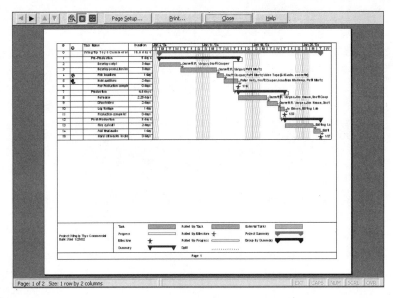

Tip

If you have a plotter (a device used to draw charts, diagrams, and other line-based graphics) selected as your default printer, or you have a different page size selected for your default printer, what you see in the Print Preview window might differ from what you see here.

21 On the Print Preview toolbar, click the Close button.

You can print the project plan now if you want, but previewing it is adequate for the purposes of this chapter. When printing in Microsoft Project, you have additional options in the Print dialog box, which you can open by clicking the Print command on the File menu. For example, you can choose to print a specific date range of a timescaled view such as the Gantt Chart view, or you can print a specific page range.

Drawing on a Gantt Chart

Microsoft Project includes a Drawing toolbar with which you can draw objects directly on the chart portion of a Gantt chart. For example, if you would like to note a particular event or graphically call out a specific item, you can draw objects such as text boxes, arrows, and other items directly on a Gantt chart. If you want, you can link a drawn object to either end of a Gantt bar or to a specific date on the timescale. Here's how to choose the kind of link you need:

■ Link objects to a Gantt bar when the object is specific to the task the Gantt bar represents. The object will move with the Gantt bar, should it be rescheduled.

■ Link objects to a date when the information the object refers to is date-sensitive. The object will remain in the same position relative to the timescale, no matter which part of the timescale is displayed.

Tip

If the Drawing toolbar does not have the type of item you would like to add, you can add bitmap images or documents using the Object command (on the Insert menu).

In this exercise, you display the Drawing toolbar and add a text box to the Custom Gantt Chart view.

1 On the View menu, point to Toolbars, and then click Drawing.

The Drawing toolbar appears.

Tip

You can also right-click any toolbar to see the Toolbars *shortcut menu*, and then display or hide a toolbar listed on that menu.

Text Box

2 On the Drawing toolbar, click the Text Box button, and then drag a small square anywhere on the chart portion of the Custom Gantt Chart view.

3 In the square you just drew, type **Film festival January 15 and 16.**

4 On the Format menu, point to Drawing, and then click Properties.

The Format Drawing dialog box appears.

Tip

You can also double-click the border of the text box to view its properties.

5 Click the Line & Fill tab if it is not already selected.

6 In the Color box under the Fill label, click Yellow.

7 Click the Size & Position tab.

In this exercise, you'll attach the text box to a specific date rather than to a specific Gantt bar.

8 Make sure that Attach To Timescale is selected, and in the Date box, type or click **1/15/04**.

9 In the Vertical box, type **2.75**, and then click the OK button to close the Format Drawing dialog box.

Microsoft Project colors the text box yellow and positions it below the timescale near the date you specified. Your screen should look similar to the following illustration:

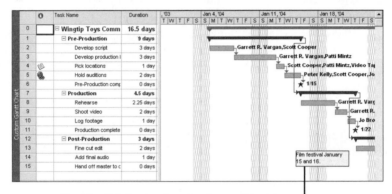

Double-click the border of a drawn object to change its formatting or other properties.

Because you attached the text box to a specific date on the timescale, it will always appear near this date, even if you zoom the timescale in or out, or scroll the chart left or right. Had you attached the text box to a Gantt bar, it would move with the Gantt bar if the task were rescheduled.

Formatting Text in a View

You can format text in tables, such as task names in a Gantt Chart view. There are two distinct ways to format text:

■   Format whole categories of text in the Text Styles dialog box, which you can open by clicking the Text Styles command on the Format menu. In this case, the formatting changes you make to a type of text (a *summary task*, for example) apply to all such types of text in the view.

■   Format individual selections of text directly. The formatting changes you make have no effect on other text in the view.

Tip

You might notice some symmetry between style-based formatting (available through the Format Bar Styles and Format Text Styles commands on the Format menu) and direct formatting of Gantt bars and text (available through the Bar and Font commands on the Format menu). This is generally consistent with formatting options you might use in a word processor.

As with all formatting options in Microsoft Project, the formatting changes you make to any view or report affect only that view or report, and only for the active project plan. Later chapters will introduce ways of copying custom views or reports between project plans.

In this exercise, you switch to a different view and then use text styles and direct formatting to change the appearance of the text in that view:

1   On the View menu, click More Views.

The More Views dialog box appears, with the current view (the Custom Gantt Chart view) selected.

2   In the Views box, click Task Sheet, and then click the Apply button.

The Task Sheet view appears. Unlike Gantt Chart views, this view does not include a chart component; it consists of a single table. Next you will change the table displayed in the Task Sheet view.

3   On the View menu, point to Table: Entry, and then click Summary.

The Summary table appears in the Task Sheet view. Like the Entry table, this table focuses on task details, but it includes a different set of *fields*. The field we're most interested in now is the Cost field. Your screen should look similar to the following illustration:

		Task Name	Duration	Start	Finish	% Comp.	Cost	Work
	0	⊟ Wingtip Toys Comm	16.5 days	Mon 1/5/04	Tue 1/27/04	0%	$8,748.90	704 hrs
	1	⊟ Pre-Production	9 days	Mon 1/5/04	Thu 1/15/04	0%	$2,789.20	176 hrs
	2	Develop script	3 days	Mon 1/5/04	Wed 1/7/04	0%	$945.00	48 hrs
	3	Develop production I	3 days	Thu 1/8/04	Mon 1/12/04	0%	$705.60	48 hrs
	4	Pick locations	1 day	Tue 1/13/04	Tue 1/13/04	0%	$250.20	16 hrs
	5	Hold auditions	2 days	Wed 1/14/04	Thu 1/15/04	0%	$888.40	64 hrs
	6	Pre-Production comp	0 days	Thu 1/15/04	Thu 1/15/04	0%	$0.00	0 hrs
	7	⊟ Production	4.5 days	Thu 1/15/04	Thu 1/22/04	0%	$4,476.70	456 hrs
	8	Rehearse	2.25 days	Thu 1/15/04	Mon 1/19/04	0%	$1,717.40	214 hrs
Task Sheet	9	Shoot video	2 days	Mon 1/19/04	Wed 1/21/04	0%	$2,409.30	226 hrs
	10	Log footage	1 day	Wed 1/21/04	Thu 1/22/04	0%	$350.00	16 hrs
	11	Production complete	0 days	Thu 1/22/04	Thu 1/22/04	0%	$0.00	0 hrs
	12	⊟ Post-Production	3 days	Thu 1/22/04	Tue 1/27/04	0%	$1,483.00	72 hrs
	13	Fine cut edit	2 days	Thu 1/22/04	Mon 1/26/04	0%	$978.00	48 hrs
	14	Add final audio	1 day	Mon 1/26/04	Tue 1/27/04	0%	$505.00	24 hrs
	15	Hand off master to c	0 days	Tue 1/27/04	Tue 1/27/04	0%	$0.00	0 hrs

Next you'll change how Microsoft Project formats an entire category of information—in this case, summary tasks.

4   On the Format menu, click Text Styles.

The Text Styles dialog box appears.

Tip

Text styles in Microsoft Project are similar to styles in Microsoft Word. The Items To Change list displays all the types of information in a project plan that you can consistently format.

5 In the Items To Change list, click Summary Tasks.

The current format settings of summary tasks appear in the dialog box, and a preview appears in the Sample box. Next you will change the formatting so that the summary tasks appear larger and in color.

6 In the Size box, click 10.

7 In the Color box, click Blue, and then click the OK button.

Microsoft Project applies the new format settings to all summary tasks in the project (except for the project summary task, which appears separately in the Items To Change list). Any new summary tasks added to the project plan will also appear with the new formatting.

8 Double-click between the text in the column labels to widen any columns that display pound signs (##).

Your screen should look similar to the following illustration:

After applying the text style formatting change, all summary tasks are reformatted.

If you see pound signs (##), double-click here to widen the column to the right.

	Task Name	Duration	Start	Finish	% Comp.	Cost	Work
0	⊟ Wingtip Toys Comm	16.5 days	Mon 1/5/04	Tue 1/27/04	0%	$8,748.90	704 hrs
1	⊟ Pre-Production	9 days	Mon 1/5/04	Thu 1/15/04	0%	$2,789.20	176 hrs
2	Develop script	3 days	Mon 1/5/04	Wed 1/7/04	0%	$945.00	48 hrs
3	Develop production l	3 days	Thu 1/8/04	Mon 1/12/04	0%	$705.60	48 hrs
4	Pick locations	1 day	Tue 1/13/04	Tue 1/13/04	0%	$250.20	16 hrs
5	Hold auditions	2 days	Wed 1/14/04	Thu 1/15/04	0%	$888.40	64 hrs
6	Pre-Production comp	0 days	Thu 1/15/04	Thu 1/15/04	0%	$0.00	0 hrs
7	⊟ Production	4.5 days	Thu 1/15/04	Thu 1/22/04	0%	$4,476.70	456 hrs
8	Rehearse	2.25 days	Thu 1/15/04	Mon 1/19/04	0%	$1,717.40	214 hrs
9	Shoot video	2 days	Mon 1/19/04	Wed 1/21/04	0%	$2,409.30	226 hrs
10	Log footage	1 day	Wed 1/21/04	Thu 1/22/04	0%	$350.00	16 hrs
11	Production complete	0 days	Thu 1/22/04	Thu 1/22/04	0%	$0.00	0 hrs
12	⊟ Post-Production	3 days	Thu 1/22/04	Tue 1/27/04	0%	$1,483.00	72 hrs
13	Fine cut edit	2 days	Thu 1/22/04	Mon 1/26/04	0%	$978.00	48 hrs
14	Add final audio	1 day	Mon 1/26/04	Tue 1/27/04	0%	$505.00	24 hrs
15	Hand off master to c	0 days	Tue 1/27/04	Tue 1/27/04	0%	$0.00	0 hrs

The format changes you've made to summary tasks apply to all tables that you can display in the Task Sheet view, but only in the Task Sheet view. If you displayed the Summary table in the Gantt Chart view, for example, these format changes would not appear there.

To conclude this exercise, you will apply direct formatting to a specific item in a view. As with styles in Word, you can use direct formatting in conjunction with text style formatting. In this project plan, you'll apply italic formatting to the production phase's cost.

9 In the Summary table, click the Cost field for task 7, the Production summary task.

10 On the Format menu, click Font.

The Font dialog box appears. This is similar to the Text Styles dialog box you worked with earlier. However, the options you choose here apply only to the selected text.

11 In the Font Style box, click Bold Italic, and then click the OK button.

Microsoft Project applies bold italic formatting to Task 7's Cost field. Your screen should look similar to the following illustration:

After applying direct formatting,
only this value is reformatted.

	Task Name	Duration	Start	Finish	% Comp.	Cost	Work
0	⊟ Wingtip Toys Comm	16.5 days	Mon 1/5/04	Tue 1/27/04	0%	$8,748.90	704 hrs
1	⊟ Pre-Production	9 days	Mon 1/5/04	Thu 1/15/04	0%	$2,789.20	176 hrs
2	Develop script	3 days	Mon 1/5/04	Wed 1/7/04	0%	$945.00	48 hrs
3	Develop production	3 days	Thu 1/8/04	Mon 1/12/04	0%	$705.60	48 hrs
4	Pick locations	1 day	Tue 1/13/04	Tue 1/13/04	0%	$250.20	16 hrs
5	Hold auditions	2 days	Wed 1/14/04	Thu 1/15/04	0%	$888.40	64 hrs
6	Pre-Production comp	0 days	Thu 1/15/04	Thu 1/15/04	0%	$0.00	0 hrs
7	⊟ Production	4.5 days	Thu 1/15/04	Thu 1/22/04	0%	*$4,476.70*	456 hrs
8	Rehearse	2.25 days	Thu 1/15/04	Mon 1/19/04	0%	$1,717.40	214 hrs
9	Shoot video	2 days	Mon 1/19/04	Wed 1/21/04	0%	$2,409.30	226 hrs
10	Log footage	1 day	Wed 1/21/04	Thu 1/22/04	0%	$350.00	16 hrs
11	Production complete	0 days	Thu 1/22/04	Thu 1/22/04	0%	$0.00	0 hrs
12	⊟ Post-Production	3 days	Thu 1/22/04	Tue 1/27/04	0%	$1,483.00	72 hrs
13	Fine cut edit	2 days	Thu 1/22/04	Mon 1/26/04	0%	$978.00	48 hrs
14	Add final audio	1 day	Mon 1/26/04	Tue 1/27/04	0%	$505.00	24 hrs
15	Hand off master to c	0 days	Tue 1/27/04	Tue 1/27/04	0%	$0.00	0 hrs

To sum up, use the Text Styles command (on the Format menu) to change the formatting of entire categories of information, such as all summary tasks. When you want to reformat a specific item (such as one task's cost value) to draw attention to it, use the Font command (on the Format menu). Note that the Font command is not available in some views, such as the Calendar view.

Tip

Some buttons on the Formatting toolbar correspond to the options available with the Font command (on the Format menu). These options control direct formatting, not the style-based formatting you might apply with the Text Styles dialog box.

Formatting and Printing Reports

Reports are predefined formats intended for printing Microsoft Project data. Unlike views, which you can either print or work with on the screen, reports are designed only for printing or for viewing in the Print Preview window. You do not enter data directly into a report. Microsoft Project includes several predefined task, resource, and assignment reports you can edit to get the information you want.

In this exercise, you view a report in the Print Preview window, and then you edit its format to include additional information.

1 On the View menu, click Reports.

The Reports dialog box appears, showing the six broad categories of reports available in Microsoft Project. Your screen should look similar to the following illustration:

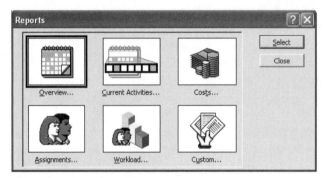

2 Click Overview, and then click the Select button.

The Overview Reports dialog box appears, listing the five predefined reports in Microsoft Project that provide project-wide overview information.

3 In the Overview Reports dialog box, click Project Summary, and then click the Select button.

Microsoft Project displays the Project Summary report in the Print Preview window. This is a handy summary of the project plan's tasks, resources, costs, and current status. You could use this report, for example, as a recurring status report that you share with the clients or other *stakeholders* of the project.

Depending on your screen resolution, the text on the report might not be readable when you zoom out to view a full page.

Tip

Here's a quick way to see vital project statistics on the screen: Click the Project Information command on the Project menu, and then click Statistics.

4 In the Print Preview window, click the upper half of the page with the mouse pointer.

Microsoft Project zooms in to show the page at a legible resolution. Your screen should look similar to the following illustration:

The project title and company
name come from the values
entered in the Properties dialog
box (File menu).

Click to zoom out.

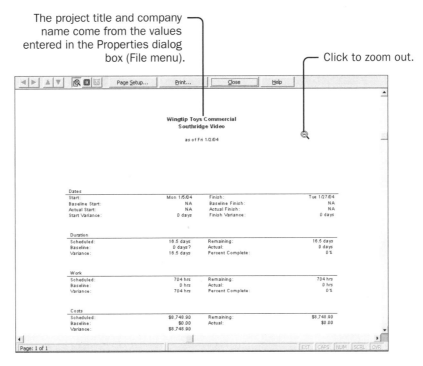

At this point in the project life cycle, the most pertinent pieces of information in the report are the planned start and finish dates and the total cost. If any of these values did not fit within the expectations of the project **sponsor** or other stakeholders, now would be a good time to find out.

5 On the Print Preview toolbar, click the Close button.

The Print Preview window closes, and the Reports dialog box reappears. Next you will preview and edit a different report.

For a small, simple project such as the TV commercial, a report is a simple way to communicate assignments to the resources involved. To do this, you will work with the Who Does What When report.

Tip

For more detailed projects, communicating resource assignments (and subsequent changes) and other project details can be a significant responsibility for a project manager. Microsoft Project Server offers an intranet-based solution for communicating such project details in conjunction with either Microsoft Project Standard or Professional editions. For more information, see Appendix A, "Introducing Microsoft Project Server."

6 Click Assignments, and then click the Select button.

The Assignment Reports dialog box appears, listing four predefined reports in Microsoft Project that provide resource assignment information.

7 In the Assignment Reports dialog box, click Who Does What When, and then click the Select button.

Microsoft Project displays the first page of the Who Does What When report in the Print Preview window. Your screen should look similar to the following illustration:

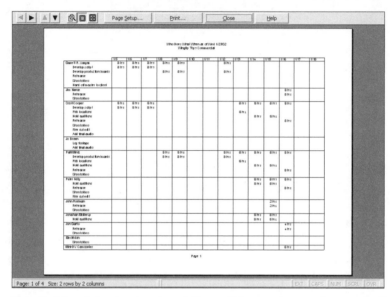

Note that the status bar message tells you this report spans four pages. To get a broader view of the output, you will switch to a multipage view.

Multiple Pages

8 On the Print Preview toolbar, click the Multiple Pages button.

The entire report appears in the Print Preview window. Your screen should look similar to the following illustration:

The multi-page Print Preview shows you the
entire printed output laid out on separate pages.
(The paper size is determined by your printer settings.)

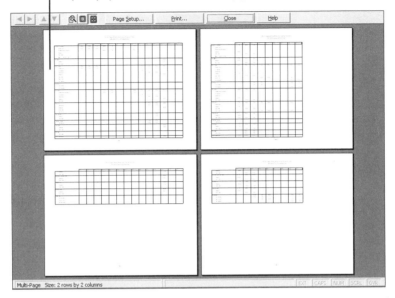

To conclude this exercise, you will customize the header that appears at the top of each printed page so that it includes a logo graphic.

9 On the Print Preview toolbar, click the Page Setup button.

The Page Setup dialog box for the Who Does What When report appears.

10 Click the Header tab.

Your screen should look similar to the following illustration:

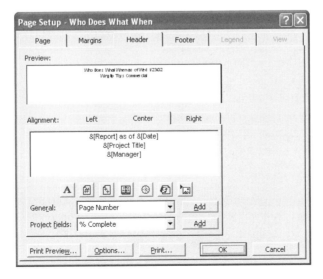

As you can see in the Preview and Alignment boxes, codes such as "&[Date]" determine the specific text that appears in the header. You will add a logo to the left side of the header.

11 Next to Alignment, click the Left tab.

As with all regions of the header and footer, you can insert standard elements, such as page numbers, as well as any Microsoft Project field. In this exercise, you'll insert a logo graphic that's supplied for you.

Insert Picture

12 Click the Insert Picture button.

13 Navigate to the Chapter 5 Simple Formatting folder and double-click the Logo file.

The logo image appears on the left side of the header in the Page Setup dialog box.

14 Click the OK button to close the Page Setup dialog box.

The updated header appears on each page in the Print Preview window.

One Page

15 To get a closer look at the updated header, on the Print Preview toolbar, click the One Page button.

Microsoft Project displays the first page of the report. Your screen should look similar to the following illustration:

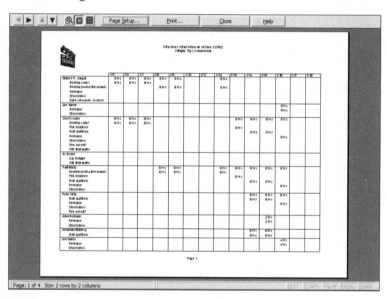

16 On the Print Preview toolbar, click the Close button.

17 Click Close again to close the Reports dialog box. The Task Sheet view reappears.

Tip

You can change the headers and footers of views in the same way you do in reports. Keep in mind that changes you make to the page setup of any view or report apply only to that view or report. However, the general way you customize the page setup is the same for any report or view.

Chapter Wrap-Up

This chapter covered how to format Gantt Chart views and work with reports.

If you are going on to other chapters:

Save

1 On the Standard toolbar, click the Save button to save changes made to Wingtip Toys Commercial 5.

2 On the File menu, click Close to close the project plan.

If you aren't continuing to other chapters:

1 On the Standard toolbar, click the Save button to save changes made to Wingtip Toys Commercial 5.

2 To quit Microsoft Project for now, on the File menu, click Exit.

First screenshot (Task Sheet)

Save a baseline and compare scheduled, baseline, and actual values, page 91

	Task Name	Start	Finish	Baseline Start	Baseline Finish	Start Var.	Finish Var.
0	⊟ **Wingtip Toys Co**	**Mon 1/5/04**	**Tue 1/27/04**	**Mon 1/5/04**	**Tue 1/27/04**	**0 days**	**0 days**
1	⊟ Pre-Productio	Mon 1/5/04	Thu 1/15/04	Mon 1/5/04	Thu 1/15/04	0 days	0 days
2	Develop script	Mon 1/5/04	Wed 1/7/04	Mon 1/5/04	Wed 1/7/04	0 days	0 days
3	Develop produc	Thu 1/8/04	Mon 1/12/04	Thu 1/8/04	Mon 1/12/04	0 days	0 days
4	Pick locations	Tue 1/13/04	Tue 1/13/04	Tue 1/13/04	Tue 1/13/04	0 days	0 days
5	Hold auditions	Wed 1/14/04	Thu 1/15/04	Wed 1/14/04	Thu 1/15/04	0 days	0 days
6	Pre-Production	Thu 1/15/04	Thu 1/15/04	Thu 1/15/04	Thu 1/15/04	0 days	0 days
7	⊟ Production	Thu 1/15/04	Thu 1/22/04	Thu 1/15/04	Thu 1/22/04	0 days	0 days
8	Rehearse	Thu 1/15/04	Mon 1/19/04	Thu 1/15/04	Mon 1/19/04	0 days	0 days
9	Shoot video	Mon 1/19/04	Wed 1/21/04	Mon 1/19/04	Wed 1/21/04	0 days	0 days
10	Log footage	Wed 1/21/04	Thu 1/22/04	Wed 1/21/04	Thu 1/22/04	0 days	0 days
11	Production com	Thu 1/22/04	Thu 1/22/04	Thu 1/22/04	Thu 1/22/04	0 days	0 days
12	⊟ Post-Productic	Thu 1/22/04	Tue 1/27/04	Thu 1/22/04	Tue 1/27/04	0 days	0 days
13	Fine cut edit	Thu 1/22/04	Mon 1/26/04	Thu 1/22/04	Mon 1/26/04	0 days	0 days
14	Add final audio	Mon 1/26/04	Tue 1/27/04	Mon 1/26/04	Tue 1/27/04	0 days	0 days
15	Hand off maste	Tue 1/27/04	Tue 1/27/04	Tue 1/27/04	Tue 1/27/04	0 days	0 days

Second screenshot (Incorporate Progress)

◆ ◆ Incorporate Progress ✕

To update your project:

1. Set the Status Date

If necessary, change the status date below, to reflect the date you want to use for submitting progress:

1/12/2004 ▾

Learn how to accurately use the status date when updating

2. Update progress

In the % Work Complete column of the table at the right, enter a value between 0 (no work has been performed on the task) and 100 (all work has been completed on the task) for each task you want to update.

Note: Microsoft Project calculates the percentage of work completed for each summary task based on the progress of its subtasks.

	Task Name	Work	% Work Complete	Jan 11, '04	Jan 18, '04
0	⊟ **Wingtip Toys Commercial**	704 hrs	16%		
1	⊟ Pre-Production	176 hrs	64%		
2	Develop script	48 hrs	100%	R. Vargas,Scott Cooper	
3	Develop production boards	48 hrs	100%	Garrett R. Vargas,Patti Min	
4	Pick locations	16 hrs	100%	Scott Cooper,Patti Mint:	
5	Hold auditions	64 hrs	0%	Peter Kelly,Scott (	
6	Pre-Production complete!	0 hrs	0%	◆ 1/15	
7	⊟ Production	456 hrs	0%		
8	Rehearse	214 hrs	0%	Garre	
9	Shoot video	226 hrs	0%	G	
10	Log footage	16 hrs	0%		
11	Production complete!	0 hrs	0%		
12	⊟ Post-Production	72 hrs	0%		
13	Fine cut edit	48 hrs	0%		
14	Add final audio	24 hrs	0%		
15	Hand off master to client	0 hrs	0%		

Enter percent work complete per task, page 94

Third screenshot

Enter actual and remaining work per task, page 96

	Task Name	Work	Actual Work	Rem	Jan 11, '04	Jan 18, '04	Jan 25, '04
0	⊟ **Wingtip Toys Commercial**	720 hrs	192 hrs				
1	⊟ Pre-Production	192 hrs	192 hrs				
2	Develop script	48 hrs	48 hrs		Garrett R. Vargas,Scott Cooper		
3	Develop production boards	48 hrs	48 hrs		Garrett R. Vargas,Patti Mintz		
4	Pick locations	16 hrs	16 hrs		100% Scott Cooper,Patti Mintz,Video Tape[4 30-min. cass		
5	Hold auditions	80 hrs	80 hrs		100% Peter Kelly,Scott Cooper,Jonathan Mollerup		
6	Pre-Production complete!	0 hrs	0 hrs		◆ 1/16		
7	⊟ Production	456 hrs	0 hrs				
8	Rehearse	214 hrs	0 hrs		0% Garrett R. Vargas,Jim Hance,Sco		
9	Shoot video	226 hrs	0 hrs		0% Garrett R. Vargas,Jim Hance		
10	Log footage	16 hrs	0 hrs		0% Jo Brown,Editing Lab		
11	Production complete!	0 hrs	0 hrs		◆ 1/22		
12	⊟ Post-Production	72 hrs	0 hrs				
13	Fine cut edit	48 hrs	0 hrs		0% Editing Lab,S		
14	Add final audio	24 hrs	0 hrs		0% Editing Lat		
15	Hand off master to client	0 hrs	0 hrs		◆ 1/27		

Chapter 6
Tracking Progress on Tasks

After completing this chapter, you will be able to:

✔ Save current values in a schedule as a baseline.

✔ Record progress on tasks through a specific date.

✔ Record a task's percentage of completion.

✔ Enter actual start, finish, work, and duration values for tasks.

Until now, you have focused on project *planning*—developing and communicating the details of a project before actual work begins. When work begins, so does the next phase of project management: tracking progress. *Tracking* means recording project details such as who did what work, when the work was done, and at what cost. These details are often called *actuals*.

Tracking actuals is essential to properly managing, as opposed to just planning, a project. The project manager must know how well the project team is performing and when to take corrective action. Properly tracking project performance and comparing it to the original plan lets you answer such questions as these:

■ Are tasks starting and finishing as planned, and, if not, what will be the impact on the project's finish date?

■ Are resources spending more or less time than planned to complete tasks?

■ Are higher-than-anticipated task costs driving up the overall cost of the project?

Microsoft Project supports several ways to track progress. Your choice of a tracking method should depend on the level of detail or control required by you, your project *sponsor*, and other *stakeholders*. Tracking the fine details of a project requires more work from you and possibly from the resources working on the project. So before you begin tracking progress, you should determine the level of detail you need. The different levels of tracking detail include the following:

■ Record project work as scheduled. This works best if everything in the project occurs exactly as planned. Hey, it could happen!

■ Record each task's percentage of completion, either at precise values or at increments such as 25, 50, 75, or 100 percent.

- Record the actual start, actual finish, actual work, and actual and remaining duration for each task or assignment.

- Track assignment-level work by time period. This is the most detailed level of tracking. Here you record actual work values per day, week, or another interval.

Because different portions of a project might have different tracking needs, you might need to apply a combination of these approaches within a single project. For example, you might want to track high-risk tasks more closely than low-risk ones. In this chapter, you will perform the first three actions in the preceding list; the fourth (tracking assignment-level work by time period) is addressed in Part 2, "Managing a Complex Project."

Wingtip Toys Commercial 6a

This chapter uses the practice file Wingtip Toys Commercial 6a. This file contains the project plan you created in previous chapters. For details about installing the practice files, see "Using the Book's CD-ROM" at the beginning of this book.

Saving a Project Baseline

One of a project manager's most important activities, after developing a project plan, is to record actuals and evaluate project performance. To judge project performance properly, you will need to compare it to your original plan. This original plan is called the baseline plan, or just the *baseline*. A baseline is a collection of important values in a project plan, such as the planned start dates, finish dates, and the costs of the tasks, resources, and assignments. When you save a baseline, Microsoft Project takes a "snapshot" of the existing values and saves it in your Microsoft Project plan for future comparison.

The specific values saved in a baseline include the task, resource, and assignment fields, and *timephased fields* listed in the following table:

Task fields	Resource fields	Assignment fields
Start	Work and timephased work	Start
Finish	Cost and timephased cost	Finish
Duration		Work and timephased work
Work and timephased work		Cost and timephased cost
Cost and timephased cost		

Tip

Timephased fields show task, resource, and assignment values distributed over time. For example, you can look at a task with five days of work planned at the weekly, daily, or hourly level and see the specific baseline work values per time increment. In Part 2, "Managing a Complex Project," you will work with timephased values.

You should save the baseline when:

■ You have developed the project plan as fully as possible. (However, this does not mean you cannot add tasks, resources, or assignments to the project after work has started. Usually this is unavoidable.)

■ You have not yet started entering actual values, such as a task's percentage of completion.

The TV commercial project plan is now fully developed, and actual work on the project will soon begin. In this exercise, you save the baseline for the TV commercial project and then view the baseline task values:

1 If Microsoft Project is not already open, start it now.

Open

2 On the Standard toolbar, click the Open button.

The Open dialog box appears.

3 Navigate to the Chapter 6 Simple Tracking folder, and double-click the Wingtip Toys Commercial 6a file.

4 On the File menu, click Save As.

The Save As dialog box appears.

5 In the File Name box, type **Wingtip Toys Commercial 6**, and then click the Save button.

6 On the Project Guide toolbar, click the Track button.

The Track pane appears.

7 In the Track pane, click the Save A Baseline Plan To Compare With Later Versions link.

The Save Baseline pane appears.

8 Click the Save Baseline button.

Microsoft Project saves the baseline, even though there's no indication in the Gantt Chart view that anything has changed. You will now see some of the changes caused by saving the baseline.

Tip

To save a baseline, you can also click the Save Baseline command. (On the Tools menu, point to Tracking and click Save Baseline.)

9 Click the Close button in the upper right corner of the Project Guide pane to close the Project Guide.

Tip

Multiple baselines
new in
Project
2002

You can save up to 11 baselines in a single plan. (The first one is called Baseline, and the rest are Baseline 1 through Baseline 10.) Saving multiple baselines can be useful for projects with exceptionally long planning phases, where you might want to compare different sets of baseline values. For example, you might want to save and compare the baseline plans every month as the planning details change. To learn more about baselines in Microsoft Project's online Help, type **All about baselines** into the Ask A Question box in the upper right corner of the Microsoft Project window.

10 On the View menu, click More Views.

The More Views dialog box appears.

11 In the Views box, click Task Sheet, and then click the Apply button.

Because the Task Sheet view does not include the Gantt chart, you have more room to see the fields in the table. Now you'll switch to a different table in the Task Sheet view.

12 On the View menu, point to Table: Summary, and click Variance.

The Variance table appears. This table includes both the scheduled and baseline start and finish columns, shown side by side for easy comparison.

Tip

If any column contains pound signs (###), double-click between the column titles to widen that column.

Your screen should look similar to the following illustration:

	Task Name	Start	Finish	Baseline Start	Baseline Finish	Start Var.	Finish Var.
0	⊟ **Wingtip Toys Co**	**Mon 1/5/04**	**Tue 1/27/04**	**Mon 1/5/04**	**Tue 1/27/04**	**0 days**	**0 days**
1	⊟ Pre-Productio	Mon 1/5/04	Thu 1/15/04	Mon 1/5/04	Thu 1/15/04	0 days	0 days
2	Develop script	Mon 1/5/04	Wed 1/7/04	Mon 1/5/04	Wed 1/7/04	0 days	0 days
3	Develop produc	Thu 1/8/04	Mon 1/12/04	Thu 1/8/04	Mon 1/12/04	0 days	0 days
4	Pick locations	Tue 1/13/04	Tue 1/13/04	Tue 1/13/04	Tue 1/13/04	0 days	0 days
5	Hold auditions	Wed 1/14/04	Thu 1/15/04	Wed 1/14/04	Thu 1/15/04	0 days	0 days
6	Pre-Production	Thu 1/15/04	Thu 1/15/04	Thu 1/15/04	Thu 1/15/04	0 days	0 days
7	⊟ Production	Thu 1/15/04	Thu 1/22/04	Thu 1/15/04	Thu 1/22/04	0 days	0 days
8	Rehearse	Thu 1/15/04	Mon 1/19/04	Thu 1/15/04	Mon 1/19/04	0 days	0 days
9	Shoot video	Mon 1/19/04	Wed 1/21/04	Mon 1/19/04	Wed 1/21/04	0 days	0 days
10	Log footage	Wed 1/21/04	Thu 1/22/04	Wed 1/21/04	Thu 1/22/04	0 days	0 days
11	Production com	Thu 1/22/04	Thu 1/22/04	Thu 1/22/04	Thu 1/22/04	0 days	0 days
12	⊟ Post-Productio	Thu 1/22/04	Tue 1/27/04	Thu 1/22/04	Tue 1/27/04	0 days	0 days
13	Fine cut edit	Thu 1/22/04	Mon 1/26/04	Thu 1/22/04	Mon 1/26/04	0 days	0 days
14	Add final audio	Mon 1/26/04	Tue 1/27/04	Mon 1/26/04	Tue 1/27/04	0 days	0 days
15	Hand off maste	Tue 1/27/04	Tue 1/27/04	Tue 1/27/04	Tue 1/27/04	0 days	0 days

At this point, because no actual work has occurred yet and no changes to the scheduled work have been made, the values in the Start and Baseline Start fields have identical values, as do the Finish and Baseline Finish fields. After actual work is recorded or later schedule adjustments are made, the scheduled start and finish values might differ from the baseline values. You would then see the differences displayed in the variance columns.

Now that you have had a look at some baseline fields, it is time to enter some actuals!

Tracking a Project as Scheduled

The simplest approach to tracking progress is to report that the actual work is proceeding exactly as planned. For example, if the first month of a five-month project has elapsed and all of its tasks have started and finished as scheduled, you can quickly record this in the Update Project dialog box.

In the TV commercial project, suppose that some time has now passed since saving the baseline. Work has started and so far, so good. In this exercise, you record project actuals by updating work to the current date:

1 On the View menu, click Gantt Chart.

The Gantt Chart view appears.

2 On the Tools menu, point to Tracking, and click Update Project.

The Update Project dialog box appears.

3 Make sure the Update Work As Complete Through option is selected. In the adjacent date list, type or select **1/12/04**, and click the OK button.

Tip

You can also click the down arrow in the Update Work As Complete Through box, and in the calendar that appears, select *January 12, 2004*.

Microsoft Project records the completion percentage for the tasks that were scheduled to start before January 12. Then it displays that progress by drawing **progress bars** in the Gantt bars for those tasks. Your screen should look similar to the following illustration:

Check marks appear in the Indicators column for tasks that have been completed.

This progress bar indicates the portion of the task that has been completed.

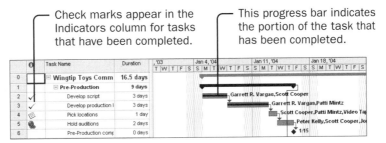

In the Gantt Chart view, the progress bar shows how much of each task has been completed. Because Tasks 2 and 3 have been completed, a check mark appears in the Indicators column for those tasks, and the progress bars extend through the full length of the tasks' Gantt bars.

Entering a Task's Completion Percentage

After work has begun on a task, you can quickly record progress on it as a percentage. When you enter a completion percentage other than 0, Microsoft Project changes the task's actual start date to match its scheduled start date. It then calculates actual duration, remaining duration, actual costs, and other values, based on the percentage you enter. For example, if you specify that a four-day task is 50 percent complete, Microsoft Project calculates that it has had two days of actual duration and has two days of remaining duration.

Here are some ways of entering completion percentage:

- Use the Tracking toolbar (on the View menu, point to Toolbars, and then click Tracking). This toolbar contains buttons for quickly recording that a task is 0, 25, 50, 75, or 100 percent complete.

- Enter any percentage value you want in the Update Tasks dialog box (on the Tools menu, point to Tracking, and then click Update Tasks).

- Use the Project Guide (as you will do in this exercise).

In this exercise, you record completion percentages of tasks via the Project Guide:

1 On the Project Guide toolbar, click the Track button.

The Track pane appears.

2 In the Track pane, click the Prepare To Track The Progress Of Your Project link.

Step 1 of the Setup Tracking pane appears. This pane controls the use of Microsoft Project Server to collect actuals from resources. For this exercise, you are not using Microsoft Project Server, so make sure that the No option is selected.

3 Click the Save And Go To Step 2 link.

Step 2 of the Setup Tracking pane appears.

4 Select the Always Track By Entering The Percent Of Work Complete option, and then click the Save And Finish link at the bottom of the Setup Tracking pane.

Microsoft Project updates the Project Guide: Custom Tracking view to the right. In the % Work Complete column in the Custom Tracking view, you will enter the completion percentage of the next few tasks.

5 In the Track pane, click the Incorporate Progress Information Into The Project link.

The Incorporate Progress pane appears. Here you can set the *status date* and read about how to enter a value in the % Work Complete field. In this chapter, you won't change the status date directly. The status date and other calculation options can help you control how Microsoft Project schedules actual and remaining work. You will work with the status date in Part 2, "Managing a Complex Project."

6 In the % Work Complete field for Task 4, type or select **100**, and then press Enter.

Microsoft Project records the actual work for the task as scheduled, and then it extends a progress line through the length of the Gantt bar. Next you'll get a better look at the task's Gantt bar.

Go To
Selected Task

7 On the Standard toolbar, click the Go To Selected Task button.

Your screen should look similar to the following illustration:

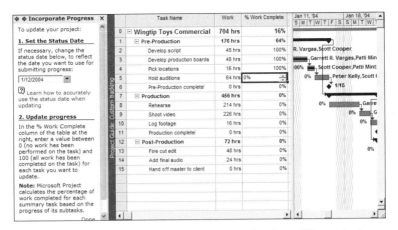

Next you will enter a completion percentage value for a different task.

8 In the % Work Complete field for Task 5, type or select **50**, and then press Enter.

Microsoft Project records the actual work for the task as scheduled, and then it draws a progress line through 50 percent of the Gantt bar.

Tip

The ScreenTip that appears when you point to a progress line in a Gantt bar tells you the task's completion percentage.

9 At the bottom of the Incorporate Progress pane, click the Done link.

So far, you have recorded actual work that started and finished on schedule. While this might prove true for some tasks, often you need to record actuals for tasks that lasted longer or shorter than planned. This is the subject of the next topic.

Entering Actual Values for Tasks

One way to keep your schedule up to date is to record what actually happens for each task in your project. You can record each task's actual start, finish, work, and duration values. When you enter these values, Microsoft Project updates the schedule and calculates the task's completion percentage. Microsoft Project uses the following rules:

■ When you enter a task's actual start date, Microsoft Project moves the scheduled start date to match the actual start date.

■ When you enter a task's actual finish date, Microsoft Project moves the scheduled finish date to match the actual finish date and sets the task to 100 percent complete.

■ When you enter a task's actual work value, Microsoft Project recalculates the task's remaining work values.

■ When you enter a task's actual duration, if it is less than the scheduled duration, Microsoft Project subtracts the actual duration from the scheduled duration to determine the remaining duration.

■ When you enter a task's actual duration, if it is equal to the scheduled duration, Microsoft Project sets the task to 100 percent complete.

■ When you enter a task's actual duration, if it is longer than the scheduled duration, Microsoft Project adjusts the scheduled duration to match the actual duration and sets the task to 100 percent complete.

Suppose that a few more days have passed and work on the TV commercial has progressed. In this exercise, you record actual work values for some tasks, and start dates and durations for other tasks:

1 In the Track pane, click the Prepare To Track The Progress Of Your Project link.

Step 1 of the Setup Tracking pane appears.

2 Click the Save And Go To Step 2 link.

3 Select the Always Track By Entering The Actual Work Done And Work Remaining option, and then click the Save And Finish link.

Microsoft Project updates the Project Guide: Custom Tracking view to the right. In the Actual Work and Remaining Work columns in the Project Guide: Custom Tracking view, you will enter actual and remaining work values of the next few tasks.

In the chart portion of the Custom Tracking view, you can see that Task 5 is currently 50 percent complete, and in the table portion of the view, you can see the resulting hour values of work that this percentage corresponds to. You want to record that the task is now complete but required more work than expected.

4 In the Track pane, click the Incorporate Progress Information Into The Project link.

The Incorporate Progress pane appears. Here you can set the *status date* and read about how to enter values in the Actual Work or Remaining Work fields. In this chapter, you won't change the status date directly.

5 In the Actual Work field for Task 5, type or select **80**, and then press Enter.

Microsoft Project records that 80 hours of work have been completed on Task 5. It extends the Gantt bar of the task to indicate its longer duration and reschedules subsequent tasks.

6   Click the Close button in the upper right corner of the Project Guide pane to close the Project Guide.

Your screen should look similar to the following illustration:

	Task Name	Work	Actual Work	Rem		
0	⊟ **Wingtip Toys Commercial**	**720 hrs**	**192 hrs**			
1	⊟ **Pre-Production**	**192 hrs**	**192 hrs**			
2	Develop script	48 hrs	48 hrs			Garrett R. Vargas,Scott Cooper
3	Develop production boards	48 hrs	48 hrs			Garrett R. Vargas,Patti Mintz
4	Pick locations	16 hrs	16 hrs		100%	Scott Cooper,Patti Mintz,Video Tape[4 30-min. cass
5	Hold auditions	80 hrs	80 hrs		100%	Peter Kelly,Scott Cooper,Jonathan Mollerup
6	Pre-Production complete!	0 hrs	0 hrs			◆ 1/16
7	⊟ **Production**	**456 hrs**	**0 hrs**			
8	Rehearse	214 hrs	0 hrs		0%	Garrett R. Vargas,Jim Hance,Sco
9	Shoot video	226 hrs	0 hrs		0%	Garrett R. Vargas,Jim Hance
10	Log footage	16 hrs	0 hrs		0%	Jo Brown,Editing Lab
11	Production complete!	0 hrs	0 hrs			◆ 1/22
12	⊟ **Post-Production**	**72 hrs**	**0 hrs**			
13	Fine cut edit	48 hrs	0 hrs		0%	Editing Lab,S
14	Add final audio	24 hrs	0 hrs		0%	Editing Lal
15	Hand off master to client	0 hrs	0 hrs			◆ 1/27

Now suppose that more time has passed. To conclude this exercise, you will enter actual start dates and durations of tasks.

7   In the Task Name column, click Task 8, **Rehearse**.

This task started one working day behind schedule (the Monday after its scheduled start date), and took a total of three days to complete. You will record this information in fields that are not in the Project Guide: Custom Tracking view by default. You could insert the fields, switch to a different table that includes them, or (as you will do now) enter the values in the Update Tasks dialog box.

8   On the Tools menu, point to Tracking, and then click Update Tasks.

The Update Tasks dialog box appears. This dialog box shows both the actual and scheduled values for the task's duration, start, and finish, as well as its remaining duration. In it, you can update the actual and remaining values.

9   In the Start field in the Actual box on the left side of the dialog box, type or select **1/19/04**.

10   In the Actual Dur field, type or select **3d**, and then click the OK button.

Microsoft Project records the actual start date and duration of the task. Your screen should look similar to the illustration on the following page.

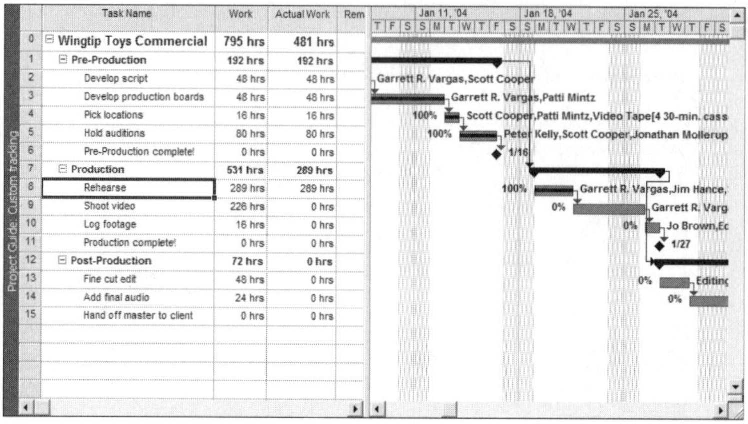

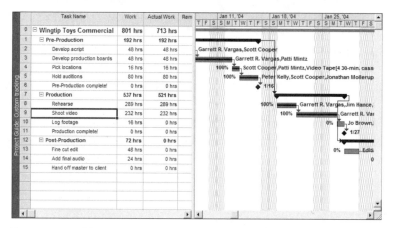

To conclude this exercise, you will record that Task 9 started on time but took longer than planned to complete.

11 In the Task Name column, click Task 9, Shoot Video.

12 On the Tools menu, point to Tracking, and then click Update Tasks.

The Update Tasks dialog box appears.

13 In the Actual Dur field, type or select **3d**, and then click the OK button.

Microsoft Project records the actual duration of the task. Your screen should look similar to the following illustration:

Because you did not specify an actual start date, Microsoft Project assumes that the task started as scheduled, but the actual duration you entered causes Microsoft Project to calculate an actual finish date that is later than the originally scheduled finish date.

Project Management Focus: Is the Project on Track?

Properly evaluating a project's status can be tricky. Consider the following issues:

- For many tasks, it is very difficult to evaluate a completion percentage. When is an engineer's design for a new motor assembly 50 percent complete? Or when is a programmer's code for a software module 50 percent complete? Reporting work in progress is in many cases a "best guess" effort and inherently risky.

- The elapsed portion of a task's duration is not always equal to the amount of work accomplished. For example, a task might require relatively little effort initially, but require more work as time passes. (This is referred to as a back-loaded task.) When 50 percent of its duration has elapsed, far less than 50 percent of its total work will have been completed.

- The resources assigned to a task might have different criteria for what constitutes the task's completion than the project manager or the resources assigned to successor tasks might.

Good project planning and communication can avoid or mitigate these and other problems that arise in project execution. For example, developing proper task durations and status-reporting periods should help you identify tasks that have substantially varied from the baseline early enough to make adjustments. Having well-documented and well-communicated task completion criteria should help prevent "downstream" surprises. Nevertheless, large, complex projects will almost always vary from the baseline.

Chapter Wrap-Up

This chapter covered how to save a project's baseline schedule and record actual progress on tasks.

If you are going on to other chapters:

Save

1 On the Standard toolbar, click the Save button to save changes made to Wingtip Toys Commercial 6.

2 On the File menu, click Close to close the project plan.

If you aren't continuing to other chapters:

1 On the Standard toolbar, click the Save button to save changes made to Wingtip Toys Commercial 6.

2 To quit Microsoft Project for now, on the File menu, click Exit.

Managing a Complex Project

2

QuickLook

Change how tasks are related to each other,
page 105

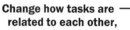

	Task Name	30	1	2	3	4	5	6	7	8	9	10	11	12
7	Paint background scenes													
8	Set up lighting													
9	Install props													

	🛈	Task Name	Duration
19		⊟ Scene 3	4 days
20	🔲	Scene 3 setup	1 day
21	🏛	This task has a 'Start No Earlier Than' constraint on Mon 5/24/04.	1 day
22			8 hrs
23		Scene 3 teardown	1 day
24		Scene 3-process da	1 day

Apply constraints to control when tasks can start or stop, page 110

	🛈	Task Name	Leveling	May 9, '04	May 16, '04	May 23, '04	May 30, '04
				T F S S M T W T F S	S M T W T F S	S M T W T F S	S M T W T F S
1		⊟ Pre-Production	0				
2		Review script					
3		Develop script breakdo					
4		Develop production boa					
5		Scout locations					
6		Select locations					
7		Hold auditions					
8		Apply for filming permit:					
9		Reserve camera equipr					
10		Reserve sound equipm					
11		Pre-Production complete		1.6 days			
12		⊟ Production	0				
13		⊟ Scene 7	0		1.6 days		
14		Scene 7 setup					
15		Scene 7 rehearsal					
16		Scene 7 shoot					
17		Scene 7 teardown					
18		Scene 7-process da		1.6 days			
19		⊟ Scene 3	0				
20	🏛	Scene 3 setup					

View the project's critical path and identify slack, page 113

◆ ◆ Change Project		Task Name	Duration	Work	Assignment Units	Details	
The view on the right shows tasks and the resource assignments for each task. You can edit the following:	2	⊟ Review script	⟨!⟩ 1 wk	80 hrs		Work	
			You just increased the duration of this task. Is it because the:				
Duration is the total time required to do a task. It is calculated by looking at the working time spanned by all the resource assignments on the task.		Clair Hector	⦿ Work required to do this task has increased, so it will take longer				
		Scott Cooper	○ Resources will work fewer hours per day, so the task will take longer				
	3	⊟ Develop script breakdown an	○ None of the above; show me more details				
		Johnathan Perrera				Work	
Work is the person-hours or effort needed to complete a task or assignment. The total work for a task is the sum of the work for all of its assignments.		Scott Cooper				Work	
	4	⊟ Develop production boards	1 mon	480 hrs		Work	
		Johnathan Perrera		160 hrs	100%	Work	
		Kim Yoshida		160 hrs	100%	Work	
Assignment Units represent the percentage of a resource's time assigned to a task. To assign multiple resources such as '3 carpenters', you can set the assignment units to '300%'.		Scott Cooper		160 hrs	100%	Work	
	5	⊟ Scout locations	2 wks	240 hrs		Work	
		Jan Miksovsky		80 hrs	100%	Work	
		Jo Brown		80 hrs	100%	Work	
		Max Benson		80 hrs	100%	Work	
	6	⊟ Select locations	1 wk	120 hrs		Work	
		Clair Hector		40 hrs	100%	Work	
◇ **Controlling Changes**		Max Benson		40 hrs	100%	Work	
		Scott Cooper		40 hrs	100%	Work	
Duration, work and units are tied, so when you change one value, the	7	⊟ Hold auditions	1 wk	100 hrs		Work	
		Clair Hector		40 hrs	100%	Work	

Change a task's duration, work, or assignment units and control how Microsoft Project handles the change, page 120

Chapter 7
Fine-Tuning Task Details

After completing this chapter, you will be able to:

✔ **Adjust task links to have more control over how tasks are related.**

✔ **Apply a constraint to a task.**

✔ **Identify the tasks on the critical path.**

✔ **Split a task to record an interruption in work.**

✔ **Create a task calendar and apply it to tasks.**

✔ **Change a task type to control how Microsoft Project schedules tasks.**

✔ **Record deadlines for tasks.**

✔ **Enter a fixed cost and specify how it should accrue.**

✔ **Set up a recurring task in the project schedule.**

In this chapter, you examine and use a variety of advanced features of Microsoft Project. These features focus on fine-tuning task details prior to saving a baseline and commencing work on the project with the goal of developing the most accurate schedule representation of the tasks you anticipate for the plan.

Short Film Project 7a

This chapter uses the practice file Short Film Project 7a. This is an initial project plan for Southridge Video, the fictitious film and video production company. If you completed the chapters in Part 1, "Managing a Simple Project," you might recognize some of the tasks and sequences in the film project plan. For details about installing the practice files, see "Using the Book's CD-ROM" at the beginning of this book.

Adjusting Task Relationships

You might recall from Chapter 2, "Creating a Task List," that there are four types of task dependencies, or relationships:

■ Finish-to-start (FS): The finish date of the predecessor task determines the start date of the successor task.

■ Start-to-start (SS): The start date of the predecessor task determines the start date of the successor task.

■ Finish-to-finish (FF): The finish date of the predecessor task determines the finish date of the successor task.

■ Start-to-finish (SF): The start date of the predecessor task determines the finish date of the successor task.

Link Tasks

When you enter tasks in Microsoft Project and link them by clicking the Link Tasks button on the Standard toolbar, the tasks are given a finish-to-start (FS) relationship. This might be fine for most tasks, but you will probably want to change some task relationships. Here are some examples of tasks that require relationships other than finish-to-start:

■ You can start setting up the lighting for a film scene as soon as you start setting up the props (start-to-start relationship). This reduces the overall time required to complete the two tasks, as they are completed in parallel.

	Task Name	30	1	2	3	4	5	6	7	8	9	10	11	12
1	Set up lighting													
2	Install props													

■ Planning the filming sequence can begin before the script is complete, but it cannot be finished until after the script is complete. You want the two tasks to finish at about the same time (finish-to-finish relationship).

	Task Name	30	1	2	3	4	5	6	7	8	9	10	11	12
4	Develop script													
5	Plan scene filming sequence													

Task relationships should reflect the sequence in which work should be done. After you have established the correct task relationships, you can fine-tune your schedule by entering overlap (called **lead time**) or delay (called **lag time**) between the finish or start dates of predecessor and successor tasks.

Assuming that two tasks have a finish-to-start relationship:

■ Lead time causes the successor task to begin before its predecessor task concludes.

■ Lag time causes the successor task to begin some time after its predecessor task concludes.

Here is an illustration of how lead and lag time affect task relationships. Let's say you initially planned the following three tasks using finish-to-start relationships:

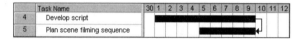

Initially the tasks are linked with finish-to-start relationships, so the successor tasks begin as soon as the predecessor tasks finish.

	Task Name	30	1	2	3	4	5	6	7	8	9	10	11	12
7	Paint background scenes													
8	Set up lighting													
9	Install props													

Before Task 8 can start, you need to allow an extra day for the paint applied in Task 7 to dry. You do not want to add a day to the duration of Task 7, because no real work will occur on that day. Instead, you enter a one-day lag between Tasks 7 and 8:

This lag time causes a delay in the start of the successor task.

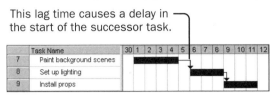

However, Task 9 can start as soon as Task 8 is halfway completed; to make this happen, enter a 50-percent lead time between Tasks 8 and 9:

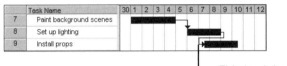

This lead time causes the successor task to start before the predecessor task finishes.

Tip

Some of the places you can enter lead or lag time include the Task Information dialog box, and the Predecessors column in the Entry table.

You can enter lead and lag time as units of time (for example, two days) or as a percentage of the duration of the predecessor task (for example, 50 percent). Lag time is entered in positive units, lead time in negative units (for example, minus two days or minus 50 percent). You can apply lead or lag time to any type of task relationship: finish-to-start, start-to-start, and so on.

In this exercise, you change task relationships and enter lead and lag time between predecessor and successor tasks:

1   If Microsoft Project is not already open, start it now.

Open

2   On the Standard toolbar, click the Open button.

The Open dialog box appears.

3   Navigate to the Chapter 7 Complex Tasks folder, and double-click the Short Film Project 7a file.

4   On the File menu, click Save As.

The Save As dialog box appears.

5   In the File Name box, type **Short Film Project 7** and then click the Save button.

6 Double-click the name of Task 9, *Reserve camera equipment*.

The Task Information dialog box appears.

7 Click the Predecessors tab.

Here you can see that Task 9 has one predecessor task, Task 8.

8 In the Lag field for predecessor Task 8, type **-50%**.

To enter lead time against a predecessor task, enter it as a negative lag time either in units of time such as days, or as a percentage of the duration of the predecessor task.

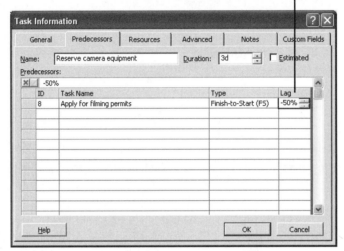

Entering lag time as a negative value produces lead time.

9 Click OK to close the Task Information dialog box.

Tip

You can also double-click a link to enter lead or lag time, change the task relationship, or delete the link.

Go To
Selected Task

10 To see how the lag time affects the scheduling of the successor task, on the Standard toolbar, click the Go To Selected Task button.

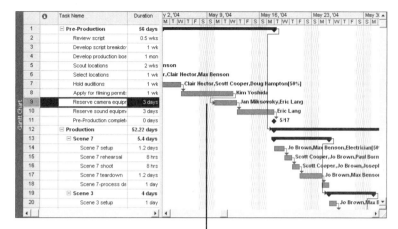

Lead time causes the successor task
to start before the predecessor task
has finished, although the two tasks
still have a finish-to-start relationship.

Microsoft Project scrolls the Gantt chart to display the Gantt bar for Task 9. Task 9
is now scheduled to start when Task 8 is 50 percent complete. Should the duration
of Task 8 change, Microsoft Project will reschedule the start of Task 9 so that it keeps
a 50 percent lead time.

Next you will change the task relationship between two tasks.

11 Double-click the name of Task 10, *Reserve sound equipment*.

The Task Information dialog box appears. The Predecessors tab should be visible.

12 Click in the Type column for predecessor Task 9. Select Start-To-Start (SS), and click OK.

Microsoft Project changes the task relationship between Tasks 9 and 10 to start-to-start.

The start-to-start task relationships cause
the two tasks to start at the same time.
Should the start date of the predecessor
task change, the start date of the
successor task would change as well.

Important

Assigning tasks start-to-start relationships and entering lead times where appropriate are both excellent techniques to shorten overall project duration. However, Microsoft Project cannot automatically make such schedule adjustments for you. As project manager, you must analyze the sequences and relationships of your tasks and make those adjustments where appropriate.

Setting Task Constraints

Every task you enter into Microsoft Project has some type of constraint applied to it. A constraint controls the start or finish date of a task and the degree to which that task can be rescheduled. There are three categories of constraints:

- *Flexible constraints*. Microsoft Project can change the start and finish dates of a task. For example, the task *Select locations to film* can start as soon as possible. This type of flexible constraint is called As Soon As Possible, or ASAP for short, and is the default constraint type in Microsoft Project. No constraint date is associated with flexible constraints.

- *Inflexible constraints*. A task must begin or end on a certain date. For example, a task such as Set up lighting must end on April 10, 2004. Inflexible constraints are sometimes called hard constraints.

- *Semi-flexible constraints*. A task has a start or finish date boundary. However, within that boundary, Microsoft Project has the scheduling flexibility to change start and finish dates of a task. For example, a task such as Install props must finish no later than March 26, 2004. However, the task could finish before this date. Semi-flexible constraints are sometimes called soft or moderate constraints.

In all, there are eight types of task constraints:

This constraint category	Includes these constraint types	And means
Flexible	As Soon As Possible (ASAP)	Microsoft Project will schedule a task to occur as soon as it can occur. This is the default constraint type applied to all new tasks when scheduling from the project start date.
	As Late As Possible (ALAP)	Microsoft Project will schedule a task to occur as late as it can occur. This is the default constraint type applied to all new tasks when scheduling from the project finish date.

This constraint category	Includes these constraint types	And means
Semi-flexible	Start No Earlier Than (SNET)	Microsoft Project will schedule a task to start on or after the constraint date you specify. Use this constraint type to ensure that a task will not start before a specific date.
	Start No Later Than (SNLT)	Microsoft Project will schedule a task to start on or before the constraint date you specify. Use this constraint type to ensure that a task will not start after a specific date.
	Finish No Earlier Than (FNET)	Microsoft Project will schedule a task to finish on or after the constraint date you specify. Use this constraint type to ensure that a task will not finish before a specific date.
	Finish No Later Than (FNLT)	Microsoft Project will schedule a task to finish on or before the constraint date you specify. Use this constraint type to ensure that a task will not finish after a specific date.
Inflexible	Must Start On (MSO)	Microsoft Project will schedule a task to start on the constraint date you specify. Use this constraint type to ensure that a task will start on an exact date.
	Must Finish On (MFO)	Microsoft Project will schedule a task to finish on the constraint date you specify. Use this constraint type to ensure that a task will finish on an exact date.

Important

Beginning Microsoft Project users are often tempted to enter start or finish dates for tasks. However, doing so applies semi-flexible constraints such as Start No Earlier Than or Finish No Earlier Than. This essentially prevents users from taking full advantage of the Microsoft Project scheduling engine. Although this is one of the most common scheduling problems people have with Microsoft Project, it is usually avoidable.

These three categories of constraints have very different effects on the scheduling of tasks:

■ Flexible constraints, such as As Soon As Possible, allow tasks to be scheduled without any limitations other than their predecessor and successor relationships. No fixed start or end dates are imposed by these constraint types. Use these constraint types whenever possible.

ASAP

■ Semi-flexible constraints, such as Start No Earlier Than or Start No Later Than, limit the rescheduling of a task within the date boundary you specify.

Constraint
Date

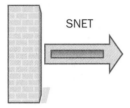

■ Inflexible constraints, such as Must Start On, completely prevent the rescheduling of a task. Use these constraint types only when absolutely necessary.

The type of constraint you apply to the tasks in your projects depends on what you need from Microsoft Project. You should use inflexible constraints only if the start or finish date of a task is fixed by factors beyond the control of the project team. Examples of such tasks include handoffs to clients and the end of a funding period. For tasks without such limitations, you should use flexible constraints. Flexible constraints give you the most discretion in adjusting start and finish dates, and they allow Microsoft Project to adjust dates if your project plan changes. For example, if you have used ASAP constraints and the duration of a predecessor task changes from four days to two days, Microsoft Project adjusts or "pulls in" the start and finish dates of all successor tasks. However, if a successor task had an inflexible constraint applied, Microsoft Project could not adjust its start or finish dates.

In this exercise, you apply a Start No Earlier Than constraint to a task:

1   On the Project Guide toolbar, click Tasks.

    The Tasks pane appears.

2   In the Tasks pane, click the Set Deadlines And Constrain Tasks link.

    The Deadlines And Constraints pane appears.

3   Select Task 20, *Scene 3 setup*.

    This scene must be shot at a location that is not available to the film crew until May 24, 2004.

4   Under Constrain A Task in the Deadlines And Constraints pane, select Start No Earlier Than.

5   In the date box below it, type or select **5/24/04**. Your screen should look like the following illustration:

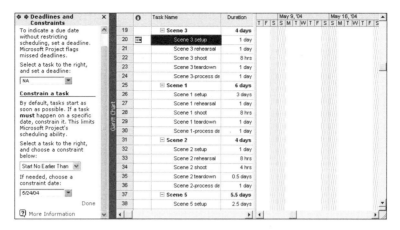

6 At the bottom of the Deadlines And Constraints pane, click the Done link.

Microsoft Project applies an SNET constraint to the task, and a constraint icon appears in the Indicators column.

You can point to the icon to see the constraint details in a ScreenTip.

Position your mouse pointer over a constraint indicator (or any icon in the Indicators column) to

	ⓘ	Task Name	Duration
19		⊟ Scene 3	**4 days**
20		Scene 3 setup	1 day
21		This task has a 'Start No Earlier Than' constraint on Mon 5/24/04.	1 day
22			8 hrs
23		Scene 3 teardown	1 day
24		Scene 3-process da	1 day

Task 20 is rescheduled to start on May 24 instead of May 20. All tasks that depend on Task 20 are also rescheduled.

7 Click the Close button in the upper right corner of the Project Guide to close it.

Here are a few more things to keep in mind when applying constraints to tasks:

■ Entering a Finish date for a task (for example, in the Finish column) applies an FNET constraint to the task.

■ Entering a Start date for a task (for example, in the Start column) or dragging a Gantt bar directly on the Gantt chart applies a SNET constraint to the task.

■ In many cases, entering a deadline date is a preferable alternative to entering a semi-flexible or inflexible constraint. You will work with deadline dates later in this chapter.

■ Unless you specify a time, Microsoft Project schedules a constraint date's start or finish time using the Default Start Time or Default End Time values on the Calendar tab (Tools menu, Options command). In this project, the default start time is 8 A.M. If you want a constrained task to be scheduled to start at a different time, enter that time along with the start date. For example, if you want to schedule a task to start at 10 A.M. on May 24, enter **5/24/04 10AM** in the Start field.

■ To remove a constraint, on the Project menu, click Task Information, and in the Task Information dialog box, click the Advanced tab. In the Constraint Type box, select As Soon As Possible or (if scheduling from the project finish date) As Late As Possible.

■ If you need to apply semi-flexible or inflexible constraints to tasks in addition to task relationships, you might create what is called negative slack. For example, you have a successor task that has a finish-to-start relationship with its predecessor task. If you entered a Must Start On constraint on the successor task earlier than the finish date of the predecessor task, this would result in negative slack and a scheduling conflict. By default, the constraint date applied to the successor task will override the relationship. However, if you prefer, you can set Microsoft Project to honor relationships over constraints. On the Tools menu, click Options, and in the Options dialog box, click the Schedule tab. Clear the Tasks Will Always Honor Their Constraint Dates check box. This setting applies only to the current project file.

■ If you must schedule a project from a finish date rather than a start date, some constraint behaviors change. For example, the ALAP (rather than the ASAP) constraint type becomes the default for new tasks. You should pay close attention to constraints when scheduling from a finish date to make sure they have the effects you intend.

Viewing the Project's Critical Path

A critical path is the series of tasks that will push out the project's end date if the tasks are delayed. The word "critical" has nothing to do with how important these tasks are to the overall project. It refers only to how their scheduling will affect the project's finish date. However, the project finish date is of great importance in most projects. If you want to shorten the duration of a project to bring in the finish date, you must begin by shortening the critical path.

Over the life of a project, the project's critical path is likely to change from time to time as tasks are completed ahead of or behind schedule. Schedule changes, such as assigning resources to tasks, can also change the critical path. After a task on the critical path is completed, it is no longer critical, because it cannot affect the project finish date. In Chapter 16, "Getting Your Project Back on Track," you will work with a variety of techniques to shorten a project's overall duration.

A key to understanding the critical path is to understand slack, also known as float. There are two types of slack: free and total. *Free slack* is the amount of time a task can be delayed before it delays another task.

Total slack is the amount of time a task can be delayed before it delays the finish of the project. A task is on the critical path if its total slack is less than a certain amount—normally, if it is zero.

In contrast, ***noncritical tasks*** have slack, meaning they can start or finish earlier or later within their slack time without affecting the completion date of a project.

In this exercise, you view the project's critical path. One way to see the critical path is to switch to the Detail Gantt view:

1 On the View menu, click More Views.

2 In the More Views dialog box, select Detail Gantt, and then click the Apply button.

The project appears in the Detail Gantt view.

3 On the Edit menu, click Go To.

Tip

Ctrl+G is the keyboard shortcut for Go To.

4 In the ID box, type **12**, and then click OK.

Microsoft Project displays Task 12, the production summary task.

Noncritical tasks have free slack, displayed here.

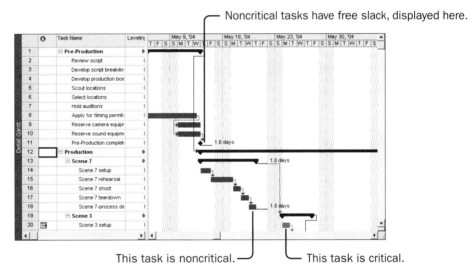

This task is noncritical. ⎯⎯⎯⎯⎯⎯⎯⎯ This task is critical.

The tasks subsequent to Scene 3 are critical tasks. In the Detail Gantt view, Microsoft Project distinguishes between critical and noncritical tasks. Critical task bars are red, but noncritical task bars are blue. In this view, you can also see tasks with free slack.

Notice the Gantt bar of Task 18, *Scene 7–process dailies*. The blue bar represents the duration of the task. The thin teal line and the number next to it represent free slack for this task. As you can see, this particular task has some slack and is therefore a non-critical task. (Remember that the term critical in this sense has nothing to do with the task's importance, only with how much or little total slack the task has.) The slack on task 18 was caused by the Start No Earlier Than constraint applied to Task 20.

5 On the View menu, click Gantt Chart.

Working with the critical path is the most important way to manage a project's overall duration. In later exercises, you will make adjustments that might extend the project's duration. Checking the project's critical path and, when necessary, shortening the overall project duration are important project management skills.

Tip

Critical path is a frequently misused phrase on many projects. Just listen for references to critical path work on your current projects to see how frequently the phrase is used correctly. Remember that critical has nothing to do with the relative importance of a task, only with its effect on the project finish date.

Here are a few more things to keep in mind when working with the critical path:

- By default, Microsoft Project defines a task as critical if it has zero slack. However you can change the amount of slack required for a task to be critical. On the Tools menu click Options, and in the Options dialog box, click the Calculation tab. In the Tasks Are Critical If Slack Is Less Than Or Equal To box, enter the number of days you want.

- Microsoft Project constantly recalculates the critical path, even if you never display it.

- You see free slack represented in the chart portion of the Detail Gantt view, and you can also see the values of free and total slack in the Schedule table. You can apply the Schedule table to any Gantt or Task Sheet view.

- To learn more about managing a critical path, type **All about the critical path** into the Ask A Question box in the upper right corner of the Microsoft Project window.

Interrupting Work on a Task

When initially planning project tasks, you might know that work on a certain task will be interrupted. You can split the task to indicate times when the work will be interrupted and when it can resume. Here are some reasons why you might want to split a task:

- You anticipate an interruption in a task. For example, a resource might be assigned to a week-long task but needs to attend an event on Wednesday that is unrelated to the task.

- A task is unexpectedly interrupted. After a task is under way, a resource might have to stop work on the task because another task has taken priority. After the second task is completed, the resource can resume work on the first task.

In this exercise, you split a task:

1   On the Edit menu, click Go To.
2   In the ID box, type **4**, and then click OK.

Microsoft Project displays Task 4, *Develop production boards*.

You know that work on this task will be interrupted for two days starting March 15.

The timescale is divided into tiers. The time setting of the lowest tier determines how you can split tasks. In this example, you can split tasks into one-day increments.

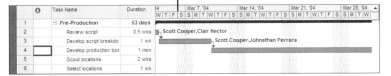

Split Task

Split Task mouse pointer

3 On the Standard toolbar, click the Split Task button.

A ScreenTip appears, and the mouse pointer changes.

4 Move the mouse pointer over the Gantt bar of Task 4.

This ScreenTip is essential for accurately splitting a task; it contains the date at which you would start the second segment of the task if you dragged the mouse pointer from its current location on the Gantt bar. As you move the mouse pointer along the Gantt bar, you will see the start date in the ScreenTip change.

Use this ScreenTip to help you accurately split tasks.

5 Move (but don't click) the mouse pointer over the Gantt bar of Task 4 until the start date of Monday, 3/15/04, appears in the ScreenTip.

6 Drag the mouse pointer to the right until the start date of Wednesday, 3/17/04, appears in the ScreenTip, and then release the mouse button.

Microsoft Project inserts a task split, represented in the Gantt chart as a dotted line, between the two segments of the task.

The split appears as a dotted line connecting the segments of the task.

Tip

Four-headed arrow mouse pointer

Splitting tasks with the mouse might take a little practice. If you didn't split Task 4 so that the second segment starts on 3/17/04, just point to it again. When the mouse pointer changes to a four-headed arrow, drag the segment to the correct start date.

Here are a few more things to keep in mind when splitting tasks:

■ Adjusting the bottom tier of the timescale is important for splitting tasks: the calibration of the bottom tier determines the smallest time increment into which you can split a task. With the bottom tier set at the Days level, you must split a task by at least a day. If you wanted to split a task at the hourly level, you would have to adjust the bottom tier further (through the Timescale command on the Format menu).

■ You can split a task into as many segments as you want.

■ You can drag a segment of a split task left or right to reschedule the split.

■ The time of the task split itself, represented by the dotted line, is not counted in the duration of the task unless the task type is Fixed Duration. No work occurs during the split.

■ If the duration of a split task changes, the last segment of the task is increased or decreased.

■ If a split task is rescheduled (for example, if its start date changes), the entire task, splits and all, is rescheduled. The task keeps the same pattern of segments and splits.

■ Resource leveling or manually contouring assignments over time can cause tasks to split. You will level resources in Chapter 8, "Fine-tuning Resource and Assignment Details," and contour assignments in Chapter 9, "Fine-tuning the Project Plan."

■ To rejoin two segments of a split task, drag one segment of the task until it touches the other segment.

■ If you do not want to display splits as a dotted line, you can remove them. On the Format menu, click Layout, and in the Layout dialog box, clear the Show Bar Splits check box.

Adjusting Working Time for Individual Tasks

Sometimes you want specific tasks to occur at times that are outside of the project calendar's (or for assigned resources, the resource calendar's) working time. To accomplish this, you apply a task calendar to these tasks. As with the project calendar, you specify which base calendar to use as a task calendar. Here are some examples of when you might need a task calendar:

■ You are using the Standard base calendar as your project calendar, and you have a task that must run overnight.

■ You have a task that must occur on a specific weekday.

■ You have a task that must occur over the weekend.

Unlike resources and resource calendars, Microsoft Project does not create task calendars as you create tasks. When you need a custom task calendar, you assign one of the base calendars provided with Microsoft Project (or more likely a new base calendar you have created) to the task.

For example, if you assign the 24 Hours base calendar to a task, Microsoft Project will schedule that task according to a 24-hour workday rather than the working time specified in the project calendar.

For tasks that have both a task calendar and resource assignments, Microsoft Project schedules work in the working times that are common between the task calendar and resource calendar(s). If there is no common working time, Microsoft Project alerts you when you apply the task calendar or assign a resource to the task.

Tip

When you assign a base calendar to a task, you can choose to ignore resource calendars for all resources assigned to the task. Doing so causes Microsoft Project to schedule the resources to work on the task according to the task calendar and not their own resource calendars (for example, to work 24 hours per day). If this would result in resources working in what would otherwise be their nonworking time, you might want to first discuss this with the affected resources.

In the film project, one of the scenes must be filmed at night. However, the project calendar does not include working time late enough to cover the filming of this scene. Because this task is really an exception to the normal working time of the project, you do not want to change the project calendar. In this exercise, you create a new base calendar and apply it to the appropriate task:

1 On the Tools menu, click Change Working Time.

2 In the Change Working Time dialog box, click the New button.

   The Create New Base Calendar dialog box appears.

3 In the Name box, type **Evening Shoot.**

4 In the Make A Copy Of box, make sure Standard is selected, and then click OK.

5 In the calendar below the Select Date(s) label, select the column headings for Monday through Friday.

6 In the upper row of the From and To boxes, enter **5:00 PM** and **11:00 PM**, and then delete the values in the second row. Your Change Working Time dialog box should look like the illustration shown on the following page.

This custom base calendar contains the unique working times not available in the built-in base calendars.

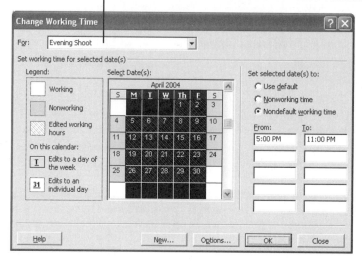

7 Click OK to close the dialog box.

Next you will apply the Evening Shoot calendar to a task that must be filmed in the evening.

8 Select the name of Task 34, *Scene 2 shoot*.

Task
Information

9 On the Standard toolbar, click the Task Information button.

The Task Information dialog box appears.

10 Click the Advanced tab.

11 In the Calendar box, select Evening Shoot from the list.

12 Click the Scheduling Ignores Resource Calendars check box, and then click OK to close the dialog box.

Microsoft Project applies the Evening Shoot calendar to Task 34. A calendar icon appears in the Indicators column, reminding you that this task has a task calendar applied to it. Because you chose to ignore resource calendars in the previous step, the resources assigned to these tasks will be scheduled at times that would otherwise be nonworking times for them.

Tip

To remove a task calendar from a task, on the Advanced tab of the Task Information dialog box, click None in the Calendar box.

Changing Task Types

You might recall from Chapter 4, "Assigning Resources to Tasks," that Microsoft Project uses the following formula, called the scheduling formula, to calculate a task's work value:

Work = Duration × Units

Remember also that a task has work when it has at least one work resource assigned to it. Each value in the scheduling formula corresponds to a task type. A task type determines which of the three scheduling formula values remains fixed if the other two values change.

The default task type is *Fixed Units*: when you change a task's duration, Microsoft Project recalculates work. Likewise, if you change a task's work, Microsoft Project recalculates the duration. In either case, the units value is unchanged. The two other task types are *Fixed Duration* and *Fixed Work*.

For a fixed-duration task, you can change the task's units or work value, and Microsoft Project will recalculate the other value. For a fixed-work task, you can change the units or duration value, and Microsoft Project will recalculate the other value. Note that you cannot turn off effort-driven scheduling for this task type.

Which is the right task type to apply to each of your tasks? It depends on how you want Microsoft Project to schedule that task. The following table summarizes the effects of changing any value for any task type. You read it like a multiplication table:

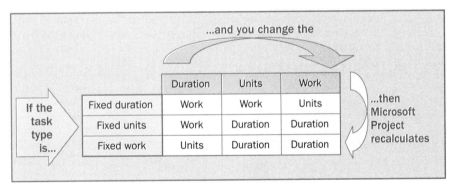

	...and you change the		
If the task type is...	Duration	Units	Work
Fixed duration	Work	Work	Units
Fixed units	Work	Duration	Duration
Fixed work	Units	Duration	Duration

...then Microsoft Project recalculates

Task Information

To see the task type of the selected task, on the Standard toolbar, click the Task Information button, and in the Task Information dialog box, click the Advanced tab. You can also see the task type in the Task Form. (When in the Gantt Chart view, you can display the Task Form by clicking the Split command on the window menu.) You can change a task type at any time. Note that characterizing a task type as *fixed* does not mean that its duration, units, or work values are unchangeable. You can change any value for any task type. In fact when you edit a task's duration, assignment units, or work values, Microsoft Project displays a Smart Tag with which you can change the result of your edit.

In this exercise, you change scheduling formula values and task types:

1 On the Project Guide toolbar, click Track.

The Track pane appears.

2 In the Track pane, click the Make Changes To The Project link.

The Change Project pane appears, and the Project Guide: Edit Assignments view replaces the Gantt Chart view. This type of view is called a usage view. This view groups the assigned resources below each task and shows you, among other things, each task's and assignment's duration, work, and assignment units values—the three variables of the scheduling formula.

3 On the Edit menu, click Go To.

4 In the ID box, type **2**, and then click OK.

Microsoft Project displays Task 2, *Review script,* and its assignments.

You can see that Task 2 has a total work value of 40 hours (that is, 20 hours each for two resources), resource units of 100 percent each, and a duration of one-half of a week. Next you will change the task's duration to see the effects on the other values.

After a discussion among all the resources who will review the script, all agree that the task's duration should double but the work required to complete the task should remain the same.

5 In the Duration field for Task 2, type or select **1w**, and press Enter.

Microsoft Project changes the duration of Task 2 to one week and increases the work per resource to 40 hours each. You want the duration to double (it did) but the work to remain the same (it didn't), so you will use the Smart Tag to adjust the results of the new task duration.

Smart Tag
Actions

6 Point at the Duration Field and then click the Smart Tag Actions button.

Look over the options in the list that appears. Your screen should look like the following illustration:

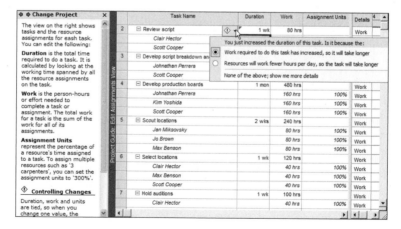

Because Task 2's task type is fixed units (the default task type), the Smart Tag's default selection is to increase work as the duration increased. However, you'd like to keep the work value the same and decrease assignment units for the task's new duration.

7 In the Smart Tag Actions list, select the option Resources Will Work Fewer Hours Per Day, So The Task Will Take Longer.

The units value of each resource decreases to 50 percent, and the total work remains fixed at 40 hours (20 hours each).

	Task Name	Duration	Work	Assignment Units	Details	4
2	⊟ Review script	1 wk	40 hrs		Work	
	Clair Hector		20 hrs	50%	Work	
	Scott Cooper		20 hrs	50%	Work	

Next you will change a task type using the Task Information dialog box.

8 On the Edit menu, click Go To.

9 In the ID box, type **67**, and then click OK.

Microsoft Project displays Task 67, *Hold formal approval showing*.

Task Information

10 On the Standard toolbar, click the Task Information button.

The Task Information dialog box appears.

11 Click the Advanced tab if it is not already selected.

The selected task describes the formal screening of the film for the financial backers of the project. You can see in the Task Type box that this task currently has a fixed-units task type.

The task is scheduled for a full day, although a few of the assigned resources will work for the equivalent of half a day. To reflect this (and properly manage resource costs for the task), you will make this a fixed duration task and adjust the assignment unit values for some of the assigned resources.

12 In the Task Type box, select Fixed Duration.

13 Click the Resources tab.

14 In the Units column, set the units values for Mark Hassall and Scott Cooper to **50%** each.

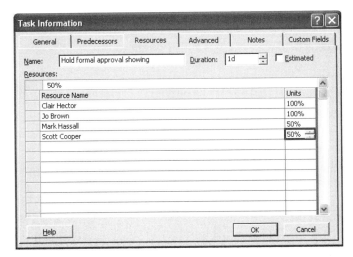

15 Click OK to close the Task Information dialog box.

You can see the updated work values of the two resources in the Project Guide: Edit Assignments view.

16 On the View menu, click Gantt Chart.

Tip

A summary task always has a fixed-duration task type, and you cannot change it. Because a summary task is based on the earliest start date and the latest finish date of its subtasks, its duration is calculated based on its subtasks and is not directly editable. If you want to confirm this, double-click Summary Task 1, Pre-Production—or another summary task—and view the Advanced tab in the Task Information dialog box.

Task Types and Effort-Driven Scheduling

Many people misunderstand task types and effort-driven scheduling and conclude that these two issues are more closely related than they really are. Both settings can affect work, duration, and units values. However, effort-driven scheduling affects your schedule only when you're assigning or removing resources from tasks, while changing a task type affects only the resources currently assigned to the task. For more information about effort-driven scheduling, see Chapter 4, "Assigning Resources to Tasks."

Entering Deadline Dates

One common mistake new Microsoft Project users make is to place semi-flexible or inflexible constraints on too many tasks in their projects. Such constraints severely limit your scheduling flexibility.

Yet if you know that a specific task must be completed by a certain date, why not enter a Must Finish On constraint? Here is why not: let's say you have a five-day task that you want to see completed by October 12, and today is October 1. If you enter a Must Finish On constraint on the task and set it to October 12, Microsoft Project will move it out so that it will, indeed, end on October 12.

	Task Name	30	1	2	3	4	5	6	7	8	9	10	11	12	13	14
15	Hand off deliverables															

This task has a Must Finish On constraint applied, so Microsoft Project schedules it to finish on the specified date, but no earlier.

Now, even if the task could be completed earlier, Microsoft Project will not reschedule it to start earlier. In fact, by applying that constraint, you have increased the risk for this task. If the task is delayed for even one day for any reason (a required resource is out sick, for example), the task will miss its planned finish date.

A better approach to scheduling this task is to use the default As Soon As Possible (ASAP) constraint and enter a deadline of October 12. A deadline is a date value you enter for a task that indicates the latest date by which you want the task to be completed, but the deadline date itself does not constrain the task.

With an ASAP constraint applied, the task starts earlier and leaves slack between the finish date and the deadline.

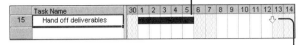

The deadline marker appears on the Gantt Chart.

Now the task has the greatest scheduling flexibility. It might be completed well before its deadline, depending on resource availability, predecessor tasks, and whatever other scheduling issues apply.

Deadline Indicator

Entering a deadline date causes Microsoft Project to display a deadline indicator on the chart portion of the Gantt Chart view. If the task's finish date moves past its deadline, Microsoft Project displays a missed deadline indicator in the Indicator field for that task.

Missed Deadline Indicator

In this exercise, you enter deadline dates for some tasks:

1 On the Edit menu, click Go To.

2 In the ID box, type **11** and click OK.

Microsoft Project displays Task 11. This task is a milestone marking the scheduled finish date of the pre-production phase of the project. You want to make sure that the pre-production tasks conclude by May 21, 2004, so you will enter a deadline date for this milestone.

3 If the Tasks pane is not already displayed, on the Project Guide toolbar, click Tasks.

The Tasks pane appears.

4 In the Tasks pane, click the Set Deadlines And Constrain Tasks link.

The Deadlines And Constraints pane appears.

5 In the Date box under Set A Deadline, type or select **5/21/04**, and then press Tab.

Microsoft Project inserts a deadline indicator in the chart portion of the Gantt Chart view. Your screen should look like the following illustration:

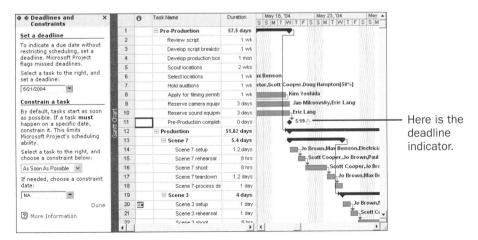

Here is the deadline indicator.

Now you can see at a glance how close the pre-production phase is to meeting or missing its deadline. Should the scheduled completion of the pre-production phase move past 5/21/04, Microsoft Project would display a missed deadline indicator in the Indicators column.

Next you will enter a deadline date for a summary task.

6   Select the name of Task 12, *Production*.

This task is the Production Summary task. You want to conclude filming by mid-August 2004.

7   In the Date box under Set A Deadline, type or select **8/13/04**, and then press Tab.

Microsoft Project inserts a deadline date marker for the summary task. If you wish to see it, scroll the chart portion of the Gantt Chart view to the right.

8   At the bottom of the Deadlines And Constraints pane, click the Done link.

9   Click the Close button in the upper right corner of the Project Guide pane to close it.

Tip

You can also enter a deadline date for the selected task on the Advanced tab in the Task Information dialog box. On the Project menu, click Task Information.

Except for one situation, entering a deadline date has no effect on the scheduling of a summary or subtask. However, a deadline date will cause Microsoft Project to alert you if the scheduled completion of a task exceeds its deadline date.

The one situation in which the deadline date can affect the scheduling of a task involves slack. When a task is given a deadline date, its slack does not extend beyond the deadline date.

Tip

To remove a deadline from a task, clear the Date field in the Deadlines And Constraints pane of the Project Guide, or clear the Deadline field on the Advanced tab of the Task Information dialog box (available by clicking Task Information on the Project menu).

Entering Fixed Costs

For most projects, financial costs are derived mainly from resource costs. Typically, you set up hourly, weekly, or monthly cost rates for resources. However, in addition to (or sometimes instead of) the resource costs associated with a task, a task might have a *fixed cost*. A fixed cost is a specific monetary amount budgeted for a task. It remains the same regardless of how much time or effort resources expend to complete the task. Here are some common examples of fixed costs in projects:

- Travel expenses for a consultant, paid in addition to an hourly or a daily fee.
- A setup fee, charged in addition to a per-day rental fee, for a piece of equipment.
- A permit to film in a public location.

If you enter both resource costs and fixed costs for a task, Microsoft Project adds the two to determine the task's total cost. If you do not enter resource cost information into a project plan (perhaps because you do not know how much your resources will be paid), you can still gain some control over the project's total cost by entering fixed costs per task.

You can specify when fixed costs should accrue:

- **Start.** The entire fixed cost is scheduled for the start of the task. When you track progress, the entire fixed cost of the task is incurred as soon as the task starts.
- **End.** The entire fixed cost is scheduled for the end of the task. When you track progress, the entire fixed cost of the task is incurred only after the task is completed.
- **Prorated.** The fixed cost is distributed evenly over the duration of the task. When you track progress, the project incurs the cost of the task at the rate at which the task is completed. For example, if a task has a $100 fixed cost and is 75 percent complete, the project has incurred $75 against that task.

When you plan a project, the *accrual* method you choose for fixed costs determines how these costs are scheduled over time. This can be important in anticipating budget and cash-flow needs. By default, Microsoft Project assigns the prorated accrual method for fixed costs, but you can change that to match your organization's cost accounting practices.

For the film project, you know from past experience that the filming permits will cost $500, payable when you apply for the permits. In this exercise, you assign a fixed cost to a task and specify its accrual method:

1 On the View menu, click More Views.

2 In the More Views dialog box, click Task Sheet, and then click the Apply button.

The Task Sheet view appears.

3 On the View menu, point to Table: Entry, and click Cost.

The Cost table appears, replacing the Entry table.

4 In the Fixed Cost field for Task 8, *Apply for filming permits*, type or select **500**, and press Tab.

5 In the Fixed Cost Accrual field, select Start, and press Tab.

	Task Name	Fixed Cost	Fixed Cost Accrual	Total Cost	Baseline	Variance	Actual	Remaining
1	⊟ Pre-Production	**$0.00**	Prorated	**$21,926.50**	**$0.00**	**$21,926.50**	**$0.00**	**$21,926.50**
2	Review script	$0.00	Prorated	$787.50	$0.00	$787.50	$0.00	$787.50
3	Develop script breakdo	$0.00	Prorated	$1,655.00	$0.00	$1,655.00	$0.00	$1,655.00
4	Develop production boa	$0.00	Prorated	$8,124.00	$0.00	$8,124.00	$0.00	$8,124.00
5	Scout locations	$0.00	Prorated	$4,920.00	$0.00	$4,920.00	$0.00	$4,920.00
6	Select locations	$0.00	Prorated	$2,535.00	$0.00	$2,535.00	$0.00	$2,535.00
7	Hold auditions	$0.00	Prorated	$1,835.00	$0.00	$1,835.00	$0.00	$1,835.00
8	Apply for filming permit:	$500.00	Start ▾	$876.00	$0.00	$876.00	$0.00	$876.00
9	Reserve camera equipr	$0.00	Prorated	$822.00	$0.00	$822.00	$0.00	$822.00

A fixed cost value is either accrued at the start or finish of a task or prorated over the duration of the task, depending on the option you choose.

Now Microsoft Project will schedule a $500 cost against the task Apply for filming permits at the task's start date, and the project will incur this cost when the task starts. This cost is independent of the task's duration and of the costs of resources assigned to it. In fact, the task's total cost (visible in the Total Cost column) includes both the $500 fixed cost and the cost of the resources assigned to the task.

Tip

To learn more about managing costs in a project plan, type **All about costs** into the Ask A Question box in the upper right corner of the Microsoft Project window.

Setting Up a Recurring Task

Many projects require repetitive tasks, such as attending project status meetings, creating and publishing status reports, or running quality control inspections. Although it is easy to overlook the scheduling of such events, you should account for them in your project plan. After all, status meetings and similar events that indirectly support the project require time from resources. And such events take time away from your resources' other assignments.

To help account for such events in your project plan, create a *recurring task*. As the name suggests, a recurring task is repeated at a specified frequency, such as daily, weekly, monthly, or yearly. When you create a recurring task, Microsoft Project creates a series of tasks with Start No Earlier Than constraints, no task relationships, and effort-driven scheduling turned off.

In this exercise, you create a recurring task:

1   On the View menu, click Gantt Chart.

The Gantt Chart view appears.

2   Select the name of Task 12, *Production*.

You want the recurring tasks to be inserted into the project as the last items in the pre-production phase, directly above Task 12.

3   On the Insert menu, click Recurring Task.

The Recurring Task Information dialog box appears.

4   In the Task Name box, type **Staff planning meeting**.

5   In the Duration box, type **2h**.

6   Under Recurrence Pattern, make sure Weekly is selected, and then select the Monday check box.

Next you will specify the date of its first occurrence. By default, it is the project start date. However, you want the weekly status meetings to begin a week later.

7   In the Start box, type or select **3/8/04**.

Next you will specify the number of recurrences. You do this by entering either an exact number of recurrences or a date by which the task should end.

8   Select End After, and type or select 12 occurrences.

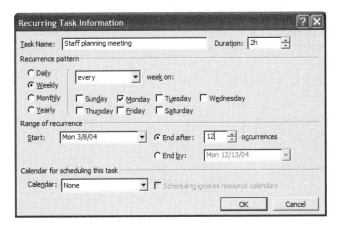

9 Click OK to create the recurring task.

Microsoft Project inserts the recurring tasks, nested within the Pre-Production phase. Initially the summary task is collapsed. A recurring task icon appears in the Indicators column.

Go To
Selected Task

10 To see the first occurrences of the recurring meeting's Gantt bars, on the Standard toolbar, click the Go To Selected Task button.

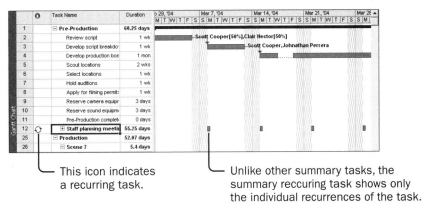

This icon indicates
a recurring task.

Unlike other summary tasks, the
summary reccuring task shows only
the individual recurrences of the task.

Note that the summary Gantt bar for the recurring task does not look like the other summary Gantt bars in the Gantt chart. A summary Gantt bar for a recurring task shows only the occurrences or *roll-ups* of the individual occurrences of the task. For example, contrast the summary Gantt bar for the recurring task with that of Task 1, Pre-Production.

Next you will assign resources to the recurring task.

Assign
Resources

11 On the Standard toolbar, click Assign Resources.

12 In the Assign Resources dialog box, click Clair Hector. Then hold down the Ctrl key while clicking Johnathan Perrera and Scott Cooper.

13 Click the Assign button, and then click Close.

The Assign Resources dialog box closes, and Microsoft Project assigns the selected resources to the recurring task. Next you will view the individual occurrences of the recurring task.

14 Click the plus sign next to the summary recurring task's title, *Staff planning meeting*. Your screen should look similar to the following illustration:

Recurring tasks are automatically numbered sequentially. You can also see resource assignments for the individual tasks.

	❶	Task Name	Duration	29, '04	Mar , '04	Mar 14, '04	Mar 21, '04	Mar 2
				M T W T F S S	M T W T F S S	M T W T F S S	M T W T F S S	M
1		⊟ **Pre-Production**	**60.25 days**					
2		Review script	1 wk		Scott Cooper[50%],Clair Hector[50%]			
3		Develop script breakdo	1 wk		Scott Cooper,Johnathan Perrera			
4		Develop production bos	1 mon					
5		Scout locations	2 wks					
6		Select locations	1 wk					
7		Hold auditions	1 wk					
8		Apply for filming permit	1 wk					
9		Reserve camera equipr	3 days					
10		Reserve sound equipm	3 days					
11		Pre-Production complet	0 days					
12	⟳	⊟ **Staff planning meeti**	**55.25 days**		■	■	■	■
13	📅	Staff planning meetir	2 hrs		■ Clair Hector,Johnathan Perrera,Scott Cooper			
14	📅	Staff planning meetir	2 hrs			■ Clair Hector,Johnathan Perrera,Scott Coop		
15	📅	Staff planning meetir	2 hrs				■ Clair Hector,Johnatha	
16	📅	Staff planning meetir	2 hrs					■ C
17	📅	Staff planning meetir	2 hrs					
18	📅	Staff planning meetir	2 hrs					
19	📅	Staff planning meetir	2 hrs					
20	📅	Staff planning meetir	2 hrs					
21	📅	Staff planning meetir	2 hrs					
22	📅	Staff planning meetir	2 hrs					

Each occurrence of the summary task is sequentially numbered (if you wish to verify this, widen the Task Name column), and the resource assignments appear for the subtasks.

15 Click the minus sign next to the summary recurring task's title, *Staff planning meeting*, to hide the subtasks.

Here are a few more things to keep in mind when creating recurring tasks:

■ By default, Microsoft Project schedules a recurring task to start at the Default Start Time value entered in the Calendar tab (on the Tools menu, click Options). In this project, that is 8 A.M. If you want to schedule a recurring task to start at a different time, enter that time along with the start date in the Start box of the Recurring Task Information dialog box. For example, if you had wanted the recurring staff meeting to be scheduled for 10 A.M. starting on March 1, you would enter **3/1/04 10AM** in the Start box.

■ When you schedule a recurring task to end on a specific date, Microsoft Project suggests the current project end date. If you use this date, be sure to manually change it if the project end date changes later.

- Microsoft Project alerts you if you create a recurring task that would occur during nonworking time (a holiday, for example). You can then choose not to create that occurrence or to schedule it for the next working day.

- You should always assign resources to recurring tasks with the Assign Resources dialog box. Entering resource names in the Resource Name field of the summary recurring task assigns the resources to the summary task, not to the individual occurrences.

Chapter Wrap-Up

This chapter covered how to address advanced issues relating to tasks in a project plan.

If you are going on to other chapters:

Save

1 On the Standard toolbar, click the Save button to save changes made to Short Film Project 7.

2 On the File menu, click Close to close the project plan.

If you aren't continuing to other chapters:

1 On the Standard toolbar, click the Save button to save changes made to Short Film Project 7.

2 To quit Microsoft Project for now, on the File menu, click Exit.

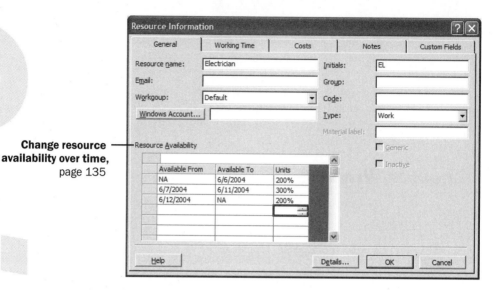

Change resource availability over time, page 135

Control when a resource starts work on an assignment, page 137

Contour resource assignments manually or with built-in contour patterns, page 138

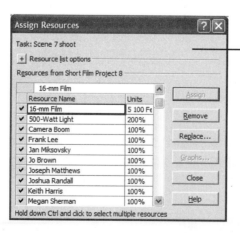

Assign material resources to tasks using variable consumption rates, page 143

Chapter 8
Fine-Tuning Resource and Assignment Details

After completing this chapter, you will be able to:

✔ **Set up different pay rates for resources.**

✔ **Set up pay rates that will change over time for a resource.**

✔ **Set resource availability to change over time.**

✔ **Delay the start of a resource assignment.**

✔ **Control how a resource's work on a task is scheduled over time by using work contours.**

✔ **Apply different cost rates for a resource assigned to different kinds of tasks.**

✔ **Enter variable consumption rates for material resources.**

Because people and equipment resources are often the most expensive part of a project, understanding how to make the best use of resources' time is an important project planning skill. In this chapter, you examine and use a variety of advanced Microsoft Project features relating to *resources* and their *assignments* to *tasks*.

Short Film Project 8a

This chapter uses the practice file Short Film Project 8a. For details about installing the practice files, see "Using the Book's CD-ROM" at the beginning of this book.

Entering Multiple Pay Rates for a Resource

Some *work resources* might perform different tasks with different pay rates. For example, in the short film project, the director of photography could also serve as a camera operator. Because the pay rates for director of photography and camera operator are different, you can enter two *cost rate tables* for the resource. Then, after you assign the resource to tasks, you specify which rate table should apply. Each resource can have up to five cost rate tables.

In this exercise, you create a second cost rate table for a resource:

1 If Microsoft Project is not already open, start it now.

Open

2 On the Standard toolbar, click the Open button.

The Open dialog box appears.

3 Navigate to the "Chapter 8 Complex Resources and Assignments" folder, and double-click the Short Film Project 8a file.

4 On the File menu, click the Save As button.

The Save As dialog box appears.

5 In the File Name box, type **Short Film Project 8**, and then click the Save button.

6 On the View menu, click Resource Sheet.

The Resource Sheet view replaces the Gantt Chart view.

7 On the Resource Sheet view, click the name of Resource 18, *Jan Miksovsky*.

Resource
Information

8 On the Standard toolbar, click the Resource Information button.

The Resource Information dialog box appears.

Tip

You can also double-click the Resource Name field to display the Resource Information dialog box.

9 Click the Costs tab.

You see Jan's default pay rate of $18.75 per hour on rate table A. Each tab (labeled *A*, *B*, and so on) corresponds to one of the five pay rates a resource can have.

10 Under Cost Rate Tables, click the B tab.

11 Select the default entry of $0.00/h in the field directly below the column heading Standard Rate, and then type **14/h**.

12 In the Overtime Rate field in the same row, type **21/h**, and then press the Enter key:

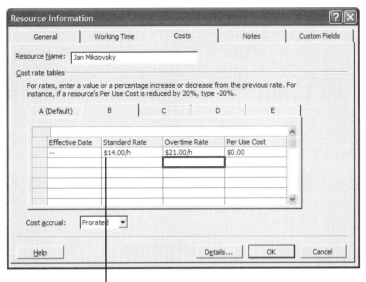

When you enter a pay rate, Microsoft Project supplies the currency symbol if you do not.

13 Click OK to close the Resource Information dialog box.

Notice that on the Resource Sheet, Jan's standard pay rate is still $18.75 per hour. (This is recorded in the Std. Rate column.) This matches the value in her rate table A, the default rate table. This rate table will be used for all of Jan's task assignments unless you specify a different rate table. You will do this in a later section.

Setting Up Pay Rates to Apply at Different Times

Resources can have both standard and overtime pay rates. By default, Microsoft Project uses these rates for the duration of the project. However, you can change a resource's pay rates to be effective as of the date you choose. For example, you could initially set up a resource on January 1 with a standard rate of $10 per hour, planning to raise the resource's standard rate to $13 per hour on July 1.

Microsoft Project uses these pay rates when calculating resource costs, based on when the resource's work is scheduled. You can assign up to 25 pay rates to be applied at different times to each of a resource's five cost rate tables.

In this exercise, you enter different pay rates for a resource to be applied at a later date:

Resource
Information

1   In the Resource Name column, select the name of Resource 11, *Doug Hampton*.

2   On the Standard toolbar, click the Resource Information button.

     The Resource Information dialog box appears.

3   Click the Costs tab.

     You'll enter a pay rate increase in cost rate table A.

4   In the Effective Date cell in the second row of cost rate table A, type or select **7/1/04**.

5   In the Standard Rate cell in the second row, type **20%**, and then press the Enter key:

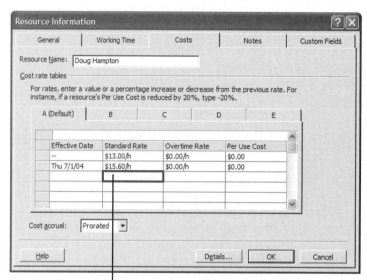

If you enter a positive or negative percentage value here, Microsoft Project automatically calculates the new rate value based on the previous rate value.

Note that Microsoft Project calculates the 20 percent increase to produce a rate of $15.60 per hour. The previous rate of $13 per hour plus 20 percent equals $15.60 per hour. You can enter a specific value or a percentage increase or decrease from the previous rate.

Tip

In addition to or instead of standard and overtime pay rates that can change over time, a resource can also have a cost per use that can change over time.

6   Click OK to close the Resource Information dialog box.

     Note that Doug Hampton's initial rate, $13.00/hr, appears in his Standard Rate field. This field will display $13 per hour until the current date changes to 7/1/04 or later. Then it will display his new standard rate of $15.60 per hour.

Setting Up Resource Availability to Apply at Different Times

One of the values Microsoft Project stores for each work resource is the resource's Max. Units value. This is the maximum capacity of a resource to accomplish tasks. A resource's working time settings (recorded in the individual resource calendars) determine when work assigned to a resource can be scheduled. However, the resource's capacity to work (measured in *units*, and limited by the resource's Max. Units value) determines the extent to which the resource can work within those hours without becoming *overallocated*.

You can specify different Max. Units values to be applied at different time periods for any resource. Setting a resource's availability over time enables you to control exactly what a resource's Max. Units value is at any time. For example, you might have two electricians available for the first eight weeks, three for the next six weeks, and then two for the remainder of the project. You set resource availability over time in the Resource Availability grid on the General tab of the Resource Information dialog box. (You can open this dialog box by clicking the Resource Information command on the Project menu when in a resource view.)

Tip

Setting the Max. Units values for different times will not prevent a resource from becoming overallocated, but Microsoft Project will indicate when the resource's assignments exceed their Max. Units capacity.

In this exercise, you customize a resource's availability over time:

1 In the Resource Name column, select the name of Resource 13, *Electrician*.

Resource
Information

2 On the Standard toolbar, click the Resource Information button.

3 Click the General tab.

You expect to have two electricians available to work on this project from the start of the project through June 6, 2004, three electricians from June 7 through June 11, and then just two for the remainder of the project.

4 Under Resource Availability, in the first row of the Available From column, leave *NA* (for Not Applicable).

5 In the Available To cell in the first row, type or select **6/6/04**.

6 In the Available From cell in the second row, type or select **6/7/04**.

7 In the Available To cell in the second row, type or select **6/11/04**.

8 In the Units cell in the second row, type or select **300%**.

9 In the Available From cell in the third row, type or select **6/12/04**.

10 Leave the Available To cell in the third row blank. (Microsoft Project will insert *NA* for you after you complete the next step.)

11 In the Units cell in the third row, type or select **200%**, and then press the Enter key:

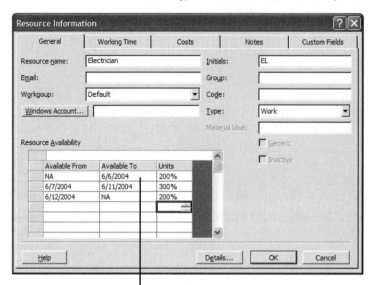

When you enter dates in an abbreviated format, such as 6/6/04, Microsoft Project converts them to this expanded format.

Now, for the period between June 7 through June 11, you can schedule up to three electricians without overallocating them. Before and after this period, you have just two electricians to schedule.

12 Click OK to close the Resource Information dialog box.

Tip

The Max. Units field for the Electricians resource will display 300% only when the current date (based on your computer's system clock) is within the June 7 through June 11 range. At other times it will display 200%.

Delaying the Start of Assignments

If more than one resource is assigned to a task, you might not want all the resources to start working on the task at the same time. You can delay the start of work for one or more resources assigned to a task.

For example, let's say a task has four resources assigned. Three of the resources initially work on the task and the fourth later inspects the quality of the work. The inspector should start work on the task later than the other resources.

Tip

If you need to delay the start of all resources assigned to a task rather than adjusting each resource's assignment, you should reschedule the start date of the task.

In this exercise, you delay the start of one resource's assignment on a task:

1 On the View menu, click Task Usage.

The Task Usage view appears. In this view, the assigned resources are listed under each task.

2 On the Edit menu, click Go To, enter **86** in the ID box, and then click OK.

Tip

Remember that Ctrl+G is a shortcut for displaying the Go To dialog box.

Microsoft Project displays task 86, *Archive master film and audio tape*:

	❶	Task Name	Work	Details	Dec 5, '04						
					W	T	F	S	S	M	T	W
86		⊟ Archive master film and	30 hrs	Work			10h			20h		
		Doug Hampton	6 hrs	Work			2h			4h		
		Editing Lab	12 hrs	Work			4h			8h		
		Michael Patten	12 hrs	Work			4h			8h		
87		⊟ Hand off masters to dis	8 hrs	Work							8h	
		Michael Patten	8 hrs	Work							8h	
				Work								
				Work								

As you can see, this task currently has three resources (two people and the editing lab) assigned to it. You want to delay the start of Doug Hampton's work on this task until Monday, December 6.

3 In the Task Name column, select the name of the resource *Doug Hampton*.

Assignment Information

4 On the Standard toolbar, click the Assignment Information button.

The Assignment Information dialog box appears.

5 Click the General tab.

6 In the Start box, type or select **12/6/04**, and then click OK to close the Assignment Information dialog box:

After delaying the start of the resource's ⌐
assignment, work is shifted to the next workday.

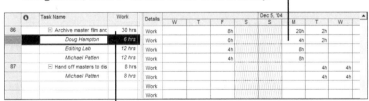

└─ The total work for the task does not change.

Tip

If you want an assignment to start at a specific time as well as on a specific date, you can specify the time in the Start box. For example, if you want Doug Hampton's assignment to start at 1 P.M. on December 16, type **12/16/04 1:00 PM**. Otherwise, Microsoft Project uses the default start time as specified in the Default Start Time box on the Calendar tab of the Options dialog box.

Microsoft Project adjusts Doug Hampton's assignment on this task so that he works no hours on it Friday but four hours on Monday and two on Tuesday. The other resources assigned to the task are not affected. Note that while the total work of this task did not change, its duration did—the work was spread from 2 days (Friday and Monday) to 3 days (Friday, Monday, and Tuesday).

Tip

You can also delay or make other changes to individual resource assignments by using the Project Guide. Click the Track button on the Project Guide toolbar, and then click the Make Changes To The Project link. In the Project Guide's Edit Assignments view, change the assignment-level details you want.

Applying Contours to Assignments

In the Resource Usage and Task Usage views, you can see exactly how long each resource is scheduled to work on each task. In addition to viewing assignment details, you can change the amount of time a resource works on a task in any given time period. There are two ways to do this:

■ Apply a predefined work *contour* to an assignment. Predefined contours generally describe how work is distributed over time in terms of graphical patterns. For example, the Bell predefined contour distributes less work to the beginning and end of the assignment, and distributes more work toward the middle. If you were to graph the work over time, the graph's shape would resemble a bell.

■ Edit the assignment details directly. For example, in the Resource Usage or Task Usage view, you can change the assignment values directly in the timescaled grid.

How you contour or edit an assignment depends on what you need to accomplish. Predefined contours work best for assignments in which you can predict a likely pattern of effort—a task that requires considerable ramp-up time might benefit from a back-loaded contour, for example, to reflect the likelihood that the resource will be most productive toward the end of the assignment.

In this exercise, you apply a predefined contour to one task's assignments, and you manually edit another assignment:

1 On the Edit menu, click Go To, enter **81** in the ID box, and then click OK.

Microsoft Project scrolls to Task 81, *Record final narration*. This task has three resources assigned to it:

	❶	Task Name	Work	Details					Oct 3, '04			
					W	T	F	S	S	M	T	W
81		⊟ Record final narration	216 hrs	Work			12h			24h	24h	24h
		David Campbell	72 hrs	Work			4h			8h	8h	8h
		Michael Patten	72 hrs	Work			4h			8h	8h	8h
		Scott Cooper	72 hrs	Work			4h			8h	8h	8h
82		⊟ Add head and tail titles	120 hrs	Work								
		Editing Lab	40 hrs	Work								
		Jo Brown	40 hrs	Work								
		Michael Patten	40 hrs	Work								

As you can see in the timescaled data at the right, all three resources are scheduled to work on this task at a regular rate of eight hours per day—except for the first and last days of the task. These assignments have a flat contour. This is the default work contour type Microsoft Project uses when scheduling work.

You want to change Michael Patten's assignment on this task so that although the other assigned resources work full-time, he starts with a brief daily assignment and increases his work time as the task progresses. He should continue working on the task after the other resources have finished their assignments. To accomplish this, you will apply a back-loaded contour to the assignment.

Tip

The reason each resource assigned to Task 81 has just four hours of work on the task's first and last day is that the task is scheduled to start halfway through the workday (at 1 P.M.) on Friday, and finish in the middle of the workday on Thursday.

2 In the Task Name column, select Michael Patten, the second resource assigned to Task 81.

Assignment Information

3 On the Standard toolbar, click the Assignment Information button.

Microsoft Project displays the Assignment Information dialog box.

4 Click the General tab.

5 In the Work Contour box, select Back Loaded, and then click OK to close the Assignment Information dialog box.

Microsoft Project applies the contour to this resource's assignment and reschedules his work on the task:

The backloaded contour causes Microsoft Project initially to assign very little work to the resource and then add more work each day.

	❶	Task Name	Work	Details					Oct 3, '04			
					W	T	F	S	S	M	T	W
81		⊟ Record final narration	216 hrs	Work			8.4h			16.8h	17.2h	17.6h
		David Campbell	72 hrs	Work			4h			8h	8h	8h
	⊿	Michael Patten	72 hrs	Work			0.4h			0.8h	1.2h	1.6h
		Scott Cooper	72 hrs	Work			4h			8h	8h	8h
82		⊟ Add head and tail titles	120 hrs	Work								
		Editing Lab	40 hrs	Work								
		Jo Brown	40 hrs	Work								
		Michael Patten	40 hrs	Work								

The contour indicator matches the type of contour applied—back loaded in this case.

If you scroll the timescaled data to the right, you see that in each successive day of the task's duration, Michael Patten is assigned slightly more time to work on the assignment. You also see a contour indicator in the Indicators column, showing the type of contour that is applied to the assignment.

6 Point to the indicator:

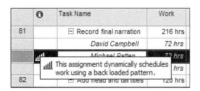

Microsoft Project displays a ScreenTip describing the type of contour applied to this assignment.

Because Michael Patten's assignment to this task finishes later than the assignments of the other resources, Michael Patten determines the finish date of the task. One common way to phrase this is that Michael Patten is the *driving resource* of this task; his assignment determines, or drives, the finish date of the task.

Next you will directly edit another task's assignment values.

Tip

Applying a contour to this assignment caused the overall duration of the task to be extended. If you do not want a contour to extend a task's duration, change the **task type** (on the Advanced tab of the Task Information dialog box) to *Fixed Duration* before applying the contour. Applying a contour after changing a task type such as Fixed Duration will cause Microsoft Project to recalculate the resource's work value so that he or she works less in the same time period.

7 On the Edit menu, click Go To, enter **2** in the ID box, and then click OK.

Microsoft Project scrolls vertically to Task 2, *Review script*:

	❶	Task Name	Work	Details			M	T	W	T	F	S	Mt ▲
					S	S							
2		⊟ Review script	40 hrs	Work			8h	8h	8h	8h	8h		
		Clair Hector	20 hrs	Work			4h	4h	4h	4h	4h		
		Scott Cooper	20 hrs	Work			4h	4h	4h	4h	4h		
3		⊟ Develop script breakdo	80 hrs	Work									
		Johnathan Perrera	40 hrs	Work									
		Scott Cooper	40 hrs	Work									

Note that Clair Hector is currently assigned four hours per day for each day of the assignment's duration. Why four hours? Clair normally has eight working hours per day on these days (as determined by her resource calendar). She was assigned to this task at 50 percent assignment units, however, so the resulting scheduled work is just four hours per day.

You want to change Clair Hector's assignment on the last two days of this task so that she will work full-time on it. To accomplish this, you will manually edit her assignment values.

8 Select Clair Hector's four-hour assignment for Thursday, March 4.

9 Type **8h**, and then press the Tab key.

10 In Clair's assignment for Friday, type **8h**, and then press Enter:

Here are Clair Hector's assigned work values
for Thursday and Friday, after you edited them.

	❶	Task Name	Work	Details	Feb 29, '04							Ma
					S	S	M	T	W	T	F	S
2		☐ Review script	48 hrs	Work			8h	8h	8h	12h	12h	
	🖉	Clair Hector	28 hrs	Work			4h	4h	4h	8h	8h	
		Scott Cooper	20 hrs	Work			4h	4h	4h	4h	4h	
3		☐ Develop script breakdo	80 hrs	Work								
		Johnathan Perrera	40 hrs	Work								
		Scott Cooper	40 hrs	Work								

After you manually edit Clair's assignment, this indicator appears.

Now Clair is assigned eight hours per day on these days. Microsoft Project displays a contour indicator in the Indicators column, this time showing that a manually edited contour has been applied to the assignment.

Tip

Assignment
Notes

If you want to document details about contouring an assignment, or anything about an assignment, you can record the details in an assignment note. In Task Usage or Resource Usage view, select the assignment, and then click the Assignment Notes button on the Standard toolbar. Assignment notes are similar to task and resource notes.

Applying Different Cost Rates to Assignments

You can set as many as five pay rates per resource. This enables you to apply different pay rates to different assignments for a resource, for example, depending on the skills required for each assignment. For each assignment, Microsoft Project initially uses rate table A by default, but you can specify that another rate table should be used.

In a previous section, you set up a second rate table for Jan Miksovsky to be applied for any assignments where she is functioning as a camera operator. Jan is currently assigned to Task 29, *Scene 7 shoot*, as a camera operator, but her assignment still reflects her default rate pay rate as director of photography. In this exercise, you change the pay rate table to be applied to Jan for her assignment to Task 29:

1 On the Edit menu, click Go To, enter **29** in the ID box, and then click OK.

Microsoft Project scrolls the Task Usage view to display Task 29, *Scene 7 Shoot*.

2 On the View menu, point to Table: Usage, and click Cost.

Microsoft Project displays the Cost Table.

3 Click the row heading directly to the left of Jan Miksovsky so that the entire assignment is selected.

4 Scroll the table portion (on the left) of the Task Usage view to the right until the Total Cost column is visible:

> In the Cost table you can see the task's and each assignment's total cost. To see other assignment cost values such as actual cost or variance, scroll the table to the right.

	Fixed Cost Accrual	Total Cost	Basel	Details	4							May 30, '04		
					M	T	W	T	F	S		S	M	T
29	Prorated	$1,483.00		Work			136h							
		$150.00		Work			24h							
		$40.00		Work			16h							
		$0.00		Work			8h							
		$112.00		Work			8h							
		$150.00		Work			8h							
		$150.00		Work			8h							
		$75.00		Work			8h							
		$96.00		Work			8h							
		$112.00		Work			8h							
		$144.00		Work			8h							
		$155.00		Work			8h							
		$75.00		Work			8h							
		$112.00		Work			8h							
		$112.00		Work			8h							
30	Prorated	$430.00		Work				20h						

Note the current cost of Jan's assignment to this task: $150.00.

Assignment Information

🗒

5 On the Standard toolbar, click the Assignment Information button.

The Assignment Information dialog box appears.

6 Click the General tab.

7 In the Cost Rate Table box, type or select **B**, and then click OK to close the Assignment Information dialog box.

Microsoft Project applies Jan's Cost rate table B to the assignment. The new cost of the assignment, $112.00, appears in the Cost column.

Tip

If you frequently change cost rate tables for assignments, you will find it quicker to display the Cost Rate Table field directly in the Resource Usage or Task Usage view. Select a column heading, and on the Insert menu, click Column. In the Field Name box, select Cost Rate Table in the drop-down list, and then click OK.

Entering Material Resource Consumption Rates

The short film project includes one *material resource*: 16-mm film. If you completed Chapter 4, "Assigning Resources to Tasks," you assigned a material resource with a fixed amount, or *fixed consumption rate*, to a task. Another way to use material resources is to assign them with a *variable consumption rate*. Here is the difference between the two rates:

■ A fixed consumption rate means that regardless of the duration of the task to which the material resource is assigned, an absolute quantity of the resource will be used. For example, pouring concrete for a house foundation requires a fixed amount of concrete, no matter how long it takes to pour it.

■ A variable consumption rate means that the quantity of the material resource consumed depends on the duration of the task. When shooting film, for example, you will shoot more film in four hours than in two, and you can determine an hourly rate at which you shoot (or consume) film. After you enter a variable consumption rate for a material resource's assignment, Microsoft Project calculates the total quantity of the material resource consumed, based on the task's duration. The advantage of using a variable rate of consumption is that the rate is tied to the task's duration. If the duration changes, the calculated quantity and cost of the material resource will change as well.

In either case, after you enter a standard pay rate for one unit of the material resource, Microsoft Project calculates the total cost of the assignment. For example, we will assume that a 100-foot spool of 16-mm film costs $20 to purchase and process.

In this exercise, you enter an hourly variable consumption rate for a task that requires shooting (or consuming) film. Then you look at the resulting quantity or number of units of film required by the duration of the task, as well as the cost of the material resource assignment:

1 On the View menu, click Gantt Chart.

The Gantt Chart view appears.

2 On the Edit menu, click Go To, enter **29** in the ID box, and then click OK.

Microsoft Project displays task 29, *Scene 7 shoot*. This is the first of several tasks that require film to be shot. Next you will assign the material resource 16-mm Film to this task.

Assign
Resources

3 On the Standard toolbar, click the Assign Resources button.

The Assign Resources dialog box appears.

4 In the Units field for 16-mm Film in the Assign Resources dialog box, type **5/h** and then click the Assign button.

Tip

Be sure to select 16-mm Film and not *16-mm Camera* in the Assign Resources dialog box.

Microsoft Project assigns the film to the task, at a consumption rate of five 100-foot spools per hour as shown in the illustration on the following page.

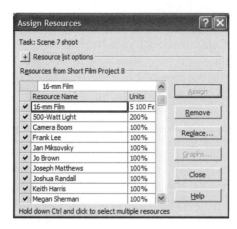

Because this task currently has an eight-hour duration, the total film assignment should be 40 spools of film. To verify this and see the resulting cost of the material resource assignment, you will change views.

5 In the Assign Resources dialog box, click the Close button.

6 On the View menu, click Task Usage.

7 Click the row heading directly to the left of 16-mm Film so that the entire assignment is selected.

8 If necessary, scroll the Cost table to the right to see the Total Cost column:

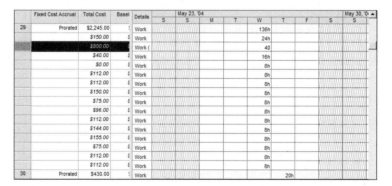

Here you can see the total cost of all assignments in the task, as well as the individual assignments. The calculated cost of the film assignment, $800, is the 40 units of the material resource for this assignment times the $20 per unit cost entered for the material resource. (This value is recorded in the Std. Rate field for the resource.) Should the duration of the task change, the number of units of film consumed and their total cost would change correspondingly.

To see the total work of this assignment, you will change tables.

9 On the View menu, point to Table: Cost, and then click Usage.

10 If necessary, scroll the Usage table to the right to see the Work column.

11 If the Work column contains pound signs (###), double-click between the column titles to widen that column:

	Work	Duration	Start	Details	May 23, '04								May 30, '04	
					S	S	M	T	W	T	F	S	S	M
29	136 hrs	8 hrs	Wed 5/2	Work					136h					
	24 hrs		Wed 5/2	Work					24h					
	40 100 Feet		Wed 5/2	Work (					40					
	16 hrs		Wed 5/2	Work					16h					
	8 hrs		Wed 5/2	Work					8h					

In the Work column, you can see that the 16-mm Film assignment to task 29 is currently 40 100-foot spools of film.

Chapter Wrap-Up

This chapter covered how to adjust a variety of resource and assignment details, mainly relating to cost and availability.

If you are going on to other chapters:

Save

1 On the Standard toolbar, click the Save button to save changes made to Short Film Project 8.

2 On the File menu, click Close to close the project plan.

If you aren't continuing to other chapters:

1 On the Standard toolbar, click the Save button to save changes made to Short Film Project 8.

2 To quit Microsoft Project for now, on the File menu, click Exit.

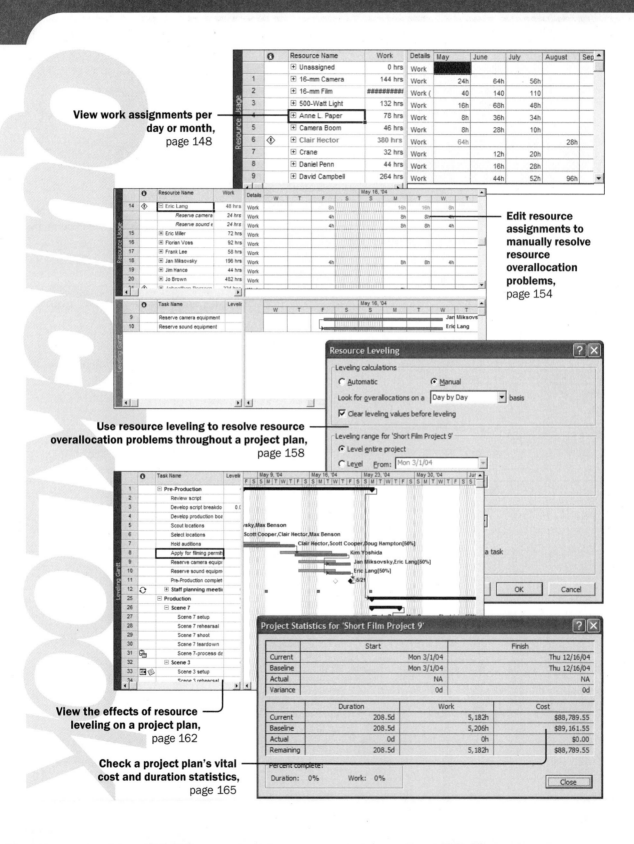

View work assignments per day or month, page 148

Edit resource assignments to manually resolve resource overallocation problems, page 154

Use resource leveling to resolve resource overallocation problems throughout a project plan, page 158

View the effects of resource leveling on a project plan, page 162

Check a project plan's vital cost and duration statistics, page 165

Chapter 9
Fine-Tuning
the Project Plan

After completing this chapter, you will be able to:

✔ Look at how resources are scheduled to work over the duration of a project.

✔ Edit a resource assignment to resolve a resource overallocation.

✔ Resolve resource overallocations automatically.

✔ See detailed and summary project costs.

✔ See tasks on the critical path that determines a project's finish date.

Up to now you have worked with tasks, resources, and assignments separately. Now you will fine-tune some settings that affect all three elements. When you build a project plan, you work with tasks, resources, and assignments together. Changes you make to tasks, for example, affect the resources assigned to those tasks.

Short Film Project 9a

This chapter uses the practice file Short Film Project 9a. For details about installing the practice files, see "Using the Book's CD-ROM" at the beginning of this book.

Examining Resource Allocations Over Time

In this exercise, you will focus on resource allocation—how the task assignments you've made affect the workloads of the people and equipment resources of a project. The relationship between a resource's capacity and his or her task assignments is called *allocation*. Each resource is in one of three states of allocation:

■ *Underallocated*.   The resource's assignments do not fill his or her maximum capacity. For example, a full-time resource who has only 25 hours of work assigned in a 40-hour work week is underallocated.

■ *Fully allocated*.   The resource's assignments fill his or her maximum capacity. For example, a full-time resource who has 40 hours of work assigned in a 40-hour work week is fully allocated.

■ ***Overallocated.*** The resource's assignments exceed his or her maximum capacity. For example, a full-time resource who has 65 hours of work assigned in a 40-hour work week is overallocated.

In Microsoft Project, a resource's capacity to work is measured in units; the maximum capacity of a given resource is called ***maximum units***. Units are measured either as numbers (for example, three units) or as a percentage (for example, 300 percent units).

Project Management Focus:
Evaluating Resource Allocation

It is tempting to say that fully allocating all resources all the time is every project manager's goal—but that would be an oversimplification. Depending on the nature of your project and the resources working on it, some underallocations might be perfectly fine. Overallocation might not always be a problem either, depending on the amount of overallocation. If one resource is overallocated for just a half hour, Microsoft Project can alert you, but such a minor overallocation might not be a problem you need to solve, depending on the resource involved and the nature of the assignment. Severe overallocation—for example, a resource being assigned twice the work he or she could possibly accomplish in one day—is always a problem, however, and you should know how to identify it and have strategies for addressing it. This chapter helps you identify and remedy resource overallocation.

In this exercise, you look at resource allocations and focus on two resources who are overallocated:

1 If Microsoft Project is not already open, start it now.

Open

2 On the Standard toolbar, click the Open button.

The Open dialog box appears.

3 Navigate to the "Chapter 9 Complex Plan" folder, and double-click the Short Film Project 9a file.

4 On the File menu, click Save As.

The Save As dialog box appears.

5 In the File Name box, type **Short Film Project 9**, and then click the Save button.

Next you will use the Project Guide to view resource usage.

6 On the Project Guide toolbar, click the Report button.

7   In the Report pane, click the See How Resources' Time Is Allocated link.

A split view, with the Resource Usage view on top and the Gantt Chart view on the bottom, appears:

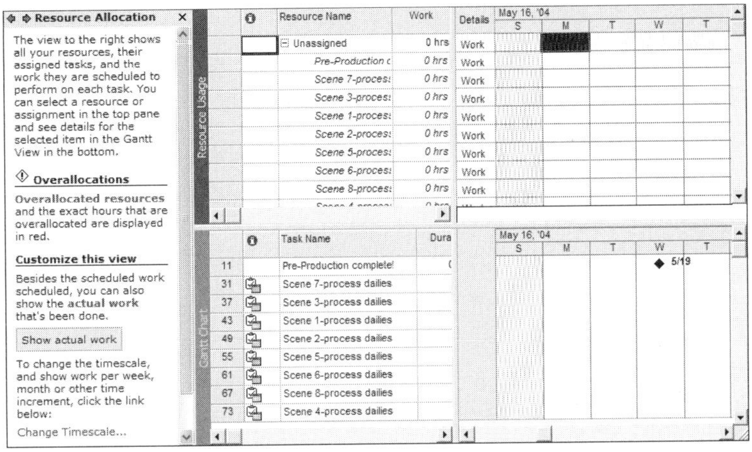

On the left side of the Resource Usage view is a table (the Usage table by default) that shows assignments grouped per resource, the total work assigned to each resource, and each assignment's work. This information is organized into an outline that you can expand or collapse.

The right side of the view contains assignment details (work, by default) arranged on a timescale. You can scroll the timescale horizontally to see different time periods. You can also change the tiers of the timescale to display data in units of weeks, days, hours, and so on.

Next you will collapse the outline in the table to see total work per resource over time.

8   Click the Resource Name column heading.

Hide Subtasks   **9**   On the Formatting toolbar, click the Hide Subtasks button.

Microsoft Project collapses the Resource Usage view. Resource assignments are hidden in the Usage Table, and the resources' total work values over time appear in the time-scaled grid on the right, as shown in the illustration on the following page.

		Resource Name	Work	Details	May 16, '04				
					S	M	T	W	T
		⊞ Unassigned	0 hrs	Work					
1		⊞ 16-mm Camera	144 hrs	Work					
2		⊞ 16-mm Film	#########	Work (					
3		⊞ 500-Watt Light	132 hrs	Work					
4		⊞ Anne L. Paper	78 hrs	Work					
5		⊞ Camera Boom	46 hrs	Work					
6	◇	⊞ Clair Hector	380 hrs	Work		2h			
7		⊞ Crane	32 hrs	Work					
8		⊞ Daniel Penn	44 hrs	Work					
9		⊞ David Campbell	364 hrs						

		Task Name	Dura		May 16, '04				
					S	M	T	W	T
2		Review script							
3		Develop script breakdown an							
4		Develop production boards							
5		Scout locations							
6		Select locations							
7		Hold auditions			pton[50%]				
8		Apply for filming permits						Kim Yoshida	
9		Reserve camera equipment						Jan Miksovsk	
10		Reserve sound equipment						Eric Lang	

Tip

Notice the name of the first resource, *Unassigned*. This resource lists all tasks to which no specific resources are assigned.

Next you will look at two people resources and their allocations.

10 In the Resource Name column, click the name of Resource 4, *Anne L. Paper*.

Go To
Selected Task

11 On the Standard toolbar, click the Go To Selected Task button.

Microsoft Project scrolls the timescaled grid to show Anne L. Paper's earliest assignment: eight hours on a Monday. Below the Resource Usage view, the Gantt Chart view shows the tasks to which Anne is assigned.

12 Point to the M column heading at the top of the timescaled grid:

In any timescaled view, you can get details about dates by hovering your mouse pointer over the timescale.

		Resource Name	Work	Details	May 30, '04				
					S	M	T	W	T
		⊞ Unassigned	0 hrs	Work		5/31/04			
1		⊞ 16-mm Camera	144 hrs	Work			16h		
2		⊞ 16-mm Film	#########	Work (			40		
3		⊞ 500-Watt Light	132 hrs	Work			32h		
4		⊞ Anne L. Paper	78 hrs	Work		8h	8h		
5		⊞ Camera Boom	46 hrs	Work			8h		
6	◇	⊞ Clair Hector	380 hrs	Work					
7		⊞ Crane	32 hrs	Work					
8		⊞ Daniel Penn	44 hrs	Work					
9		⊞ David Campbell	364 hrs						

A ScreenTip appears with the date of the assignment: 5/31/04. Such ScreenTips are handy in any timescaled view, such as the Resource Usage view or the Gantt Chart.

Currently the timescale is set to display weeks in the middle tier and days in the bottom tier. Now you'll change the timescale to see the work data summarized more broadly.

13 At the bottom of the Resource Allocation pane in the Project Guide, click the Change Timescale link.

The Timescale dialog box appears.

Tip

You can also click Timescale on the Format menu.

Three-tiered Timescale

new in Project 2002

The timescale can display up to three tiers, typically in descending order of detail, such as years, months, and days. However, the top tier is disabled by default.

14 Make sure that the Middle Tier tab is selected, and in the Units box under Middle Tier Formatting, click Months.

15 In the Show box under Timescale Options, click One Tier (Middle), and then click OK to close the Timescale dialog box.

Microsoft Project changes the timescaled grid to show work values per month:

	🛈	Resource Name	Work	Details	May	June	July	August	Sep
		⊞ Unassigned	0 hrs	Work					
1		⊞ 16-mm Camera	144 hrs	Work	24h	64h	56h		
2		⊞ 16-mm Film	########	Work (	40	140	110		
3		⊞ 500-Watt Light	132 hrs	Work	16h	68h	48h		
4		⊞ Anne L. Paper	78 hrs	Work	8h	36h	34h		
5		⊞ Camera Boom	46 hrs	Work	8h	28h	10h		
6	◈	⊞ Clair Hector	380 hrs	Work	64h			28h	
7		⊞ Crane	32 hrs	Work		12h	20h		
8		⊞ Daniel Penn	44 hrs	Work		16h	28h		
9		⊞ David Campbell	264 hrs	Work		44h	52h	96h	

As you can see in the timescaled grid, Anne L. Paper is underallocated in each of the three months in which she has assignments in the project: May, June, and July. Anne is one of the actors assigned to the scenes in which her character is needed, so this underallocation is really not a problem you need to address.

Notice that the names of Clair Hector and other resources appear in red. The red formatting means that these resources are overallocated: at one or more points in the schedule their assigned tasks exceed their capacity to work. You will focus on Clair Hector, first by changing the timescale settings.

16 At the bottom of the Resource Allocation pane, click the Change Timescale link.

The Timescale dialog box appears.

17 Make sure that the Middle Tier tab is selected, and in the Units box, click Weeks.

18 In the Show box under Timescale Options, click Two Tiers (Middle, Bottom), and then click OK to close the Timescale dialog box.

19 In the Resource Name column, click the name of Resource 6, *Clair Hector*.

20 On the Standard toolbar, click the Go To Selected Task button.

Microsoft Project scrolls the timescaled grid to show Clair Hector's earliest assignments. For the week of February 29, Clair has no overallocations.

21 Scroll the Resource Usage view so that *Clair Hector* appears at the top of the view, and then scroll the timescaled portion of view (using the scroll bars at the bottom of the screen) to display the week of March 7, 2004.

Monday, March 8 shows Clair's first overallocation: 10 hours. In the Gantt Chart view below, you can see the two tasks to which Clair is assigned on Monday.

22 Click the plus sign next to Clair Hector's name in the Resource Name column.

Microsoft Project expands the Resource Usage view to show Clair Hector's individual assignments.

23 Scroll the Resource Usage view to see all of Clair's assignments on Monday, March 8:

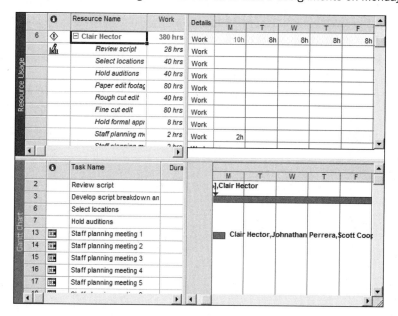

Clair has two assignments on March 8: the two-hour task *Staff planning meeting 1* and the eight-hour task *Develop script breakdown and schedule*. These two tasks have been scheduled at times that overlap between the hours of 8 A.M. and 10 A.M. (If you want to see this, format the timescale to display days in the middle tier and hours in the bottom tier.) This is a real overallocation: Clair probably cannot complete both tasks simultaneously. However, it is a relatively minor overallocation given the scope of the project, and you don't need to be too concerned about resolving this level of overallocation.

There are other, more serious overallocations in the schedule, however, which you will remedy later in this chapter.

Here are a few more things to keep in mind when viewing resource allocation:

■ By default, the Resource Usage view displays the Usage table. You can display different tables, however. On the View menu, click Table: Usage, and then click the table you want displayed.

■ By default, the Resource Usage view displays work values in the timescaled grid. However, you can display additional assignment values, such as cost and remaining availability. On the Format menu, click Details, and then click the value you want displayed.

Zoom In
Zoom Out

■ Instead of using the Timescale command on the Format menu to change the tiers of the timescale, you can click the Zoom In and Zoom Out buttons on the Standard toolbar. However, this method might not produce the exact level of detail you want. If it does not, use the Timescale command on the Format menu.

■ To see allocations for each resource graphed against a timescale, you can display the Resource Graph view by clicking the Resource Graph command on the View menu. Use the arrow keys or horizontal scroll bar to switch between resources in this view.

Manually Resolving Resource Overallocations

In this exercise and the next, you will continue to focus on resource allocation—how the task assignments you have made affect the workloads of the people and equipment resources of the project. In this exercise, you will manually edit an assignment to resolve a resource overallocation. In the next exercise, you will automatically resolve resource overallocations.

Manually editing an assignment is just one way to resolve a resource overallocation. Other solutions include the following:

■ Replace the overallocated resource with another resource using the Replace button in the Assign Resources dialog box.

■ Reduce the value in the Units field in the Assignment Information or Assign Resources dialog box.

If the overallocation is not too severe (for example, 10 hours of work assigned in a normal eight-hour workday), you can often leave the overallocation in the schedule.

Tip

To learn more about resolving resource overallocation problems, type **Resolve resource over-allocation problems** into the Ask A Question box in the upper right corner of the Microsoft Project window.

In this exercise, you will use the Resource Allocation view to examine one overallocated resource's assignments, and edit the assignment to eliminate the overallocation:

1 On the Window menu, click Remove Split.

2 If the Project Guide is visible, click the Close button in the upper right corner of the Project Guide pane to close it.

3 On the View menu, click More Views, click Resource Allocation, and then click the Apply button:

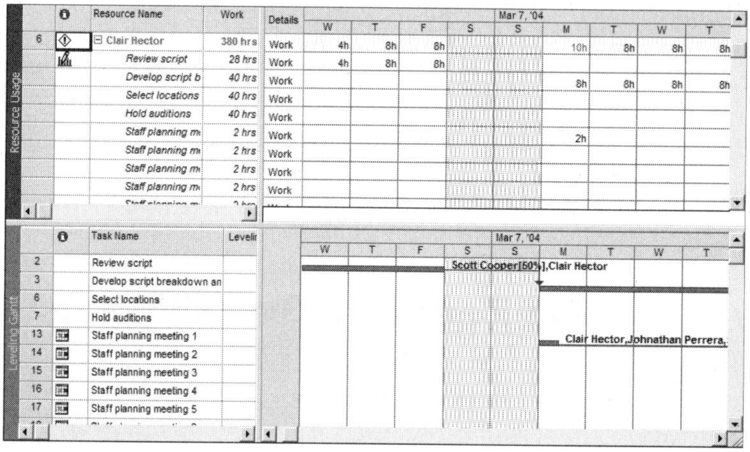

Microsoft Project switches to the Resource Allocation view. This view is a combination view that displays the Resource Usage view in the top pane and the Leveling Gantt view in the bottom pane.

4 In the Resource Usage view, scroll vertically through the Resource Name column.

Note that several names appear in red. These are overallocated resources.

5 In the Resource Name column, click the name of Resource 14, *Eric Lang*.

6 Click the plus sign next to Eric Lang's name to display his assignments.

Go To
Selected Task

7 On the Standard toolbar, click the Go To Selected Task button.

Your screen should look similar to the following illustration:

Even though this resource's assignments on this day don't exceed his capacity to work, they have been scheduled at times that overlap, resulting in an hour-by-hour overallocation.

	❶	Resource Name	Work	Details	W	T	F	S	S	M	T	W	T
14	◈	⊟ Eric Lang	48 hrs	Work			8h			16h	16h	8h	
		Reserve camera	24 hrs	Work			4h			8h	8h	4h	
		Reserve sound e	24 hrs	Work			4h			8h	8h	4h	
15		⊞ Eric Miller	72 hrs	Work									
16		⊞ Florian Voss	92 hrs	Work									
17		⊞ Frank Lee	58 hrs	Work									
18		⊞ Jan Miksovsky	196 hrs	Work			4h			8h	8h	4h	
19		⊞ Jim Hance	44 hrs	Work									
20		⊞ Jo Brown	482 hrs	Work									
21	⚠	⊞ Johnathan Perera	334 hrs										

Resource Usage

	❶	Task Name	Levelir	W	T	F	S	S	M	T	W	T
9		Reserve camera equipment										Jan Miksovs
10		Reserve sound equipment										Eric Lang

Leveling Gantt

In the upper pane you see that Eric is assigned full time to two tasks that both start on Friday, May 14. He is overallocated for the duration of both tasks. In the lower pane, you see the Gantt bars for the specific tasks that have caused Eric to be overallocated on these days. For tasks 9 and 10, Eric is assigned eight hours of work on each task Monday and Tuesday. This results in 16 hours of work per day, which is beyond Eric's capacity to work.

You might also notice that Eric is assigned a total of eight hours of work on Friday, and then again on the following Wednesday. These values also appear in red, indicating that Eric is overallocated on those days as well. This is because the two tasks are scheduled to start at the same time Friday and end at the same time Wednesday. So even though Eric has a total of eight hours of work assigned on Friday and Wednesday, he really has two four-hour assignments in parallel. This is an overallocation.

Next you will manually resolve this overallocation.

8 In the Resource Name column, click Eric's first assignment, *Reserve camera equipment*.

Assignment Information

9 On the Standard toolbar, click the Assignment Information button.

The Assignment Information dialog box appears.

10 Click the General tab.

11 In the Units box, type or click 50%, and then click OK to close the Assignment Information dialog box:

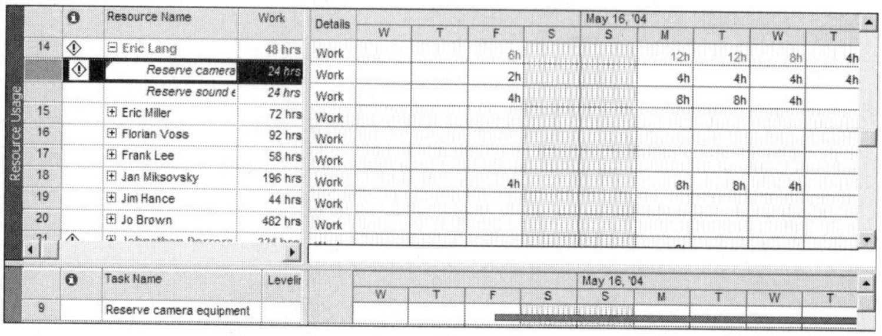

Eric's daily work assignments on this task are reduced to two or four hours per day, but the task duration increased. You'd like to reduce the work but not extend the duration of the task. Note the Smart Tag indicator that appears next to the name of assignment. You will use the Smart Tag to change the scheduling effect of the new assignment units.

12 Click the Smart Tag Actions button.

Look over the options in the list that appears. Your screen should look like the following illustration:

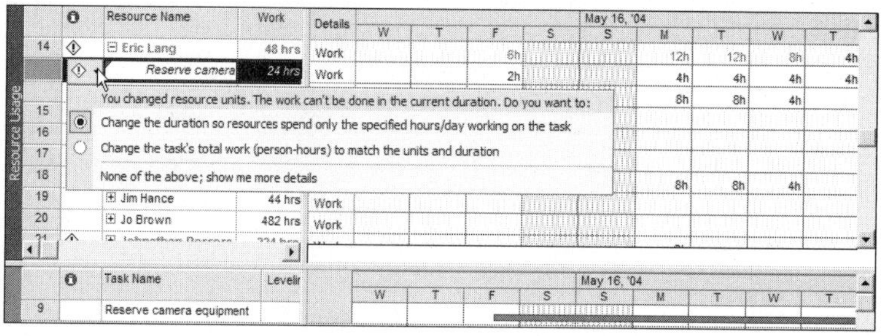

13 In the Smart Tag Actions list, click Change The Task's Total Work (Person-Hours) To Match The Units And Duration.

Microsoft Project reduces Eric's work assignments on the task and restores the task to its original duration.

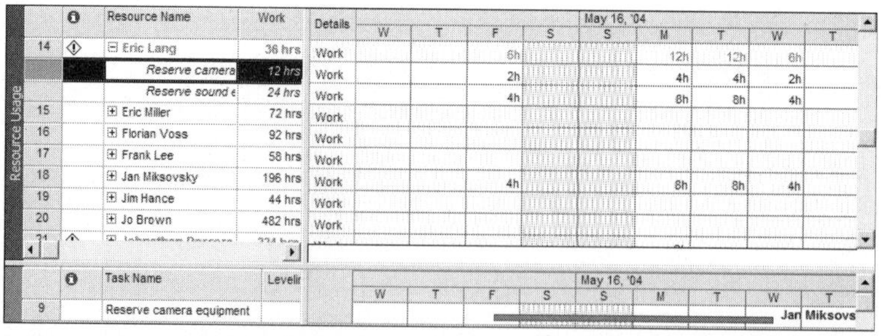

However, Eric is still overallocated. To remedy this, you will reduce his assignment units on his second task.

14 In the Resource Name column, click Eric's second assignment, *Reserve sound equipment*.

15 On the Standard toolbar, click the Assignment Information button.

The Assignment Information dialog box appears.

16 Click the General tab.

17 In the Units box, type or click 50%, and then click OK to close the Assignment Information dialog box.

18 Click the Smart Tag Actions button.

19 In the Smart Tag Actions list, click Change The Task's Total Work (Person-Hours) To Match The Units And Duration.

Your screen should look like the following illustration:

	●	Resource Name	Work	Details	W	T	F	S	S	M	T	W	T
14		⊟ Eric Lang	24 hrs	Work			4h			8h	8h	4h	
		Reserve camera	_12 hrs_	Work			2h			4h	4h	2h	
		Reserve sound e	_12 hrs_	Work			2h			4h	4h	2h	
15		⊞ Eric Miller	72 hrs	Work									
16		⊞ Florian Voss	92 hrs	Work									
17		⊞ Frank Lee	58 hrs	Work									
18		⊞ Jan Miksovsky	196 hrs	Work			4h			8h	8h	4h	
19		⊞ Jim Hance	44 hrs	Work									
20		⊞ Jo Brown	482 hrs	Work									
21		⊞ Johnathan Perera	224 hrs										

	●	Task Name	Leveli		W	T	F	S	S	M	T	W	T
10		Reserve sound equipment											Eric Lang[50'

Eric's total assignments on Monday and Tuesday are now reduced to eight hours each day. He is fully allocated. By manually editing Eric's assignments to reduce his work on these days, you have resolved his overallocation. There are other resource overallocations in the short film project that you can resolve automatically with resource leveling, however. You will do this in the next section.

Leveling Overallocated Resources

In the previous section, you read about resource allocation, learned what causes overallocation, and manually resolved an overallocation. ***Resource leveling*** is the process of delaying a resource's work on a task to resolve an overallocation. The options in the Level Resources dialog box enable you to set parameters about how you want Microsoft Project to resolve resource overallocations, and it will attempt to do so when you choose to level resources. Depending on the options you choose, this might involve delaying the start date of an assignment or task or splitting up the work on the task.

For example, consider the following tasks, all of which have the same full-time resource assigned:

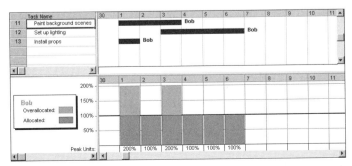

In this split view, the Resource Graph view appears below the Gantt Chart view. On day 1, the resource is overallocated at 200 percent. On day 2, the resource is fully allocated at 100 percent. On day 3, he is overallocated at 200 percent again. After day 3, the resource is fully allocated at 100 percent.

When you perform resource leveling, Microsoft Project delays the start dates of the second and third tasks so that the resource is not overallocated, as shown in the following figure:

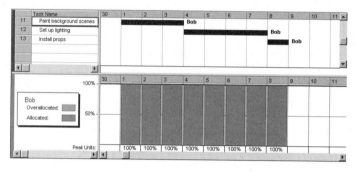

Note that the finish date of the latest task has moved from day 6 to day 8. This is common with resource leveling, which often pushes out the project finish date. Before leveling, there was a total of eight days of work, but two of those days overlapped, causing the resource to be overallocated on those days. After leveling, all eight days of work are still there, but the resource is no longer overallocated.

Resource leveling is a powerful tool, but it does only a few basic things: it delays tasks, splits tasks, and delays resource assignments. It does this following a fairly complex set of rules and options you specify in the Resource Leveling dialog box. (These options are explained in the following exercise.) Resource leveling is a great fine-tuning tool, but it cannot replace your good judgment about resource availability, task durations, relationships, and constraints. Resource leveling will work with all this information as it is entered into your project plan, but it might not be possible to fully resolve all resource overallocations within the time frame you want unless you change some of the basic task and resource information.

Tip

To learn more about resource leveling, type **All about resource leveling** into the Ask A Question box in the upper right corner of the Microsoft Project window.

In this exercise, you level resources and look at the effects on assignments and the project finish date:

1   On the Window menu, click Remove Split.

2   On the View menu, click Resource Sheet.

The Resource Sheet view appears. Note that several resource names appear in red and have the Overallocated icon in the Indicators column.

Tip

Overallocated
Icon

If you do not see the Overallocated icon for any resources, try the following: On the Tools menu, click Level Resources. In the Resource Leveling dialog box, make sure that Day By Day is selected in the Look For Overallocations On A ... Basis box and then click OK.

3 On the Tools menu, click Level Resources.

The Resource Leveling dialog box appears. In the next several steps, you will walk through the options in this dialog box.

4 Under Leveling Calculations, click Manual.

These settings determine whether Microsoft Project levels resources constantly (Automatic) or only when you tell it to (Manual). Automatic leveling occurs as soon as a resource becomes overallocated.

Tip

All settings in the Resource Leveling dialog box apply to all project plans you work with in Microsoft Project, not to just the active project plan. Using automatic leveling might sound tempting, but it will cause frequent adjustments to project plans whether you want them or not. For that reason, we recommend you keep this setting on Manual.

5 In the Look For Overallocations On A box, click Day By Day.

This setting determines the time frame in which Microsoft Project will look for overallocations. If a resource is overallocated at all, its name will be formatted in red. If it's overallocated at the level you choose here, Microsoft Project will also show the Overallocated indicator next to its name.

Tip

On most projects, leveling in finer detail than day by day can result in unrealistically precise adjustments to assignments.

6 Select the Clear Leveling Values Before Leveling check box.

Sometimes you will need to level resources repeatedly to get the results you want. For example, you might initially attempt to level week by week, and then switch to day by day. If the Clear Leveling Values Before Leveling check box is selected, Microsoft Project removes any existing leveling delays from all tasks and assignments before leveling. If, for example, you previously leveled the project plan and then added more assignments, you might clear this check box before leveling again so that you wouldn't lose the previous leveling results.

7 Under Leveling Range For "Short Film Project 9," click Level Entire Project.

Here you choose to level either the entire project or only those assignments that fall within a date range you specify. Leveling within a date range is most useful after you have started tracking actual work and you want to level only the remaining assignments in a project.

8 In the Leveling Order box, click Standard.

You control the priority Microsoft Project uses to determine which tasks it should delay to resolve a resource conflict. The ID Only option delays tasks only according to their ID numbers: numerically higher ID numbers will be delayed before numerically lower ID numbers. You might want to use this option when your project plan has no task relationships or constraints. The Standard option delays tasks according to predecessor relationships, start dates, task constraints, *slack*, priority, and IDs. The Priority, Standard option looks at the *task priority* value before the other standard criteria. (Task priority is a numeric ranking between 0 and 1000 that indicates the task's appropriateness for leveling. Tasks with the lowest priority are delayed or split first.)

9 Clear the Level Only Within Available Slack check box.

Tip

Remember that to *clear* a check box means to remove a check from the check box, and to *select* a check box means to put a check in it. You can toggle the selection state of a check box by clicking it.

Clearing this check box allows Microsoft Project to extend the project's finish date, if necessary, to resolve resource allocations.

Selecting this check box would prevent Microsoft Project from extending the project's finish date in order to resolve resource overallocations. Instead, Microsoft Project would use only the free slack within the existing schedule. Depending on the project, this might not be adequate to fully resolve resource overallocations.

10 Select the Leveling Can Adjust Individual Assignments On A Task check box.

This allows Microsoft Project to add leveling delay (or split work on assignments if Leveling Can Create Splits In Remaining Work is also selected) independently of any other resources assigned to the same task. This might cause resources to start and finish work on a task at different times.

11 Select the Leveling Can Create Splits In Remaining Work check box.

This allows Microsoft Project to split work on a task (or on an assignment if Leveling Can Adjust Individual Assignments On A Task is also selected) as a way of resolving an overallocation. Your screen should look similar to the following illustration:

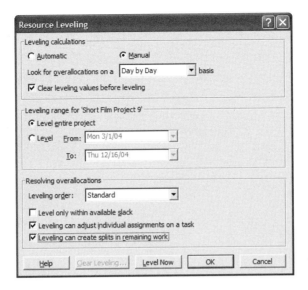

12 Click the Level Now button.

13 Microsoft Project asks whether you want to level the entire pool or only selected resources. Leave Entire Pool selected, and click OK.

Microsoft Project levels the overallocated resources.

	❶	Resource Name	Type	Material Label	Initials	Group	Max. Units	Std. Rate	Ovt. Rate	Cost/Use	A ▲
1		16-mm Camera	Work		16mm		300%	$250.00/wk	$0.00/hr	$0.00	St
2		16-mm Film	Material	100 Feet	Film			$20.00		$0.00	Pr
3		500-Watt Light	Work		5000WL		400%	$100.00/wk	$0.00/hr	$0.00	Pr
4		Anne L. Paper	Work		AP		100%	$75.00/day	$0.00/hr	$0.00	Pr
5		Camera Boom	Work		Boom		200%	$0.00/hr	$0.00/hr	$0.00	Pr
6		Clair Hector	Work		CH		100%	$800.00/wk	$0.00/hr	$0.00	Pr
7		Crane	Work		Crane		100%	$0.00/hr	$0.00/hr	$0.00	Pr
8		Daniel Penn	Work		DP		100%	$75.00/day	$0.00/hr	$0.00	Pr
9		David Campbell	Work		DC		100%	$75.00/day	$0.00/hr	$0.00	Pr
10		Dolly	Work		Dolly		200%	$0.00/hr	$0.00/hr	$0.00	Pr
11		Doug Hampton	Work		DH		100%	$13.00/hr	$0.00/hr	$0.00	Pr
12		Editing Lab	Work		EL		100%	$200.00/day	$0.00/hr	$25.00	Pr
13		Electrician	Work		EL		200%	$22.00/hr	$33.00/hr	$0.00	Pr
14		Eric Lang	Work		EL		100%	$15.50/hr	$0.00/hr	$0.00	Pr
15		Eric Miller	Work		EM		100%	$75.00/day	$0.00/hr	$0.00	Pr
16		Florian Voss	Work		FV		100%	$22.00/hr	$0.00/hr	$0.00	Pr
17		Frank Lee	Work		FL		100%	$14.00/hr	$21.00/hr	$0.00	Pr
18		Jan Miksovsky	Work		JM		100%	$18.75/hr	$28.12/hr	$0.00	Pr
19		Jim Hance	Work		JH		100%	$75.00/day	$0.00/hr	$0.00	Pr
20		Jo Brown	Work		JB		100%	$18.75/hr	$0.00/hr	$0.00	Pr
21		Johnathan Perrera	Work		JP		100%	$22.00/hr	$0.00/hr	$0.00	Pr
22		Joseph Matthews	Work		JM		100%	$75.00/day	$0.00/hr	$0.00	Pr ▼

Notice that the Overallocated indicators are gone, although some resource names still appear in red. This means that some resources are still overallocated hour by hour (or minute by minute) but not day by day.

Next you will look at the project plan before and after leveling, using the Leveling Gantt view.

14 On the View menu, click More Views, click Leveling Gantt, and then click the Apply button.

Microsoft Project switches to the Leveling Gantt view.

15 Click the name of Task 8, *Apply for filming permits*.

Go To
Selected Task

16 On the Standard toolbar, click the Go To Selected Task button.

This gives you a better look at some of the tasks that were affected by leveling:

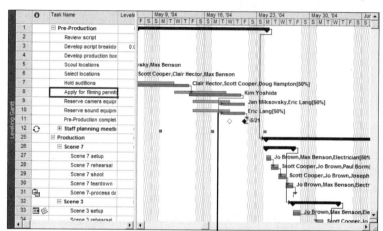

In the Leveling Gantt view, the bar on top represents the prelevel schedule of the task. The bar below represents the schedule after leveling.

Notice that each task now has two bars. The green bar on top represents the preleveled task. You can see a task's preleveled start, finish, and duration by pointing to a green bar. The blue bar on the bottom represents the leveled task.

Microsoft Project was able to resolve the resource overallocations. For this particular project, leveling did not affect the project finish date. The pre-production phase of the project had some slack, and leveling was able to adjust the pre-production tasks within the available slack.

Examining Project Costs

Not all project plans include cost information, but for those that do, keeping track of project costs can be as important as or more important than keeping track of the scheduled finish date. Two factors to consider when examining project costs are the specific types of costs you want to see and how you can best see them.

The types of costs you might have over the life of a project include the following:

- Baseline costs are the original planned task, resource, or assignment costs saved as part of a baseline plan.

- Current (or scheduled) costs are the calculated costs of tasks, resources, and assignments in a project plan. As you make adjustments in a project plan, such as assigning or removing resources, Microsoft Project recalculates current costs, just as it recalculates task start and finish dates. After you start incurring actual costs (normally by tracking actual work), the current cost equals the actual cost plus remaining cost per task, resource, or assignment. Current costs are the values you see in fields labeled *Cost* or *Total Cost.*

- Actual costs are the costs that have been incurred for tasks, resources, or assignments.

- Remaining costs are the difference between the current or scheduled costs and the actual costs for tasks, resources, or assignments.

You might need to compare these costs (baseline vs. actual, for example), or examine them individually per task, resource, or assignment. Or you might need to examine cost values for summary tasks or for an entire project plan. Some common ways to see these types of costs include the following:

- See the entire project's current, baseline, actual, and remaining costs in the Project Statistics dialog box (on the Project menu, click Project Information, and then click Statistics).

- See or print formatted reports that include cash flow, budget, over-budget tasks or resources, and earned value (on the View menu, click Reports, and then click the Costs button).

Tip

Earned value is a powerful schedule analysis tool that relies on cost information in a project plan. For more information, see Chapter 19, "Measuring Performance with Earned Value Analysis."

- See task, resource, or assignment-level cost information in usage views by displaying the Cost table (on the View menu, point to Table:Entry, and then click Cost).

Tip

Row and column totals
new in
Project
2002

When printing usage views, you can include cost totals. You can include row totals when printing date ranges from a usage view (on the File menu, click Page Setup, and in the Page Setup dialog box, click the View tab, and select the Print Row Totals For Values Within Print Date Range check box). You can also include column totals in usage views (on the File menu, click Page Setup, in the Page Setup dialog box, click the View tab, and select the Print Column Totals check box).

In this exercise, you look at the overall project costs and at individual task costs:

1 On the View menu, click More Views, click Task Sheet, and then click the Apply button.

Microsoft Project switches to the Task Sheet view. Next you will display the project summary task to see the top-level or rolled-up values of the project.

2 On the Tools menu, click Options.

3 In the Options dialog box, click the View tab.

4 Under the Outline Options For label, select the Show Project Summary Task check box, and then click the OK button.

Microsoft Project displays the project summary task at the top of the Task Sheet view. Next you will switch to the Cost table.

5 On the View menu, point to Table: Entry, and click Cost.

The Cost table appears.

6 Double-click between the text in the column labels to widen any columns that display pound signs (##).

Your screen should look like the following illustration:

	Task Name	Fixed Cost	Fixed Cost Accrual	Total Cost	Baseline	Variance	Actual	Remaining
0	⊟ Short Film Project 9	$0.00	Prorated	$88,789.55	$89,161.55	($372.00)	$0.00	$88,789.55
1	⊟ Pre-Production	$0.00	Prorated	$23,987.50	$24,359.50	($372.00)	$0.00	$23,987.50
2	Review script	$0.00	Prorated	$947.50	$947.50	$0.00	$0.00	$947.50
3	Develop script breal	$0.00	Prorated	$2,455.00	$2,455.00	$0.00	$0.00	$2,455.00
4	Develop production	$0.00	Prorated	$8,124.00	$8,124.00	$0.00	$0.00	$8,124.00
5	Scout locations	$0.00	Prorated	$4,920.00	$4,920.00	$0.00	$0.00	$4,920.00
6	Select locations	$0.00	Prorated	$2,535.00	$2,535.00	$0.00	$0.00	$2,535.00
7	Hold auditions	$0.00	Prorated	$1,835.00	$1,835.00	$0.00	$0.00	$1,835.00
8	Apply for filming per	$500.00	Start	$876.00	$876.00	$0.00	$0.00	$876.00
9	Reserve camera equ	$0.00	Prorated	$636.00	$822.00	($186.00)	$0.00	$636.00
10	Reserve sound equi	$0.00	Prorated	$186.00	$372.00	($186.00)	$0.00	$186.00
11	Pre-Production com	$0.00	Prorated	$0.00	$0.00	$0.00	$0.00	$0.00
12	⊞ Staff planning me	$0.00	Prorated	$1,473.00	$1,473.00	$0.00	$0.00	$1,473.00
25	⊟ Production	$0.00	Prorated	$36,334.15	$36,334.15	$0.00	$0.00	$36,334.15
26	⊟ Scene 7	$0.00	Prorated	$3,702.50	$3,702.50	$0.00	$0.00	$3,702.50
27	Scene 7 setup	$0.00	Prorated	$322.50	$322.50	$0.00	$0.00	$322.50
28	Scene 7 rehears	$0.00	Prorated	$705.00	$705.00	$0.00	$0.00	$705.00
29	Scene 7 shoot	$0.00	Prorated	$2,245.00	$2,245.00	$0.00	$0.00	$2,245.00
30	Scene 7 teardow	$0.00	Prorated	$430.00	$430.00	$0.00	$0.00	$430.00
31	Scene 7-process	$0.00	Prorated	$0.00	$0.00	$0.00	$0.00	$0.00
32	⊟ Scene 3	$0.00	Prorated	$4,170.00	$4,170.00	$0.00	$0.00	$4,170.00
33	Scene 3 setup	$0.00	Prorated	$518.00	$518.00	$0.00	$0.00	$518.00

Here you can see many types of cost values for the overall project, project phases (summary tasks), and individual tasks. At this point in the project life cycle, the project plan includes a baseline, so you see values in the Baseline column; it has had some assignment adjustments made earlier in this chapter, so you see some values in the Variance column; but it does not yet contain any actual progress, so the Actual column contains only zero values.

Checking the Project's Finish Date

A project's finish date is a function of its duration and start date. Most projects have a desired, or *soft*, finish date, and many projects have a "must hit," or hard, finish date. When managing projects like these, it is essential that you know the project's current or scheduled finish date and understand how the adjustments you make in the planning stage affect the finish date.

In the language of project management, a project's finish date is determined by its *critical path*. The critical path is the series of tasks that will push out the project's end date if the tasks are delayed. For this reason, when evaluating the duration of a project, you should focus mainly on the tasks on the critical path, called critical tasks.

Tip

Remember that the word *critical* has nothing to do with how important these tasks are to the overall project. The word refers only to how their scheduling will affect the project's finish date.

In this exercise, you look at the project's critical path and finish date:

1   On the Project menu, click Project Information.

The Project Information dialog box appears.

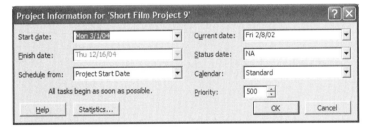

In it you can see the current or scheduled finish date for the project: December 16, 2004. Note that you can edit the start date of the project here, but not its finish date. Microsoft Project has calculated this finish date based on the start date plus the overall duration of the project. This project is scheduled from the start date, as the Schedule From box indicates. In some cases you might want to schedule a project from a finish date, in which case you enter the finish date and task information and Microsoft Project calculates the start date.

Tip

It might sound tempting to schedule a project from a finish date, especially if it has a hard "must-hit" deadline. However, in nearly all cases you should resist this temptation and instead schedule from a start date. To learn more about the effects of scheduling from a finish date, type **Strategies for scheduling a project from a finish date** into the Ask A Question box in the upper right corner of the Microsoft Project window.

Next you will look at the duration values for this project.

2 In the Project Information dialog box, click the Statistics button.

The Project Statistics dialog box appears:

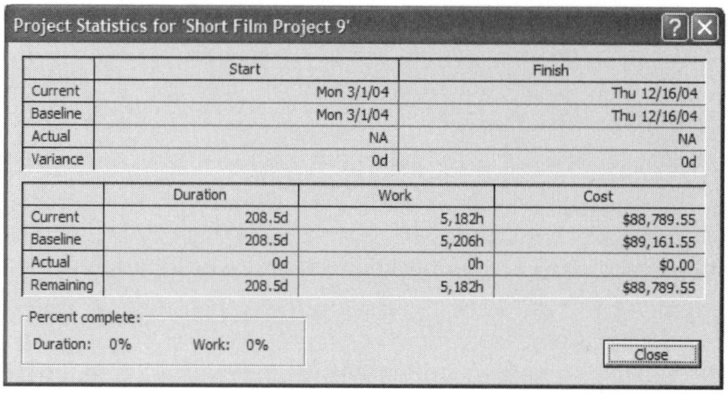

Project Statistics for 'Short Film Project 9'				? ✕
	Start		Finish	
Current		Mon 3/1/04		Thu 12/16/04
Baseline		Mon 3/1/04		Thu 12/16/04
Actual		NA		NA
Variance		0d		0d

	Duration	Work	Cost
Current	208.5d	5,182h	$88,789.55
Baseline	208.5d	5,206h	$89,161.55
Actual	0d	0h	$0.00
Remaining	208.5d	5,182h	$88,789.55

Percent complete:
Duration: 0%   Work: 0%   [Close]

Here you can see the project's current, baseline, and actual start and finish dates, as well as its schedule variance.

You might recall from the previous section that assignment adjustments you made earlier in this chapter introduced some cost variance into the plan, but they did not cause any schedule variance—the project plan has zero schedule variance. This is indicated by the 0d values in the Variance row.

This project currently has no actual work reported, so you also see zero values in the Actual Duration and Actual Work fields. The project's current scheduled and baseline duration values as well as work values are also reported here.

3 Click the Close button to close the Project Statistics dialog box. To conclude this exercise, you will look at the critical path.

4 On the Project Guide toolbar, click the Report button.

5 In the Report pane, click the See The Project's Critical Tasks link.

The Project Guide: Critical Tasks view replaces the Task Sheet view. In the Critical Path pane, you can see the current scheduled finish date and apply a *filter* to the view.

6 Click the Close button in the upper right corner of the Project Guide pane to close the Project Guide.

7 On the Edit menu, click Go To.

8 In the ID box, type **25**, and then click OK.

Microsoft Project scrolls the view to show Task 25, the Production summary task. Your screen should look like the following illustration:

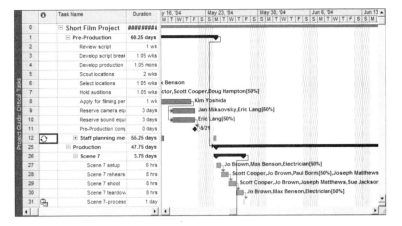

Here you can see both critical tasks (their Gantt bars are red) and non-critical tasks (blue). Any changes to the durations of critical tasks will affect the project finish date. However, changes to the non-critical tasks won't necessarily affect the project finish date, depending on available slack. When you make adjustments to the project plan, and especially after you start tracking actual work, the specific tasks on the critical path are likely to change. For this reason you should frequently check the project finish date and the critical tasks that determine it.

Chapter Wrap-Up

This chapter covered how to work with a variety of features to fine-tune a project plan prior to tracking actual work.

If you are going on to other chapters:

Save

1   On the Standard toolbar, click the Save button to save changes made to Short Film Project 9.

2   On the File menu, click Close to close the project plan.

If you aren't continuing to other chapters:

1   On the Standard toolbar, click the Save button to save changes made to Short Film Project 9.

2   To quit Microsoft Project for now, on the File menu, click Exit.

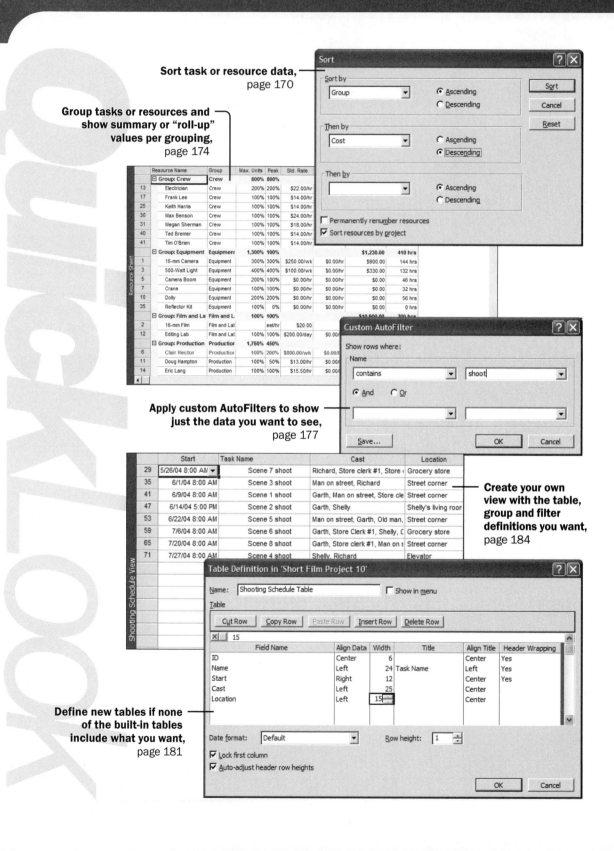

Sort task or resource data,
page 170

Group tasks or resources and show summary or "roll-up" values per grouping,
page 174

Apply custom AutoFilters to show just the data you want to see,
page 177

Create your own view with the table, group and filter definitions you want,
page 184

Define new tables if none of the built-in tables include what you want,
page 181

Chapter 10
Organizing and Formatting Project Details

After completing this chapter, you will be able to:

✔ Sort task and resource data.

✔ Display task and resource data in groups.

✔ Filter or highlight task and resource data.

✔ Create a custom table.

✔ Create a custom view.

After you've built a project plan, chances are you will need to examine specific aspects of it for your own analysis or to share with other *stakeholders*. Although the built-in views, tables, and reports in Microsoft Project provide many ways to examine a project plan, you might need to organize information to suit your own specific needs.

In this chapter, you use some of the formatting tools in Microsoft Project to change the way your data appears. Microsoft Project includes powerful features that enable you to organize and analyze data that otherwise would require separate tools, such as a spreadsheet application.

Short Film
Project 10a

This chapter uses the practice file Short Film Project 10a. For details about installing the practice files, see "Using the Book's CD-ROM" at the beginning of this book.

Sorting Project Details

Sorting is the simplest way to reorganize task or resource data in Microsoft Project. You can sort tasks or resources by predefined criteria, or you can create your own sort order with up to three levels of nesting. For example, you can sort resources by resource group, and then sort by cost within each resource group.

Like grouping and filtering, which you will work with in later sections, sorting does not (with one exception) change the underlying data of your project plan; it simply reorders the data you have. The one exception is the option it offers to renumber task or resource IDs after sorting. After tasks or resources are renumbered, you cannot restore their original numbered sequence.

However, it's fine to permanently renumber tasks or resources if that's what you intend to do. For example, when building a resource list, you might enter resource names in the order in which the resources join your project. Later, when the list is complete, you might want to sort them alphabetically by name and permanently renumber them.

Each resource in the Short Film Project plan is assigned to one of several resource groups. These groups have names like *Crew*, *Production*, *Talent*, and other names that make sense in a film production company. For your project plans, you might use resource groups to represent functional teams, departments, or whatever most logically describes collections of similar resources.

Sorting all resources by resource group enables you to see more easily the costs associated with each resource group. This can help you plan your project's budget. You can also sort resources within each group by cost from most to least expensive.

Important

The Permanently Renumber Tasks (or when in a resource view, the Permanently Renumber Resources) check box in the Sort dialog box is a Microsoft Project–level setting; if selected, it permanently renumbers tasks or resources in any Microsoft Project plan in which you sort. Because you might not want to permanently renumber tasks or resources every time you sort, it's a good idea to clear this check box.

In this exercise, you sort a resource view:

1 If Microsoft Project is not already open, start it now.

Open

2 On the Standard toolbar, click the Open button.

The Open dialog box appears.

3 Navigate to the Chapter 10 Complex Formatting folder, and double-click the Short Film Project 10a file.

4 On the File menu, click Save As.

The Save As dialog box appears.

5 In the File Name box, type **Short Film Project 10**, and then click the Save button.

6 On the View menu, click Resource Sheet.

The Resource Sheet view appears. By default, the Entry table appears in the Resource Sheet view; however, the Entry table does not display the cost field per resource. You will switch to the Summary table instead.

7 On the View menu, point to Table: Entry, and then click Summary.

The Summary table appears. Your screen should look similar to the following illustration:

	Resource Name	Group	Max. Units	Peak	Std. Rate	Ovt. Rate	Cost	Work
1	16-mm Camera	Equipment	300%	300%	$250.00/wk	$0.00/hr	$900.00	144 hrs
2	16-mm Film	Film and Lab		eet/hr	$20.00		$5,800.00	290 100 Feet
3	500-Watt Light	Equipment	400%	400%	$100.00/wk	$0.00/hr	$330.00	132 hrs
4	Anne L. Paper	Talent	100%	100%	$75.00/day	$0.00/hr	$731.25	78 hrs
5	Camera Boom	Equipment	200%	100%	$0.00/hr	$0.00/hr	$0.00	46 hrs
6	Clair Hector	Production	100%	200%	$800.00/wk	$0.00/hr	$7,600.00	380 hrs
7	Crane	Equipment	100%	100%	$0.00/hr	$0.00/hr	$0.00	32 hrs
8	Daniel Penn	Talent	100%	100%	$75.00/day	$0.00/hr	$412.50	44 hrs
9	David Campbell	Talent	100%	100%	$75.00/day	$0.00/hr	$2,475.00	264 hrs
10	Dolly	Equipment	200%	200%	$0.00/hr	$0.00/hr	$0.00	56 hrs
11	Doug Hampton	Production	100%	50%	$13.00/hr	$0.00/hr	$1,788.80	121 hrs
12	Editing Lab	Film and Lab	100%	100%	$200.00/day	$0.00/hr	$5,100.00	200 hrs
13	Electrician	Crew	200%	200%	$22.00/hr	$33.00/hr	$2,178.00	99 hrs
14	Eric Lang	Production	100%	100%	$15.50/hr	$0.00/hr	$372.00	24 hrs
15	Eric Miller	Talent	100%	100%	$75.00/hr	$0.00/hr	$675.00	72 hrs
16	Florian Voss	Production	100%	100%	$22.00/hr	$0.00/hr	$2,024.00	92 hrs
17	Frank Lee	Crew	100%	100%	$14.00/hr	$21.00/hr	$812.00	58 hrs
18	Jan Miksovsky	Production	100%	100%	$18.75/hr	$28.12/hr	$3,637.00	196 hrs
19	Jim Hance	Talent	100%	100%	$75.00/day	$0.00/hr	$412.50	44 hrs
20	Jo Brown	Production	100%	100%	$18.75/hr	$0.00/hr	$9,037.50	482 hrs
21	Johnathan Perrera	Production	100%	100%	$22.00/hr	$0.00/hr	$4,928.00	224 hrs
22	Joseph Matthews	Talent	100%	100%	$75.00/day	$0.00/hr	$356.25	38 hrs

Now you are ready to sort the Resource Sheet view.

8   On the Project menu, point to Sort, and click Sort By.

The Sort dialog box appears.

9   Under Sort By, click Cost in the drop-down list, and next to that, click Descending.

10   Make sure that the Permanently Renumber Resources check box is cleared, and then click the Sort button.

The Summary table in the Resource Sheet view is sorted by the Cost column, in descending order. Your screen should look similar to the following illustration:

The Resource Sheet view is now — ⌐
sorted by cost, in descending order.

	Resource Name	Group	Max. Units	Peak	Std. Rate	Ovt. Rate	Cost	Work
38	Scott Cooper	Production	100%	200%	$775.00/wk	$0.00/hr	$10,346.25	534 hrs
20	Jo Brown	Production	100%	100%	$18.75/hr	$0.00/hr	$9,037.50	482 hrs
30	Max Benson	Crew	100%	100%	$24.00/hr	$0.00/hr	$8,592.00	358 hrs
6	Clair Hector	Production	100%	200%	$800.00/wk	$0.00/hr	$7,600.00	380 hrs
32	Michael Patten	Production	100%	100%	$700.00/wk	$0.00/hr	$6,230.00	356 hrs
2	16-mm Film	Film and Lab		eet/hr	$20.00		$5,800.00	290 100 Feet
12	Editing Lab	Film and Lab	100%	100%	$200.00/day	$0.00/hr	$5,100.00	200 hrs
21	Johnathan Perrera	Production	100%	100%	$22.00/hr	$0.00/hr	$4,928.00	224 hrs
18	Jan Miksovsky	Production	100%	100%	$18.75/hr	$28.12/hr	$3,637.00	196 hrs
26	Kim Yoshida	Production	100%	100%	$9.40/hr	$0.00/hr	$3,384.00	360 hrs
36	Richard Lum	Production	100%	100%	$625.00/wk	$0.00/hr	$3,125.00	200 hrs
9	David Campbell	Talent	100%	100%	$75.00/day	$0.00/hr	$2,475.00	264 hrs
13	Electrician	Crew	200%	200%	$22.00/hr	$33.00/hr	$2,178.00	99 hrs
16	Florian Voss	Production	100%	100%	$22.00/hr	$0.00/hr	$2,024.00	92 hrs
11	Doug Hampton	Production	100%	50%	$13.00/hr	$0.00/hr	$1,788.80	121 hrs
28	Lisa Garmaise	Production	100%	100%	$9.00/hr	$0.00/hr	$1,440.00	160 hrs
31	Megan Sherman	Crew	100%	100%	$18.00/hr	$0.00/hr	$972.00	54 hrs
34	Paul Borm	Production	50%	50%	$200.00/day	$0.00/hr	$950.00	38 hrs
39	Sue Jackson	Talent	100%	100%	$75.00/day	$0.00/hr	$937.50	100 hrs
1	16-mm Camera	Equipment	300%	300%	$250.00/wk	$0.00/hr	$900.00	144 hrs
17	Frank Lee	Crew	100%	100%	$14.00/hr	$21.00/hr	$812.00	58 hrs
25	Keith Harris	Crew	100%	100%	$14.00/hr	$21.00/hr	$812.00	58 hrs

This arrangement is fine for looking at resource costs in the entire project, but you'd like to see this data organized by resource group. To see this, you'll apply a two-level sort order.

Tip

When you sort data, the sort order applies to the active view, regardless of the specific table currently displayed in the view. For example, if you sort the Gantt Chart view by start date while displaying the Entry table and then switch to the Cost table, you'll see the tasks sorted by start date in the Cost table.

11 On the Project menu, point to Sort, and then click Sort By.

The Sort dialog box appears. In it, you can apply up to three nested levels of sort criteria.

12 Under Sort By, click Group in the drop-down list, and next to that, click Ascending.

Tip

You can sort by any field, not just the fields visible in the active view.

13 Under Then By (in the center of the dialog box), click Cost in the drop-down list, and next to that, click Descending.

14 Make sure that the Permanently Renumber Resources check box is cleared.

Your screen should look similar to the following illustration:

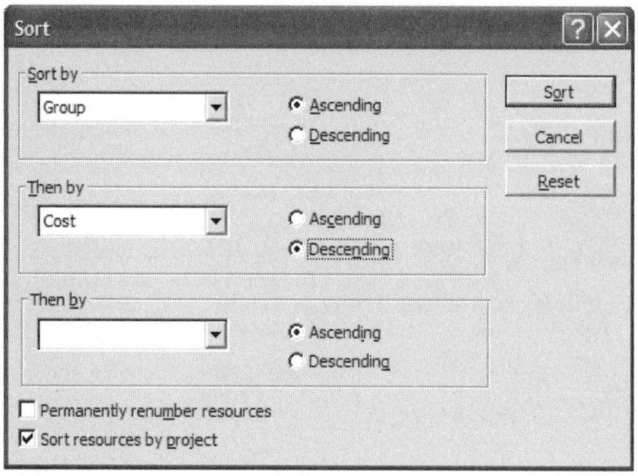

15 Click the Sort button.

Microsoft Project sorts the Resource Sheet view to display resources by group (Crew, Equipment, and so on) and then by cost within each group. Your screen should look similar to the following illustration:

Now the Resource Sheet view is sorted first by
resource group, and within each group by cost.

	Resource Name	Group	Max. Units	Peak	Std. Rate	Ovt. Rate	Cost	Work
30	Max Benson	Crew	100%	100%	$24.00/hr	$0.00/hr	$8,592.00	358 hrs
13	Electrician	Crew	200%	200%	$22.00/hr	$33.00/hr	$2,178.00	99 hrs
31	Megan Sherman	Crew	100%	100%	$18.00/hr	$0.00/hr	$972.00	54 hrs
17	Frank Lee	Crew	100%	100%	$14.00/hr	$21.00/hr	$812.00	58 hrs
25	Keith Harris	Crew	100%	100%	$14.00/hr	$21.00/hr	$812.00	58 hrs
40	Ted Bremer	Crew	100%	100%	$14.00/hr	$21.00/hr	$812.00	58 hrs
41	Tim O'Brien	Crew	100%	100%	$14.00/hr	$21.00/hr	$784.00	56 hrs
1	16-mm Camera	Equipment	300%	300%	$250.00/wk	$0.00/hr	$900.00	144 hrs
3	500-Watt Light	Equipment	400%	400%	$100.00/wk	$0.00/hr	$330.00	132 hrs
5	Camera Boom	Equipment	200%	100%	$0.00/hr	$0.00/hr	$0.00	46 hrs
7	Crane	Equipment	100%	100%	$0.00/hr	$0.00/hr	$0.00	32 hrs
10	Dolly	Equipment	200%	200%	$0.00/hr	$0.00/hr	$0.00	56 hrs
35	Reflector Kit	Equipment	100%	0%	$0.00/hr	$0.00/hr	$0.00	0 hrs
2	16-mm Film	Film and Lat		eet/hr	$20.00		$5,800.00	290 100 Feet
12	Editing Lab	Film and Lat	100%	100%	$200.00/day	$0.00/hr	$5,100.00	200 hrs
38	Scott Cooper	Production	100%	200%	$775.00/wk	$0.00/hr	$10,346.25	534 hrs
20	Jo Brown	Production	100%	100%	$18.75/hr	$0.00/hr	$9,037.50	482 hrs
6	Clair Hector	Production	100%	200%	$800.00/wk	$0.00/hr	$7,600.00	380 hrs
32	Michael Patten	Production	100%	100%	$700.00/wk	$0.00/hr	$6,230.00	356 hrs
21	Johnathan Perrera	Production	100%	100%	$22.00/hr	$0.00/hr	$4,928.00	224 hrs
18	Jan Miksovsky	Production	100%	100%	$18.75/hr	$28.12/hr	$3,637.00	196 hrs
26	Kim Yoshida	Production	100%	100%	$9.40/hr	$0.00/hr	$3,384.00	360 hrs

This is an easy way to identify the most expensive resources in each resource group
working on the short film project.

To conclude this exercise, you'll re-sort the resource information to return it to its original
order.

16 On the Project menu, point to Sort, and then click By ID.

Microsoft Project re-sorts the resource list by resource ID.

Note that there is no visual indication that a task or resource view has been sorted other
than the order in which the rows of data appear. You cannot save custom sort settings that
you have specified, as you can with grouping and filtering. However, the sort order you
most recently specified will remain in effect until you re-sort the view.

Grouping Project Details

As you develop a project plan, you can use the default views available in Microsoft Project
to view and analyze your data in several ways. One important way to see the data in task
and resource views is by *grouping*. Grouping allows you to organize task or resource information (or, when in a usage view, assignment information) according to criteria you choose.
For example, rather than viewing the resource list in the Resource Sheet view sorted by ID,
you can view resources sorted by cost. Grouping goes a step beyond just sorting, however.
Grouping adds summary values, or "roll-ups," at intervals that you can customize. For
example, you can group resources by their cost with a $1,000 interval between groups.

Tip

In some respects, grouping in Microsoft Project is similar to the Subtotals feature in Microsoft Excel. In fact, grouping allows you to reorganize and analyze your Microsoft Project data in ways that would otherwise require you to export your Microsoft Project data to a spreadsheet program.

Grouping can significantly change the way you view your task or resource data, allowing for a more refined level of data analysis and presentation. Grouping doesn't change the underlying structure of your project plan; it simply reorganizes and summarizes the data. As with sorting, when you group data in a view, the grouping applies to all tables you can display in the view. You can also group the Network Diagram view, which does not contain a table.

Microsoft Project includes several predefined task and resource groups, such as grouping tasks by duration or resources by standard pay rate. You can also customize any of the built-in groups or create your own.

Tip

You can also use the Project Guide to apply a filter or group to a table or to sort information in a table. On the Project Guide toolbar, click Report. In the Reports pane, click the Change The Content Or Order Of Information In A View link.

In this exercise, you group resources by their Group name (this is the value in the *Group field—Crew, Equipment,* and so on). This is similar to the sorting you did in the previous section, but this time you will see summary cost values for each resource group:

1 On the Project menu, point to Group By: No Group, and then click Resource Group.

Microsoft Project reorganizes the resource data into resource groups, adds summary cost values per group, and presents the data in an expanded outline form. Your screen should look similar to the following illustration:

After grouping resources by the Group field, Microsoft Project adds summary values per group.

	Resource Name	Group	Max. Units	Peak	Std. Rate	Ovt. Rate	Cost	Work
	⊟ Group: Crew	Crew	800%	800%			$14,962.00	741 hrs
13	Electrician	Crew	200%	200%	$22.00/hr	$33.00/hr	$2,178.00	99 hrs
17	Frank Lee	Crew	100%	100%	$14.00/hr	$21.00/hr	$812.00	58 hrs
25	Keith Harris	Crew	100%	100%	$14.00/hr	$21.00/hr	$812.00	58 hrs
30	Max Benson	Crew	100%	100%	$24.00/hr	$0.00/hr	$8,592.00	358 hrs
31	Megan Sherman	Crew	100%	100%	$18.00/hr	$0.00/hr	$972.00	54 hrs
40	Ted Bremer	Crew	100%	100%	$14.00/hr	$21.00/hr	$812.00	58 hrs
41	Tim O'Brien	Crew	100%	100%	$14.00/hr	$21.00/hr	$784.00	56 hrs
	⊟ Group: Equipment	Equipment	1,300%	100%			$1,230.00	410 hrs
1	16-mm Camera	Equipment	300%	300%	$250.00/wk	$0.00/hr	$900.00	144 hrs
3	500-Watt Light	Equipment	400%	400%	$100.00/hr	$0.00/hr	$330.00	132 hrs
5	Camera Boom	Equipment	200%	100%	$0.00/hr	$0.00/hr	$0.00	46 hrs
7	Crane	Equipment	100%	100%	$0.00/hr	$0.00/hr	$0.00	32 hrs
10	Dolly	Equipment	200%	200%	$0.00/hr	$0.00/hr	$0.00	56 hrs
35	Reflector Kit	Equipment	100%	0%	$0.00/hr	$0.00/hr	$0.00	0 hrs
	⊟ Group: Film and La	Film and L	100%	100%			$10,900.00	200 hrs
2	16-mm Film	Film and Lat		eet/hr	$20.00		$5,800.00	290 100 Feet
12	Editing Lab	Film and Lat	100%	100%	$200.00/day	$0.00/hr	$5,100.00	200 hrs
	⊟ Group: Production	Production	1,750%	450%			$54,957.55	3,171 hrs
6	Clair Hector	Production	100%	200%	$800.00/wk	$0.00/hr	$7,600.00	380 hrs
11	Doug Hampton	Production	100%	50%	$13.00/hr	$0.00/hr	$1,788.80	121 hrs
14	Eric Lang	Production	100%	100%	$15.50/hr	$0.00/hr	$372.00	24 hrs

Microsoft Project applies colored formatting (in this case, a yellow background) to the summary data rows. Because the summary data is derived from subordinate data, you cannot edit it directly. Displaying these summary values has no effect on the cost or schedule calculations of the project plan.

This arrangement of the resource cost information is similar to the sorting you did in the previous section. To give yourself more control over how Microsoft Project organizes and presents the data, you'll now create a group.

2 On the Project menu, point to Group By: Resource Group, and then click More Groups.

The More Groups dialog box appears. In it, you can see all the available predefined groups for tasks (when in a task view) and resources (when in a resource view). Your new group will be most similar to the Resource Group, so you'll start by copying it.

3 Make sure that Resource Group is selected, and then click the Copy button.

The Group Definition In dialog box appears.

4 In the Name box, type **Resource Groups by Cost**.

5 In the Field Name column, click the first empty cell below Group.

6 Type or click **Cost**.

7 In the Order column, click Descending for the Cost field.

The resources will be sorted within their groups by cost from highest to lowest values.

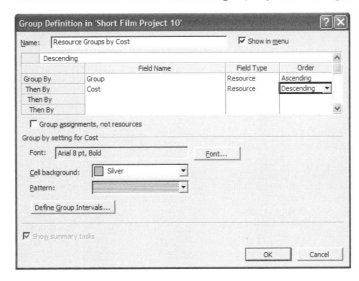

Next you'll fine-tune the cost intervals at which Microsoft Project will group the resources.

8 Click the Define Group Intervals button.

The Define Group Interval dialog box appears.

9 In the Group On box, click Interval.

10 In the Group Interval box, type **1000**, and then click the OK button.

11 Click OK again to close the Group Definition In dialog box.

Resource Groups by Cost appears as a new group in the More Groups dialog box.

12 Click the Apply button.

Microsoft Project applies the new group to the Resource Sheet view. To get a better look at the groupings, you'll widen the Resource Name column.

13 Double-click the Resource Name column heading.

The Column Definition dialog box appears.

14 Click the Best Fit button.

Microsoft Project widens the Column Definition dialog box. Your screen should look similar to the following illustration:

After applying a two-level group, information is grouped first by Resource Group, and within each group by cost.

Resource Name	Group	Max. Units	Peak	Std. Rate	Ovt. Rate	Cost	Work
⊟ Group: Crew	Crew	800%	800%			$14,962.00	741 hrs
⊟ Cost: $8,000.00 - <$9,000.00	Crew	100%	100%			$8,592.00	358 hrs
30　　Max Benson	Crew	100%	100%	$24.00/hr	$0.00/hr	$8,592.00	358 hrs
⊟ Cost: $2,000.00 - <$3,000.00	Crew	200%	200%			$2,178.00	99 hrs
13　　Electrician	Crew	200%	200%	$22.00/hr	$33.00/hr	$2,178.00	99 hrs
⊟ Cost: $0.00 - <$1,000.00	Crew	500%	500%			$4,192.00	284 hrs
17　　Frank Lee	Crew	100%	100%	$14.00/hr	$21.00/hr	$812.00	58 hrs
25　　Keith Harris	Crew	100%	100%	$14.00/hr	$21.00/hr	$812.00	58 hrs
31　　Megan Sherman	Crew	100%	100%	$18.00/hr	$0.00/hr	$972.00	54 hrs
40　　Ted Bremer	Crew	100%	100%	$14.00/hr	$21.00/hr	$812.00	58 hrs
41　　Tim O'Brien	Crew	100%	100%	$14.00/hr	$21.00/hr	$784.00	56 hrs
⊟ Group: Equipment	Equipment	1,300%	100%			$1,230.00	410 hrs
⊟ Cost: $0.00 - <$1,000.00	Equipment	1,300%	100%			$1,230.00	410 hrs
1　　16-mm Camera	Equipment	300%	300%	$250.00/wk	$0.00/hr	$900.00	144 hrs
3　　500-Watt Light	Equipment	400%	400%	$100.00/wk	$0.00/hr	$330.00	132 hrs
5　　Camera Boom	Equipment	200%	100%	$0.00/hr	$0.00/hr	$0.00	46 hrs
7　　Crane	Equipment	100%	100%	$0.00/hr	$0.00/hr	$0.00	32 hrs
10　　Dolly	Equipment	200%	200%	$0.00/hr	$0.00/hr	$0.00	56 hrs
35　　Reflector Kit	Equipment	100%	0%	$0.00/hr	$0.00/hr	$0.00	0 hrs
⊟ Group: Film and Lab	Film and L	100%	100%			$10,900.00	200 hrs
⊟ Cost: $5,000.00 - <$6,000.00	Film and L	100%	100%			$10,900.00	200 hrs
2　　16-mm Film	Film and Lat		eet/hr	$20.00		$5,800.00	290 100 Feet

The resources are grouped by their resource group value (the yellow bands that bind together *Crew*, *Equipment*, and so on) and within each group by cost values at $1,000 intervals (the gray bands).

To conclude this exercise, you'll remove the grouping.

15 On the Project menu, point to Group By: Resource Groups By Cost, and click No Group.

Microsoft Project removes the summary values and outline structure, leaving the original data. Displaying or removing a group has no effect on the subordinate data.

Tip

All predefined groups and any groups you create are available to you through the Group By button on the Standard toolbar. The name of the active group appears on this button, which resembles a box with a drop-down list. Click the arrow in the Group By button to see other group names. If no group is applied to the current table, *No Group* appears on the button.

Group By

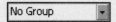

To learn more about using groups, type **Work with groups** or **Available groups** into the Ask A Question box.

Filtering Project Details

Another useful way to change the way you view Microsoft Project task and resource information is by *filtering*. As the name suggests, filtering hides task or resource data that does not meet the criteria you specify, displaying only the data you're interested in. Like grouping, filtering does not change the data in your Microsoft Project plan; it just changes the way that data appears.

There are two ways to use filters. Either apply predefined filters to a view, or apply an *AutoFilter* to a view:

■ Apply a predefined or custom filter to see or highlight only the task or resource information that meets the criteria of the filter. For example, the Critical Task filter displays only the tasks on the critical path. Some predefined filters, such as the Task Range filter, prompt you to enter specific criteria—for example, a range of task IDs. If a task or resource sheet view has a filter applied, the filter name appears in the Filter button on the Formatting toolbar.

■ Use AutoFilters for ad hoc filtering in any table in Microsoft Project. When the AutoFilter feature is turned on, small arrows appear next to the names of column headings. Click the arrow to display a list of criteria by which you can filter the data. The criteria you see depends on the type of data contained in the column— for example, AutoFilter criteria in a date column include choices like *Today* and *This month*, as well as a *Custom* option with which you can specify your own criteria. You use AutoFilter in Microsoft Project in the same way you might use AutoFilter in Microsoft Excel.

Both types of filters hide rows in task or resource sheet views that do not meet the criteria you specify. You might see gaps in the task or resource ID numbers. The "missing" data is only hidden and not deleted. As with sorting and grouping, when you filter data in a view, the filtering applies to all tables you can display in the view. Views that do not include tables, such as the Calendar and Network Diagram views, also support filtering (through the Filtered For command on the Project menu), but not AutoFilters.

A commonly used format for communicating schedule information on a film project is called a *shooting schedule*. In this exercise, you create a filter that displays only the uncompleted film shoot tasks. In later sections, you'll combine this filter with a custom table and a custom view to create a complete shooting schedule that will inform everyone on the film project:

1 On the View menu, click Gantt Chart.

The Gantt Chart view appears. Before you create a filter, you'll quickly see the tasks you're interested in by applying an AutoFilter.

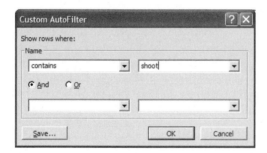

2 On the Formatting toolbar, click the AutoFilter button.

Microsoft Project displays arrows to the right of the column headings. Your screen should look like the following illustration:

After turning on AutoFilter, these arrows appear next to column headings. Click them to choose the AutoFilter you want.

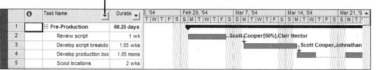

3 Click the down arrow in the Task Name column heading, and then click (Custom...).

The Custom AutoFilter dialog box appears. You'd like to see just the tasks that contain the word *shoot*.

4 Under Name, make sure *Contains* appears in the first box.

5 In the adjacent box, type **shoot**.

6 Click OK to close the Custom AutoFilter dialog box.

Microsoft Project filters the task list to show only the tasks that contain the word *shoot*, and their summary tasks. Your screen should look similar to the following illustration:

After applying an AutoFilter, the filtered column name and its AutoFilter arrow are formatted in blue.

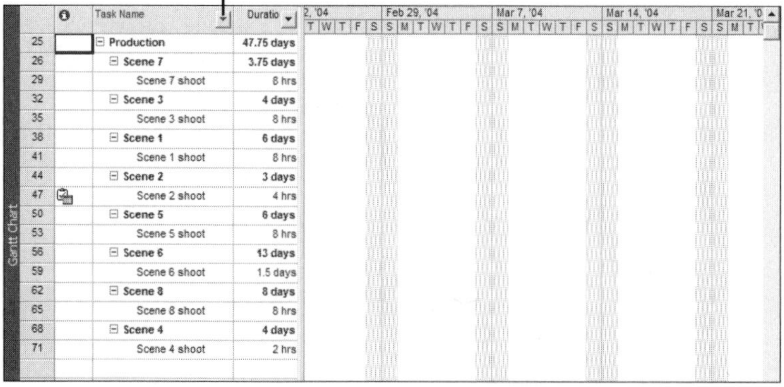

Note that the Task Name column heading and arrow appear in blue. These are visual indicators that an AutoFilter has been applied to this view.

Next you turn off the AutoFilter and create a custom filter.

7 On the Formatting toolbar, click the AutoFilter button.

Microsoft Project toggles the AutoFilter off, redisplaying all tasks in the project plan. Now you are ready to create a custom filter.

8 On the Project menu, point to Filtered For: All Tasks, and then click More Filters.

The More Filters dialog box appears. In it, you can see all the predefined filters for tasks (when in a task view) and resources (when in a resource view) available to you.

9 Click the New button.

The Filter Definition In dialog box appears.

10 In the Name box, type **Uncompleted Shoots**.

11 In the first row in the Field Name column, type or click **Name**.

12 In the first row in the Test column, type or click **contains**.

13 In the first row in the Value(s) column, type **shoot**.

That covers the first criterion for the filter; next you'll add the second criterion.

14 In the second row in the And/Or column, type or click **And**.

15 In the second row in the Field Name column, type or click **Actual Finish**.

16 In the second row in the Test column, type or click **equals**.

17 In the second row in the Value(s) column, type **NA**.

NA means "not applicable" and is the way Microsoft Project marks some fields that have no value yet. In other words, any shooting task that does not have an actual finish date must be uncompleted.

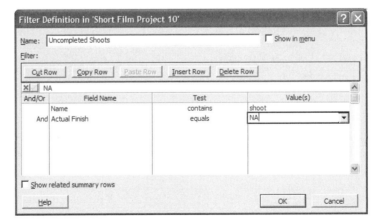

18 Click OK to close the Filter Definition In dialog box.

The new filter appears in the More Filters dialog box.

19 Click the Apply button.

Microsoft Project applies the new filter to the Gantt Chart view. Your screen should look similar to the following illustration:

After applying a filter, Microsoft Project hides information that does not meet the filter's criteria. Note the gaps in the Task IDs; this is one visual clue that a filter has been applied.

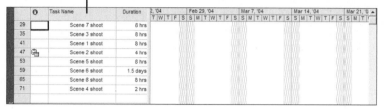

Now the tasks are filtered to show only the uncompleted shooting tasks. Because we haven't started tracking actual work yet, all the shooting tasks are uncompleted at this time.

Tip

Rather than hiding tasks that do not meet the filter criteria, you can highlight those that do in blue. Click the Highlight button instead of the Apply button in the More Filters dialog box.

To conclude this exercise, you will remove the filtering.

20 On the Project menu, point to Filtered For: Uncompleted Shoots, and then click All Tasks.

Microsoft Project removes the filter. As always, displaying or removing a filter has no effect on the original data.

Tip

All filters are also available to you through the Filter button on the Formatting toolbar. The name of the active filter appears in this button; click the arrow next to the filter name to see other filters. If no filter is applied to the current view, *All Tasks* or *All Resources* appears on the button, depending on the type of view currently displayed.

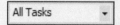

To learn more about the filters available in Microsoft Project, type **Available filters** into the Ask A Question box.

Customizing Tables

As you might already know, a table is a spreadsheet-like presentation of project data, organized into vertical columns and horizontal rows. Each column represents one of the many fields in Microsoft Project, and each row represents a single task or resource (or in usage views, an assignment). The intersection of a column and a row can be called a cell (if you're oriented toward spreadsheets) or a field (if you think in database terms).

Microsoft Project includes several tables that can be applied in views. You've already used some of these tables, such as the Entry table and the Summary table. Chances are that these tables will contain the fields you want most of the time. However, you can modify any predefined table, or you can create your own table with just the data you want.

In this exercise, you create a table to display the information found on a shooting schedule, a common format for presenting schedule information in film projects:

1 On the View menu, click More Views.

The More Views dialog box appears.

2 Click Task Sheet, and then click the Apply button.

Microsoft Project displays the Task Sheet view.

3 On the View menu, point to Table: Entry, and then click More Tables.

The More Tables dialog box appears. In it, you can see all the available predefined tables for tasks (when in a task view) and resources (when in a resource view).

4 Make sure that Task is the active option, and then in the list of tables, make sure that Entry is selected.

5 Click the Copy button.

The Table Definition In dialog box appears.

6 In the Name box, type **Shooting Schedule Table**.

Next you will remove several fields, add others, and then put the remaining fields in the order you want.

7 In the Field Name column, click each of the following field names, and then click the Delete Row button after clicking each field name:

Indicators

Duration

Finish

Predecessors

Resource Names

After you've deleted these fields, your screen should look similar to the illustration on the following page:

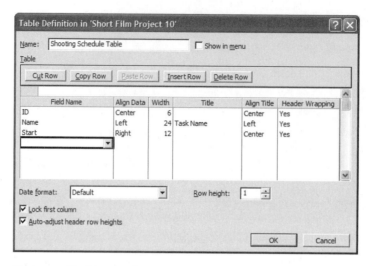

Next you will add some fields to this table definition.

8 In the Field Name column, click the down arrow in the next empty cell below Start, and then click Cast (Text9) in the drop-down list.

9 In the Align Data column in the same row, click Left.

As soon as you click in the Align Data column, Microsoft Project completes row entries for the Cast field name by adding data to the Width and Align Title columns.

10 In the Width column, type or click **25**.

11 In the Field Name column in the next empty row below Cast, click Location (Text10) in the drop-down list.

12 In the Align Data column, click Left.

13 In the Width column, type or click **15**.

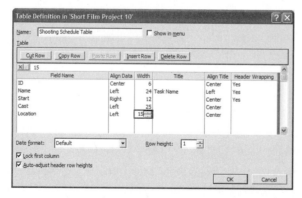

The two customized text fields Cast (Text9) and Location (Text10) contain the character names and film locations for the shooting tasks. These were previously customized in the project plan.

The remaining work to complete this table definition is to reorder the fields to match the order commonly found on a shooting schedule.

14 In the Field Name column, click Start, and then click the Cut Row button.

15 In the Field Name column, click Name, and then click the Paste Row button.

16 In the Date Format box, click 1/28/02 12:33PM.

Your screen should look similar to the following illustration:

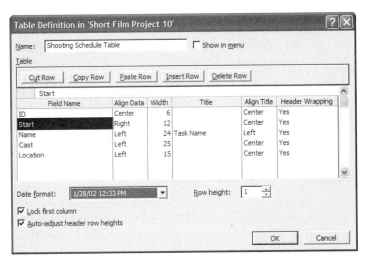

This matches the order in which information is commonly listed on a film-shooting schedule.

17 Click OK to close the Table Definition In dialog box.

The new table appears in the More Tables dialog box.

18 Click the Apply button.

Microsoft Project applies the new table to the Task Sheet view. If the Start column displays pound signs (###), double-click the column heading's right edge to widen it.

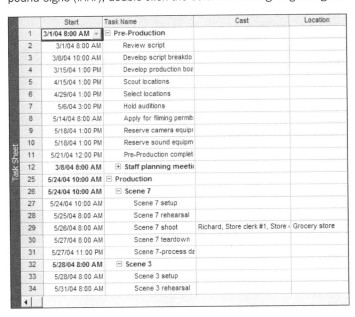

In the next section, you will combine the custom filter with this custom table to create a shooting schedule view for the film project.

Tip

To learn more about how to change the way information in a project plan is organized and displayed, type **Display the details you want using tables, filters, grouping, or sorting** into the Ask A Question box.

To learn more about the tables available in Microsoft Project, type **Available tables** into the Ask A Question box.

Customizing Views

Nearly all work you perform in Microsoft Project occurs in a *view*. A view might contain elements such as tables, groups, and filters. You can combine these with other elements (such as a timescaled grid in a usage view) or with graphic elements (such as the graphic representation of tasks in the chart portion of the Gantt Chart view).

Microsoft Project includes dozens of views that organize information for specific purposes. You might find that you need to see your project information in some way not available in the predefined views. Should this happen, you can edit an existing view or create your own view.

In this exercise, you create a film shooting schedule view that combines the custom filter and custom table you created in the previous sections. The view you create will more closely match a standard format used in the film industry:

1 On the View menu, click More Views.

The More Views dialog box appears. In it, you can see all the predefined views available to you.

2 Click the New button.

The Define New View dialog box appears. Most views occupy a single pane, but a view can consist of two separate panes.

3 Make sure Single View is selected, and then click OK.

The View Definition In dialog box appears.

4 In the Name box, type **Shooting Schedule View**.

5 In the Screen box, click Task Sheet in the drop-down list.

6 In the Table box, click Shooting Schedule Table in the drop-down list.

The specific tables listed in the drop-down list depend on the type of view you selected in step 5: task-related tables or resource-related tables.

7 In the Group box, click No Group in the drop-down list.

The specific groups listed in the drop-down list depend on the type of view you selected in step 5.

8 In the Filter box, click Uncompleted Shoots in the drop-down list.

The specific filters listed in the drop-down list depend on the type of view you selected in step 5.

9 Select the Show In Menu check box.

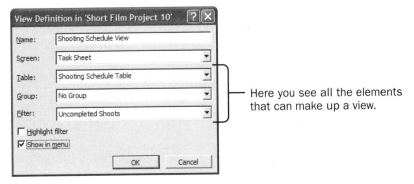

Here you see all the elements that can make up a view.

10 Click OK to close the View Definition dialog box.

The new view appears in the More Views dialog box.

11 Click the Apply button.

Microsoft Project applies the new view. Your screen should look similar to the following illustration:

The custom view is arranged like a shooting schedule, a standard format in the film industry.

	Start	Task Name	Cast	Location
29	5/26/04 8:00 AM	Scene 7 shoot	Richard, Store clerk #1, Store	Grocery store
35	6/1/04 8:00 AM	Scene 3 shoot	Man on street, Richard	Street corner
41	6/9/04 8:00 AM	Scene 1 shoot	Garth, Man on street, Store cle	Street corner
47	6/14/04 5:00 PM	Scene 2 shoot	Garth, Shelly	Shelly's living roor
53	6/22/04 8:00 AM	Scene 5 shoot	Man on street, Garth, Old man,	Street corner
59	7/6/04 8:00 AM	Scene 6 shoot	Garth, Store Clerk #1, Shelly, C	Grocery store
65	7/20/04 8:00 AM	Scene 8 shoot	Garth, Store clerk #1, Man on s	Street corner
71	7/27/04 8:00 AM	Scene 4 shoot	Shelly, Richard	Elevator

Now only uncompleted shoots are displayed, and the fields appear in an order consistent with a standard shooting schedule for a film project. Also, Microsoft Project added the Shooting Schedule view to the View menu. This view will be saved with this Microsoft Project plan, and you can use it whenever you want.

To conclude this exercise, you will adjust row height and column width to display some information that is not currently visible.

12 While holding down the Ctrl key, click the task ID numbers for Tasks 29, 41, 53, 59, and 65.

In each of these selected rows, the names in the Cast column exceed the width of the column.

13 Drag the bottom edge of the task ID for Task 29 down approximately one row.

Microsoft Project resizes the selected rows.

14 Double-click the right edge of the Location column heading.

Microsoft Project resizes the column width to accommodate the widest value in the column. Your screen should look similar to the following illustration:

To resize a column's width, drag the right edge of the column label.

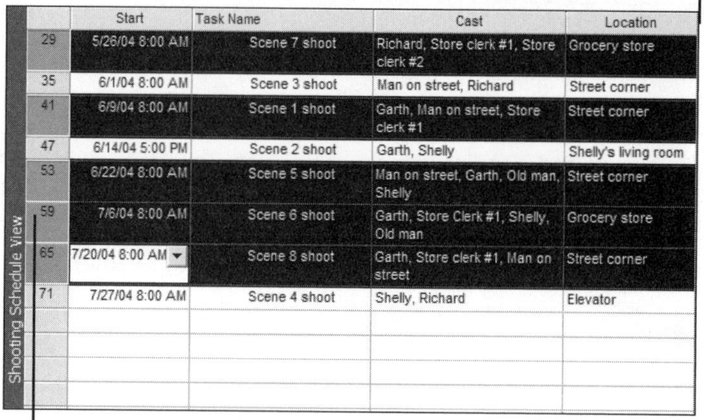

	Start	Task Name	Cast	Location
29	5/26/04 8:00 AM	Scene 7 shoot	Richard, Store clerk #1, Store clerk #2	Grocery store
35	6/1/04 8:00 AM	Scene 3 shoot	Man on street, Richard	Street corner
41	6/9/04 8:00 AM	Scene 1 shoot	Garth, Man on street, Store clerk #1	Street corner
47	6/14/04 5:00 PM	Scene 2 shoot	Garth, Shelly	Shelly's living room
53	6/22/04 8:00 AM	Scene 5 shoot	Man on street, Garth, Old man, Shelly	Street corner
59	7/6/04 8:00 AM	Scene 6 shoot	Garth, Store Clerk #1, Shelly, Old man	Grocery store
65	7/20/04 8:00 AM ▼	Scene 8 shoot	Garth, Store clerk #1, Man on street	Street corner
71	7/27/04 8:00 AM	Scene 4 shoot	Shelly, Richard	Elevator

To resize a row's height, drag the bottom edge of the task ID. If you previously selected multiple rows, all selected rows are also resized.

Tip

To learn more about working with views and the views available in Microsoft Project, type **All about views or Available views** into the Ask A Question box.

Chapter Wrap-Up

This chapter covered how to use sorting, filtering, grouping, and other formatting features to change the way task and resource information appears, without changing the underlying data.

If you are going on to other chapters:

Save

1   On the Standard toolbar, click the Save button to save changes made to Short Film Project 10.

2   On the File menu, click Close to close the project plan.

If you aren't continuing to other chapters:

1   On the Standard toolbar, click the Save button to save changes made to Short Film Project 10.

2   To quit Microsoft Project for now, on the File menu, click Exit.

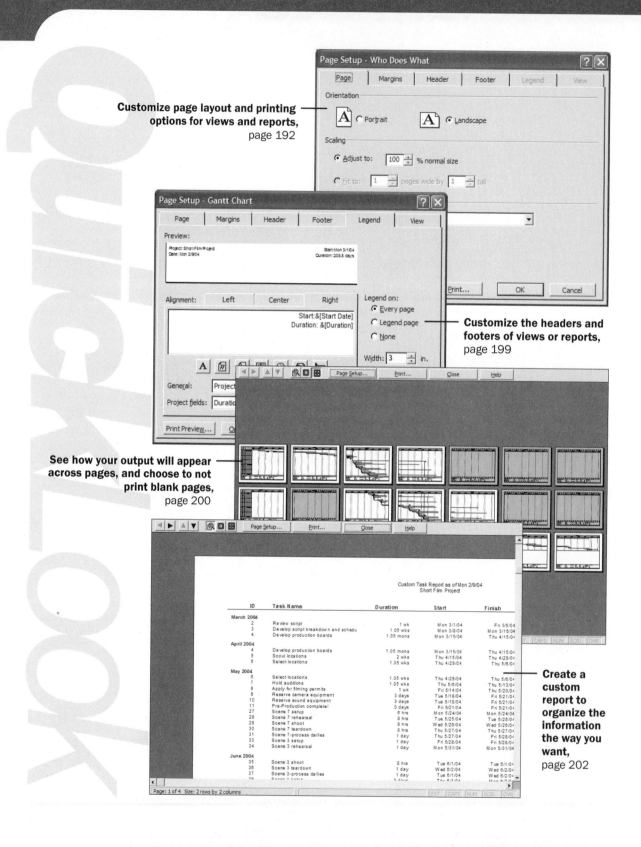

Customize page layout and printing
options for views and reports,
page 192

Page Setup - Who Does What

Page | Margins | Header | Footer | Legend | View

Orientation
○ Portrait   ● Landscape

Scaling
● Adjust to: 100 ÷ % normal size
○ Fit to: 1 ÷ pages wide by 1 ÷ tall

Print... | OK | Cancel

Page Setup - Gantt Chart

Page | Margins | Header | Footer | Legend | View

Preview:
Project: Short Film Project   Start: Mon 3/1/04
Date: Mon 2/9/04   Duration: 208.5 days

Alignment: Left | Center | Right

Start: &[Start Date]
Duration: &[Duration]

Legend on:
● Every page
○ Legend page
○ None

Width: 3 ÷ in.

General: Project
Project fields: Duratic

Print Preview... | O

Customize the headers and
footers of views or reports,
page 199

Page Setup... | Print... | Close | Help

See how your output will appear
across pages, and choose to not
print blank pages,
page 200

Page Setup... | Print... | Close | Help

Custom Task Report as of Mon 2/9/04
Short Film Project

ID	Task Name	Duration	Start	Finish
March 2004				
2	Review script	1 wk	Mon 3/1/04	Fri 3/5/04
3	Develop script breakdown and schedu	1.05 wks	Mon 3/8/04	Mon 3/15/04
4	Develop production boards	1.05 mons	Mon 3/15/04	Thu 4/15/04
April 2004				
4	Develop production boards	1.05 mons	Mon 3/15/04	Thu 4/15/04
5	Scout locations	2 wks	Thu 4/15/04	Thu 4/29/04
6	Select locations	1.05 wks	Thu 4/29/04	Thu 5/6/04
May 2004				
6	Select locations	1.05 wks	Thu 4/29/04	Thu 5/6/04
7	Hold auditions	1.05 wks	Thu 5/6/04	Thu 5/13/04
8	Apply for filming permits	1 wk	Fri 5/14/04	Thu 5/20/04
9	Reserve camera equipment	3 days	Tue 5/18/04	Fri 5/21/04
10	Reserve sound equipment	3 days	Tue 5/18/04	Fri 5/21/04
11	Pre-Production complete!	0 days	Fri 5/21/04	Fri 5/21/04
27	Scene 7 setup	6 hrs	Mon 5/24/04	Mon 5/24/04
28	Scene 7 rehearsal	8 hrs	Tue 5/25/04	Tue 5/25/04
29	Scene 7 shoot	8 hrs	Wed 5/26/04	Wed 5/26/04
30	Scene 7 teardown	8 hrs	Thu 5/27/04	Thu 5/27/04
31	Scene 7-process dailies	1 day	Thu 5/27/04	Fri 5/28/04
33	Scene 3 setup	1 day	Fri 5/28/04	Fri 5/28/04
34	Scene 3 rehearsal	1 day	Mon 5/31/04	
June 2004				
35	Scene 3 shoot	8 hrs	Tue 6/1/04	Tue 6/1/04
36	Scene 3 teardown	1 day	Wed 6/2/04	Wed 6/2/04
37	Scene 3-process dailies	1 day	Tue 6/1/04	Wed 6/2/04

Create a
custom
report to
organize the
information
the way you
want,
page 202

Page: 1 of 4 Size: 2 rows by 2 columns

Chapter 11
Printing Project Information

After completing this chapter, you will be able to:

✔ **Change page setup options for views and reports.**

✔ **Print a view.**

✔ **Print a report.**

In this chapter, you work with some of the many views and reports in Microsoft Project to print your project plan. One of the most important tasks of any project manager is communicating project information to *stakeholders*, and that often means printing. To communicate project details in printed form, you can use the predefined views and reports as they are or customize them to better suit your needs.

Short Film
Project 11a

This chapter uses the practice file Short Film Project 11a. For details about installing the practice files, see "Using the Book's CD-ROM" at the beginning of this book.

Printing Your Project Plan

Printing information from a project plan to share with stakeholders is a common activity for most project managers. In Microsoft Project, printing focuses on *views* and *reports*.

You've probably already seen several views and a few reports, such as the Gantt Chart view and the Project Summary report. Both views and reports organize details of a project plan into specific formats for specific purposes. In a view you can enter, read, edit, and print information, while in a report you can only print information. Think of views as your general working environment in Microsoft Project, and think of reports as specific formats for printing.

You can customize the way you print both views and reports; however, your options for printing reports are not as broad. When printing, you have many of the same options with both views and reports, as well as some specific options unique to views or reports. To customize printing for a view or report, you use the Page Setup and Print dialog boxes.

First let's look at the Page Setup dialog box. To see the Page Setup dialog box for views, click Page Setup on the File menu. To see this dialog box for reports, first display a report in the Print Preview window, and then click the Page Setup button.

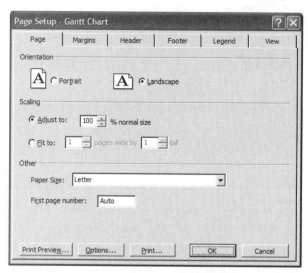

In the Page Setup dialog box, the Page and Margins tabs are available for both views and reports. However, the specific options you choose in the Page Setup dialog box for any view or report affect only that view or report; the settings are not shared between views or reports.

Some page setup options are unique to views or reports, and a few options are available to only specific views or reports. Here is a summary of unique page setup options:

■ You can use options on the Header, Footer, and View tabs in the Page Setup dialog box for all views. The View tab in particular includes options that vary depending on which view is currently active. For views that include a legend (such as the Gantt Chart, Network Diagram, and Calendar views), the Legend tab is also available.

■ You can use options on the Header and Footer tabs in most reports, but the View and Legend tabs are not available for any reports.

Next let's look at the Print dialog box. To see the Print dialog box for views, click Print on the File menu. To see this dialog box for reports, first display the report in the Print Preview window, and then click the Print button.

Project Management Focus:
Communicating with Stakeholders

Besides knowing how to print, it's important to know what to print. Most project managers find that they have different stakeholders with different information needs. For example, what the project's financial supporters need to see at the planning stage of a project might be quite different from what the project's resources need to see after work has begun. The built-in views and reports in Microsoft Project should cover nearly all stakeholder communication needs (at least when printing is the solution). Here is a summary of which views and reports best communicate project plan details to various stakeholders.

If this stakeholder	Is most interested in	Provide this printed view	Or this printed report
Project sponsor or client	Overall project duration information	Gantt Chart with project summary task displayed, filtered for summary tasks	Project Summary
	Overall project cost information	Task Sheet with project summary task displayed and Cost table applied	Budget or other reports in the Cost category
	Schedule status after work has begun	Tracking Gantt with Tracking table applied	Project Summary, Completed Tasks, or Tasks Starting Soon
Resources assigned to tasks in the project	The tasks to which they are assigned	Calendar or Resource Usage view, filtered for the specific resource	To-Do List, Who Does What, or Who Does What When
Resource managers in your organization	The scope of work their resources have in the project	Resource Sheet, Resource Graph, or Resource Usage	Resource Usage, Who Does What, or other reports in the Assignments category
Other project managers in your organization	Schedule logic, critical path, and task relationships	Network Diagram, Detail Gantt, or Tracking Gantt	Critical Tasks

This table lists just some of the many built-in views and reports in Microsoft Project. If you have a specific information need, explore all the views and reports before you attempt to build your own. Chances are, Microsoft Project has a view or report that will meet your needs or serve as a starting point for further customization.

Tip

Depending on the printer or plotter to which you are printing, you might also have additional options unique to that device. To set these options, click the Properties button for your selected printer in the Print dialog box.

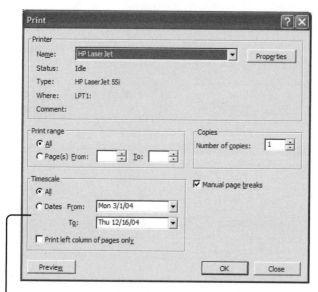

Depending on the active view or report, the Timescale options might not be available.

In the Print dialog box, most options available for views are also available for reports. For example, some views and some reports support timescale options in the Print dialog box, but others do not. The Gantt Chart view and the Who Does What When report, for example, both include a timescale. In the Print dialog boxes for both, you can print specific ranges from the timescale if you wish.

Tip

To learn more about which views or reports best convey specific project information, type **All about printing and reporting** into the Ask A Question box in the upper right corner of the Microsoft Project window.

In this exercise, you compare the page setup options of views and reports:

1 If Microsoft Project is not already open, start it now.

Open

2 On the Standard toolbar, click the Open button.

The Open dialog box appears.

3 Navigate to the Chapter 11 Printing folder, and double-click the Short Film Project 11a file.

4 On the File menu, click Save As.

The Save As dialog box appears.

5 In the File Name box, type **Short Film Project 11**, and then click the Save button.

Next you will look at page setup options.

6 On the File menu, click Page Setup.

The Page Setup dialog box appears. Note the title of the dialog box: *Page Setup – Gantt Chart*. Because the Page Setup dialog box changes depending on the active view, Microsoft Project includes the view name in the dialog box title bar.

7 Click the View tab.

Your screen should look similar to the following illustration:

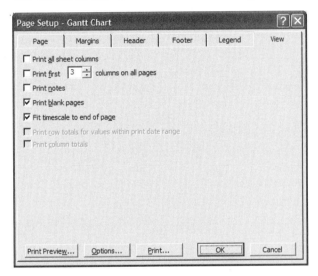

Because the Gantt Chart view includes a table, the View tab includes some options relating to columns. The Gantt chart also includes a timescale, so you also see an option relating to the timescale.

8 Click Cancel.

The Page Setup dialog box closes. Next you'll switch to another view and see how the page setup options differ.

9 On the View menu, click Calendar.

The Calendar view appears. This view lacks both the table and chart elements you saw in the Gantt Chart view, and instead represents tasks in a month-at-a-glance arrangement.

10 On the File menu, click Page Setup.

The Page Setup dialog box appears. Note again the title of the dialog box: *Page Setup – Calendar*.

11 Click the View tab if it is not already active.

Your screen should look similar to the following illustration:

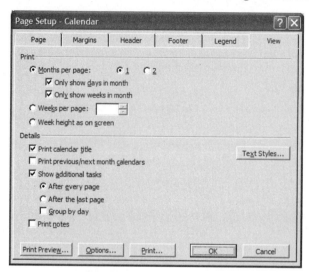

The options available for the Calendar view are quite different from those of the Gantt Chart view. Here you have several options for controlling how details are organized on the Calendar view when printed.

The Print Notes check box, however, is available for both the Gantt Chart and Calendar views.

12 Click Cancel.

The Page Setup dialog box closes.

To conclude this exercise, you will see the page setup options for a report.

13 On the View menu, click Reports.

The Reports dialog box appears.

14 Click Custom, and then click the Select button.

Tip

You can also double-click the Custom button.

The Custom Reports dialog box appears.

15 In the Custom Reports box, click Who Does What, and then click the Setup button.

The Page Setup dialog box appears. Note again the title of the dialog box: *Page Setup – Who Does What*. Your screen should look similar to the following illustration:

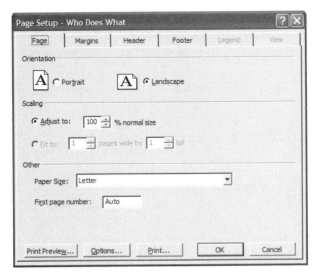

Most of the tabs you've seen for views are also available for reports, but the Legend and View tabs are not.

16 Click Cancel to close the Page Setup dialog box, and click Cancel again to close the Custom Reports dialog box.

17 Click the Close button to close the Reports dialog box.

18 On the View menu, click Gantt Chart.

Tip

All the views available in Microsoft Project are listed in the More Views dialog box. (On the View menu, click More Views.) Likewise, all available reports are listed in the Custom Reports dialog box. (On the View menu, click Reports, click Custom, and then click Select.) Another handy way to display a view or report is through the Project Guide. (On the Project Guide toolbar, click Report, and then click the Select A View Or Report link.)

Printing Views

Printing a view enables you to get on paper just about anything you see on your screen. Any customization you apply to a view, such as applying different *tables* or *groups*, will be printed as well. With a few exceptions, you can print any view you see in Microsoft Project. Here are the exceptions:

■ You cannot print form views, such as the Task Form and the Relationship Diagram.

■ If you have two views displayed in a combination view (one view in the top pane and the other view in the bottom pane), only the view in the active pane will be printed.

Tip

To see descriptions of all of the views available in Microsoft Project, type **Available views** into the Ask A Question box in the upper right corner of the Microsoft Project window.

Keep in mind that the part of your project plan that you see on your screen at one time might be a relatively small portion of the full project, which could require a large number of pages to print. For example, the Gantt Chart view of a six-month project with 85 tasks can require 14 or more letter-size pages to print in its entirety. Printing Gantt Chart or Network Diagram views can use quite a bit of paper; in fact, some heavy-duty Microsoft Project users make poster-size printouts of their project plans using plotters.

Whether you have a printer or a plotter, it's a good idea to preview any views you intend to print. By using the Page Setup dialog box in conjunction with the Print Preview window, you can control many aspects of the view to be printed. For example, you can control the number of pages on which the view will be printed, apply headers and footers, and determine content that appears in the legend of the Gantt Chart and some other views.

Tip

When printing Gantt Chart views and other views that include a timescale, adjusting the time-scale before printing affects the number of pages required. To adjust the timescale so it shows the largest time span in the smallest number of pages, on the View menu, click Zoom; then in the Zoom dialog box, click Entire Project.

To further reduce the number of pages required, you can collapse a project plan's outline to summary tasks. Click the Show button on the Formatting toolbar, and then click the outline level you want. A collapsed view showing only summary tasks and milestones might be informative enough for people who want just an overall sense of the project plan. If you're interested in a specific time period, you can print just that portion of the timescale. Or you might apply a filter to display only the information that's of greatest interest to a particular audience: late or overbudget tasks, for example.

In this exercise, you preview the Gantt Chart view and change options in the Page Setup dialog box:

1   On the File menu, click Print Preview.

Microsoft Project displays the Gantt Chart view in the Print Preview window. Your screen should look similar to the following illustration:

The Print Preview toolbar contains buttons for navigating between pages, zooming in or out, setting Page Setup options, printing, and exiting Print Preview.

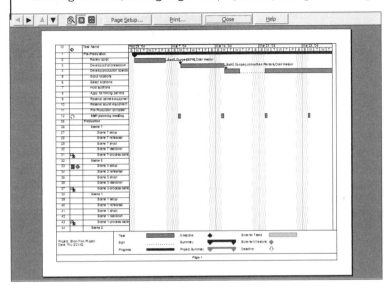

The Print Preview window has several options to explore. Let's start with the page navigation buttons.

Page Right

2 On the Print Preview toolbar, click the Page Right button several times to display different pages.

Page Down

3 Click the Page Down button once.

To get a broader view of the output, you'll switch to a multi-page view.

Multiple Pages

4 Click the Multiple Pages button.

The entire Gantt Chart view appears in the Print Preview window. Your screen should look similar to the illustration on the following page.

The multiple page Print Preview shows you the entire printed output laid out on separate sheets (the paper size is determined by your printer settings).

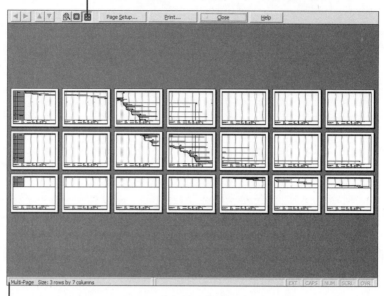

This status bar message refers to rows and columns of printed sheets as they are laid out in the Print Preview window.

If you have a plotter selected as your default printer, or you have a different page size selected for your default printer, what you see in the Print Preview window will differ from what's shown here.

The status bar text reads *3 rows by 7 columns*. We refer to rows and columns on the Gantt Chart and in other views; in the Print Preview window, however, these terms denote rows and columns of pages—in this case, three rows of pages by seven columns of pages, for a total of 21 pages. The status bar text can help you quickly determine the size (in pages) your printed view will be.

Next you'll change some options in the Page Setup dialog box.

One Page

5 On the Print Preview toolbar, click the One Page button.

Microsoft Project displays the first page of the Gantt chart.

6 Click the Page Setup button.

Page Setup...

The Page Setup dialog box appears. This is the same dialog box you'd see if you clicked Page Setup on the File menu. The first change we'll make to the printed Gantt char is to add the company name to the header that is printed on every page.

7 Click the Header tab.

8 On the Header tab are Alignment tabs. Make sure that Center is selected.

9 In the General box, click Company Name in the drop-down list, and then click the Add button.

Microsoft Project inserts the &[Company] code into the header and displays a preview in the Preview window of the Page Setup dialog box. The company name comes from the Properties dialog box. Next you'll change the content of the Gantt Chart view's legend.

10 Click the Legend tab.

11 On the Legend tab are Alignment tabs. Click the Right tab.

With the current settings, Microsoft Project will print the project title and the current date on the left side of the legend. You will also print the project start date and duration on the right side of the legend.

12 Click the Right Alignment box, and type **Start:**, followed by a space.

13 In the General box, click Project Start Date in the drop-down list, and then click the Add button.

Microsoft Project adds the label and code for the project start date to the legend.

14 Press the Enter key to add a second line to the legend, and then type **Duration:**, followed by a space.

15 In the Project Fields box, click Duration in the drop-down list, and then click the Add button.

Microsoft Project adds the label and code for project duration to the legend.

16 In the Width box, type or click **3**.

This increases the width of the box on the left side of the legend.

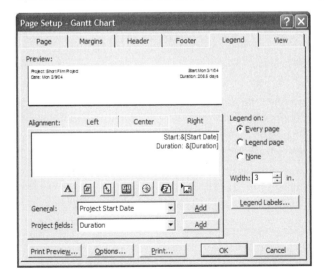

17 Click OK to close the Page Setup dialog box.

Microsoft Project applies the changes you specified to the legend. To get a closer look, zoom in on the legend.

18 In the Print Preview window, click the lower left corner of the page with the magnifying-glass pointer.

Microsoft Project zooms in to show the page at a legible resolution. Your screen should look similar to the following illustration:

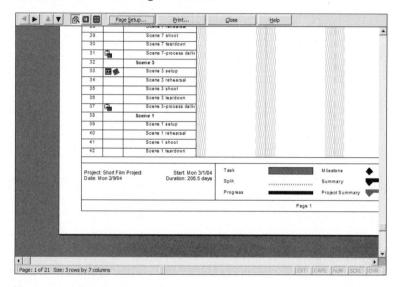

You can see the data you added to the legend, which will be printed on every page of the printed output.

To conclude this exercise, you will choose not to print pages that do not include any Gantt bars.

19 Click the Multiple Pages button again.

Note that several of the pages in the lower left and upper right range of the Gantt Chart view do not contain any Gantt bars. If you intend to print a Gantt Chart view and stitch the pages together, these pages don't add any information, so you don't need to print them.

20 Click the Page Setup button.

21 In the Page Setup dialog box, click the View tab.

22 Clear the Print Blank Pages box, and then click OK.

Your screen should look similar to the following illustration:

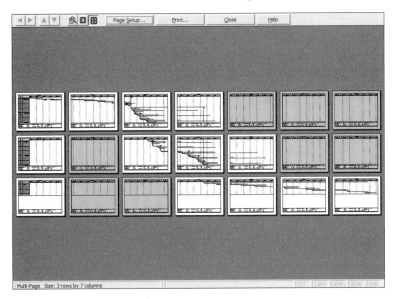

In the Print Preview window, the blank pages are formatted with a gray pattern, indicating that they will not be printed. The two pages in the lower left corner will be printed, however, because they contain the table portion of the Gantt Chart view.

23 On the Print Preview toolbar, click the Close button.

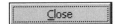

The Print Preview window closes, and the Gantt Chart view appears. Although you did not print, your changes to the header and the legend will be saved when you save the project file.

Tip

You can print the project plan now if you wish; however, previewing the project plan is adequate for the purposes of the lesson. When printing in Microsoft Project, you have additional options in the Print dialog box, which you can open by clicking the Print command on the File menu. For example, you can choose to print a specific date range of a timescaled view, such as the Gantt Chart view, or you can print a specific page range.

Printing Reports

Reports are predefined formats intended for printing Microsoft Project data. Unlike views, which you can either print or work with onscreen, reports are designed only for printing. You don't enter data directly into a report. Microsoft Project includes several predefined reports you can edit to get the information you want.

Although reports are distinct from views, some settings you specify for a view might affect some reports. For example:

- If subtasks are collapsed or hidden under summary tasks in a view, reports that include task lists will show only the summary tasks and not the subtasks.

- In usage views, if assignments are collapsed or hidden under tasks or resources, the usage reports (Task Usage or Resource Usage) likewise hide assignment details.

In this exercise, you see a report in the Print Preview window, and then you edit its definition (that is, the set of elements that make up the report) to include additional information.

1 On the View menu, click Reports.

The Reports dialog box appears, showing the broad categories of reports available in Microsoft Project.

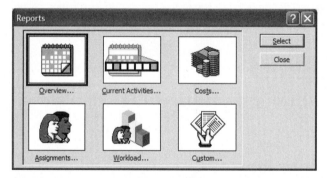

2 Click Custom, and then click the Select button.

The Custom Reports dialog box appears, listing all predefined reports in Microsoft Project and any custom reports that have been added.

3   In the Reports box, click Task, and then click the Preview button.

Microsoft Project displays the Task report in the Print Preview window. Your screen should look similar to the following illustration:

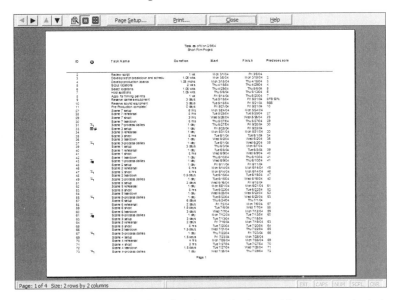

This report is a complete list of project tasks (except for summary tasks), similar to what you'd see in the Entry table of the Gantt Chart view. You'd like to see this data presented in a different way, so you'll edit this report.

4   On the Print Preview toolbar, click the Close button.

The Print Preview window closes, and the Custom Reports dialog box reappears. Next you'll create a copy of a built-in report and modify the copy.

5   In the Reports box, ensure that Task is still selected, and then click the Copy button.

The Task Report dialog box appears.

6   In the Name box, click the displayed text, and then type **Custom Task Report**.

7   In the Period box, click Months in the drop-down list.

Choosing Months here groups tasks by the month in which they occur. Because the report now includes a time period element, the Timescale options in the Print dialog box become available, enabling you to print data within a specific date range if you want.

8 In the Table box, click Summary in the drop-down list.

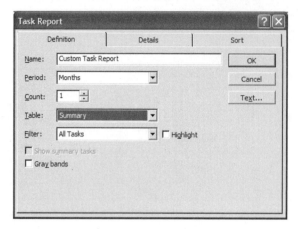

Tip

The tables listed in the Task Report dialog box are the same as those you can apply to any view that shows tasks in a table. In fact, if you completed Chapter 10, "Organizing and Formatting Project Details," the Shooting Schedule table you created there appears in the list here. When editing a report format, you can apply predefined or custom tables and filters, choose additional details to include in the report, and apply a sort order to the information—all in the dialog box for the report you're editing.

9 Click OK to close the Task Report dialog box.

10 In the Custom Reports dialog box, make sure that Custom Task Report is selected in the Reports box, and then click the Preview button.

Microsoft Project applies the custom report settings you chose to the report, and the report appears in the Print Preview window. Next you will zoom in to see the report in more detail.

11 In the Print Preview window, click the upper left corner of the page with the magnifying-glass pointer.

Your screen should look similar to the following illustration:

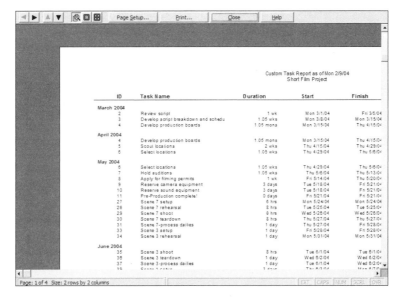

This custom report shows the fields displayed on the Summary Task table but divides the tasks by month.

12 On the Print Preview toolbar, click the Close button.

13 In the Custom Reports dialog box, click the Close button.

14 Click the Close button again to close the Reports dialog box.

The Gantt Chart view reappears.

Chapter Wrap-Up

This chapter covered how to customize the printing options for views and reports.

If you are going on to other chapters:

Save

1 On the Standard toolbar, click the Save button to save changes made to Short Film Project 11.

2 On the File menu, click Close to close the project plan.

If you aren't continuing to other chapters:

1 On the Standard toolbar, click the Save button to save changes made to Short Film Project 11.

2 To quit Microsoft Project for now, on the File menu, click Exit.

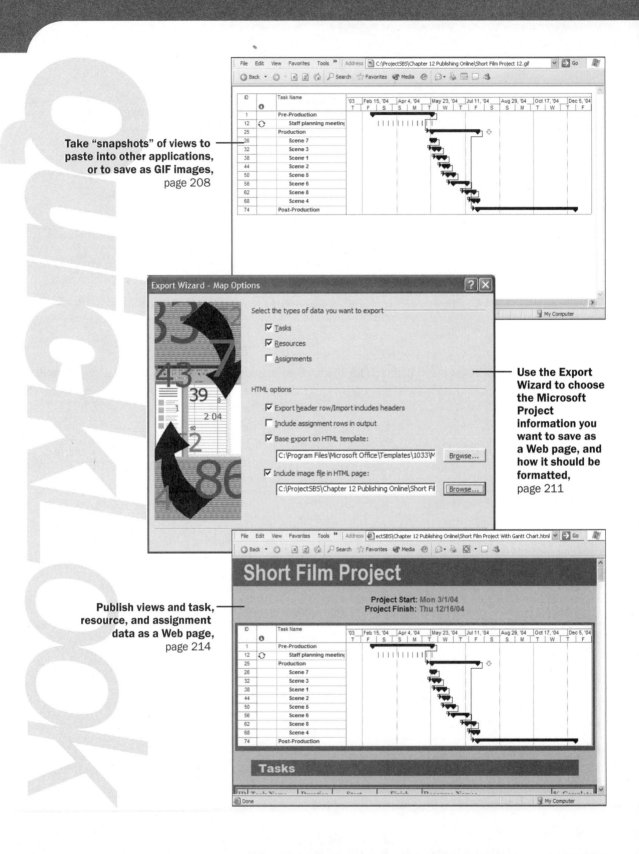

Take "snapshots" of views to paste into other applications, or to save as GIF images, page 208

Use the Export Wizard to choose the Microsoft Project information you want to save as a Web page, and how it should be formatted, page 211

Publish views and task, resource, and assignment data as a Web page, page 214

Chapter 12
Publishing Project Information Online

After completing this chapter, you will be able to:

✔ Take a "snapshot" of a Gantt Chart view as a GIF image.

✔ Publish Microsoft Project information in HTML format.

✔ Control how Microsoft Project information is saved in HTML format by customizing a map.

Printing Microsoft Project information is a common way to share project details with others, but it has its limitations. Project details can be out of date almost as soon as you commit them to paper. You're also limited to duplicating and distributing copies of the printed output, which has some overhead. Publishing project information online, on the other hand, enables you to more easily update published project details and share them with a wide audience of online viewers.

In this chapter, you work with the Web publishing features of Microsoft Project. These features include the Copy Picture feature, which enables you to take a "snapshot" of the active view and save it as a GIF image. You also export Microsoft Project information to HTML format and control how the exported information appears. In many organizations, publishing in HTML format on an intranet is the primary means by which project details are communicated to stakeholders.

Short Film
Project 12a

This chapter uses the practice file Short Film Project 12a. For details about installing the practice files, see "Using the Book's CD-ROM" at the beginning of this book.

Important

This chapter describes sharing Microsoft Project information online by saving HTML or GIF format files. However, both Microsoft Project Standard and Professional editions can be used with Microsoft Project Server to provide much more sophisticated ways of not only publishing project information online, but collecting information (such as actual work) from resources and other stakeholders as well. To learn more about the workgroup and enterprise collaboration tools available with Microsoft Project Server, see Appendix A, "Introducing Microsoft Project Server."

Copying Project Information as a GIF Image

When communicating project details to resources, managers, and other stakeholders, chances are you'll need to copy information from Microsoft Project and paste it into other programs and formats. Microsoft Project supports the standard copy-and-paste functionality of most Windows programs, and it has an additional feature called ***Copy Picture*** that takes "snapshots" of a view. You can take these snapshots by choosing the Copy Picture command on the Edit menu or clicking the Copy Picture button on the Standard toolbar.

Copy Picture

With the Copy Picture feature, you have the following options when taking snapshots of the active view:

■ Copy the entire view visible on the screen or selected rows of a table in a view.

■ Copy a range of time that you specify or display on the screen.

Either way, you can save the snapshot to a Graphics Interchange Format (GIF) file in a location you specify. After you save the image as a GIF file, you can use it in any of the many programs that support the GIF format. You can also combine it with HTML content on a Web page, as you'll do later in this chapter. You can also use the Copy Picture feature to copy an image onto the Windows Clipboard and later paste it into another program for onscreen viewing (Microsoft PowerPoint, for example) or for printing (Microsoft Word, for example).

Tip

If you want to copy portions of a table (to paste a task list into a spreadsheet, for example) rather than copying a graphic image, use the Copy Cell command on the Edit menu.

In this exercise, you change what appears in the Gantt Chart view and then use the Copy Picture feature to save a snapshot of this view as a GIF file. To begin, you filter the Gantt chart to show only summary tasks:

1 If Microsoft Project is not already open, start it now.

Open

2 On the Standard toolbar, click the Open button.

The Open dialog box appears.

3 Navigate to the Chapter 12 Publishing Online folder, and double-click the Short Film Project 12a file.

4 On the File menu, click Save As.

The Save As dialog box appears.

5 In the File Name box, type **Short Film Project 12**, and then click the Save button.

6 On the Project menu, point to Filtered For: All Tasks, and then click Summary Tasks.

Microsoft Project filters the Gantt chart to display only summary tasks. Next you'll zoom out on the *timescale* to see the entire project.

7 On the View menu, click Zoom.

The Zoom dialog box appears.

8 Click Entire Project, and then click OK.

Microsoft Project adjusts the timescale in the Gantt Chart view to display the entire project's duration in the window. Your screen should look similar to the following illustration:

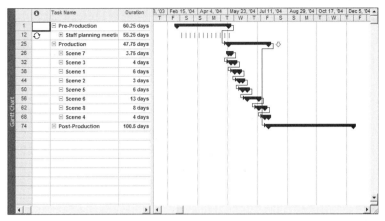

Copy Picture

9 On the Standard toolbar, click the Copy Picture button.

The Copy Picture dialog box appears.

Tip

You can also click Copy Picture on the Edit menu.

10 Under Render Image, click To GIF Image File.

Microsoft Project prompts you to save the file in the same location as the practice file and with the same name, except with a .gif extension. Your screen should look similar to the following illustration:

When taking a snapshot of a view, select how you want the image rendered here: the first two options copy the image to the Windows Clipboard, whereas the third enables you to save the image as a GIF file.

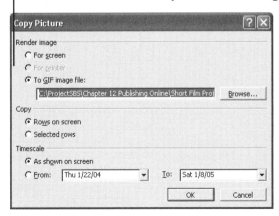

11 Click OK to close the Copy Picture dialog box.

The GIF image is saved.

You can open your browser or a graphics program to view the GIF image you just saved, but you can also view it from within Microsoft Project.

12 On the View menu, point to Toolbars, and then click Web.

The Web toolbar appears.

13 On the Web toolbar, click the Go button, and then click Open Hyperlink in the drop-down list.

The Open Internet Address dialog box appears.

14 Click the Browse button.

The Browse dialog box appears.

15 In the Files Of Type box, click GIF Files in the drop-down list.

16 Locate the GIF image named *Short Film Project 12* in your Chapter 12 Publishing Online folder.

17 Click the GIF image, and then click the Open button.

18 In the Open Internet Address dialog box, click OK.

Microsoft Project opens the GIF image. If you have Microsoft Internet Explorer as your default program for viewing GIF files, your screen should look similar to the following illustration:

The Gantt Chart view snapshot is saved to a GIF image, which you can view in a browser or graphics editing program.

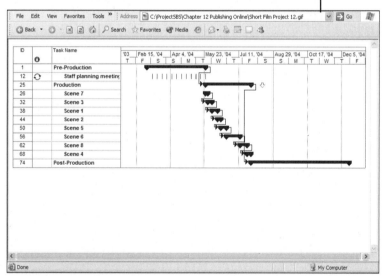

As noted earlier, what you see is a graphic image of the Gantt Chart view. The GIF image displays the view you displayed in Microsoft Project, almost exactly as you had it set up.

19 Close the program you used to view the GIF file, and then return to Microsoft Project.

Tip

The Copy Picture feature is unavailable when a form view, such as the Task Form or Relationship Diagram view, is displayed.

GIF images of views in Microsoft Project are useful on their own. However, you can also combine them with other Microsoft Project content and save the results as a Web page for publication to the Web or to an intranet site. You will do this in the following section.

Saving Project Information as a Web Page

Another way to publish Microsoft Project information is to save it as a Web page. Unlike the Copy Picture feature, the Save As Web Page feature is geared toward publishing text. Microsoft Project uses maps (also called **export maps** or **data maps**) that specify the exact data to export and how to structure it. Maps organize Microsoft Project data into HTML tables; the predefined maps resemble some of the predefined tables and reports in Microsoft Project. You can use maps as they are or customize them to export only the Microsoft Project data you want.

In this exercise, you save Microsoft Project data as a Web page using a map, and then you view the results in your browser:

1 On the File menu, click Save As Web Page.

The Save As dialog box appears. Microsoft Project prompts you to save the information as a Web page in the same location from which you opened the practice file. If you see a different location in the Save In box, navigate to the Chapter 12 Publishing Online folder on your hard disk.

2 Click the Save button.

Export Wizard
new in
Project
2002

The Export Wizard appears. This wizard helps you export the structured data from Microsoft Project to a different format.

3 Click the Next button.

The second page of the Export Wizard appears. Your screen should look similar to the following illustration:

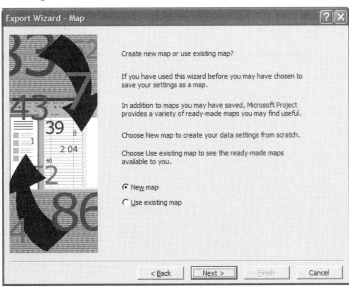

The Export Wizard uses maps to organize the way fields from a Microsoft Project plan are exported to another file format. For this exercise, you will use one of the maps included with Microsoft Project.

4 Select the Use Existing Map option, and then click the Next button.

5 Under Choose A Map For Your Data, click Export To HTML Using Standard Template.

Your screen should look similar to the following illustration:

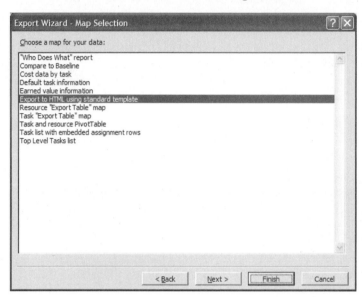

6 Click the Finish button.

Microsoft Project saves the data in HTML format. This particular map produces three tables that contain task, resource, and assignment information from the short film project. All three tables will appear on the single Web page that you saved. Next you will view the Web page.

7 On the Web toolbar, click Go, and then click Open Hyperlink in the drop-down list.

The Open Internet Address dialog box appears.

8 Click the Browse button.

The Browse dialog box appears.

9 In the Files Of Type box, click Web Pages in the drop-down list.

10 Locate the Web page named Short Film Project 12 in the Chapter 12 Publishing Online folder on your hard disk.

11 Click the name of the Web page, and then click the Open button.

12 In the Open Internet Address dialog box, click OK.

Microsoft Project opens the Web page in your browser. If you have Microsoft Internet Explorer, your screen should look similar to the following illustration:

This is the result of saving Microsoft Project data as a Web page using a standard HTML template.

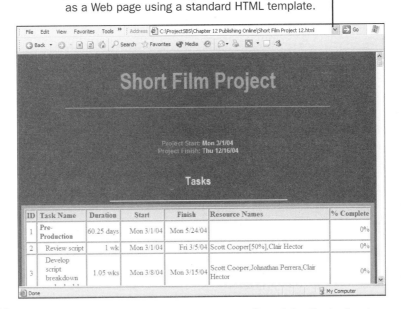

13 Scroll through the Web page. As you can see, it contains the task, resource, and assignment information from the project plan.

14 Close your browser, and return to Microsoft Project.

Saving information as a Web page enables you to publish large volumes of project information in HTML format. The data you can export when using the Save To Web Page command is not tied to the specific view you happen to be in at the time you save.

You can do a few things to fine-tune the Web pages you publish from Microsoft Project:

■ You can edit the map. After you select the map in the Export Wizard, click Next repeatedly to see the other options in the wizard. You have a great deal of flexibility in choosing the exact task, resource, and assignment fields you want to export and how you want the exported data organized.

■ You can apply a different HTML template to the Web page when you save it. This changes the format of the Web page, and it is the subject of the next section.

■ If you're HTML-savvy, you can edit the resulting Web page after saving it in Microsoft Project. For example, you can add several Microsoft Project–specific tags to a Web page. For a list of those tags, type **HTML export templates and tags** into the Ask A Question box in the upper right corner of the Microsoft Project window.

Changing the Look of a Project Web Page

Although maps determine which Microsoft Project data you save as a Web page and how it's organized, *HTML templates* determine how that data is formatted. Microsoft Project includes several HTML templates that you can apply as you save data as a Web page. You can experiment with different formats to find those you like best.

In this exercise, you save project information as a Web page, apply a different template, and include the GIF image you created earlier:

1 On the File menu, click Save As Web Page.

The Save As dialog box appears. Microsoft Project prompts you to save the information as a Web page in the same location from which you opened the practice file.

2 In the File Name box, type **Short Film Project 12 With Gantt Chart**, and click the Save button.

The Export Wizard appears.

3 Click the Next button.

4 Select the Use Existing Map option, and then click the Next button.

5 Under Choose A Map For Your Data, click Export To HTML Using Standard Template, and then click the Next button.

The Map Options page of the Export Wizard appears. Your screen should look similar to the following illustration:

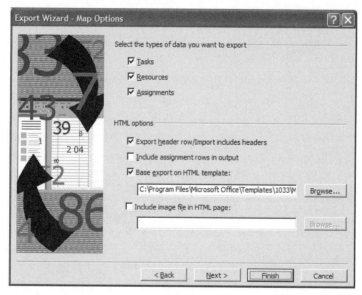

In the previous section, you saw that more information was exported to the Web page than you need, so you'll publish just task and resource information this time.

6 Under Select The Type of Data You Want To Export, clear the Assignments check box.

Next you will pick a different HTML template to use. Under HTML Options, the Base Export On HTML Template check box is selected by default, and the path to the current template appears.

7 Click the Browse button next to the path to the current template.

The Browse dialog box appears, displaying all of the HTML templates that are included with Microsoft Project.

Tip

If you installed Microsoft Project to the default location, the HTML templates it includes are in the following folder:
C:\Program Files\Microsoft Office\Templates\1033\Microsoft Project Web

8 In the list of templates, click Stripes Ivy, and then click OK.

There's just one more thing to do before creating the Web page. Earlier in this chapter, you created a GIF image of the Gantt Chart view named *Short Film Project 12.gif*. You'd like to include this image in the Web page.

9 Select the Include Image File In HTML Page check box.

If the GIF image file has the same name and is in the same folder as the Project file you're saving as a Web page, the path to that image file appears by default. Had you selected a different name or folder when creating the GIF image, you'd need to click the Browse button to locate it.

Your screen should look similar to the following illustration:

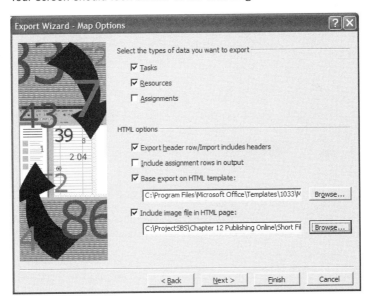

10 Click the Finish button.

Microsoft Project saves your Microsoft Project data in HTML format. Next you will view the Web page you just created.

11 On the Web toolbar, click Go, and then click Open Hyperlink in the drop-down list.

The Open Internet Address dialog box appears.

12 Click the Browse button.

The Browse dialog box appears.

13 In the Files Of Type box, click Web Pages.

14 Locate the Web page named *Short Film Project 12 With Gantt Chart* in your Chapter 12 Publishing Online folder.

15 Click the name of Web page, and then click the Open button.

16 In the Open Internet Address dialog box, click OK.

The Web page appears in your browser. If you have Internet Explorer, your screen should look similar to the following illustration:

With a different template and the GIF image included, this is the result of saving Microsoft Project data as a Web page.

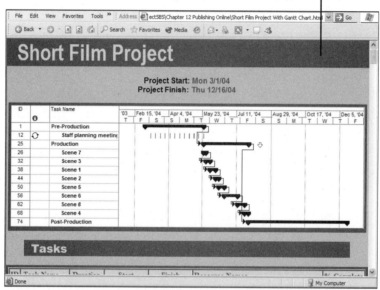

17 Scroll through the Web page to view the Gantt chart image, the Tasks table, and the Resources table. The new Web page doesn't have the Assignments table, and it shows different formatting from the page you created earlier.

18 Close your browser, and return to Microsoft Project.

19 Right-click any toolbar. In the shortcut menu that appears, click Web.

The Web toolbar disappears.

You've only scratched the surface of Microsoft Project's Web publishing capabilities. Depending on the communication needs you have as a project manager, you might use these features extensively. By modifying export maps, applying HTML templates, or editing the resulting Web pages, you can carefully tailor the information you provide over the Web.

Chapter Wrap-Up

This chapter covered how to use Microsoft Project's Web publishing features. You learned how to save GIF images of views, change the information you export to HTML, and format the Web pages you create.

If you are going on to other chapters:

Save

1   On the Standard toolbar, click the Save button to save changes made to Short Film Project 12.

2   On the File menu, click Close to close the project plan.

If you aren't continuing to other chapters:

1   On the Standard toolbar, click the Save button to save changes made to Short Film Project 12.

2   To quit Microsoft Project for now, on the File menu, click Exit.

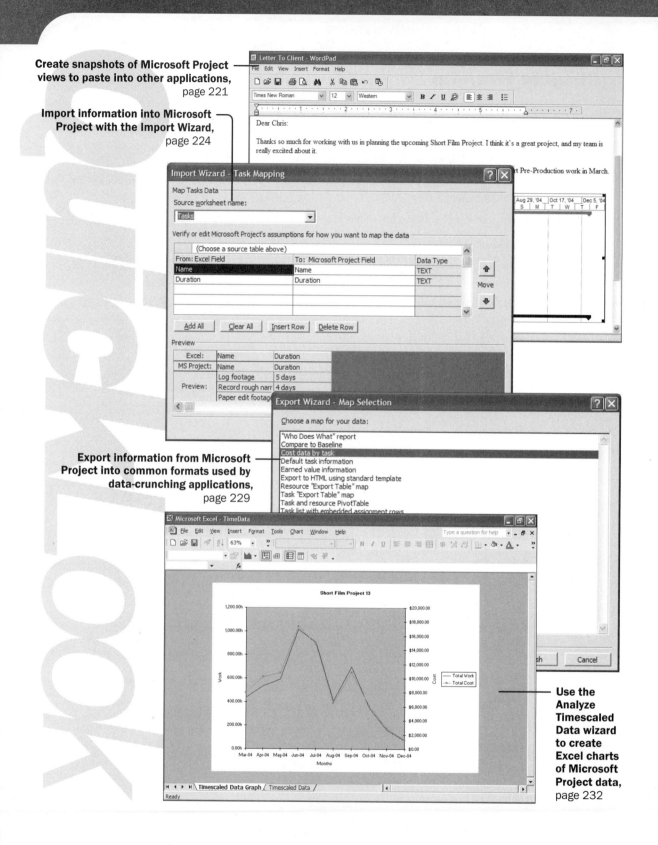

Create snapshots of Microsoft Project views to paste into other applications, page 221

Import information into Microsoft Project with the Import Wizard, page 224

Export information from Microsoft Project into common formats used by data-crunching applications, page 229

Use the Analyze Timescaled Data wizard to create Excel charts of Microsoft Project data, page 232

Chapter 13
Sharing Project Information with Other Programs

After completing this chapter, you will be able to:

✔ Copy and paste data to and from Microsoft Project.

✔ Use Microsoft Project to open a file produced in another program.

✔ Save Microsoft Project data to other file formats using import/export maps.

In this chapter, you focus on various ways of getting data into and out of Microsoft Project. In addition to the standard Windows copy and paste features with which you might be familiar, Microsoft Project offers a variety of options for importing and exporting data.

Throughout this chapter, you'll see the following terms:

■ The *source program* is the program from which you copy information.

■ The *destination program* is the program to which you paste information.

Important

This chapter describes various ways of sharing information between Microsoft Project and other applications, usually to communicate project details with *stakeholders*. Both Microsoft Project Standard and Professional editions, when used with Microsoft Project Server, offer much more sophisticated ways of communicating with resources and other stakeholders online. To learn more about the workgroup and enterprise collaboration tools available with Microsoft Project Server, see Appendix A, "Introducing Microsoft Project Server."

Short Film Project 13a

This chapter uses the practice file Short Film Project 13a. For details about installing the practice files, see "Using the Book's CD-ROM" at the beginning of this book.

Copying and Pasting with Microsoft Project

You can copy and paste data to and from Microsoft Project by clicking the Copy Cell, Copy Picture, Paste, and Paste Special commands on the Edit menu (or the corresponding buttons on the Standard toolbar). When copying data from Microsoft Project, you can choose one of two options, depending on the results you want:

- You can copy text (such as task names and dates) from a table and paste it as text into a destination program.

- You can copy a graphic image of a view from Microsoft Project and paste it as a graphic image in the destination program. With the Copy Picture command on the Edit menu, you can create a graphic image of a view or a selected portion of a view. Use the Copy Picture feature to optimize the image for onscreen viewing (in Microsoft PowerPoint, for example) or for printing (in Microsoft Word, for example).

Tip

The Copy Picture command also includes an option to save the snapshot to a GIF image file. You can then include the GIF image in a Word document or e-mail message, or post it directly to an intranet site.

There is an important distinction between using Copy and Copy Picture. If you use Copy, you can edit the data in the destination program. However, Copy Picture yields an image that you can edit only with a graphics editing program, such as Microsoft Paint.

Tip

Many Windows programs, such as Microsoft Word and Microsoft Excel, have a Paste Special command on their Edit menus. This command gives you more options for pasting text from Microsoft Project into the destination program. For example, you can use the Paste Special command in Word to paste formatted or unformatted text, a picture, or a Microsoft Project Document Object (an *OLE* object). You can also choose to paste just the data or paste it with a link to the source data in Microsoft Project. For more information about using OLE with Microsoft Project, type **About linked and embedded objects** into the Ask A Question box.

You also have two options when pasting data into Microsoft Project from other programs:

- You can paste text (such as a list of task or resource names) into a table in Microsoft Project. For example, you can paste a range of cells from Excel or a sequence of paragraphs from Word into Microsoft Project. You might paste a series of task names that are organized in a vertical column from Excel or Word into the Task Name column in Microsoft Project, for instance.

■ You can paste a graphic image or an OLE object from another program into a graphical portion of a Gantt Chart view. You can also paste a graphic image or an OLE object into a task, resource, or assignment note; into a form view, such as the Task or Resource Form views; or into the header, footer, or legend of a view or report.

Tip

Pasting text as multiple columns requires some planning. First make sure that the order of the information in the source program matches the order of the columns in the Microsoft Project table. You can either rearrange the data in the source program to match the column order in the Microsoft Project table, or vice versa. Second make sure that the columns in the source program support the same types of data—text, numbers, dates, and so on—as do the columns in Microsoft Project.

For the short film project, you'd like to add a Gantt chart image to a document you've prepared for a stakeholder of the project. In this exercise, you copy a snapshot of a Gantt chart and paste it into WordPad (or Word, if you prefer). You copy the same way regardless of the destination program you have in mind. For example, you could paste the snapshot into a word processor file or an e-mail message. To begin, you'll format the Gantt Chart view to show the information you want.

In this exercise, you copy an image of a Gantt Chart view to the Windows Clipboard and then paste it into another document:

1 If Microsoft Project is not already open, start it now.

Open

2 On the Standard toolbar, click the Open button.

The Open dialog box appears.

3 Navigate to the Chapter 13 Sharing folder, and double-click the Short Film Project 13a file.

4 On the File menu, click Save As.

The Save As dialog box appears.

5 In the File Name box, type **Short Film Project 13**, and then click the Save button.

6 On the Project menu, point to Filtered For: All Tasks, and then click Summary Tasks.

Microsoft Project displays only the summary tasks in the project.

7 On the View menu, click Zoom.

The Zoom dialog box appears.

8 In the Zoom dialog box, click Entire Project, and then click OK.

Microsoft Project adjusts the timescale of the Gantt chart to show the entire project. Your screen should look similar to the following illustration:

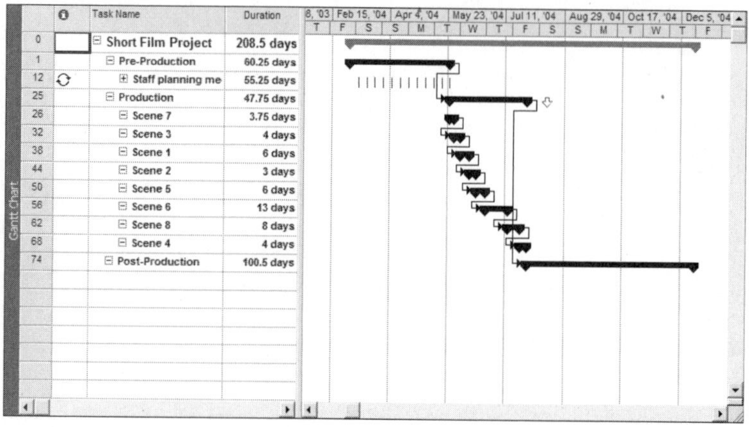

Copy Picture

9 On the Standard toolbar, click the Copy Picture button.

The Copy Picture dialog box appears.

10 Under the Render Image label, select For Screen, and then click OK.

Microsoft Project copies a snapshot of the Gantt Chart view to the Windows Clipboard.

Next you'll open a proposal that's been created in a word processor. You can open this in WordPad or in Word if you have it.

11 Do one of the following:

- If you do not have Word installed, click the Windows Start button, point to All Programs, point to Accessories, and then click WordPad.

- If you have Word installed, start it.

12 In WordPad or Word, on the File menu, click Open.

13 Locate and open the document named Letter To Client in your Chapter 13 Sharing folder (you may have to select All Files in the Files Of Type box).

14 Select the paragraph (*insert Gantt Chart picture here*).

15 On the Edit menu, click Paste.

16 Microsoft Project pastes the snapshot of the Gantt Chart view from the Windows Clipboard into the document. If you are using WordPad, your screen should look similar to the following illustration:

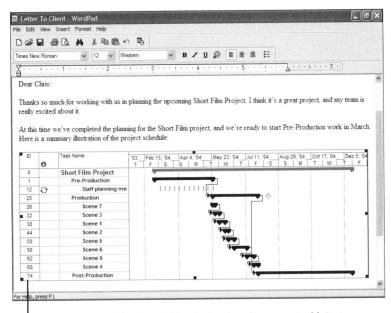

The image of the Gantt Chart view has been pasted into a WordPad document. The Gantt Chart cannot be edited in this format except as a graphic image.

Again, note that rather than pasting the image into a Word or WordPad document, you could paste this image into an e-mail message or another type of document.

17 On the WordPad or Word File menu, click Exit. When prompted to save the document, click No.

Opening Other File Formats in Microsoft Project

Information that you need to incorporate into a Microsoft Project document can come from a variety of sources. A task list from a spreadsheet or resource costs from a database are two examples. You might want to use the unique features of Microsoft Project to analyze data from another program. For example, many people keep task lists and simple project schedules in Excel, but accounting for basic scheduling issues like working and nonworking time is impractical in Excel.

As you might recall from Chapter 12, "Publishing Project Information Online," Microsoft Project uses maps when saving data to HTML and other formats. Microsoft Project also uses maps when opening data from another file format. In fact, the same maps are used for both opening and saving data, so they are known as *import/export maps*. (You might also hear these referred to as *data maps* or just *maps*.) You use import/export maps to specify how you want individual fields in the source program's file to correspond to individual fields in the destination program. After you set up an import/export map, you can use it over and over again.

Tip

If you have Excel installed on your computer, open the workbook named Sample Task List in the Chapter 13 Sharing folder. The important things to note about the workbook are the names and the order of the columns, the presence of a header row (the labels at the top of the columns), and that the data is in a worksheet named Tasks. When you're done viewing the workbook, close it without saving changes.

In this exercise, a colleague has sent you an Excel workbook that contains her recommended tasks, durations, and sequence of activities for some work Southridge Video will do in the future. You open the Excel workbook in Microsoft Project and set up an import/export map to control how the Excel data is imported into Microsoft Project:

1 In Microsoft Project, on the File menu, click Open.

   The Open dialog box appears.

2 Locate the Chapter 13 Sharing folder in the MS Project 2002 SBS Practice folder on your hard disk.

3 In the Files Of Type box, select Microsoft Excel Workbooks.

Tip

While scrolling through the Files Of Type box, you can see the several file formats Microsoft Project can import. If you work with programs that can save in any of these file formats, you can import their data into Microsoft Project. For more information, type **File formats supported by Microsoft Project** into the Ask A Question box.

4 Double-click the Sample Task List file.

   The Import Wizard appears. This wizard helps you import structured data from a different format to Microsoft Project.

Tip

If you completed Chapter 12, "Publishing Project Information Online," you will find the Import Wizard to be very similar to the Export Wizard. Remember that Microsoft Project uses basically the same process and maps for importing as it does for exporting.

5 Click the Next button.

   The second page of the Import Wizard appears. Your screen should look similar to the following illustration:

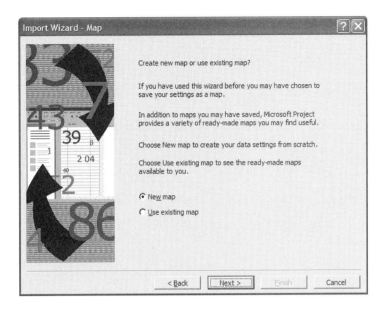

The Import Wizard uses maps to organize the way structured data from another file format is imported into Microsoft Project. For this exercise, you will create a new map.

6 Make sure that New Map is selected, and then click the Next button.

The Import Mode page of the Import Wizard appears. Your screen should look similar to the following illustration:

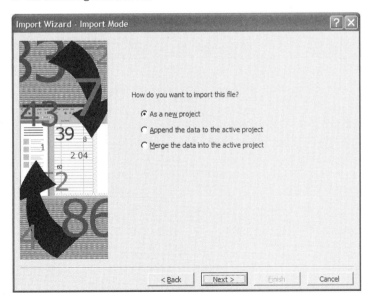

7 Make sure that As A New Project is selected, and then click the Next button.

The Map Options page of the Import Wizard appears.

8 Select the Tasks check box, and make sure that Import Includes Headers is selected as well.

Your screen should look similar to the following illustration:

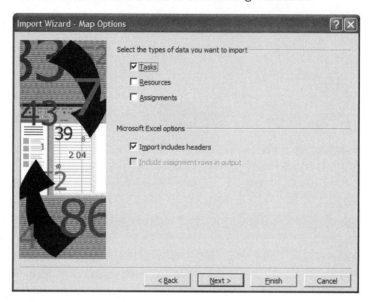

9 Click the Next button.

The Task Mapping page of the Import Wizard appears. Here you identify the source workbook and specify how you want to map the data from the source workbook to Microsoft Project fields.

10 In the Source Worksheet Name list, select Tasks.

Microsoft Project analyzes the header row names from the workbook and suggests the Microsoft Project field names that are probable matches. Your screen should look similar to the following illustration:

On this page of the Import Wizard, you specify how Microsoft Project should import data from other file formats—in this case an Excel workbook.

Use the Preview area here to see how the data from another file format will be mapped to Microsoft Project fields, based on the setting you've made above.

11 Click the Next button.

The final page of the Import Wizard appears. Here you have the option of saving the settings for the new import map. This would be useful if you anticipate importing similar data into Microsoft Project in the future. This time you'll skip this step.

12 Click the Finish button.

Microsoft Project imports the Excel data into a new Microsoft Project file. Your screen should look similar to the illustration on the following page. (The dates you see on the timescale will differ from those shown because Microsoft Project uses the current date as the project start date in the new file.)

After importing the task names and durations, they appear as an unlinked sequence of tasks, ready for editing.

	ⓘ	Task Name	Duration	Feb 8, '04	Feb 15, '04	Feb
1		Log footage	5 days			
2		Record rough narration	4 days			
3		Paper edit footage	10 days			
4		Rough cut edit	8 days			
5		Fine cut edit	7 days			
6		Hold formal approval show	1 day			
7		Add dialog	2 days			
8		Record final narration	5 days			
9		Add head and tail titles	5 days			
10		Add final music	3 days			
11		Print internegative of film	3 days			
12		Clone dubbing masters of	4 days			
13		Archive master film and au	0.5 days			
14		Hand off masters to distrib	0 days	◆ 2/10		

This task list will become a more fully developed schedule that you'll use in a later chapter.

13 Close the new file without saving changes.

Tip

If you find that others need to give you task lists for creating a plan in Microsoft Project and you must reorganize or clean up the lists you get, try using the Microsoft Project Task List Import Template. Microsoft Project 2002 installs this Microsoft Excel template. In Excel, this template appears on the Spreadsheet Solutions tab of the Templates dialog box. The Excel template is set up with the proper field headings and column order to make importing a clean task list in Microsoft Project easy.

Saving to Other File Formats from Microsoft Project

Pasting Microsoft Project data into other programs might be fine for one-time or infrequent needs, but this technique might not work as well if you need to export a large volume of data from Microsoft Project. Instead, you can save Microsoft Project data in a variety of file formats. You can take one of two approaches to saving Microsoft Project data in other file formats:

■ You can save the entire project as a database. In fact, you can store multiple projects in a single database file for centralized administration or for other purposes. Saving a project in a database format might also help if you need to report or analyze data in ways that Microsoft Project doesn't support. The supported formats include Microsoft Project Database (.mpd) and Access Database (.mdb). These two formats are almost identical. One important difference is that the Microsoft Project Database format requires you to save the entire project, but the Access Database format allows you to save either the entire project or just the data you specify in an export map. You can also save an entire project to Extensible Markup Language (XML) format for structured data exchange with other applications that support it.

■ You can save just the data you specify in a different format. The supported formats include Access database, Web page, Excel workbook, Excel PivotTable, and tab-delimited or comma-delimited text. If you completed Chapter 12, "Publishing Project Information Online," you worked with an export map when saving Microsoft Project data to a Web page. You use the same approach when specifying data you want to save in any format. You choose the format in which you want to save, pick a built-in export map (or create your own), and export the data.

Tip

Microsoft Project includes thorough documentation for the Microsoft Project Database format. If you installed Microsoft Project in the default location, you'll find the documentation file at C:\Program Files\Microsoft Office\Office10\1033\Projdb.htm.

For more information about the file formats Microsoft Project can work with, type **File formats supported by Microsoft Project** into the Ask A Question box in the upper right corner of the Microsoft Project window.

Although the short film project has not yet started, the project file already contains quite a bit of planned cost data. You'd like to give this data to the financial planner of Southridge Video so she can start work on detailed budgets. However, the financial planner uses a budget program that can't work directly with Microsoft Project files. You decide to provide her with cost data as tab-delimited text. This will allow her the greatest flexibility in importing the data into her budget program.

In this exercise, you save project cost data to a text file using a built-in export map. At this point, you should still have Short Film Project 13 open in Microsoft Project:

1 On the File menu, click Save As.

The Save As dialog box appears. Microsoft Project suggests saving the file in the same location from which you opened the practice file. If you see anything different in the Save As dialog box, locate the Chapter 13 Sharing folder.

2 In the File Name box, type **Short Film Project 13 Costs**.

3 In the Save As Type box, click Text (Tab Delimited) from the list, and then click the Save button.

The Export Wizard appears.

Tip

Remember that when you use import/export maps, it makes no difference what the current view is in Microsoft Project.

4 Click the Next button.

The second page of the Export Wizard appears.

Working with Microsoft Project File Formats

Prior to Microsoft Project 2000, the Microsoft Project file format changed significantly with every major release. Starting with Microsoft Project 2000, however, Microsoft developed a file format that "grows" with each new release of Microsoft Project but is still usable with previous versions. This means that you can create a project plan in Microsoft Project 2002 and open it directly in Microsoft Project 2000. Features that are new in the 2002 version, such as multiple baselines, will not be visible when the file is opened in the 2000 version. Otherwise, you can freely exchange files between the 2002 and 2000 versions.

Microsoft Project 2002 can open Microsoft Project 98 files, as well as save in Microsoft Project 98 format. Features that were introduced after the 98 version, such as deadline dates and multiple baselines, will not appear when saving a file in 98 format.

Microsoft Project 2002 can open files in the MPX format, which is supported by a variety of project management programs. Previous versions of Microsoft Project up to 98 can save in the MPX format. If you need to migrate project plans from versions of Microsoft Project prior to 98 to Microsoft Project 2002, use the MPX format. Note that Microsoft Project 2002 can open, but not save in, MPX format.

Microsoft Project 2002 can also export files to the Extensible Markup Language (XML) format. XML is an excellent format for exchanging structured data between Microsoft Project and other applications that support it.

5 Click Use Existing Map, and then click the Next button.

6 Under Choose A Map For Your Data, select Cost Data By Task.

Your screen should look similar to the following illustration:

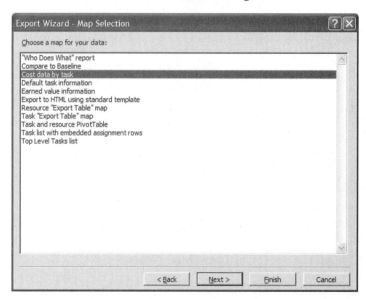

7 Click the Finish button.

Microsoft Project saves the text file. To view it, you will open it in Notepad.

8 On the Windows Start menu, point to All Programs, point to Accessories, and click Notepad.

Notepad starts.

9 In Notepad, make sure that Word Wrap is turned off. (Word Wrap on the Format menu should not be selected.)

10 On the File menu, click Open.

11 Open the document named Short Film Project 13 Costs in your Chapter 13 Sharing folder. If you are running Notepad, your screen should look like the following illustration:

```
ID	Task Name	Fixed Cost	Total Cost	Baseline Cost	Cost Variance	Actual Co
0	Short Film Project	$0.00	"$88,789.55"	"$89,161.55"	($372.00)	$0.00	"
1	Pre-Production	$0.00	"$23,987.50"	"$24,359.50"	($372.00)	$0.00	"$23,987.
2	Review script	$0.00	$947.50	$947.50	$0.00	$0.00	$947.50
3	Develop script breakdown and schedule	$0.00	"$2,455.00"	"$2,455.00"	$0.00	$
4	Develop production boards	$0.00	"$8,124.00"	"$8,124.00"	$0.00	$0.00	"
5	Scout locations	$0.00	"$4,920.00"	"$4,920.00"	$0.00	$0.00	"$4,920.00"
6	Select locations	$0.00	"$2,535.00"	"$2,535.00"	$0.00	$0.00	"$2,535.0
7	Hold auditions	$0.00	"$1,835.00"	"$1,835.00"	$0.00	$0.00	"$1,835.00"
8	Apply for filming permits	$500.00	$876.00	$876.00	$0.00	$0.00	$876.00
9	Reserve camera equipment	$0.00	$636.00	$822.00	($186.00)	$0.00	$636.00
10	Reserve sound equipment	$0.00	$186.00	$372.00	($186.00)	$0.00	$186.00
11	Pre-Production complete!	$0.00	$0.00	$0.00	$0.00	$0.00	$0.00
12	Staff planning meeting	$0.00	"$1,473.00"	"$1,473.00"	$0.00	$0.00	"$1,473.0
13	Staff planning meeting 1	$0.00	$122.75	$122.75	$0.00	$0.00	$122.75
14	Staff planning meeting 2	$0.00	$122.75	$122.75	$0.00	$0.00	$122.75
15	Staff planning meeting 3	$0.00	$122.75	$122.75	$0.00	$0.00	$122.75
16	Staff planning meeting 4	$0.00	$122.75	$122.75	$0.00	$0.00	$122.75
17	Staff planning meeting 5	$0.00	$122.75	$122.75	$0.00	$0.00	$122.75
18	Staff planning meeting 6	$0.00	$122.75	$122.75	$0.00	$0.00	$122.75
19	Staff planning meeting 7	$0.00	$122.75	$122.75	$0.00	$0.00	$122.75
20	Staff planning meeting 8	$0.00	$122.75	$122.75	$0.00	$0.00	$122.75
21	Staff planning meeting 9	$0.00	$122.75	$122.75	$0.00	$0.00	$122.75
22	Staff planning meeting 10	$0.00	$122.75	$122.75	$0.00	$0.00	$122.75
23	Staff planning meeting 11	$0.00	$122.75	$122.75	$0.00	$0.00	$122.75
24	Staff planning meeting 12	$0.00	$122.75	$122.75	$0.00	$0.00	$122.75
25	Production	$0.00	"$36,334.15"	"$36,334.15"	$0.00	$0.00	"$36,334.15"
26	Scene 7	$0.00	"$3,702.50"	"$3,702.50"	$0.00	$0.00	"$3,702.50"
27	Scene 7 setup	$0.00	$322.50	$322.50	$0.00	$0.00	$322.50
28	Scene 7 rehearsal	$0.00	$705.00	$705.00	$0.00	$0.00	$705.00
29	Scene 7 shoot	$0.00	"$2,245.00"	"$2,245.00"	$0.00	$0.00	"$2,245.00"
30	Scene 7 teardown	$0.00	$430.00	$430.00	$0.00	$0.00	$430.00
31	Scene 7-process dailies	$0.00	$0.00	$0.00	$0.00	$0.00	$0.00
32	Scene 3	$0.00	"$4,170.00"	"$4,170.00"	$0.00	$0.00	"$4,170.00"
33	Scene 3 setup	$0.00	$518.00	$518.00	$0.00	$0.00	$518.00
34	Scene 3 rehearsal	$0.00	$755.00	$755.00	$0.00	$0.00	$755.00
35	Scene 3 shoot	$0.00	"$2,379.00"	"$2,379.00"	$0.00	$0.00	"$2,379.00"
36	Scene 3 teardown	$0.00	$518.00	$518.00	$0.00	$0.00	$518.00
37	Scene 3-process dailies	$0.00	$0.00	$0.00	$0.00	$0.00	$0.00
38	Scene 1	$0.00	"$5,950.00"	"$5,950.00"	$0.00	$0.00	"$5,950.00"
```

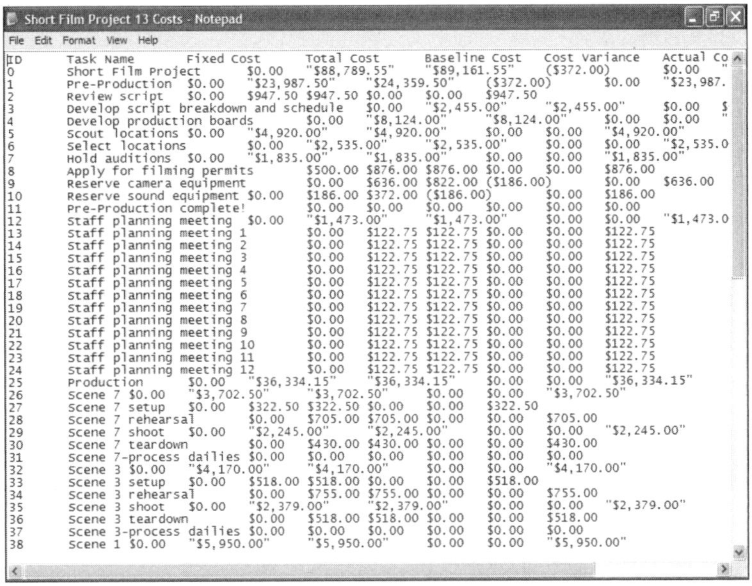

In this file, the fields are separated by tabs. It might not be easy for you to read, but this format is easily imported into virtually any data-crunching program.

12 On the File menu, click Exit.

Notepad closes, and you return to Microsoft Project.

Charting Data in Excel with the Analyze Timescaled Data Wizard

You can create charts of timephased task or resource information in Microsoft Excel using a wizard in Microsoft Project. The wizard is called the Analyze Timescaled Data Wizard. To start it, on the View menu, point to Toolbars, and then click Analysis. On the Analysis toolbar, click the Analyze Timescaled Data In Excel button. With the Analyze Timescaled Data Wizard, you can see trends of either planned or actual values distributed over time (in daily up to yearly increments) for tasks or resources. You can choose to export the entire project or just selected tasks or resources.

If you have a task view (such as the Gantt Chart) displayed when you start the wizard, you can use the wizard to export any timephased task-related values you want. For example, in the planning stage of a project, you could export and chart the planned Work and Cost totals per month and see the monthly totals charted over time. Here is what such a chart for the Short Film Project 13 file looks like:

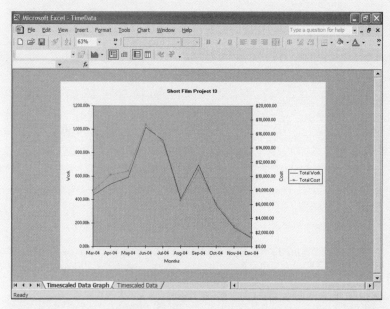

After work has begun, some useful values to chart include Baseline Work with Actual Work and Baseline Cost with Actual Cost.

If you have a resource view (such as the Resource Sheet) displayed when you start the wizard, you can use the wizard to export any timephased resource-related values you want.

You could manually do everything the wizard does for you, but the wizard is faster. The wizard does require that you have Excel installed on the same system as Microsoft Project, however. In the Excel workbook created by the wizard you also get the detailed, timephased data from which the chart is generated. Here is the timephased data that the chart above is derived from:

			3/1/2004	4/1/2004	5/1/2004	6/1/2004	7/1/2004	8/1/2004	9/1/2004	10/1/2004	11/1/2004	12/1/2004
1	Short Film Project 13											
2	Months		3/1/2004	4/1/2004	5/1/2004	6/1/2004	7/1/2004	8/1/2004	9/1/2004	10/1/2004	11/1/2004	12/1/200
3	Pre-Production											
4	Work											
5	Cost											
6	Review script											
7	Work		48.00h	0.00h	0.00h	0.00h	0.00h	0.00h	0.00h	0.00h	0.00h	0.00
8	Cost		$947.50	$0.00	$0.00	$0.00	$0.00	$0.00	$0.00	$0.00	$0.00	$0.0
9	Develop script breakdown and schedule											
10	Work		120.00h	0.00h	0.00h	0.00h	0.00h	0.00h	0.00h	0.00h	0.00h	0.00
11	Cost		$2,455.00	$0.00	$0.00	$0.00	$0.00	$0.00	$0.00	$0.00	$0.00	$0.0
12	Develop production boards											
13	Work		244.00h	236.00h	0.00h	0.00h	0.00h	0.00h	0.00h	0.00h	0.00h	0.00
14	Cost		$4,099.60	$4,024.40	$0.00	$0.00	$0.00	$0.00	$0.00	$0.00	$0.00	$0.0
15	Scout locations											
16	Work		0.00h	240.00h	0.00h	0.00h	0.00h	0.00h	0.00h	0.00h	0.00h	0.00
17	Cost		$0.00	$4,920.00	$0.00	$0.00	$0.00	$0.00	$0.00	$0.00	$0.00	$0.0
18	Select locations											
19	Work		0.00h	36.00h	84.00h	0.00h	0.00h	0.00h	0.00h	0.00h	0.00h	0.00
20	Cost		$0.00	$760.50	$1,774.50	$0.00	$0.00	$0.00	$0.00	$0.00	$0.00	$0.0
21	Hold auditions											
22	Work		0.00h	0.00h	100.00h	0.00h	0.00h	0.00h	0.00h	0.00h	0.00h	0.00
23	Cost		$0.00	$0.00	$1,835.00	$0.00	$0.00	$0.00	$0.00	$0.00	$0.00	$0.0
24	Apply for filming permits											
25	Work		0.00h	0.00h	40.00h	0.00h	0.00h	0.00h	0.00h	0.00h	0.00h	0.00
26	Cost		$0.00	$0.00	$876.00	$0.00	$0.00	$0.00	$0.00	$0.00	$0.00	$0.0

C265 — fx =SUMIF($B$4:$B$263,$B265,C$4:C$263)

Chapter Wrap-Up

This chapter covered how to exchange data between Microsoft Project and other programs. You learned how to use the Copy and Paste commands, and how to import and export Microsoft Project information to and from different file formats.

If you are going on to other chapters:

Save

1 On the Standard toolbar, click the Save button to save changes made to Short Film Project 13.

2 On the File menu, click Close to close the project plan.

If you aren't continuing to other chapters:

1 On the Standard toolbar, click the Save button to save changes made to Short Film Project 13.

2 To quit Microsoft Project for now, on the File menu, click Exit.

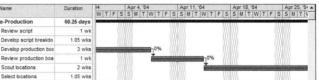

Update a baseline prior to tracking actual work, page 237

Enter actual work for tasks and assignments, page 241

Enter timephased actual work for tasks and assignments, page 248

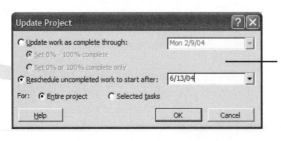

Interrupt work on the project to restart after the date you specify, page 253

Chapter 14
Tracking Progress on Tasks and Assignments

After completing this chapter, you will be able to:

✔ Update a previously saved baseline plan.

✔ Record actual work for tasks and assignments.

✔ Record daily actual work values.

✔ Interrupt work on a task and specify the date on which the task should start again.

Building, verifying, and communicating a sound project plan might take much or even most of your time as a project manager. However, planning is only the first phase of managing your projects. After the *planning* is completed, the implementation of the project starts—carrying out the plan that was previously developed. Ideally, projects are implemented just as planned, but this is seldom the case. In general, the more complex the project plan and the longer its planned duration, the more opportunity there is for *variance* to appear. Variance is the difference between what you thought would happen (as recorded in the project plan) and what really happened (as recorded by your tracking method).

Properly *tracking* actual work and comparing it against the plan enables you to identify variance early and adjust the incomplete portion of the plan when necessary. If you completed Chapter 6, "Tracking Progress on Tasks," you were introduced to the simpler ways of tracking *actuals* in a project plan. These include recording the percentage of a task that has been completed as well as its actual start and finish dates. These methods of tracking progress are fine for many projects, but Microsoft Project also supports more detailed ways of tracking.

In this chapter, you track task-level and assignment-level work totals and work per time period, such as work completed per week or per day. Information distributed over time is commonly known as *timephased*, so tracking work by time period is sometimes referred to as *tracking timephased actuals*. This is the most detailed level of tracking progress available in Microsoft Project.

As with simpler tracking methods, tracking timephased actuals is a way to address the most basic questions of managing a project:

- Are tasks starting and finishing as planned? If not, what will be the impact on the project's finish date?
- Are resources spending more or less time than planned to complete tasks?
- Is it taking more or less money than planned to complete tasks?

As a project manager, you must determine what level of tracking best meets the needs of your project plan and your stakeholders. As you might expect, the more detailed the tracking level, the more effort required from you and the resources assigned to tasks. This chapter exposes you to the most detailed tracking methods available in Microsoft Project.

Tip

Besides completing this chapter, you can read more about tracking methods in Microsoft Project's online Help to help you determine what approach best suits your needs. Type **All about picking a tracking method** into the Ask A Question box in the upper right corner of the Microsoft Project window.

In this chapter, you work with different means of tracking work and handling incomplete work. You begin, however, by updating the project baseline.

Important

This chapter describes entering actual values directly in Microsoft Project. Both Microsoft Project Standard and Professional editions, when used with Microsoft Project Server, offer much more sophisticated ways of collecting information (such as actual work) from resources and other stakeholders. To learn more about the workgroup and enterprise collaboration tools available with Microsoft Project Server, see Appendix A, "Introducing Microsoft Project Server."

Short Film
Project 14a

This chapter uses a sequence of practice files, beginning with Short Film Project 14a. This file contains the project plan you've developed in previous chapters, and has had an initial baseline saved. For details about installing the practice files, see "Using the Book's CD-ROM" at the beginning of this book.

Updating a Baseline

If you completed Chapter 6, "Tracking Progress on Tasks," you saved a baseline plan for a project plan. Recall that a *baseline* is a collection of important values in a project plan, such as the planned start dates, finish dates, and costs of tasks, resources and assignments. When you save a baseline, Microsoft Project takes a "snapshot" of the existing values and saves it in the Microsoft Project file for future comparison.

Keep in mind that the purpose of the baseline is to record what you expected the project plan to look like at one point in time. As time passes, however, you might need to change your expectations. After saving an initial baseline plan, you might need to fine-tune the project plan by adding or removing tasks or assignments, and so on. To keep an accurate baseline for later comparison, you have several options:

- Update the baseline for the entire project. This simply replaces the original baseline values with the currently scheduled values.

- Update the baseline for selected tasks. This does not affect the baseline values for other tasks, or resource baseline values in the project plan.

- Save a second or subsequent baseline. You can save up to 11 baselines in a single plan. The first one is called Baseline, and the rest are Baseline 1 through Baseline 10.

Tip

To learn more about baselines in Microsoft Project's online Help, type **All about baselines** into the Ask A Question box in the upper right corner of the Microsoft Project window.

Since you completed the initial planning for the short film project and saved an initial baseline, the project plan has undergone some additional fine-tuning. This included some adjustments to assignments and task durations and a new task in the pre-production phase of the project. Because of these changes, the initial baseline does not quite match the project plan as it is currently scheduled. In this exercise, you compare the project plan as it is currently scheduled with the baseline plan, and update the baseline for the project plan:

1   If Microsoft Project is not already open, start it now.

Open   **2**   On the Standard toolbar, click the Open button.

The Open dialog box appears.

3   Navigate to the Chapter 14 Complex Tracking folder, and double-click the Short Film Project 14a file.

4   On the File menu, click Save As.

The Save As dialog box appears.

5 In the File Name box, type **Short Film Project 14 Baseline**, and then click the Save button.

Next you will switch to a different view to see baseline and scheduled values arranged for easy comparison.

6 On the View menu, click Tracking Gantt.

The Tracking Gantt view appears. Your screen should look similar to the following illustration:

In the Tracking Gantt view, the Gantt bars for the tasks as they are currently scheduled appear in blue (or, if critical, red) and their baseline schedule values appear in gray.

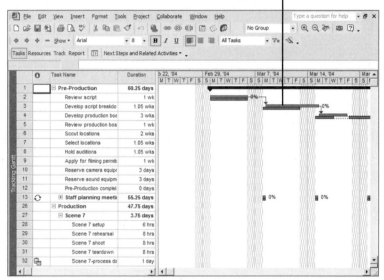

In the chart portion of this view, the tasks as they are currently scheduled appear as blue bars (if they are not critical tasks) or red bars (if they are critical). Below them, the baseline values of each task appear as gray bars.

Tip

In Gantt Chart views, the colors, patterns, and shapes of the bars represent specific things. To see what these are, on the Format menu, click Bar Styles.

7 On the Edit menu, click Go To, enter **5** in the ID box, and then click OK.

Tip

Remember that Ctrl+G is a shortcut for displaying the Go To dialog box.

The Tracking Gantt view scrolls to display the Gantt bars for Task 5, *Review production boards*. This task was added to the plan after the initial baseline was saved. Your screen should look similar to the following illustration:

This task was added to the project plan after its initial baseline was saved, so this task has no baseline.

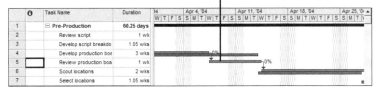

As you can see in the Tracking Gantt view, this task has no baseline values.

To conclude this exercise, you will resave the baseline for the project plan.

8 On the Tools menu, point to Tracking, and then click Save Baseline.

The Save Baseline dialog box appears.

9 Select the Save Baseline option. In the For area, select the Entire Project option.

Tip

To update a baseline just for selected tasks, click Selected Tasks in the For area. When you do this, the options under Roll Up Baselines become available. You can control how baseline updates should affect the baseline values for summary tasks. For example, you could resave a baseline for a subtask and update its related summary task baseline values if you wanted.

10 Click OK to update the baseline.

Microsoft Project alerts you that you are about to overwrite the previously saved baseline values.

11 Click the Yes button.

Microsoft Project updates the baseline values for the project plan.

Your screen should look similar to the following illustration:

After resaving the baseline for the entire project, the baseline start, finish, and duration values (among others) match the scheduled values.

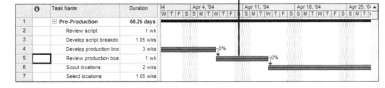

Task 5 now has a baseline, and all of the other tasks' baseline values now match their scheduled values.

Save

12 On the Standard toolbar, click the Save button.

13 On the File menu, click Close to close the project plan.

Tip

To learn more about interim plans, type **Save an interim plan** into the Ask A Question box in the upper right corner of the Microsoft Project window.

Saving Interim Plans

After you've started tracking actual values, or any time you've adjusted your schedule, you might want to take another snapshot of the current start and finish dates. You can do this with an *interim plan*. Like a baseline, an interim plan is a set of current values from the project plan that Microsoft Project saves with the file. Unlike the baseline, however, an interim plan saves only the start and finish dates of tasks, not resource or assignment values. You can save up to 10 different interim plans during a project. (If you find that you need multiple snapshots of scheduled values in addition to start and finish dates, you should instead save additional baselines.)

Depending on the scope and duration of your projects, you might want to save an interim plan at any of the following junctures:

- At the conclusion of a major phase of work
- At preset time intervals, such as weekly or monthly
- Just before or after entering a large number of actual values

To save an interim plan, on the Tools menu, point to Tracking, and then click Save Baseline. In the Save Baseline dialog box, select the Save Interim Plan option.

Tracking Actual and Remaining Values for Tasks and Assignments

If you completed Chapter 6, "Tracking Progress on Tasks," you entered actual start, finish, and duration values for individual tasks. For tasks that have resources assigned to them, you can enter actual and remaining work values for the task as a whole or for specific assignments to that task. To help you understand how Microsoft Project handles the actual values you enter, consider the following:

- If a task has a single resource assigned to it, the actual work values you enter for the task or the assignment apply equally to both the task and the resource. For example, if you record that the assignment started on March 20 and has five hours of actual work, those values apply equally to the task as well.

- If a task has multiple resources assigned to it, the actual work values you enter for the task are distributed among or *rolled down* to the assignments according to their assignment units. This level of detail is appropriate if you aren't concerned about the details at the individual assignment level.

- If a task has multiple resources assigned to it, the actual work values you enter for one assignment are *rolled up* to the task, but don't affect the other assignments to the task. This level of detail is appropriate if details at the individual assignment level are important to you.

In this exercise, you record task-level and assignment-level actuals, and see how the information is rolled up or down between tasks and assignments:

Open

1 On the Standard toolbar, click the Open button.

The Open dialog box appears.

2 Double-click Short Film Project 14b.

3 On the File menu, click Save As.

The Save As dialog box appears.

4 In the File Name box, type **Short Film Project 14 Actuals**, and then click the Save button.

This version of the project plan includes the updated baseline values you previously saved, as well as the first actuals reported against the first pre-production task.

5 On the View menu, click Task Usage.

The Task Usage view appears. This usage view lists resources under the tasks to which they're assigned in a table on the left side of the view. On the right side of the view, you see rows organized under a timescale. The rows next to each task name show you the scheduled work values for the task. The rows next to the resource names show you the scheduled work values for each resource—in other words, the scheduled work per assignment. These are the timephased values of the assignments. The two sides of the view are split by a vertical divider bar.

6 In the Task Name column, click the name of Task 3, Develop script breakdown and schedule.

7 On the Standard toolbar, click the Go To Selected Task button.

The timephased grid on the right side of the view scrolls to display the first scheduled work for the task.

Next you'll switch the table and details shown in the view.

8 On the View menu, point to Table: Usage, and then click Work.

The Work table appears. Your screen should look similar to the following illustration:

In usage view, a table appears in the left pane
and a timephased grid appears in the right pane.

	Task Name	Work	Details	Mar 7, '04 S	S	M	T	W	T	F	S	Mar 14, S
1	⊟ Pre-Production	1,215.78 hrs	Work	▓▓▓		24h	24h	24h	24h	24h		
2	⊟ Review script	48 hrs	Work									
	Clair Hector	28 hrs	Work									
	Scott Cooper	20 hrs	Work									
3	⊟ Develop script breakdo	120 hrs	Work			18h	24h	24h	24h	24h		
	Clair Hector	40 hrs	Work			6h	8h	8h	8h	8h		
	Johnathan Perrera	40 hrs	Work			6h	8h	8h	8h	8h		
	Scott Cooper	40 hrs	Work			6h	8h	8h	8h	8h		
4	⊟ Develop production boa	347.78 hrs	Work									
	Johnathan Perrera	114.6 hrs	Work									
	Kim Yoshida	118.6 hrs	Work									
	Scott Cooper	114.6 hrs	Work									
5	⊟ Review production boa	80 hrs	Work									
	Clair Hector	40 hrs	Work									
	Scott Cooper	40 hrs	Work									
6	⊟ Scout locations	240 hrs	Work									
	Jan Miksovsky	80 hrs	Work									
	Jo Brown	80 hrs	Work									
	Max Benson	80 hrs	Work									
7	⊟ Select locations	120 hrs	Work									

Currently this timephased grid displays only scheduled work per day for each assignment and task. Changing the timescale of the grid changes the level of detail it reports, though the underlying timephased data does not change.

This table includes the Actual Work and Remaining Work columns you will work with shortly, though they might not yet be visible. The values in the Work column are the task and assignment totals for scheduled work. Note that each task's work value is the sum of its assignment work values. For example, the work total for Task 2, 48 hours, is the sum of Clair Hector's 28 hours of work on the task and Scott Cooper's 20 hours.

Next you'll change the details shown on the timephased grid on the right side of the view.

9 On the Format menu, point to Details, and then click Actual Work.

For each task and assignment, Microsoft Project displays the Work and Actual Work rows on the timephased grid on the right side of the view. Your screen should look similar to the following illustration:

When you display the actual work details, the Act. Work row appears in the timephased grid for every assignment, task, and summary task.

	Task Name	Work	Details	Mar 7, '04								Mar 14,
				S	S	M	T	W	T	F	S	S
1	⊟ Pre-Production	1,215.78 hrs	Work			24h	24h	24h	24h	24h		
			Act. W									
2	⊟ Review script	48 hrs	Work									
			Act. W									
	Clair Hector	28 hrs	Work									
			Act. W									
	Scott Cooper	20 hrs	Work									
			Act. W									
3	⊟ Develop script breakdo	120 hrs	Work			18h	24h	24h	24h	24h		
			Act. W									
	Clair Hector	40 hrs	Work			6h	8h	8h	8h	8h		
			Act. W									
	Johnathan Perrera	40 hrs	Work			6h	8h	8h	8h	8h		
			Act. W									
	Scott Cooper	40 hrs	Work			6h	8h	8h	8h	8h		
			Act. W									
4	⊟ Develop production boz	347.78 hrs	Work									
			Act. W									
	Johnathan Perrera	114.6 hrs	Work									
			Act. W									
	Kim Yoshida	118.6 hrs	Work									
			Act. W									
	Scott Cooper	114.6 hrs	Work									

In the timephased grid, you see the scheduled work values per day. If you were to add up the daily work values for a specific task or assignment, the total would equal the value in the Work column for that task or assignment. In a usage view, you see work values at two different levels of detail: the total value for a task or assignment and the more detailed timephased level. These two sets of values are directly related.

Next you'll enter task-level and assignment-level actual work values, and see how they are reflected in the timephased details.

10 Using the mouse, drag the vertical divider bar to the right until you can see all the columns in the Work table.

Tip

Vertical Divider Pointer

⊣|⊢

When the mouse pointer is in the right position to drag the vertical divider bar, it changes to a two-headed arrow.

Your screen should look similar to the illustration on the following page.

To see more or less of the table on the left and the timephased grid on the right, drag this divider bar left or right.

#	Task Name	Work	Baseline	Variance	Actual	Remaining	% W. Comp.	Details	M
1	⊟ Pre-Production	1,215.78 hrs	1,215.78 hrs	0 hrs	48 hrs	1,167.78 hrs	4%	Work	24h
								Act. W	
2	⊟ Review script	48 hrs	48 hrs	0 hrs	48 hrs	0 hrs	100%	Work	
								Act. W	
	Clair Hector	28 hrs	28 hrs	0 hrs	28 hrs	0 hrs	100%	Work	
								Act. W	
	Scott Cooper	20 hrs	20 hrs	0 hrs	20 hrs	0 hrs	100%	Work	
								Act. W	
3	⊟ Develop script breakdo	120 hrs	120 hrs	0 hrs	0 hrs	120 hrs	0%	Work	18h
								Act. W	
	Clair Hector	40 hrs	40 hrs	0 hrs	0 hrs	40 hrs	0%	Work	6h
								Act. W	
	Johnathan Perrers	40 hrs	40 hrs	0 hrs	0 hrs	40 hrs	0%	Work	6h
								Act. W	
	Scott Cooper	40 hrs	40 hrs	0 hrs	0 hrs	40 hrs	0%	Work	6h
								Act. W	
4	⊟ Develop production boe	347.78 hrs	347.78 hrs	0 hrs	0 hrs	347.78 hrs	0%	Work	
								Act. W	
	Johnathan Perrers	114.6 hrs	114.6 hrs	0 hrs	0 hrs	114.6 hrs	0%	Work	
								Act. W	
	Kim Yoshida	118.6 hrs	118.6 hrs	0 hrs	0 hrs	118.6 hrs	0%	Work	
								Act. W	
	Scott Cooper	114.6 hrs	114.6 hrs	0 hrs	0 hrs	114.6 hrs	0%	Work	

11 In the Actual column for Task 3, Develop script breakdown and schedule, type or click **42h**, and then press Enter.

Your screen should look similar to the following illustration:

Entering an actual value for the task causes Microsoft Project to distribute the actual values among the assigned resources and adjust remaining work and other values.

#	Task Name	Work	Baseline	Variance	Actual	Remaining	% W. Comp.	Details	M
1	⊟ Pre-Production	1,215.78 hrs	1,215.78 hrs	0 hrs	90 hrs	1,125.78 hrs	7%	Work	24h
								Act. W	18h
2	⊟ Review script	48 hrs	48 hrs	0 hrs	48 hrs	0 hrs	100%	Work	
								Act. W	
	Clair Hector	28 hrs	28 hrs	0 hrs	28 hrs	0 hrs	100%	Work	
								Act. W	
	Scott Cooper	20 hrs	20 hrs	0 hrs	20 hrs	0 hrs	100%	Work	
								Act. W	
3	⊟ Develop script breakdo	120 hrs	120 hrs	0 hrs	42 hrs	78 hrs	35%	Work	18h
								Act. W	18h
	Clair Hector	40 hrs	40 hrs	0 hrs	14 hrs	26 hrs	35%	Work	6h
								Act. W	6h
	Johnathan Perrera	40 hrs	40 hrs	0 hrs	14 hrs	26 hrs	35%	Work	6h
								Act. W	6h
	Scott Cooper	40 hrs	40 hrs	0 hrs	14 hrs	26 hrs	35%	Work	6h
								Act. W	6h
4	⊟ Develop production boe	347.78 hrs	347.78 hrs	0 hrs	0 hrs	347.78 hrs	0%	Work	
								Act. W	
	Johnathan Perrera	114.6 hrs	114.6 hrs	0 hrs	0 hrs	114.6 hrs	0%	Work	
								Act. W	
	Kim Yoshida	118.6 hrs	118.6 hrs	0 hrs	0 hrs	118.6 hrs	0%	Work	
								Act. W	
	Scott Cooper	114.6 hrs	114.6 hrs	0 hrs	0 hrs	114.6 hrs	0%	Work	

Several important things happened when you pressed Enter:

- The amount of actual work you entered was subtracted from the Remaining column.

- The actual work is distributed to the three assignments on the task, resulting in 14 hours of actual work being recorded for each resource. Likewise, the updated remaining work value was recalculated for each assignment.

- The updated actual and remaining work values were "rolled up" to the pre-production summary task.

- The actual work values were also redistributed to the task and assignment timephased values. Next you'll take a closer look at these values.

12 Drag the vertical divider bar to the left until you see just the Task Name column in the Work table.

Your screen should look similar to the following illustration:

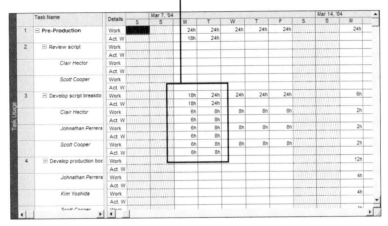

The actual work value entered for the task is also distributed among the assigned resources in the timephased grid.

In the timephased grid side of the view, you can see the daily scheduled work and actual work values for the three resources on Monday and Tuesday, March 8 and 9. Because you entered an actual work value for the entire task, Microsoft Project assumes that the work was done as scheduled (six hours of scheduled work per resource on Monday and eight hours on Tuesday) and records these timephased values for the resources.

To conclude this exercise, you will enter assignment work values and see the effect on the task.

13 Drag the vertical divider bar back to the right until you see all the columns in the Work table.

14 In the Actual column for Clair Hector's assignment to Task 3, type or click **30h**, and then press Enter.

Your screen should look similar to the illustration on the following page.

Entering an actual value for the assignment causes Microsoft Project to roll up the actual value to the task, but does not affect the other assignments.

	Task Name	Work	Baseline	Variance	Actual	Remaining	% W. Comp.	Details	M
1	⊟ Pre-Production	1,215.78 hrs	1,215.78 hrs	0 hrs	106 hrs	1,109.78 hrs	9%	Work	24h
								Act. W	18h
2	⊟ Review script	48 hrs	48 hrs	0 hrs	48 hrs	0 hrs	100%	Work	
								Act. W	
	Clair Hector	28 hrs	28 hrs	0 hrs	28 hrs	0 hrs	100%	Work	
								Act. W	
	Scott Cooper	20 hrs	20 hrs	0 hrs	20 hrs	0 hrs	100%	Work	
								Act. W	
3	⊟ Develop script breakdo	120 hrs	120 hrs	0 hrs	58 hrs	62 hrs	48%	Work	18h
								Act. W	18h
	Clair Hector	40 hrs	40 hrs	0 hrs	30 hrs	10 hrs	75%	Work	6h
								Act. W	6h
	Johnathan Perrera	40 hrs	40 hrs	0 hrs	14 hrs	26 hrs	35%	Work	6h
								Act. W	6h
	Scott Cooper	40 hrs	40 hrs	0 hrs	14 hrs	26 hrs	35%	Work	6h
								Act. W	6h
4	⊟ Develop production boc	347.78 hrs	347.78 hrs	0 hrs	0 hrs	347.78 hrs	0%	Work	
								Act. W	
	Johnathan Perrera	114.6 hrs	114.6 hrs	0 hrs	0 hrs	114.6 hrs	0%	Work	
								Act. W	
	Kim Yoshida	118.6 hrs	118.6 hrs	0 hrs	0 hrs	118.6 hrs	0%	Work	
								Act. W	
	Scott Cooper	114.6 hrs	114.6 hrs	0 hrs	0 hrs	114.6 hrs	0%	Work	

Clair Hector's actual and remaining work values are updated, and those updates also roll up to the task and its summary task. However, the actual and remaining work values for the other two resources assigned to the task are not affected.

15 Drag the vertical divider bar back to the left to see the updated timephased values for the task.

Your screen should look similar to the following illustration:

The actual work value entered for the assignment is rolled up to the task and distributed among the assigned resources in the timephased grid.

	Task Name	Details	Mar 7, '04							Mar 14, '04		
			S	S	M	T	W	T	F	S	S	M
1	⊟ Pre-Production	Work			24h	24h	24h	24h	24h			24h
		Act. W			18h	24h	8h	8h				
2	⊟ Review script	Work										
		Act. W										
	Clair Hector	Work										
		Act. W										
	Scott Cooper	Work										
		Act. W										
3	⊟ Develop script breakdo	Work			18h	24h	24h	24h	24h			6h
		Act. W			18h	24h	8h	8h				
	Clair Hector	Work			6h	8h	8h	8h	8h			2h
		Act. W			6h	8h	8h	8h				
	Johnathan Perrera	Work			6h	8h	8h	8h	8h			2h
		Act. W			6h	8h						
	Scott Cooper	Work			6h	8h	8h	8h	8h			2h
		Act. W			6h	8h						
4	⊟ Develop production boc	Work										12h
		Act. W										
	Johnathan Perrera	Work										4h
		Act. W										
	Kim Yoshida	Work										4h
		Act. W										
	Scott Cooper	Work										

Again Microsoft Project assumes that the actual work value you entered for Clair was completed as scheduled, so her work and actual work timephased values match through Thursday, March 11.

Save

16 On the Standard toolbar, click the Save button.

17 On the File menu, click Close to close the project plan.

Tip

In this exercise, you're entering actual work values but you can also enter remaining work values or percentage of work complete. All these values are related to each other—a change to one affects the others. You can update these values in the Work table or on the Tracking tab of the Assignment Information dialog box (when an assignment is selected).

Tracking a task's actual work complete value is more detailed than entering a simple percentage complete on a task. However, neither method is as detailed as entering time-phased actual work for tasks or assignments (as you will see in the next section). There's nothing wrong with tracking actual work at the task or assignment level (or just entering a percentage complete, for that matter) if that level of detail meets your needs. In fact, whether you see the timephased details or not, Microsoft Project always distributes any percentage complete or task-level or assignment-level actual work value you enter into corresponding timephased values, as you saw earlier. This is one reason why new Microsoft Project users sometimes are surprised to encounter extremely detailed timephased values, such as 1.67 hours of work, scheduled for a day. If you generally understand the math Microsoft Project is following, however, you can figure out where such numbers come from. On the other hand, you might not care about this level of scheduling detail—and that's OK too.

Manually Entering Actual Costs

Whenever you've entered actual work values in this chapter, Microsoft Project has calculated actual cost values for the affected task, its summary task, the resources assigned to the task, and the entire project. By default, Microsoft Project calculates actual costs and doesn't allow you to enter them directly. In most cases this is what we recommend, however if you want to enter actual cost values yourself, follow these steps:

1 On the Tools menu, click the Options command.

2 The Options dialog box appears.

3 Click the Calculation tab.

4 Under the Calculation Options label, clear the Actual Costs Are Always Calculated By Microsoft Project check box.

5 Click OK.

After automatic cost calculation is turned off, you can enter or import task-level or assignment-level actual costs in the Actual field. This field is available in several locations, such as the Cost table. You can also enter actual cost values on a daily or other interval in any timescale view, such as the Task Usage or the Resource Usage. On the Format menu, point to the Details command, and then click Actual Cost.

Tracking Timephased Actual Work for Tasks and Assignments

Tip

When you need to track actual work at the most detailed level possible, use the timephased grid in the Task Usage or the Resource Usage view. In either view, you can enter actual work values for individual assignments daily, weekly, or at whatever time period you want. For example, if a task has three resources assigned to it, and you know that two resources worked on the task for eight hours one day and the third worked for six hours, you can enter these as three separate values on a timephased grid.

If your organization uses a timesheet reporting system for tracking actual work, you might be able to use this timesheet data in Microsoft Project as timephased actuals. You might not need to track at this level, but if resources complete timesheets for other purposes (billing other departments within the organization, for example), you can use their data and save yourself some work.

Entering timephased actuals requires more work on the project manager's part and might require more work from resources to inform the project manager of their daily actuals. However, doing so gives you far more detail about the project's task and resource status than the other methods of entering actuals. Entering timephased values might be the best approach to take if you have a group of tasks or an entire project that have the following qualities:

- High-risk tasks
- Relatively short-duration tasks in which a variance of even a fraction of a day could put the overall project at risk
- Tasks in which sponsors or other stakeholders have an especially strong interest
- Tasks that require hourly billing for labor

At this point in the short film project, the pre-production work has been completed, and the production phase has just begun. Because of the large number of resources involved, the high setup and teardown costs, and the limited availability of sites at which some scenes must be filmed, these tasks are the riskiest ones of the project. In this exercise, you enter daily actuals for production tasks in the Task Usage view:

Open

1   On the Standard toolbar, click the Open button.

The Open dialog box appears.

2   Double-click Short Film Project 14c.

3 On the File menu, click Save As.

The Save As dialog box appears.

4 In the File Name box, type **Short Film Project 14 Timephased Actuals**, and then click the Save button.

5 Click the minus sign next to Task 1, *Pre-Production*, to collapse this phase of the project plan.

Go To
Selected Task

6 Click the name of Task 28, Scene 7 setup, and then on the Standard toolbar, click the Go To Selected Task button.

Microsoft Project scrolls the timephased grid to display the first scheduled work values of the Production phase. Your screen should look similar to the following illustration:

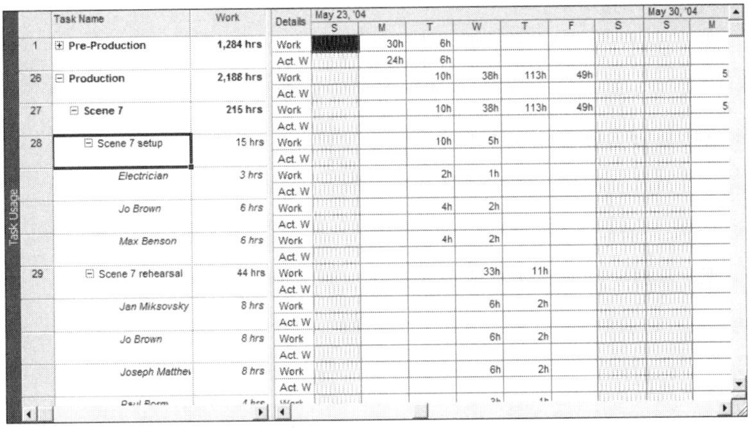

	Task Name	Work	Details	May 23, '04							May 30, '04	
				S	M	T	W	T	F	S	S	M
1	⊞ Pre-Production	1,284 hrs	Work		30h	6h						
			Act. W		24h	6h						
26	⊟ Production	2,188 hrs	Work			10h	38h	113h	49h			5
			Act. W									
27	⊟ Scene 7	215 hrs	Work			10h	38h	113h	49h			5
			Act. W									
28	⊟ Scene 7 setup	15 hrs	Work			10h	5h					
			Act. W									
	Electrician	3 hrs	Work			2h	1h					
			Act. W									
	Jo Brown	6 hrs	Work			4h	2h					
			Act. W									
	Max Benson	6 hrs	Work			4h	2h					
			Act. W									
29	⊟ Scene 7 rehearsal	44 hrs	Work				33h	11h				
			Act. W									
	Jan Miksovsky	8 hrs	Work				6h	2h				
			Act. W									
	Jo Brown	8 hrs	Work				6h	2h				
			Act. W									
	Joseph Matthei	8 hrs	Work				6h	2h				
			Act. W									
	Paul Born	4 hrs	Work				3h	1h				

The first timephased actual work values you will enter are at the task level, and not for specific assignments.

7 In the timephased grid, click the cell at the intersection of the Tuesday, May 25 column and the Task 28 actual work row.

Tip

If you point to the name of a day on the timescale, Microsoft Project will display the full date of that day in a ScreenTip.

You can change the formatting of the timescale to control the time period in which you enter actual values in the timephased grid. For example, you can format it to show weeks rather than days, and when you enter an actual value at the weekly level, that value is distributed over the week. For more information about adjusting the timescale, type **Change timescale** into the Ask A Question box in the upper right corner of the Microsoft Project window.

8   Type **10h**, and then press the Right Arrow key.

Your screen should look similar to the following illustration:

Here is the first timephased
actual work value you entered.

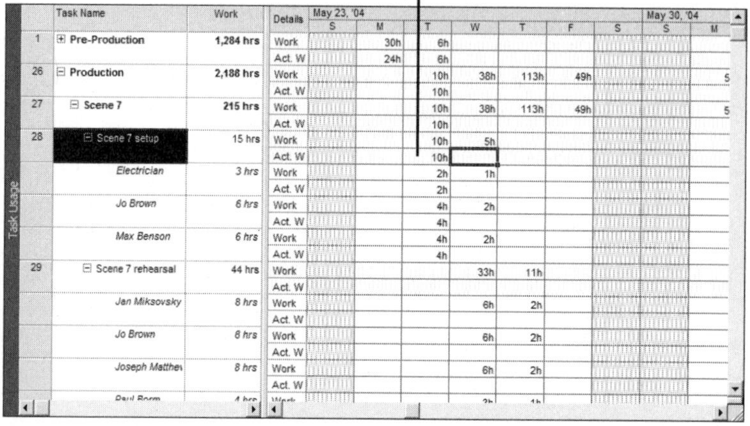

As soon as you entered the first actual value for the task, the scheduled work value changed to match it. Both work and actual work values rolled up to the task and summary task levels and were distributed among the specific assignments to the task. You can see this happen in the timephased grid.

9   In the Wednesday, May 26 actual work cell, type **5h**, and then press Enter.

Your screen should look similar to the following illustration:

Here is the second timephased actual
work value you entered. The timephased
values for the task are distributed to the
timephased assignment values and
affect the task and assignment
totals on the left.

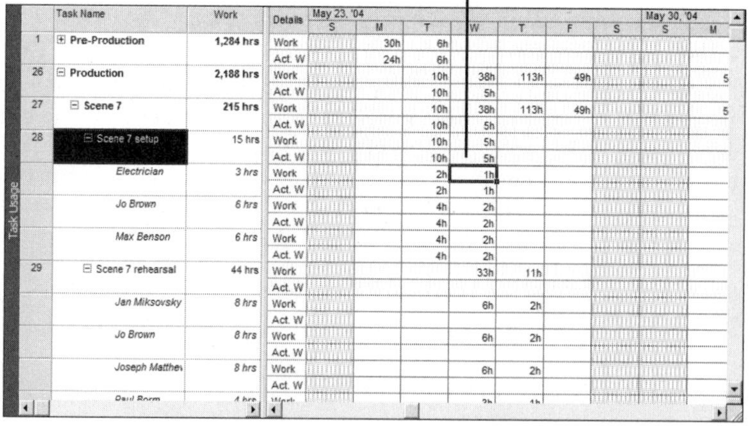

That concludes the actual work for this task. Next you'll enter actual work values for the assignments on the next task.

For Task 29, *Scene 7 rehearsal*, you have the following individual resources' actual work values for Wednesday and Thursday, July 11 and 12, 2004.

10 Scroll the Task Usage view up so that all of the assignments to Task 29 are visible.

11 In the timephased grid, click the cell at the intersection of the Wednesday, May 26 column and Jan Miksovsky's actual work row for her assignment to Task 29.

12 Enter the following actual work values into the timescale grid:

Resource name	Wednesday's actual work	Thursday's actual work
Jan Miksovsky	3h	5h
Jo Brown	3h	5h
Joseph Matthews	2h	7h
Paul Borm	3h	1h
Scott Cooper	2.5h	5.5h
Sue Jackson	6h	2h

When you are finished, your screen should look similar to the following illustration:

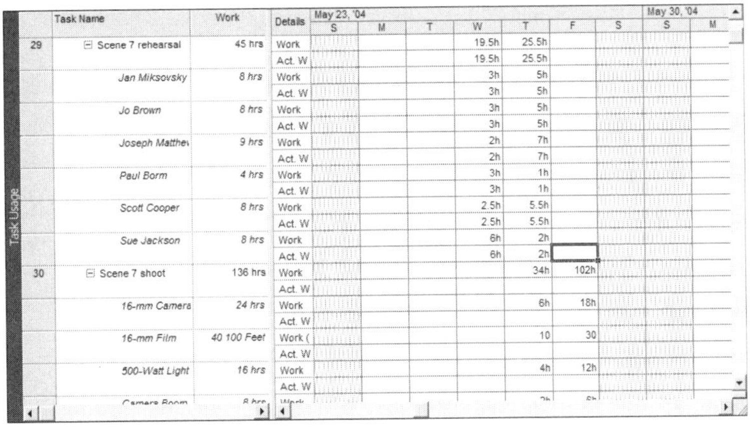

Again, the individual resources' actual work values were rolled up to the tasks' actual work values.

13 On the Standard toolbar, click the Save button.

14 On the File menu, click Close to close the project plan.

Save

Tip

In this exercise, you have seen how task and assignment values are directly related; an update to one directly affects the other. However, if you want, you can break this relationship. Doing so enables you to record progress for resource assignments, for example, and manually enter schedule values for the tasks to which those resources are assigned. You normally should not break this relationship unless you have special reporting needs within your organization— for example, you must follow a status reporting methodology based on something other than the actual values recorded for assignments in project plans. To break this relationship, on the Tools menu, click Options. On the Calculation tab of the Options dialog box, clear the Updating Task Status Updates Resource Status check box. This setting applies to the entire project plan you have open at the time; you cannot apply it just to some tasks within a project plan.

Project Management Focus: Collecting Actuals from Resources

The table you used in the previous exercise is similar to a time card. In fact, to enter assignment-level actual work values, you need some form of paper time card or its electronic equivalent. Several methods are used to collect such data from resources, assuming that you need to track actuals at this level of detail. Some collection methods include the following:

■ Use Microsoft Project in conjunction with Microsoft Project Server for intranet-based team collaboration, tracking, and status reporting. To learn more about Microsoft Project 2002 Server, see Appendix A, "Introducing Microsoft Project Server."

■ Collect actual values yourself. This method is feasible if you communicate with only a small group of resources on a frequent basis. It's also a good opportunity to talk directly to the resources about any surprises they might have encountered (either positive or negative) while performing the work.

■ Collect actuals through a formal status reporting system. This technique might work through the already existing hierarchy of your organization and serve additional purposes besides project status reporting.

■ Use Microsoft Project's e-mail-based collaboration features to collect assignment status data.

Tip

For more information, type **About using a MAPI-based e-mail system for team communication** into the Ask A Question box in the upper right corner of the Microsoft Project window.

Rescheduling Incomplete Work

During the course of a project, from time to time work might be interrupted for a specific task or for the entire project. Should this happen, you can have Microsoft Project reschedule the remaining work to restart after the date you specify.

When you reschedule incomplete work, you specify the date after which work can resume—the rescheduled date. Here is how Microsoft Project handles tasks in relation to the rescheduled date:

■ If the task does not have any actual work recorded for it prior to the rescheduled date and does not have a constraint applied, the entire task is rescheduled to begin after that date.

■ If the task has some actual work recorded prior to but none after the rescheduled date, the task is split so that all remaining work starts after the rescheduled date. The actual work is not affected.

■ If the task has some actual work recorded for it prior to as well as after the rescheduled date, the task is not affected.

At this point in the short film project, work on the first two scenes has been completed and the team is about to start work on the next scheduled scene, Scene 1. In this exercise, you troubleshoot a delay in work caused by a problem at the studio:

Open

1 On the Standard toolbar, click the Open button.

The Open dialog box appears.

2 Double-click Short Film Project 14d.

3 On the File menu, click Save As.

The Save As dialog box appears.

4 In the File Name box, type **Short Film Project 14 Reschedule**, and then click the Save button.

5 On the Edit menu, click Go To, enter **40** in the ID box, and then click OK.

The Gantt Chart view scrolls to display the Gantt bar for Task 40, *Scene 1 setup*. Currently this task has one day of actual work completed and two days of scheduled work remaining.

6 Scroll the Gantt Chart view up so that the Scene 1 summary task appears near the top.

Your screen should look similar to the following illustration:

Progress bars indicate the portion of the task that has been completed—in this case, one day of a three-day task.

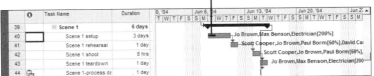

You have learned that on the evening of Tuesday, June 8, a water pipe burst in the studio where Scene 1 was to be shot. None of the project's equipment was damaged, but the cleanup will delay work until the following Monday, June 14. This effectively stops work on the production tasks for the rest of the week. Next you will reschedule incomplete work so the project can start again on Monday.

7 On the Tools menu, point to Tracking, and then click Update Project.

The Update Project dialog box appears.

8 Select the Reschedule Uncompleted Work To Start After option, and in the date box, type or click **6/13/04**.

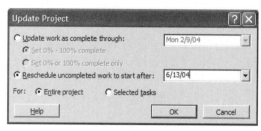

9 Click OK to close the Update Project dialog box.

10 If the Planning Wizard displays an alert, click OK.

Microsoft Project splits Task 40 so that the incomplete portion of the task is delayed until Monday. Your screen should look similar to the following illustration:

Rescheduling work for the project causes Microsoft Project to split this task, and then reschedule the remainder of it (and all subsequent tasks) after the date you specified.

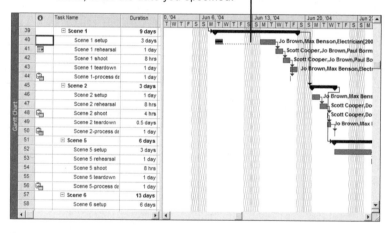

As you can see, although the duration of Task 40 remains at three days, its finish date and subsequent start dates for successor tasks have been pushed out. So although we have addressed a specific problem, in doing so we have created other problems in the remainder of the project. You will address this and other problems in the project plan in later chapters.

Tip

You can turn off Microsoft Project's ability to reschedule incomplete work on tasks that have any actual work. On the Tools menu, click the Options command. In the Options dialog box, click the Schedule tab, and then clear the Split In-Progress Tasks box.

Reschedule around status date
new in
Project 2002

If you use status dates for reporting actuals, Microsoft Project supports several options for controlling the way completed and incomplete segments of a task are scheduled around the status date. On the Tools menu, click the Options command. In the Options dialog box, click the Calculation tab. The options that control scheduling around the status date are Move End Of Completed Parts After Status Date Back To Status Date and the three other check boxes below it.

For more information about these and other options on these tabs of the Options dialog box, click the Help button that appears in the dialog box. To learn more about working with status dates in Microsoft Project, type **About the status date** into the Ask A Question box in the upper right corner of the Microsoft Project window.

Chapter Wrap-Up

This chapter covered how to update a baseline, enter task-level and assignment-level actual work and timephased actual work values, and reschedule incomplete work.

If you are going on to other chapters:

Save

1 On the Standard toolbar, click the Save button to save changes made to Short Film Project 14 Reschedule.

2 On the File menu, click Close to close the project plan.

If you aren't continuing to other chapters:

1 On the Standard toolbar, click the Save button to save changes made to Short Film Project 14 Reschedule.

2 To quit Microsoft Project for now, on the File menu, click Exit.

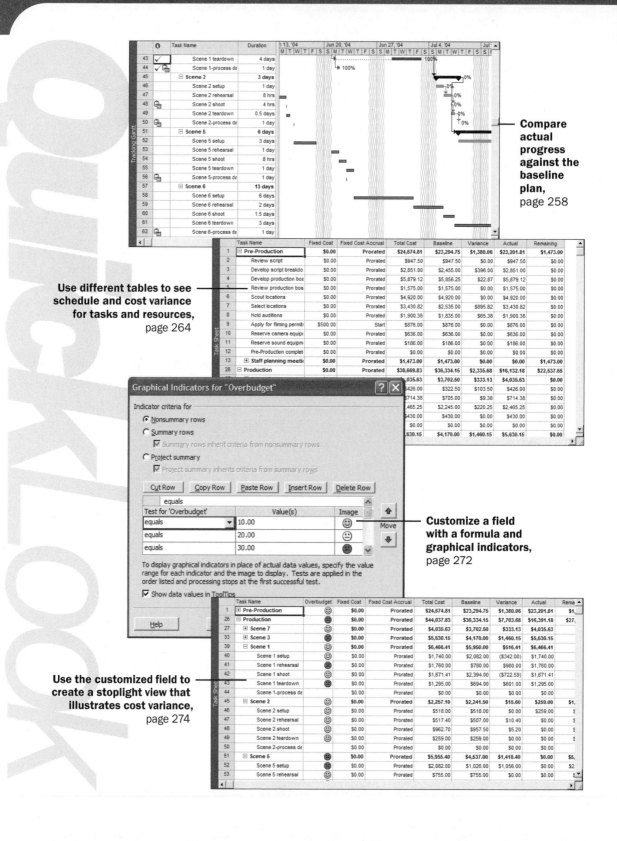

Compare actual progress against the baseline plan, page 258

Use different tables to see schedule and cost variance for tasks and resources, page 264

Graphical Indicators for "Overbudget"

Indicator criteria for
- ○ Nonsummary rows
- ○ Summary rows
  - ☑ Summary rows inherit criteria from nonsummary rows
- ○ Project summary
  - ☑ Project summary inherits criteria from summary rows

Cut Row | Copy Row | Paste Row | Insert Row | Delete Row

equals

Test for 'Overbudget'	Value(s)	Image
equals	10.00	☺
equals	20.00	☺
equals	30.00	☹

Move

To display graphical indicators in place of actual data values, specify the value range for each indicator and the image to display. Tests are applied in the order listed and processing stops at the first successful test.

☑ Show data values in ToolTips

Help

Customize a field with a formula and graphical indicators, page 272

Use the customized field to create a stoplight view that illustrates cost variance, page 274

Chapter 15
Viewing and Reporting Project Status

After completing this chapter, you will be able to:

✔ **Determine which tasks were started or completed late.**

✔ **View task costs at summary and detail levels.**

✔ **Examine resource costs and variance.**

✔ **Use custom fields to create a stoplight view that illustrates each task's cost variance.**

After a project's *baseline* has been set and work has begun, the primary focus of the project manager shifts from planning to collecting, entering, and analyzing project performance details. For most projects, these performance details boil down to three primary questions or vital signs:

■ How much work was required to complete a task?

■ Did the task start and finish on time?

■ What was the cost of completing the task?

Comparing the answers to these questions against the baseline gives the project manager and other *stakeholders* a good way to measure the project's progress and to know when corrective action might be necessary.

Communicating project status to key stakeholders such as customers and sponsors is arguably the most important function of a project manager, and one that might occupy much of your working time. Although perfect flow of communication can't guarantee a project's success, a project with poor communications flow is almost guaranteed to fail.

A key to properly communicating project status is knowing the following:

■ Who needs to know the project's status and for what purpose?

■ What format or level of detail do these people need?

The time to answer these questions is in the initial planning phase of the project. After work on the project is under way, your main communications task will be reporting project status. This can take several forms:

■ Status reports that describe where the project is in terms of cost, scope, and schedule (these are the three sides of the *project triangle*)

■ Progress reports that document the specific accomplishments of the project team

■ Forecasts that predict future project performance

Where the scheduled or actual project performance differs from the baseline plan, you have *variance*. Variance is usually measured as time, such as days behind schedule, or as cost, such as dollars over budget. After initial project planning is complete, many project managers spend most of their time identifying, justifying, and, in many cases, responding to variance. However, before you can respond to variance, you must first identify, document, and report it. That is the subject of this chapter.

Short Film
Project 15a

This chapter uses the practice file Short Film Project 15a. For details about installing the practice files, see "Using the Book's CD-ROM" at the beginning of this book.

Identifying Tasks That Have Slipped

One cause of variance is delays in starting or finishing tasks. You'd certainly want to know about tasks that started late or future tasks that might not start as scheduled. It's also helpful to identify completed tasks that did not start on time, and to try to determine why.

There are different ways to see delayed tasks, depending on the type of information you want:

■ Apply the Tracking Gantt view to graphically compare tasks' baseline dates with their actual or scheduled dates.

■ Apply the Variance table to a task view to see the number of days of variance for each task's start and finish dates.

■ Filter for delayed or slipping tasks with the Slipped/Late Progress or Slipping Tasks filters.

In this exercise, you apply these and other methods to identify variance:

1 If Microsoft Project is not already open, start it now.

Open

2 On the Standard toolbar, click the Open button.

The Open dialog box appears.

3 Navigate to the Chapter 15 Reporting Status folder, and double-click the Short Film Project 15a file.

4 On the File menu, click Save As.

The Save As dialog box appears.

5 In the File Name box, type **Short Film Project 15**, and then click the Save button.

To begin your analysis of tasks that have slipped, you'll start at the highest level—the project summary information.

6 On the Project menu, click Project Information.

The Project Information dialog box appears.

7 Click the Statistics button.

The Project Statistics dialog box appears.

Here you can see the start and finish values for the project, including the finish date's variance.

Project Statistics for 'Short Film Project 15'

	Start	Finish
Current	Mon 3/1/04	Fri 1/7/05
Baseline	Mon 3/1/04	Thu 12/16/04
Actual	Mon 3/1/04	NA
Variance	0d	16d

	Duration	Work	Cost
Current	224.5d	5,300h	$91,812.55
Baseline	208.5d	5,206h	$89,161.55
Actual	87.08d	2,121h	$39,334.00
Remaining	137.42d	3,179h	$52,478.55

Percent complete:

Duration: 39%   Work: 40%

[Close]

In this dialog box you can see, among other things, that the project currently has 16 days of schedule variance on the finish date. In effect, the overall project finish date has slipped out this number of days.

8 Click the Close button to close the Project Statistics dialog box.

For the remainder of this exercise, you will use various techniques to examine the specific task variance.

9 On the View menu, click Tracking Gantt.

Microsoft Project displays the Tracking Gantt view.

10 In the Task Name column, click the name of Task 3, *Develop script breakdown and schedule.*

Go To
Selected Task

11 On the Standard toolbar, click the Go to Selected Task button.

In the chart portion of this view, the tasks as they are currently scheduled appear as blue bars (if they are not critical tasks) or red bars (if they are critical). In the lower half of each task's row, the baseline values of each task appear as gray bars.

Your screen should look similar to the following illustration:

These blue bars represent the task as they are currently scheduled or were completed. — The original baseline schedule appears as gray bars in the Tracking Gantt view.

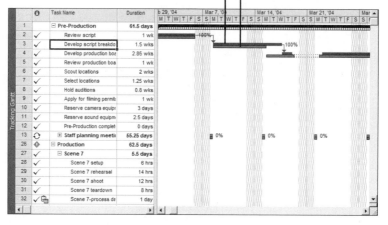

Here you can see where tasks began to vary from their baselines. Tasks 2 and 3 started as planned, but Task 3 finished later than planned.

12 On the Edit menu, click Go To.

The Go To dialog box appears.

Tip

Remember that Ctrl+G is a keyboard shortcut for displaying the Go To dialog box.

13 In the ID box, type **43**, and click OK.

Microsoft Project scrolls the Tracking Gantt view to display Task 43 and its adjacent tasks. Your screen should look similar to the following illustration:

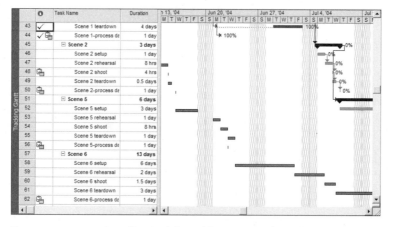

Here, you can see baseline task bars (the patterned gray bars), completed task bars (the solid blue bars), and bars for tasks scheduled but not yet not started (the red bars).

Tip

To see details about any bar or other item in a Gantt Chart view, position the mouse pointer over it. After a moment, a ScreenTip appears with details. To see a legend of all Gantt bar color coding and symbols, on the Format menu, click Bar Styles, and in the Bar Styles dialog box, look at the Name and Appearance columns.

To focus in on just the slipping tasks, you will apply a filter.

14 On the Project menu, point to Filtered For: All Tasks, and then click More Filters.

The More Filters dialog box appears. In it, you can see all the predefined filters for tasks (when in a task view) and resources (when in a resource view) available to you.

15 In the More Filters box, click Slipping Tasks, and then click the Apply button.

Microsoft Project filters the task list to show only those tasks that, as they are now scheduled, have slipped from their baseline plan. Your screen should look similar to the following illustration:

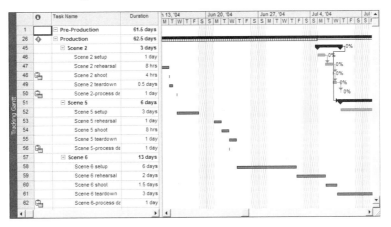

Note the gaps in the Task ID numbers. Tasks 2 through 25, for example, do not appear with the filter applied, because they are already complete.

Tip

All filters are also available to you via the Filter button on the Formatting toolbar. The name of the active filter appears in this button; click the arrow next to the filter name to see other filters. If no filter is applied to the current view, *All Tasks* or *All Resources* appears on the button, depending on the type of view currently displayed.

Filter

| All Tasks | ▼ |

You can see the criteria that most filters use to determine which tasks or resources they will display or hide. On the Project menu, point to Filter For: AllTasks, and then click More Filters. In the More Filters dialog box, click a filter and click the Edit button. In the Filter Definition dialog box, you can see the tests applied to various fields for the filter.

16 In the table portion of the view on the left, click the name of Task 45, *Scene 2*.

17 On the Standard toolbar, click the Go to Selected Task button.

The timescale side of the view scrolls to show you the scheduled duration for this and adjacent tasks. Your screen should look similar to the following illustration:

These red bars in the Tracking Gantt view represent tasks that are on the critical path; any delays in completing these tasks will delay the project finish date.

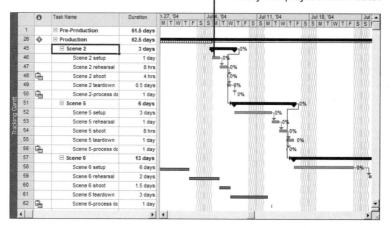

At this point in the schedule, the scheduled start date of tasks has slipped quite a bit. (To visually verify how much these tasks have slipped, you can scroll the chart portion of the Tracking Gantt view to the left to see the baseline Gantt bars for each task.) These tasks' scheduled Gantt bars are formatted red to indicate that they are critical, meaning that any delay in completing these tasks will delay the project's finish date.

Tip

The Slipping Tasks report describes tasks that are off schedule. On the View menu, click Reports. In the Reports dialog box, double-click Current Activities, and then double-click Slipping Tasks.

18 On the Project menu, point to Filtered For: Slipping Tasks, and then click All Tasks.

Microsoft Project removes the filter. As always, displaying or removing a filter has no effect on the original data.

The Tracking Gantt view graphically illustrates the difference between scheduled, actual, and baseline project performance. To see this information in a table format, you will display the Variance table in the Task Sheet view.

19 On the View menu, click More Views.

The More Views dialog box appears.

20 In the Views list, click Task Sheet, and then click the Apply button.

Microsoft Project displays the Task Sheet view. Next you'll switch to the Variance table.

21 On the View menu, point to Table: Entry, and then click Variance.

Tip

You also can right-click the Select All button in the upper left corner of the active table to switch to a different table.

The Variance table appears in the Task Sheet view. Your screen should look similar to the following illustration:

To quickly switch to a different table, right-click here, and then click the table you want.

	Task Name	Start	Finish	Baseline Start	Baseline Finish	Start Var.	Finish Var.
1	⊟ Pre-Production	Mon 3/1/04	Tue 5/25/04	Mon 3/1/04	Mon 5/24/04	0 days	1.25 days
2	Review script	Mon 3/1/04	Fri 3/5/04	Mon 3/1/04	Fri 3/5/04	0 days	0 days
3	Develop script bre	Mon 3/8/04	Wed 3/17/04	Mon 3/8/04	Mon 3/15/04	0 days	2.25 days
4	Develop productio	Wed 3/17/04	Thu 4/8/04	Mon 3/15/04	Wed 4/7/04	2.25 days	1.68 days
5	Review productior	Fri 4/9/04	Fri 4/16/04	Wed 4/7/04	Wed 4/14/04	1.68 days	2.68 days
6	Scout locations	Mon 4/19/04	Fri 4/30/04	Wed 4/14/04	Wed 4/28/04	2.68 days	2.68 days
7	Select locations	Mon 5/3/04	Tue 5/11/04	Wed 4/28/04	Wed 5/5/04	2.68 days	4.43 days
8	Hold auditions	Wed 5/12/04	Mon 5/17/04	Wed 5/5/04	Wed 5/12/04	4.43 days	3.18 days
9	Apply for filming p	Tue 5/18/04	Mon 5/24/04	Wed 5/12/04	Wed 5/19/04	3.18 days	3.18 days
10	Reserve camera e	Thu 5/20/04	Tue 5/25/04	Mon 5/17/04	Thu 5/20/04	3.18 days	3.18 days
11	Reserve sound eq	Thu 5/20/04	Mon 5/24/04	Mon 5/17/04	Thu 5/20/04	3.18 days	2.68 days
12	Pre-Production cor	Mon 5/24/04	Mon 5/24/04	Thu 5/20/04	Thu 5/20/04	2.68 days	2.68 days
13	⊞ Staff planning m	Mon 3/8/04	Mon 5/24/04	Mon 3/8/04	Mon 5/24/04	0 days	0 days
26	⊟ Production	Tue 5/25/04	Fri 8/20/04	Mon 5/24/04	Thu 7/29/04	1.25 days	16 days
27	⊟ Scene 7	Tue 5/25/04	Wed 6/2/04	Mon 5/24/04	Fri 5/28/04	1.25 days	3 days
28	Scene 7 setup	Tue 5/25/04	Wed 5/26/04	Mon 5/24/04	Mon 5/24/04	1.25 days	1.25 days
29	Scene 7 reheal	Wed 5/26/04	Thu 5/27/04	Tue 5/25/04	Tue 5/25/04	1.25 days	2 days
30	Scene 7 shoot	Fri 5/28/04	Mon 5/31/04	Wed 5/26/04	Wed 5/26/04	2 days	2.5 days
31	Scene 7 teardo	Mon 5/31/04	Tue 6/1/04	Thu 5/27/04	Thu 5/27/04	2.5 days	2.5 days
32	Scene 7-proce	Tue 6/1/04	Wed 6/2/04	Thu 5/27/04	Fri 5/28/04	3 days	3 days
33	⊟ Scene 3	Wed 6/2/04	Fri 6/11/04	Fri 5/28/04	Wed 6/2/04	3 days	7 days

In this table you can see the scheduled, baseline, and variance values per task.

Project Management Focus: Getting the Word Out

If you work in an organization that is highly focused on projects and project management, chances are that standard methods and formats already exist within your organization for reporting project status. If not, you might be able to introduce project status formats that are based on clear communication and project management principles.

Techniques you can use in Microsoft Project to help you report project status include the following:

- Printing the Project Summary report.

- Copying Microsoft Project data to other applications—for example, copying the Gantt Chart view to Microsoft Word or to Microsoft PowerPoint.

- Saving Microsoft Project data in other formats, such as HTML, using the Compare To Baseline export map.

- Sharing project status through Microsoft Project Server, enabling the stakeholders you choose to view project details through their Web browsers.

All these status-reporting tools are described elsewhere in this book.

Tip

In this exercise you have viewed variance for a task. To see variance for assignments to a task, switch to the Task Usage view, and then apply the Variance table (to see scheduled variance) or the Work table (to see work variance).

Examining Task Costs

The schedule's status (Did tasks start and finish on time?), although critical to nearly all projects, is only one indicator of overall project health. For projects that include cost information, another critical indicator is cost variance: Are tasks running over or under budget? Task costs in Microsoft Project consist of fixed costs applied directly to tasks, resource costs derived from assignments, or both. When tasks cost more or less than planned to complete, cost variance is the result. Evaluating cost variance enables you to make incremental budget adjustments for individual tasks to avoid exceeding your project's overall budget.

Tip

Another way of using project costs to measure past performance and predict future performance is earned value analysis. For more information about earned value analysis, type **All about earned value** into the Ask A Question box in the upper right corner of the Microsoft Project window. You can also see Chapter 19, "Measuring Performance with Earned Value Analysis."

Although tasks and resources (and their costs) are directly related, it's informative to evaluate each individually. In this exercise, you view task cost variance. Again you'll start at the highest level—the project summary information:

1 On the Project menu, click Project Information.

The Project Information dialog box appears.

2 Click the Statistics button.

The Project Statistics dialog box appears.

Here you can see the project's cost values.

Project Statistics for 'Short Film Project 15'

	Start	Finish
Current	Mon 3/1/04	Fri 1/7/05
Baseline	Mon 3/1/04	Thu 12/16/04
Actual	Mon 3/1/04	NA
Variance	0d	16d

	Duration	Work	Cost
Current	224.5d	5,300h	$91,812.55
Baseline	208.5d	5,206h	$89,161.55
Actual	87.08d	2,121h	$39,334.00
Remaining	137.42d	3,179h	$52,478.55

Percent complete:

Duration: 39%   Work: 40%

Close

In the Cost column, you can see the current, baseline, actual, and remaining cost values for the entire project:

■ The current cost value is the sum of the actual and remaining cost values.

■ The baseline cost value is the project's total planned cost when its baseline was saved.

■ The actual cost is the cost that's been incurred so far, after 39 percent of the project's duration and 40 percent of the total work have been completed.

■ The remaining cost is the difference between the current cost and actual cost.

■ Clearly, some cost variance has occurred, but you can't tell from this information when or where it occurred.

3 Click the Close button to close the Project Statistics dialog box.

Next you will switch to views where you can examine cost variance more closely, starting with the Cost table.

4 On the View menu, point to Table: Variance, and click Cost.

Tip

You also can right-click the upper left corner of the active table, and in the shortcut menu that appears, click Cost.

The Cost table appears in the Task Sheet view. Your screen should look similar to the following illustration:

	Task Name	Fixed Cost	Fixed Cost Accrual	Total Cost	Baseline	Variance	Actual	Remaining
1	⊟ Pre-Production	$0.00	Prorated	$24,674.81	$23,294.75	$1,380.06	$23,201.81	$1,473.00
2	Review script	$0.00	Prorated	$947.50	$947.50	$0.00	$947.50	$0.00
3	Develop script breakdo	$0.00	Prorated	$2,851.00	$2,455.00	$396.00	$2,851.00	$0.00
4	Develop production boa	$0.00	Prorated	$5,879.12	$5,856.25	$22.87	$5,879.12	$0.00
5	Review production boa	$0.00	Prorated	$1,575.00	$1,575.00	$0.00	$1,575.00	$0.00
6	Scout locations	$0.00	Prorated	$4,920.00	$4,920.00	$0.00	$4,920.00	$0.00
7	Select locations	$0.00	Prorated	$3,430.82	$2,535.00	$895.82	$3,430.82	$0.00
8	Hold auditions	$0.00	Prorated	$1,900.38	$1,835.00	$65.38	$1,900.38	$0.00
9	Apply for filming permit	$500.00	Start	$876.00	$876.00	$0.00	$876.00	$0.00
10	Reserve camera equipr	$0.00	Prorated	$636.00	$636.00	$0.00	$636.00	$0.00
11	Reserve sound equipm	$0.00	Prorated	$186.00	$186.00	$0.00	$186.00	$0.00
12	Pre-Production complet	$0.00	Prorated	$0.00	$0.00	$0.00	$0.00	$0.00
13	⊞ Staff planning meeti	$0.00	Prorated	$1,473.00	$1,473.00	$0.00	$0.00	$1,473.00
26	⊟ Production	$0.00	Prorated	$38,669.83	$36,334.15	$2,335.68	$16,132.18	$22,537.65
27	⊟ Scene 7	$0.00	Prorated	$4,035.63	$3,702.50	$333.13	$4,035.63	$0.00
28	Scene 7 setup	$0.00	Prorated	$426.00	$322.50	$103.50	$426.00	$0.00
29	Scene 7 rehearsal	$0.00	Prorated	$714.38	$705.00	$9.38	$714.38	$0.00
30	Scene 7 shoot	$0.00	Prorated	$2,465.25	$2,245.00	$220.25	$2,465.25	$0.00
31	Scene 7 teardown	$0.00	Prorated	$430.00	$430.00	$0.00	$430.00	$0.00
32	Scene 7-process da	$0.00	Prorated	$0.00	$0.00	$0.00	$0.00	$0.00
33	⊟ Scene 3	$0.00	Prorated	$5,630.15	$4,170.00	$1,460.15	$5,630.15	$0.00

In this table, you can see each task's baseline cost, scheduled cost (in the Total Cost column), actual cost, and variance. The variance is the difference between the baseline cost and the scheduled cost. Of course, costs aren't scheduled in the same sense that work is scheduled; however, costs (other than fixed costs) are derived directly from the scheduled work.

Next you'll focus on the top-level costs.

5 Click the Task Name column heading.

6 On the Formatting toolbar, click the Hide Subtasks button.

Microsoft Project displays only the top three summary tasks, which in this project correspond to the major phases of the short film project. Because we're currently working on tasks in the production phase, we'll direct our attention there.

7 Click the plus sign next to Task 26, *Production*.

Microsoft Project expands the Production summary task to show the summary tasks for the individual scenes. Your screen should look similar to the following illustration:

Here is the most significant variance — in the production phase at this point.

	Task Name	Fixed Cost	Fixed Cost Accrual	Total Cost	Baseline	Variance	Actual	Remaining
1	⊞ Pre-Production	$0.00	Prorated	$24,674.81	$23,294.75	$1,380.06	$23,201.81	$1,473.00
26	⊟ Production	$0.00	Prorated	$38,669.83	$36,334.15	$2,335.68	$16,132.18	$22,537.65
27	⊞ Scene 7	$0.00	Prorated	$4,035.63	$3,702.50	$333.13	$4,035.63	$0.00
33	⊞ Scene 3	$0.00	Prorated	$5,630.15	$4,170.00	$1,460.15	$5,630.15	$0.00
39	⊞ Scene 1	$0.00	Prorated	$6,466.41	$5,950.00	$516.41	$6,466.41	$0.00
45	⊞ Scene 2	$0.00	Prorated	$2,257.10	$2,241.50	$15.60	$0.00	$2,257.10
51	⊞ Scene 5	$0.00	Prorated	$4,547.40	$4,537.00	$10.40	$0.00	$4,547.40
57	⊞ Scene 6	$0.00	Prorated	$8,723.40	$8,723.40	$0.00	$0.00	$8,723.40
63	⊞ Scene 8	$0.00	Prorated	$5,278.20	$5,278.20	$0.00	$0.00	$5,278.20
69	⊞ Scene 4	$0.00	Prorated	$1,731.55	$1,731.55	$0.00	$0.00	$1,731.55
75	⊞ Post-Production	$0.00	Prorated	$28,467.90	$28,467.90	$0.00	$0.00	$28,467.90

Looking at the Variance column, you can see that Scenes 7 and 1 had some variance, and Scene 3 had significantly more. Next you'll focus on the details for Scene 3.

8 Click the plus sign next to summary Task 33, *Scene 3*.

Microsoft Project expands the Scene 3 summary task to show the subtasks. Your screen should look similar to the following illustration:

	Task Name	Fixed Cost	Fixed Cost Accrual	Total Cost	Baseline	Variance	Actual	Remaining
1	⊞ Pre-Production	$0.00	Prorated	$24,674.81	$23,294.75	$1,380.06	$23,201.81	$1,473.00
26	⊟ Production	$0.00	Prorated	$38,669.83	$36,334.15	$2,335.68	$16,132.18	$22,537.65
27	⊞ Scene 7	$0.00	Prorated	$4,035.63	$3,702.50	$333.13	$4,035.63	$0.00
33	⊟ Scene 3	$0.00	Prorated	$5,630.15	$4,170.00	$1,460.15	$5,630.15	$0.00
34	Scene 3 setup	$0.00	Prorated	$606.00	$518.00	$88.00	$606.00	$0.00
35	Scene 3 rehearsal	$0.00	Prorated	$1,510.00	$755.00	$755.00	$1,510.00	$0.00
36	Scene 3 shoot	$0.00	Prorated	$2,634.15	$2,379.00	$255.15	$2,634.15	$0.00
37	Scene 3 teardown	$0.00	Prorated	$880.00	$518.00	$362.00	$880.00	$0.00
38	Scene 3-process da	$0.00	Prorated	$0.00	$0.00	$0.00	$0.00	$0.00
39	⊞ Scene 1	$0.00	Prorated	$6,466.41	$5,950.00	$516.41	$6,466.41	$0.00
45	⊞ Scene 2	$0.00	Prorated	$2,257.10	$2,241.50	$15.60	$0.00	$2,257.10
51	⊞ Scene 5	$0.00	Prorated	$4,547.40	$4,537.00	$10.40	$0.00	$4,547.40
57	⊞ Scene 6	$0.00	Prorated	$8,723.40	$8,723.40	$0.00	$0.00	$8,723.40
63	⊞ Scene 8	$0.00	Prorated	$5,278.20	$5,278.20	$0.00	$0.00	$5,278.20
69	⊞ Scene 4	$0.00	Prorated	$1,731.55	$1,731.55	$0.00	$0.00	$1,731.55
75	⊞ Post-Production	$0.00	Prorated	$28,467.90	$28,467.90	$0.00	$0.00	$28,467.90

Looking at the Variance column, you can see that the Scene 3 rehearsal accounts for most of the variance for the Scene 3 summary task. Later you'll investigate this issue further and determine whether changes to the remaining rehearsal tasks are required.

9 Click the Task Name column heading.

Show Subtasks

10 On the Formatting toolbar, click the Show Subtasks button.

Microsoft Project expands the task list to show all subtasks.

To conclude this exercise, you will use the Project Guide to examine task costs. The information is similar to what you've seen before, but the Project Guide includes a handy explanation of variance and a short list of the most relevant filters.

11 On the Project Guide toolbar, click the Report button.

12 In the Report pane, click the See Project Costs link.

The Project Guide: Analyze Costs view appears. Your screen should look similar to the following illustration:

	Task Name	Total Cost	Baseline	Variance	Actual	Rem
1	☐ Pre-Production	$24,674.81	$23,294.75	$1,380.06	$23,201.81	$1,
2	Review script	$947.50	$947.50	$0.00	$947.50	
3	Develop script breakdown and schedule	$2,851.00	$2,455.00	$396.00	$2,851.00	
4	Develop production boards	$5,879.12	$5,856.25	$22.87	$5,879.12	
5	Review production boards	$1,575.00	$1,575.00	$0.00	$1,575.00	
6	Scout locations	$4,920.00	$4,920.00	$0.00	$4,920.00	
7	Select locations	$3,430.82	$2,535.00	$895.82	$3,430.82	
8	Hold auditions	$1,900.38	$1,835.00	$65.38	$1,900.38	
9	Apply for filming permits	$876.00	$876.00	$0.00	$876.00	
10	Reserve camera equipment	$636.00	$636.00	$0.00	$636.00	
11	Reserve sound equipment	$186.00	$186.00	$0.00	$186.00	
12	Pre-Production complete!	$0.00	$0.00	$0.00	$0.00	
13	⊞ Staff planning meeting	$1,473.00	$1,473.00	$0.00	$0.00	$1,
26	☐ Production	$38,669.83	$36,334.15	$2,335.68	$16,132.18	$22,
27	☐ Scene 7	$4,035.63	$3,702.50	$333.13	$4,035.63	
28	Scene 7 setup	$426.00	$322.50	$103.50	$426.00	
29	Scene 7 rehearsal	$714.38	$705.00	$9.38	$714.38	
30	Scene 7 shoot	$2,465.25	$2,245.00	$220.25	$2,465.25	
31	Scene 7 teardown	$430.00	$430.00	$0.00	$430.00	
32	Scene 7-process dailies	$0.00	$0.00	$0.00	$0.00	
33	☐ Scene 3	$5,630.15	$4,170.00	$1,460.15	$5,630.15	

Project Costs pane text:

Usually the cost of a task is based on its resource cost - the cost of the resources assigned to the task. Microsoft Project calculates this based on the resource rates you entered.

Cost Variance

The **Variance** column shows the difference between **total cost** and **baseline** cost for each task. Tasks with a positive variance are overbudget. The **Actual Cost** column shows costs incurred for work already done on the task. **Remaining Cost** shows the remaining scheduled expense.

Apply a filter

To focus on only certain tasks, you can apply a filter to this view:

No Filter Applied ▾

More filters...

This view is similar to the Task Sheet view with the Cost table applied, which you displayed in step 4 of this exercise. In the Project Costs pane, you also have quick access to the filters most relevant to project costs.

13 In the Project Costs pane, under Apply A Filter, click Cost Overbudget in the drop-down list.

Tip

This filter and all the other filters in the Project Costs pane are also available in the More Filters dialog box (on the Project menu, point to Filtered For: AllTasks, and then click More Filters) and through the Filter button on the Formatting toolbar.

Microsoft Project filters the task list to show only those tasks that had actual and scheduled costs greater than their baseline costs. Your screen should look similar to the illustration on the following page.

◈ ◈ Project Costs ✕		Task Name	Total Cost	Baseline	Variance	Actual	Rem ▲
Usually the cost of a task is based on its resource cost - the cost of the resources assigned to the task. Microsoft Project calculates this based on the resource rates you entered.	1	☐ Pre-Production	$24,674.81	$23,294.75	$1,380.06	$23,201.81	$1,
	3	Develop script breakdown and schedule	$2,851.00	$2,455.00	$396.00	$2,851.00	
	4	Develop production boards	$5,879.12	$5,856.25	$22.87	$5,879.12	
	7	Select locations	$3,430.82	$2,535.00	$895.82	$3,430.82	
	8	Hold auditions	$1,900.38	$1,835.00	$65.38	$1,900.38	
Cost Variance	26	☐ Production	$38,669.83	$36,334.15	$2,335.68	$16,132.18	$22,
The **Variance** column shows the difference between **total cost** and **baseline** cost for each task. Tasks with a positive variance are overbudget. The **Actual Cost** column shows costs incurred for work already done on the task. **Remaining Cost** shows the remaining scheduled expense.	27	☐ Scene 7	$4,035.63	$3,702.50	$333.13	$4,035.63	
	28	Scene 7 setup	$426.00	$322.50	$103.50	$426.00	
	29	Scene 7 rehearsal	$714.38	$705.00	$9.38	$714.38	
	30	Scene 7 shoot	$2,465.25	$2,245.00	$220.25	$2,465.25	
	33	☐ Scene 3	$5,630.15	$4,170.00	$1,460.15	$5,630.15	
	34	Scene 3 setup	$606.00	$518.00	$88.00	$606.00	
	35	Scene 3 rehearsal	$1,510.00	$755.00	$755.00	$1,510.00	
	36	Scene 3 shoot	$2,634.15	$2,379.00	$255.15	$2,634.15	
Apply a filter	37	Scene 3 teardown	$880.00	$518.00	$362.00	$880.00	
To focus on only certain tasks, you can apply a filter to this view:	39	☐ Scene 1	$6,466.41	$5,950.00	$516.41	$6,466.41	
	41	Scene 1 rehearsal	$1,760.00	$780.00	$980.00	$1,760.00	
	43	Scene 1 teardown	$1,295.00	$694.00	$601.00	$1,295.00	
Cost Overbudget ▾	45	☐ Scene 2	$2,257.10	$2,241.50	$15.60	$0.00	$2,
	47	Scene 2 rehearsal	$517.40	$507.00	$10.40	$0.00	$
More filters...	48	Scene 2 shoot	$962.70	$957.50	$5.20	$0.00	$

Note the gaps in the Task ID numbers, indicating which tasks are not shown with this filter applied.

14 In the Apply A Filter box, click No Filter Applied.

Microsoft Project removes the filter.

15 Click the Close button in the upper right corner of the Project Guide pane to close the Project Guide.

Tip

You can use the Overbudget Tasks report to list tasks that are over budget. On the View menu, click Reports. In the Reports dialog box, double-click Costs, and then double-click Overbudget Tasks.

What caused the task cost variance in the short film project? Because this project's costs are almost entirely derived from work performed by resources, we can conclude that more work than scheduled has been required to complete the tasks up to now.

Tip

You can see work variance in the Work table. In a task view, on the View menu, point to Table:, and then click Work. You can also compare timephased baseline and scheduled work in a usage view. For example, in the Task Usage view, on the Format menu, point to Details, and click Baseline Work.

As we noted earlier, task and resource costs are closely related; in most cases the task costs are mostly or fully derived from the costs of resources assigned to tasks. Examining resource costs is the subject of the next exercise.

Tip

In this exercise, you have viewed cost variance for a task. To see cost variance for assignments to a task, switch to the Task Usage view, and then apply the Cost table.

Examining Resource Costs

Project managers sometimes focus on resource costs as a means of measuring progress and variance within a project. However, resource cost information also serves other people and other needs. For many organizations, resource costs are the primary or even the only costs of doing projects, so keeping an eye on resource costs might directly relate to the financial health of an organization. It might not be a project manager, but an executive, cost accountant, or resource manager who is most interested in resource costs on projects as they relate to organizational costs.

Another common reason to track resource costs is for billing either within an organization (for example, billing another department for services your department has provided), or billing externally. In either case, the resource cost information stored in project plans can serve as the basis for billing out your department's or organization's services to others.

Because cost values in the short film project are almost entirely derived from the costs of resource assignments, you'll look at resource cost variance next:

1   On the View menu, click Resource Sheet.

The Resource Sheet view appears.

2   On the View menu, point to Table: Entry and click Cost.

The Cost table appears. Your screen should look similar to the following illustration:

	Resource Name	Cost	Baseline Cost	Variance	Actual Cost	Remaining
1	16-mm Camera	$736.76	$900.00	($163.24)	$236.76	$500.00
2	16-mm Film	$5,800.00	$5,800.00	$0.00	$2,400.00	$3,400.00
3	500-Watt Light	$264.71	$330.00	($65.29)	$74.71	$190.00
4	Anne L. Paper	$821.72	$731.25	$90.47	$240.47	$581.25
5	Camera Boom	$0.00	$0.00	$0.00	$0.00	$0.00
6	Clair Hector	$8,791.33	$7,600.00	$1,191.33	$4,151.33	$4,640.00
7	Crane	$0.00	$0.00	$0.00	$0.00	$0.00
8	Daniel Penn	$412.50	$412.50	$0.00	$0.00	$412.50
9	David Campbell	$2,514.69	$2,475.00	$39.69	$189.69	$2,325.00
10	Dolly	$0.00	$0.00	$0.00	$0.00	$0.00
11	Doug Hampton	$1,917.27	$1,788.80	$128.47	$466.47	$1,450.80
12	Editing Lab	$5,100.00	$5,100.00	$0.00	$0.00	$5,100.00
13	Electrician	$3,124.00	$2,178.00	$946.00	$2,860.00	$264.00
14	Eric Lang	$372.00	$744.00	($372.00)	$372.00	$0.00
15	Eric Miller	$805.15	$675.00	$130.15	$430.15	$375.00
16	Florian Voss	$2,024.00	$2,024.00	$0.00	$0.00	$2,024.00
17	Frank Lee	$838.37	$812.00	$26.37	$362.37	$476.00
18	Jan Miksovsky	$3,925.31	$3,637.00	$288.31	$3,100.31	$825.00
19	Jim Hance	$502.97	$412.50	$90.47	$240.47	$262.50
20	Jo Brown	$9,297.81	$9,037.50	$260.31	$3,822.81	$5,475.00
21	Johnathan Perrera	$1,727.03	$1,828.00	($600.97)	$3,788.03	$528.00

In the Cost table you can see each resource's cost, baseline cost, and related cost values. In most cases, the resource cost values are derived from each resource's cost rate multiplied by the work on their assignments to tasks in the project plan.

Tip

Note that the names of some resources, such as Clair Hector, appear in red. The red formatting does not relate to their cost variance, but to the fact that they are currently overallocated.

Currently, the resource sheet is sorted by Resource ID. Next you will sort it by resource cost.

3   On the Project menu, point to Sort and click Sort By.

The Sort dialog box appears.

4   In the Sort By box, click Cost in the drop-down list, and click Descending.

5   Make sure the Permanently Renumber Resources check box is cleared, and then click the Sort button.

Microsoft Project sorts the resources by cost, from highest to lowest. Your screen should look similar to the following illustration:

With resources sorted by cost in descending order, you can quickly identify the most expensive resources working on the project.

	Resource Name	Cost	Baseline Cost	Variance	Actual Cost	Remaining
38	Scott Cooper	$10,891.33	$10,346.25	$545.08	$7,287.58	$3,603.75
20	Jo Brown	$9,297.81	$9,037.50	$260.31	$3,822.81	$5,475.00
6	Clair Hector	$8,791.33	$7,600.00	$1,191.33	$4,151.33	$4,640.00
30	Max Benson	$8,660.40	$8,592.00	$68.40	$4,436.40	$4,224.00
32	Michael Patten	$6,230.00	$6,230.00	$0.00	$0.00	$6,230.00
2	16-mm Film	$5,800.00	$5,800.00	$0.00	$2,400.00	$3,400.00
12	Editing Lab	$5,100.00	$5,100.00	$0.00	$0.00	$5,100.00
21	Johnathan Perrera	$4,327.03	$4,928.00	($600.97)	$3,799.03	$528.00
18	Jan Miksovsky	$3,925.31	$3,637.00	$288.31	$3,100.31	$825.00
36	Richard Lum	$3,125.00	$3,125.00	$0.00	$0.00	$3,125.00
13	Electrician	$3,124.00	$2,178.00	$946.00	$2,860.00	$264.00
26	Kim Yoshida	$3,013.80	$3,384.00	($370.20)	$1,509.80	$1,504.00
9	David Campbell	$2,514.69	$2,475.00	$39.69	$189.69	$2,325.00
16	Florian Voss	$2,024.00	$2,024.00	$0.00	$0.00	$2,024.00
11	Doug Hampton	$1,917.27	$1,788.80	$128.47	$466.47	$1,450.80
28	Lisa Garmaise	$1,440.00	$1,440.00	$0.00	$0.00	$1,440.00
34	Paul Borm	$1,255.83	$950.00	$305.83	$605.83	$650.00
39	Sue Jackson	$977.19	$937.50	$39.69	$339.69	$637.50
31	Megan Sherman	$933.90	$972.00	($38.10)	$393.90	$540.00
17	Frank Lee	$838.37	$812.00	$26.37	$362.37	$476.00
4	Anne L. Paper	$821.72	$731.25	$90.47	$240.47	$581.25

This sort quickly tells you who the most and least expensive resources are, but it doesn't help you see variance patterns. You will do that next.

6   On the Project menu, point to Sort and click Sort By.

The Sort dialog box appears.

7   In the Sort By box, click Cost Variance, and make sure Descending is still selected.

8   Make sure the Permanently Renumber Resources check box is cleared, and then click the - Sort button.

Microsoft Project re-sorts the resources by cost variance, from highest to lowest. Your screen should look similar to the following illustration:

With resources sorted by variance in descending order, you can quickly identify those whose cost varied the most from planned costs.

	Resource Name	Cost	Baseline Cost	Variance	Actual Cost	Remaining
8	Clair Hector	$8,791.33	$7,600.00	$1,191.33	$4,151.33	$4,640.00
13	Electrician	$3,124.00	$2,178.00	$946.00	$2,860.00	$264.00
38	Scott Cooper	$10,891.33	$10,346.25	$545.08	$7,287.58	$3,603.75
34	Paul Borm	$1,255.83	$950.00	$305.83	$605.83	$650.00
18	Jan Miksovsky	$3,925.31	$3,637.00	$288.31	$3,100.31	$825.00
20	Jo Brown	$9,297.81	$9,037.50	$260.31	$3,822.81	$5,475.00
15	Eric Miller	$805.15	$675.00	$130.15	$430.15	$375.00
11	Doug Hampton	$1,917.27	$1,788.80	$128.47	$466.47	$1,450.80
22	Joseph Matthews	$474.84	$356.25	$118.59	$418.59	$56.25
4	Anne L. Paper	$821.72	$731.25	$90.47	$240.47	$581.25
19	Jim Hance	$502.97	$412.50	$90.47	$240.47	$262.50
30	Max Benson	$8,660.40	$8,592.00	$68.40	$4,436.40	$4,224.00
9	David Campbell	$2,514.69	$2,475.00	$39.69	$189.69	$2,325.00
39	Sue Jackson	$977.19	$937.50	$39.69	$339.69	$637.50
17	Frank Lee	$838.37	$812.00	$26.37	$362.37	$476.00
41	Tim O'Brien	$810.37	$784.00	$26.37	$362.37	$448.00
23	Joshua Randall	$264.00	$240.00	$24.00	$120.00	$144.00
2	16-mm Film	$5,800.00	$5,800.00	$0.00	$2,400.00	$3,400.00
5	Camera Boom	$0.00	$0.00	$0.00	$0.00	$0.00
7	Crane	$0.00	$0.00	$0.00	$0.00	$0.00
8	Daniel Penn	$412.50	$412.50	$0.00	$0.00	$412.50

With the resource list sorted by cost variance, you can quickly zero in on those resources with the greatest variance, and, if you want, begin to investigate why.

9 On the Project menu, point to Sort, and then click By ID.

Microsoft Project resorts the resources by ID.

Tip

You can use the Overbudget Resources report to list resources who are over budget. On the View menu, click Reports. In the Reports dialog box, double-click Costs, and then double-click Overbudget Resources.

You can also see timephased cost values in a usage view. For example, in the Resource Usage view, on the Format menu, click Detail Styles. In the Usage Details tab, show the Baseline Cost and Cost fields. This also works in the Task Usage view.

Project Management Focus:
What About All Those Other Costs?

In many projects, cost budgets don't fully reflect all the costs of completing the project. For example, in the short film project, we're not accounting for such overhead costs as renting or acquiring studio space, electricity, or replacement parts for equipment. Depending on your organization's needs and practices, you might need to track such overhead costs in your project plan. If you do need to track overhead costs, you might be able to use a *burdened labor rate*—resource rates that factor in such overhead costs. Using burdened labor rates has the additional benefit of hiding each resource's exact pay rate—often considered highly confidential information—in the project plan. Here's one caveat, though: if you plan to use cost information from your project plan for accounting purposes, especially for capitalizing specific task types, check with an accounting expert about how salary, benefit, and overhead cost rates should be handled.

Reporting Project Cost Variance with a Stoplight View

There are many different ways to report a project's status in terms of task or budget variance, or other measures. There is no shortage of features in Microsoft Project that support reporting project status, but the main thing to keep in mind is that how you report project status is less of a technical question and really a communications question. For example, what format and level of detail do your stakeholders need to see? Should project sponsors see different aspects of a project's performance than its resources see? These questions are central to the job of the project manager. Fortunately, as noted earlier, Microsoft Project is a rich communications tool that you can use to put together the type of project status information that best meets the needs of your stakeholders.

Tip

Creating a stoplight view involves using formulas in custom fields. Custom fields are a very powerful and flexible feature, and the stoplight view is just one example of what you can do with them. To learn more about custom fields, type **All about custom fields** into the Ask A Question box in the upper right corner of the Microsoft Project window.

In this exercise, you focus on creating what is often called a *stoplight* report. This status report represents key indicators for tasks, such as schedule or budget status, as a simple red, yellow, or green light, much as you'd find on a traffic signal. Such status reports are easy for anybody to understand, and they quickly provide a general sense of the health of a project. Strictly speaking, what you'll create here is not a *report* in Microsoft Project, so we'll call it a stoplight *view* instead:

1 On the View menu, click More Views.

The More Views dialog box appears.

2 Click Task Sheet, and click the Apply button.

Microsoft Project displays the Task Sheet view. It currently contains the Cost table.

To save you time, we have added a customized field in this project file containing a formula that evaluates each task's cost variance. Next you will view the formula to understand what it does and then view the graphical indicators assigned to the field.

3 On the Tools menu, point to Customize, and then click Fields.

The Customize Fields dialog box appears.

4 Click the Custom Fields tab.

5 In the Type box, click Number in the drop-down list.

6 In the list box, click Overbudget (Number3).

Your screen should look similar to the following illustration:

The Number3 field has been renamed "Overbudget" and customized with a formula and graphical indicators.

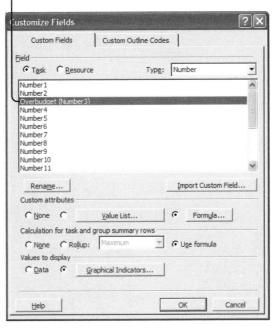

7 Under the Custom Attributes label, click the Formula button.

The Formula dialog box appears. Your screen should look similar to the following illustration:

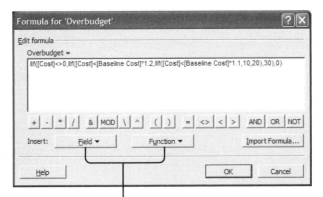

When writing a formula, use these buttons to insert Microsoft Project fields or functions into your formula.

This formula evaluates each task's cost variance. If the task's cost is 10 percent or less above baseline, the formula assigns the number 10 to the task. If the cost is between 10 and 20 percent above baseline, it is assigned a 20. If the cost is more than 20 percent above baseline, it receives a 30.

8 Click Cancel to close the Formula dialog box.

9 In the Customize Fields dialog box, under the Values To Display label, click the Graphical Indicators button.

The Graphical Indicators dialog box appears. Here you specify a unique graphical indicator to display, depending on the value of the field for each task. Again, to save you time, the indicators are already selected.

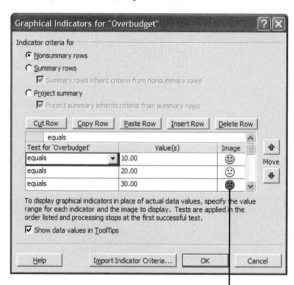

Depending on the value returned by the formula, Microsoft Project will display one of these three graphical indicators in the Overbudget column.

10 In the first cell under the Image column heading, click the drop-down arrow.

Here you can see the many graphical indicators you can associate with the values of fields.

11 Click Cancel to close the Graphical Indicators dialog box, and then click Cancel again to close the Customize Fields dialog box.

To conclude this exercise, you will display the Overbudget (Number3) column in the Cost table.

12 Click the Fixed Cost column heading.

13 On the Insert menu, click Column.

The Column Definition dialog box appears.

14 In the Field Name box, click Overbudget (Number3) in the drop-down list, and then click OK.

Microsoft Project displays the Overbudget column in the Cost table. Your screen should look similar to the following illustration:

The custom field Overbudget (Number3) displays a graphical indicator that represents one of three different levels of cost variance. Now anyone can quickly scan the column to locate tasks that need further investigation.

	Task Name	Overbudget	Fixed Cost	Fixed Cost Accrual	Total Cost	Baseline	Variance	Actual	Rema
1	⊟ Pre-Production	☺	$0.00	Prorated	$24,674.81	$23,294.75	$1,380.06	$23,201.81	$1,
2	Review script	☺	$0.00	Prorated	$947.50	$947.50	$0.00	$947.50	
3	Develop script breakdo	☺	$0.00	Prorated	$2,851.00	$2,455.00	$396.00	$2,851.00	
4	Develop production boa	☺	$0.00	Prorated	$5,879.12	$5,856.25	$22.87	$5,879.12	
5	Review production boa	☺	$0.00	Prorated	$1,575.00	$1,575.00	$0.00	$1,575.00	
6	Scout locations	☺	$0.00	Prorated	$4,920.00	$4,920.00	$0.00	$4,920.00	
7	Select locations	☻	$0.00	Prorated	$3,430.82	$2,535.00	$895.82	$3,430.82	
8	Hold auditions	☺	$0.00	Prorated	$1,900.38	$1,835.00	$65.38	$1,900.38	
9	Apply for filming permit:	☺	$500.00	Start	$876.00	$876.00	$0.00	$876.00	
10	Reserve camera equip	☺	$0.00	Prorated	$636.00	$636.00	$0.00	$636.00	
11	Reserve sound equip	☺	$0.00	Prorated	$186.00	$186.00	$0.00	$186.00	
12	Pre-Production comple		$0.00	Prorated	$0.00	$0.00	$0.00	$0.00	
13	⊞ Staff planning meeti	☺	$0.00	Prorated	$1,473.00	$1,473.00	$0.00	$0.00	$1,
26	⊟ Production	☺	$0.00	Prorated	$38,669.83	$36,334.15	$2,335.68	$16,132.18	$22,
27	⊟ Scene 7	☺	$0.00	Prorated	$4,035.63	$3,702.50	$333.13	$4,035.63	
28	Scene 7 setup	☻	$0.00	Prorated	$426.00	$322.50	$103.50	$426.00	
29	Scene 7 rehearsal	☺	$0.00	Prorated	$714.38	$705.00	$9.38	$714.38	
30	Scene 7 shoot	☺	$0.00	Prorated	$2,465.25	$2,245.00	$220.25	$2,465.25	
31	Scene 7 teardown	☺	$0.00	Prorated	$430.00	$430.00	$0.00	$430.00	
32	Scene 7-process d		$0.00	Prorated	$0.00	$0.00	$0.00	$0.00	
33	⊟ Scene 3	☻	$0.00	Prorated	$5,630.15	$4,170.00	$1,460.15	$5,630.15	

Because this task has no cost, the graphical indicator settings do not display any indicator for this task.

As each task's cost variance changes, so do the graphical indicators according to the ranges specified in the formula. This is a handy format for identifying tasks whose cost variance is higher than you'd like, as indicated by the yellow and red lights.

Tip

To see a graphical indicators value in a ScreenTip, just point to the indicator.

Up to now, you've identified schedule and budget variance in a task view and budget variance in a resource view—each an important measure of project status. This is a good time to remind yourself that the final qualifier of project status is not the exact formatting of the data in Microsoft Project, but the needs of your project's stakeholders. Determining what these needs are requires your good judgment and communication skills.

Chapter Wrap-Up

This chapter covered how to address locating schedule and cost variance for tasks and resources in a project plan, after you've started tracking actual work.

If you are going on to other chapters:

Save

1   On the Standard toolbar, click the Save button to save changes made to Short Film Project 15.

2   On the File menu, click Close to close the project plan.

If you aren't continuing to other chapters:

1   On the Standard toolbar, click the Save button to save changes made to Short Film Project 15.

2   To quit Microsoft Project for now, on the File menu, click Exit.

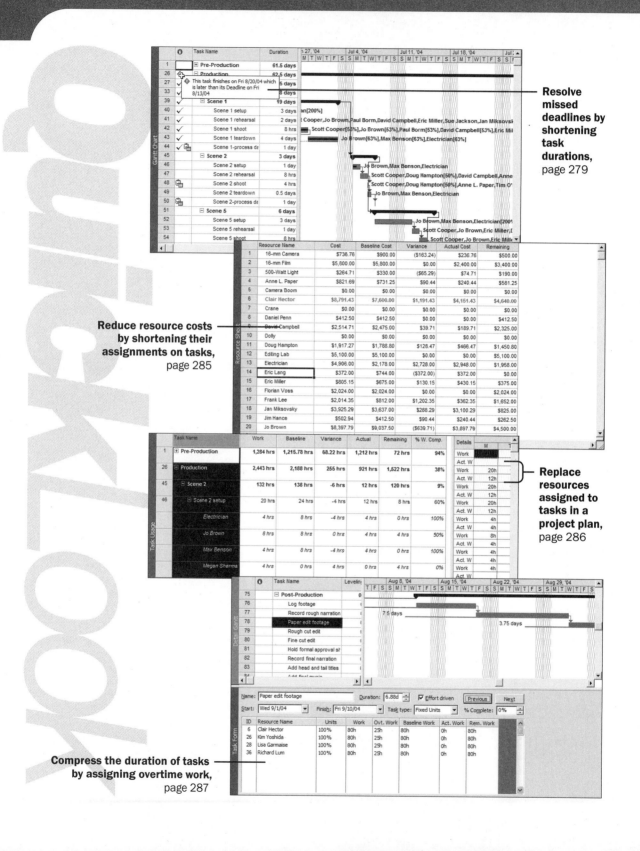

Resolve missed deadlines by shortening task durations, page 279

Reduce resource costs by shortening their assignments on tasks, page 285

Replace resources assigned to tasks in a project plan, page 286

Compress the duration of tasks by assigning overtime work, page 287

Chapter 16
Getting Your Project Back on Track

After completing this chapter, you will be able to:

✔ Assign additional resources to tasks to reduce task durations.

✔ Edit work values for resource assignments, and replace resources assigned to tasks.

✔ Assign overtime work to assignments, and change task relationships to compress the overall project duration.

After work has started on a project, addressing *variance* is not a one-time event. Instead it is an ongoing effort by the project manager. The specific way you should respond to variance depends on the type of variance and the nature of the project. In this chapter, we'll focus on some of the many variance problems that can arise during a project as work progresses. We'll frame these problems around the *project triangle* described in detail in Appendix B, "A Short Course in Project Management."

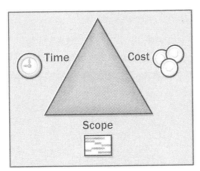

In short, the project triangle model frames a project in terms of the *time* (or duration), *cost* (or budget), and *scope* (the project work required to produce a satisfactory *deliverable*). In virtually any project of any complexity, one of these factors will be more important than the other two. The most important factor is sometimes called the *driving constraint* because meeting it drives your actions as a project manager. For example, for a project that must be concluded by a specific date, you might have to make cost and scope compromises to meet the deadline. Working with the project triangle gives you a good way to think about the inevitable trade-offs that nearly always must be made in projects. Just as importantly, it gives you a clear way of explaining the pros and cons of trade-offs to the project's *resources*, *sponsors*, and other *stakeholders*.

In the project triangle model, time, cost, and scope are interconnected; changing one element can affect the other two. However, for purposes of identifying, analyzing, and addressing problems in project management, it's useful to fit problems into one of these three categories.

The specific issues we'll focus on in this chapter aren't necessarily the most common problems you'll face in your own projects. Because every project is unique, there's no way to anticipate what you'll run into. However, we've attempted to highlight the most pressing issues at the midpoint of the short film project's duration and to apply solutions that address many of the problems that tend to surface in projects. Note that some of the features you'll use in this chapter you might also use when planning a project. Here, however, your intent is different.

Short Film Project 16a

This chapter uses the practice file Short Film Project 16a. This file describes the short film project midway through completion, with some variance that must be addressed. For details about installing the practice files, see "Using the Book's CD-ROM" at the beginning of this book.

Troubleshooting Time and Schedule Problems

Schedule variance will almost certainly appear in any lengthy project. Maintaining control over the schedule requires that the project manager know when variance has occurred and to what extent, and then take timely corrective action to stay on track. To help you identify when variance has occurred, the short film project plan includes the following:

■ Deadline dates applied to key milestones.

■ A project baseline to compare actual performance against.

The deadline dates and project baseline will help you troubleshoot time and schedule problems. In this exercise, you address the missed deadline for the production phase of the short film project and shorten the durations of some tasks on the critical path:

1 If Microsoft Project is not already open, start it now.

Open

2 On the Standard toolbar, click the Open button.

The Open dialog box appears.

3 Navigate to the Chapter 16 Getting Back On Track folder, and double-click the Short Film Project 16a file.

4 On the File menu, click Save As.

The Save As dialog box appears.

5 In the File Name box, type **Short Film Project 16**, and then click the Save button.

To begin troubleshooting the time and schedule issues, you'll get a top-level view of the degree of schedule variance in the project plan now.

6 On the Project menu, click Project Information.

The Project Information dialog box appears.

The current date will probably differ. ⎯

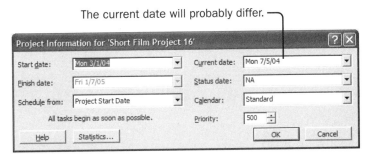

In it you can see the current or scheduled finish date for the project: January 7, 2005. However, you know this date must be pulled in so the project concludes before the end of 2004.

Next you will look at the duration values for this project.

7 In the Project Information dialog box, click the Statistics button.

The Project Statistics dialog box appears:

Based on current project performance and the ⎯
remaining work as scheduled, the project will finish
16 days later than planned in the baseline.

Project Statistics for 'Short Film Project 16'

	Start	Finish
Current	Mon 3/1/04	Fri 1/7/05
Baseline	Mon 3/1/04	Thu 12/16/04
Actual	Mon 3/1/04	NA
Variance	0d	16d

	Duration	Work	Cost
Current	224.5d	5,544h	$97,180.55
Baseline	208.5d	5,206h	$89,161.55
Actual	87.56d	2,133h	$39,593.00
Remaining	136.94d	3,411h	$57,587.55

Percent complete:

Duration: 39%   Work: 38%

Here you can see, among other things, that overall the project plan now has 16 days of finish variance.

The Project Statistics dialog box also indicates some cost variance—the difference between the current and baseline cost values. You will examine this more closely in a later exercise.

8 Click the Close button to close the Project Statistics dialog box.

Before you address the overall project duration, you'll examine the missed deadline for the production phase.

9 Point to the missed deadline indicator in the Indicators column for Task 26, the *Production* summary task.

Your screen should look similar to the following illustration:

Positioning the mouse pointer over the missed deadline indicator displays a ScreenTip in which you can see the details of the deadline and the task's finish date.

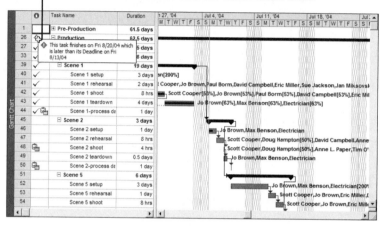

Enough schedule variance has occurred in the pre-production phase and the completed portion of the production phase to cause the scheduled completion of the production phase to move out beyond its deadline date of August 13.

Take a moment to look over the remaining tasks in the production phase. These consist of several more scenes to be shot. Because of the nature of this work, you can't change task relationships (for example, from finish-to-start to start-to-start) to decrease the duration of each scene's summary task; the tasks follow a logical finish-to-start relationship. Nor can you schedule two or more scenes to be shot in parallel, because many of the same resources are required for all of them. To get the production phase back down to an acceptable duration, you'll have to shorten the duration of some of its subtasks. To do this, you'll assign additional resources to some tasks.

Looking over the remaining production tasks, you see that some of the setup and tear-down tasks seem to be the longest, so you'll focus on these.

10 Click the name of Task 52, Scene 5 Setup, and then scroll the Gantt Chart view up so it appears at the top.

This three-day task currently has three resources assigned. After conferring with these resources, you all agree that they could get the task completed more quickly with additional resources.

Assign
Resources

11 On the Standard toolbar, click the Assign Resources button.

12 In the Assign Resources dialog box, under the Resource Name column, click Frank Lee, and then click the Assign button.

Microsoft Project assigns Frank Lee to the task, and because *effort-driven scheduling* is enabled for this task, Microsoft Project reduces the duration of the task to 2.4 days. Your screen should look similar to the following illustration:

Because effort-driven scheduling is enabled for this task, assigning an additional resource reduces the task's duration.

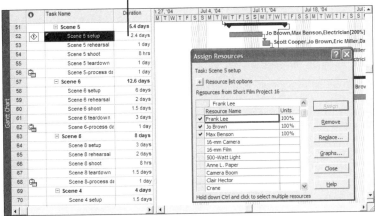

To further reduce the task's duration, you'll assign another resource.

13 In the Resource Name column, click Keith Harris, and then click the Assign button.

Microsoft Project further reduces the duration of the task. Next you will reduce the durations of the setup and teardown tasks of Scene 6.

14 In the Task Name column, click the name of Task 58, Scene 6 Setup. While holding down the Ctrl key, click the name of Task 61, Scene 6 Teardown.

15 In the Resource Name column, make sure that Keith Harris is still selected, and then click the Assign button.

Microsoft Project reduces the durations of the two tasks.

16 In the Resource Name column, click Frank Lee, and then click the Assign button.

Microsoft Project further reduces the durations of the two tasks. Your screen should look similar to the following illustration:

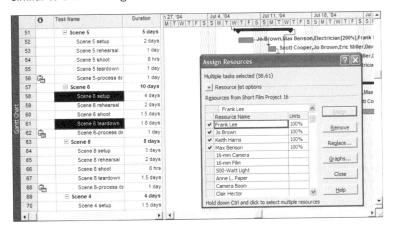

17 In the Task Name column, click the name of Task 64, *Scene 8 Setup*. While holding down the Ctrl key, click the name of Task 67, *Scene 8 Teardown*.

18 In the Resource Name column, make sure that Frank Lee is still selected, and then click the Assign button.

19 In the Resource Name column, click Keith Harris, and then click the Assign button.

20 Click the Close button to close the Assign Resources dialog box.

21 Scroll up to see Task 26, the *Production* summary task.

Your screen should look similar to the following illustration:

Reducing the durations of subtasks also reduces
the duration of this summary task enough that as
scheduled, it will not miss its deadline.

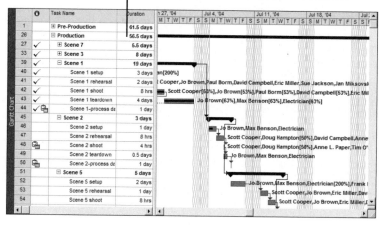

The missed deadline indicator is gone. Next you'll see how the production phase is now scheduled. Recall that the deadline date of the *Production* summary task was August 13.

22 On the Edit menu, click Go To.

23 In the Date box (not the ID box), type or click **8/13/04**, and then click OK.

Microsoft Project scrolls the Gantt Chart to show the end of the *Production* summary task. Your screen should look similar to the following illustration:

You can visually verify that the
summary task concludes prior
to its deadline in the chart portion
of the Gantt Chart view.

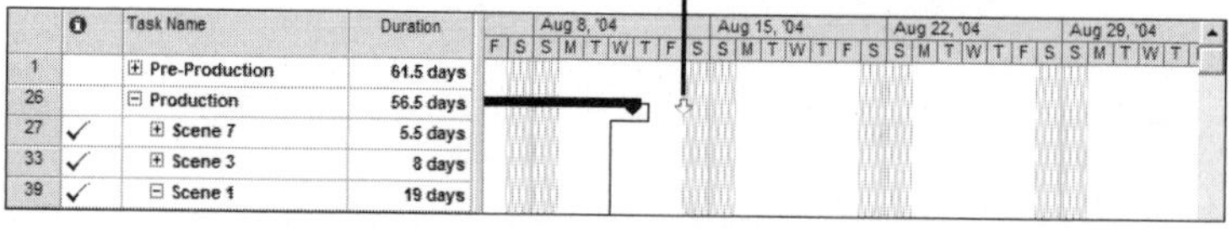

Tip

Task
Information

You can also see the summary task's scheduled finish date and deadline date by clicking the Task Information button on the Standard toolbar.

With the updated setup and teardown durations, the overall duration of the production phase now ends on August 12, just one day before its deadline. Given the amount of variance that occurred in the production phase already, however, you should keep a close watch on this phase as work progresses.

Troubleshooting Cost and Resource Problems

In projects where you've entered cost information for resources, you might find that to address many cost problems you must fine-tune resource and assignment details. Whether or not it's your intention, changing resource assignment details not only affects costs, but it can also affect task durations.

As you saw in the previous exercise, the short film project plan has some cost variance. As it is currently scheduled, the project plan will end up costing about $8,000 more than planned, or about 9 percent over budget. This cost variance has resulted from longer-than-expected assignment durations and the resulting higher costs of the assigned resources.

After doing some research into the high cost of the electricians on the setup and teardown assignments, you learn that in most cases, they're really needed for only a portion of the tasks' durations. After discussing the issue with the production manager, you agree that the electricians' assignments on the remaining setup and teardown tasks should be halved. While you're updating the project, you'll also handle the upcoming departure of another resource.

In this exercise, you adjust work values for resource assignments and replace one resource with another on upcoming assignments. You begin, however, by checking the total cost of the electricians' assignments:

1   On the View menu, click Resource Sheet.

The Resource Sheet view appears. Note the current total cost of Resource 13, Electrician: $6,908. This is a combination of the electricians' actual cost to date and their anticipated cost for scheduled assignments yet to be completed. You would like to reduce this cost by reducing the electricians' work on tasks.

2   On the View menu, click Resource Usage.

The Resource Usage view appears.

3   In the Resource Name column, click the plus sign next to the name of Resource 13, Electrician. Then scroll the Resource Usage view so all of the electricians' assignments are visible.

Because scenes 7, 3, and 1 have already been completed, you'll focus on the electricians' assignments to the remaining scenes.

4   In the Work column for Scene 2 Setup, type **4h**, and then press the Enter key.

Microsoft Project adjusts the work of the electricians on this task to four hours.

5 Enter the new work values in the following table for the electricians' remaining assignments:

For this assignment	Enter this work value
Scene 2 teardown	2h
Scene 5 setup	16h
Scene 5 teardown	8h
Scene 6 setup	32h
Scene 6 teardown	7h
Scene 8 setup	8h
Scene 8 teardown	4h
Scene 4 setup	6h
Scene 4 teardown	6h

When you're done, your screen should look similar to the following illustration:

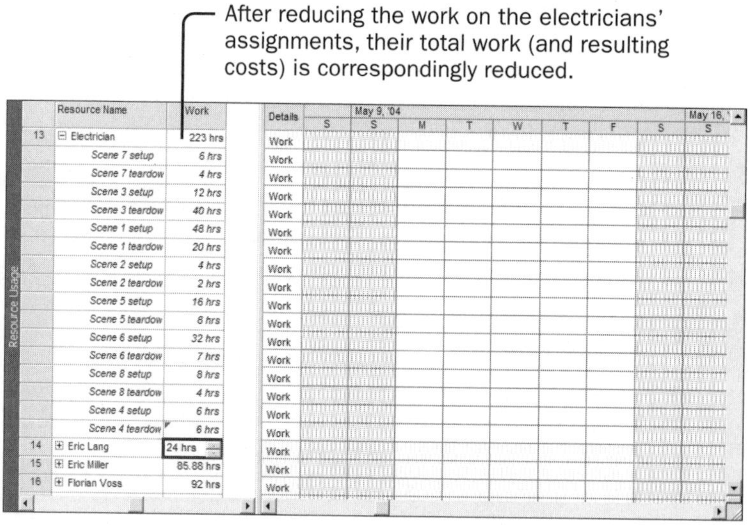

After reducing the work on the electricians' assignments, their total work (and resulting costs) is correspondingly reduced.

Note that because the electricians were not the only resource assigned to these tasks, reducing the electricians' scheduled work in this way will reduce the cost of their assignments, but not necessarily the durations of these tasks. The other resources assigned to these tasks may have assignments of longer durations.

To verify the reduction in the electricians' costs, you'll switch back to the Resource Sheet view.

6   On the View menu, click Resource Sheet.

The Resource Sheet view appears. Your screen should look similar to the following illustration:

The electricians' updated cost includes their actual cost plus remaining cost. Only remaining cost is effected by changing the upcoming assignments for the electricians.

	Resource Name	Cost	Baseline Cost	Variance	Actual Cost	Remaining
1	16-mm Camera	$736.76	$900.00	($163.24)	$236.76	$500.00
2	16-mm Film	$5,800.00	$5,800.00	$0.00	$2,400.00	$3,400.00
3	500-Watt Light	$264.71	$330.00	($65.29)	$74.71	$190.00
4	Anne L. Paper	$821.69	$731.25	$90.44	$240.44	$581.25
5	Camera Boom	$0.00	$0.00	$0.00	$0.00	$0.00
6	Clair Hector	$8,791.43	$7,600.00	$1,191.43	$4,151.43	$4,640.00
7	Crane	$0.00	$0.00	$0.00	$0.00	$0.00
8	Daniel Penn	$412.50	$412.50	$0.00	$0.00	$412.50
9	David Campbell	$2,514.71	$2,475.00	$39.71	$189.71	$2,325.00
10	Dolly	$0.00	$0.00	$0.00	$0.00	$0.00
11	Doug Hampton	$1,917.27	$1,788.80	$128.47	$466.47	$1,450.80
12	Editing Lab	$5,100.00	$5,100.00	$0.00	$0.00	$5,100.00
13	Electrician	$4,906.00	$2,178.00	$2,728.00	$2,948.00	$1,958.00
14	Eric Lang	$372.00	$744.00	($372.00)	$372.00	$0.00
15	Eric Miller	$805.15	$675.00	$130.15	$430.15	$375.00
16	Florian Voss	$2,024.00	$2,024.00	$0.00	$0.00	$2,024.00
17	Frank Lee	$2,014.35	$812.00	$1,202.35	$362.35	$1,652.00
18	Jan Miksovsky	$3,925.29	$3,637.00	$288.29	$3,100.29	$825.00
19	Jim Hance	$502.94	$412.50	$90.44	$240.44	$262.50
20	Jo Brown	$8,397.79	$9,037.50	($639.71)	$3,897.79	$4,500.00
21	Johnathan Perrera	$4,327.17	$4,928.00	($600.83)	$3,799.17	$528.00

Note the updated total cost of Resource 13, Electrician: $4,906. Only the Cost and Remaining Cost values changed; the costs relating to work already performed are not affected, nor is the baseline cost.

To conclude this exercise, you will update the project plan to reflect that a resource will be leaving the project early and his assignments will be taken over by another resource. Max Benson will be leaving the project just after the start of work on scene 2. You will reassign Max Benson's work on subsequent tasks to Megan Sherman. Megan also happens to be a slightly less expensive resource, so the replacement will help a little with the cost variance too.

7   On the View menu, click Task Usage.

The Task Usage view appears.

8   On the View menu, point to Table: Entry, and then click Work.

The Work table appears.

9   Drag the vertical divider bar to the right to show all columns in the Work table.

10   On the Edit menu, click Go To.

11   In the ID box, type **46**, and then click OK.

Microsoft Project displays the assignments for the last task for which Max Benson has any actual work reported.

Your screen should look similar to the illustration on the following page.

Task Name	Work	Baseline	Variance	Actual	Remaining	% W. Comp.	Details	M	
46 ⊟ Scene 2 setup	20 hrs	24 hrs	-4 hrs	12 hrs	8 hrs	60%	Work	20h	
							Act. W	12h	
Electrician	4 hrs	8 hrs	-4 hrs	4 hrs	0 hrs	100%	Work	4h	
							Act. W	4h	
Jo Brown	8 hrs	8 hrs	0 hrs	4 hrs	4 hrs	50%	Work	8h	
							Act. W	4h	
Max Benson	8 hrs	8 hrs	0 hrs	4 hrs	4 hrs	50%	Work	8h	
							Act. W	4h	
47 ⊟ Scene 2 rehearsal	36 hrs	36 hrs	0 hrs	0 hrs	36 hrs	0%	Work		
							Act. W		
Anne L. Paper	8 hrs	8 hrs	0 hrs	0 hrs	8 hrs	0%	Work		
							Act. W		
David Campbel	8 hrs	8 hrs	0 hrs	0 hrs	8 hrs	0%	Work		
							Act. W		
Doug Hampton	4 hrs	4 hrs	0 hrs	0 hrs	4 hrs	0%	Work		
							Act. W		
Jan Miksovsky	8 hrs	8 hrs	0 hrs	0 hrs	8 hrs	0%	Work		
							Act. W		
Scott Cooper	8 hrs	8 hrs	0 hrs	0 hrs	8 hrs	0%	Work		
							Act. W		
48 ⊟ Scene 2 shoot	66 hrs	66 hrs	0 hrs	0 hrs	66 hrs	0%	Work		
							Act. W		
16 mm Camera	8 hrs	8 hrs	0 hrs	0 hrs	8 hrs	0%	Work		

You can see that Max Benson's assignment to Task 46, *Scene 2 setup*, is 50 percent complete.

Next you'll filter the Task Usage view to show only incomplete tasks. That way, when you replace Max Benson with Megan Sherman, the replacement will affect only the incomplete tasks to which Max Benson is assigned.

12 On the Project menu, point to Filtered For: All Tasks, and then click Incomplete Tasks.

Microsoft Project filters the Task Usage view to show only those tasks that are not yet complete. Next you will make the resource replacement. Keep an eye on Max Benson's partial work on Task 46.

13 Click the Task Name column heading.

Assign Resources

14 On the Standard toolbar, click the Assign Resources button.

The Assign Resources dialog box appears.

15 In the Resource Name column, click Max Benson, and then click the Replace button.

The Replace Resource dialog box appears.

16 In the Resource Name column, click Megan Sherman, and then click OK.

Microsoft Project replaces Max Benson's future assignments with Megan Sherman.

17 Click Close to close the Assign Resources dialog box.

Your screen should look similar to the following illustration:

After replacing Max Benson with Megan Sherman, Max's actual work on the partially completed task is preserved...

Task Name	Work	Baseline	Variance	Actual	Remaining	% W. Comp.	Details	M	T
1 ⊞ Pre-Production	1,284 hrs	1,215.76 hrs	68.22 hrs	1,212 hrs	72 hrs	94%	Work		
							Act. W		
26 ⊟ Production	2,443 hrs	2,188 hrs	255 hrs	921 hrs	1,522 hrs	38%	Work	20h	
							Act. W	12h	
45 ⊟ Scene 2	132 hrs	138 hrs	-6 hrs	12 hrs	120 hrs	9%	Work	20h	
							Act. W	12h	
46 ⊟ Scene 2 setup	20 hrs	24 hrs	-4 hrs	12 hrs	8 hrs	60%	Work	20h	
							Act. W	12h	
Electrician	4 hrs	8 hrs	-4 hrs	4 hrs	0 hrs	100%	Work	4h	
							Act. W	4h	
Jo Brown	8 hrs	8 hrs	0 hrs	4 hrs	4 hrs	50%	Work	8h	
							Act. W	4h	
Max Benson	4 hrs	8 hrs	-4 hrs	4 hrs	0 hrs	100%	Work	4h	
							Act. W	4h	
Megan Sherma	4 hrs	0 hrs	4 hrs	0 hrs	4 hrs	0%	Work	4h	
							Act. W		

...And his remaining work on the task is assigned to Megan.

Note that for Task 46, Microsoft Project preserved Max Benson's four hours of work on the task and assigned the remainder of his work on the task (four hours) to Megan. For the subsequent tasks to which Max was assigned, he has been replaced by Megan.

18 On the Project menu, point to Filtered For: Incomplete Tasks, and then click All Tasks.

Microsoft Project unfilters the Task Usage view. Note that Max's historical actual work is still recorded in the project plan.

Troubleshooting Scope-of-Work Problems

The project's scope includes all the work required—and only the work required—to successfully deliver the product of the project to its intended customer. After project work has started, managing its scope usually requires making trade-offs: trading time for money, quality for time, and so on. You might have the goal of never making such trade-offs, but a more realistic goal might be to make the best-informed trade-offs possible.

Recall from the previous exercises that the project finish date extended into 2005. With the actions taken in the previous exercise, the finish date has been pulled into 2004, but you want it to end around mid-December 2004 at the latest. In this exercise, you focus on the project's finish date and make several trade-offs to ensure that the project will deliver its product within the time frame that you want:

1 On the Project menu, click Project Information.

The Project Information dialog box appears. As the schedule is now, if all the remaining work is completed as scheduled, the project will be completed on December 30, 2004. However, realistically, you expect the holiday season to interfere with concluding the project, so you'll need to take steps to pull in the finish date.

2 Click Cancel to close the Project Information dialog box.

Because the project finish date is controlled by tasks on the critical path, you'll begin by viewing only those tasks.

3 On the View menu, click More Views.

4 In the More Views dialog box, click Detail Gantt, and then click the Apply button.

The Detail Gantt view appears.

5 On the Project menu, point to Filtered For: All Tasks, and then click Critical.

Microsoft Project displays only the critical tasks. The remaining production tasks are already as compressed as they can be, so you'll focus on compressing the post-production tasks. To begin, you'll allow overtime work for several tasks, to shorten their durations.

6 On the Edit menu, click Go To.

7 In the ID box, type **76**, and then click OK.

Microsoft Project displays Task 76, *Log footage*.

Your screen should look similar to the following illustration:

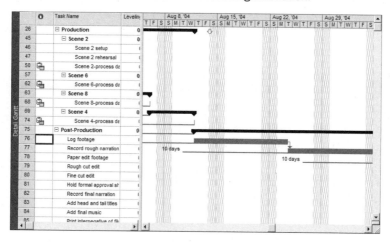

8 On the Window menu, click Split.

The Task Form appears below the Detail Gantt view.

9 Click anywhere in the Task Form. Then on the Format menu, point to Details, and click Resource Work.

The Resource Work details appear in the Task Form.

10 To see the effect of the following steps on the duration of Task 76, scroll the Detail Gantt view in the upper pane until Task 76 is visible.

11 In the Task Form, in the Ovt. Work column for the resource named Editing Lab, type or click **20h**, and press Enter.

12 In the Ovt. Work column for Florian Voss, type or click **20h**, and click OK in the upper right corner of the Task Form.

The overtime work values cause Microsoft Project to adjust the daily work assignments for these resources and to shorten the overall duration of the task. Your screen should look similar to the following illustration:

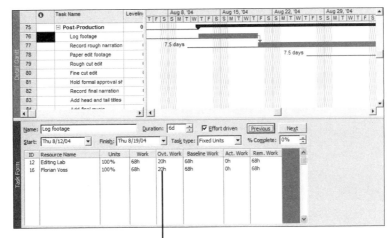

Assigning overtime work reduces the duration of the task, but not the total amount of work required to complete the task.

Note that each resource's total work on this task remains at 68 hours. Now, however, 20 of those 68 hours per resource will be scheduled as overtime. The same amount of work will be performed, but in a shorter time span. Microsoft Project will apply overtime cost rates, if they have been set up, to the overtime portion of the assignment.

13 In the Gantt Chart view, click the name of Task 77, Record Rough Narration.

14 In the Task Form, enter 30 hours (**30h**) of overtime work for both of the assigned resources, and then click OK.

Microsoft Project schedules the overtime work and recalculates the task's duration.

15 In the Gantt Chart view, click the name of Task 78, Paper Edit Footage.

16 In the Task Form, enter 25 hours (**25h**) of overtime work for each of the four assigned resources, and then click OK.

Microsoft Project schedules the overtime work and recalculates the task's duration.

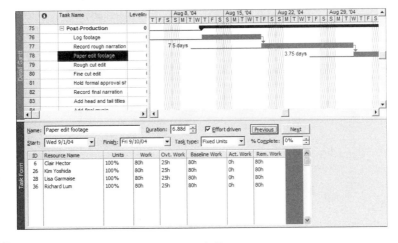

17 On the Window menu, click Remove Split.

18 On the Project menu, click Project Information.

The Project Information dialog box appears. The adjustments you've made to the schedule have pulled in the project's finish date to 12/17/04. Although that meets the target you had in mind, given the overall performance to date, you can expect some additional variance. In anticipation of this, you'll make further adjustments to the post-production tasks.

19 Click Cancel to close the Project Information dialog box.

Task 83, *Add head and tail titles*, is a fairly long task. After talking with the resources assigned to it and its predecessor task, you all agree that given the schedule crunch, work on Task 83 can begin at the same time as its predecessor, Task 82.

20 In the Task Name column, click the name of Task 83, Add Head And Tail Titles.

Task
Information

21 On the Standard toolbar, click the Task Information button.

The Task Information dialog box appears.

22 Click the Predecessors tab.

23 In the Type field for the task's predecessor, click Start-to-Start (SS) in the drop-down list.

24 Click OK to close the Task Information dialog box.

Go To
Selected Task

25 On the Standard toolbar, click the Go To Selected Task button.

Your screen should look similar to the following illustration:

Changing the predecessor relationship
between these tasks to start-to-start
decreases the overall duration of the
project because these tasks are on the
critical path.

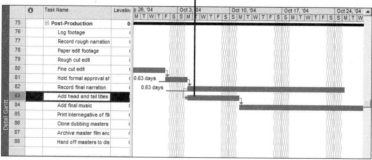

Microsoft Project reschedules Task 83 to start when 82 starts, and reschedules all subsequent linked tasks as well.

26 On the Project menu, click Project Information.

The Project Information dialog box appears. The project's finish date is now pulled back to late November—a workable date at this time.

To conclude this exercise, you'll see what effects these final adjustments you've made have had on the project's final cost values as well.

27 Click the Statistics button.

The Project Statistics dialog box appears.

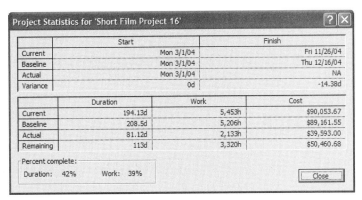

The current cost calculation is very close to its baseline cost, although you know it's likely to go up.

28 Click the Close button to close the Project Statistics dialog box.

You confer with the project sponsors, who are pleased that you can wrap up the short film project before the holiday season. Although producing the project deliverable within these constraints will be a challenge, you're both realistic and optimistic about the project's future performance, and comfortable with your project management skills and your knowledge of Microsoft Project. Good luck!

Chapter Wrap-Up

This chapter covered how to troubleshoot time, cost, and scope issues after project work has begun and variance in the project plan has appeared.

If you are going on to other chapters:

Save

1 On the Standard toolbar, click the Save button to save changes made to Short Film Project 16.

2 On the File menu, click Close to close the project plan.

If you aren't continuing to other chapters:

1 On the Standard toolbar, click the Save button to save changes made to Short Film Project 16.

2 To quit Microsoft Project for now, on the File menu, click Exit.

3
Special
Subjects

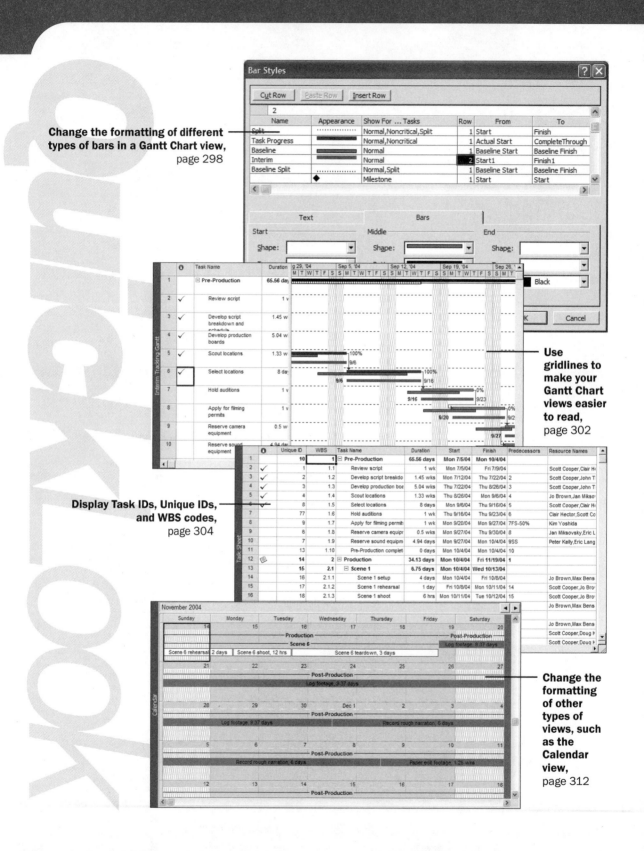

Change the formatting of different types of bars in a Gantt Chart view, page 298

Use gridlines to make your Gantt Chart views easier to read, page 302

Display Task IDs, Unique IDs, and WBS codes, page 304

Change the formatting of other types of views, such as the Calendar view, page 312

Chapter 17
Applying Advanced Formatting

After completing this chapter, you will be able to:

✔ **Format items in a Gantt Chart view.**

✔ **Display Task IDs, outline codes, and WBS codes.**

✔ **Format the Network Diagram view.**

✔ **Format the Calendar view.**

This chapter introduces you to some of the more advanced formatting features in Microsoft Project. A well-formatted project plan is essential for communicating details to resources, customers, and other stakeholders. Some of the formatting capabilities in Microsoft Project are similar to those of a style-based word processor such as Microsoft Word, in which defining a style once affects all content in the document to which that style has been applied. In Microsoft Project you can use styles to change the appearance of a specific type of Gantt bar, such as a summary bar, throughout a project plan. Other formatting options you're introduced to in this chapter focus on the different ways of identifying tasks and formatting some of the more commonly used views.

Parnell
Film 17a

This chapter uses the practice file Parnell Film 17a. For details about installing the practice files, see "Using the Book's CD-ROM" at the beginning of this book.

Formatting Bar Styles in a Gantt Chart View

You can directly format specific items (a milestone, for example) in a Gantt chart view or use the Gantt Chart Wizard (on the Format menu) to change the look of a Gantt chart view in limited ways. To change the overall appearance of a Gantt chart view, however, you use the Bar Styles command on the Format menu.

Tip

Remember that several views are Gantt chart views, even though only one view is specifically called the Gantt Chart view. Other Gantt chart views include the Detail Gantt, Leveling Gantt, Multiple Baselines Gantt, and Tracking Gantt. *Gantt chart view* generally refers to a type of presentation that shows Gantt bars organized along a timescale.

In addition to changing the formatting of objects that appear by default in a Gantt chart view (such as a tasks' Gantt bar), you can add or remove objects. For example, it is useful to compare *baseline*, *interim*, and *actual* plans in a single view. Doing so helps you evaluate the schedule adjustments you have made.

In this exercise, you display the current schedule along with the baseline and the interim plan. (The baseline and interim plans were previously saved in the project plan.) You begin by customizing a copy of the Tracking Gantt chart view:

1 If Microsoft Project is not already open, start it now.

Open

2 On the Standard toolbar, click the Open button.

The Open dialog box appears.

3 Navigate to the Chapter 17 Advanced Formatting folder, and double-click the Parnell Film 17a file.

4 On the File menu, click Save As.

The Save As dialog box appears.

5 In the File Name box, type **Parnell Film 17**, and then click the Save button.

6 On the View menu, click More Views.

The More Views dialog box appears.

7 In the Views list, click Tracking Gantt, and click the Copy button.

The View Definition dialog box appears:

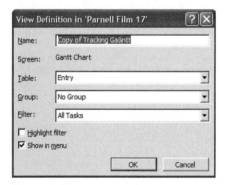

8 In the Name box, type **Interim Tracking Gantt**, and click OK.

The new view is listed in the More Views dialog box.

9 Click the Apply button.

Microsoft Project displays the new view, which at this point is identical to the Tracking Gantt view.

Next you will add the interim plan bars to the view.

10 On the Format menu, click Bar Styles.

The Bar Styles dialog box appears.

Tip

You can also display this dialog box by double-clicking the background of the chart portion of a Gantt chart view.

11 Scroll down the list of the bar styles, and in the Name column, click Baseline Split.

12 Click the Insert Row button.

Microsoft Project inserts a row for a new bar style in the table.

13 In the new cell, type **Interim**.

14 In the same row, click the cell under the Show For…Tasks column heading, and then click Normal in the drop-down list.

15 Click the cell under the From column heading, and click Start1 in the drop-down list.

16 Click the cell under the To column heading, and then click Finish1 in the drop-down list.

Your screen should look similar to the following illustration:

— Here is the new bar style you are creating.

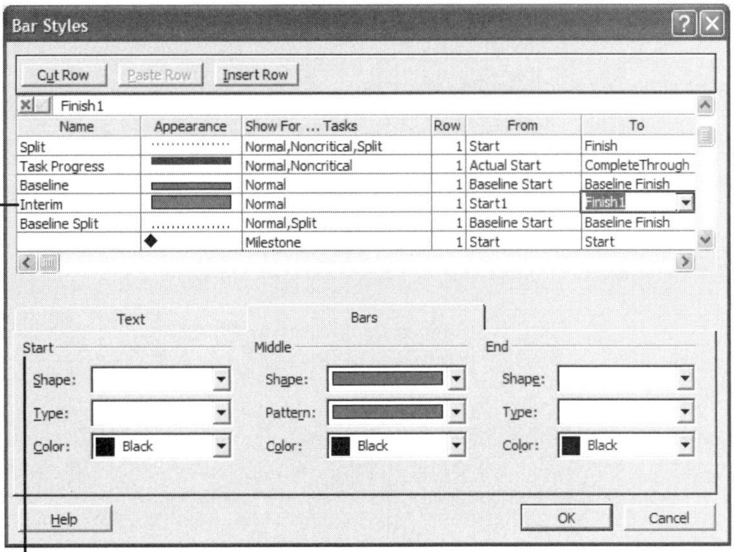

— The options on these tabs apply to the active bar style above; in this case, "Interim."

The Start1 and Finish1 items are the fields in which the first interim plan values were previously saved for you in the project plan. The current start date and finish date of each task in the project were saved to these fields when the interim plan was saved.

You have now instructed Microsoft Project to display the first interim plan start and finish dates as bars; next you will specify what these bars should look like.

17 Click the cell under the Row column heading, and click 2 in the drop-down list.

This causes Microsoft Project to display multiple rows of Gantt bars for each task in the view. Next focus your attention on the lower half of the Bar Styles dialog box.

18 In the Shape box under the Middle label, click the half-height bar, the third option from the top of the list.

19 In the Pattern box under the Middle label, click the solid bar, the second option from the top of the list.

20 In the Color box, click Green.

Your screen should look similar to the following illustration:

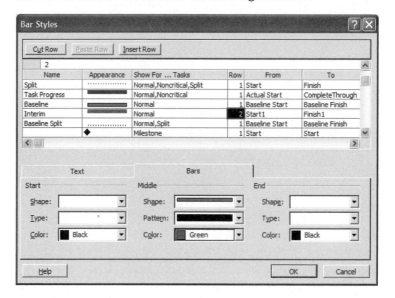

Tip

To view Help about this dialog box, click the Help button. To view Help about individual items in the dialog box, click the question mark button in the upper right corner of the dialog box, and then click the item you want to know more about.

Because this custom view focuses on the interim plan, next you'll format the interim bars to include their start and finish dates.

21 In the Bar Styles dialog box, click the Text tab.

22 In the Left box, click Start1 in the drop-down list.

Tip

You can type a letter in a field name list to go directly to fields that begin with that letter. For example, you can type **S** to go to the items that begin with S.

23 In the Right box, click Finish1 in the drop-down list.

Your screen should look similar to the following illustration:

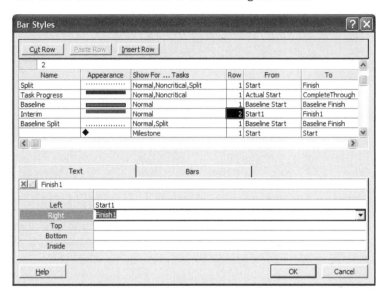

24 Click OK to close the Bar Styles dialog box.

Microsoft Project displays the interim bars on the Interim Tracking Gantt view, although it's possible that no Gantt bars will be visible on your screen yet. Next you will get a better look at the Gantt bars.

25 On the Edit menu, click Go To.

The Go To dialog box appears.

26 In the ID box, type **6** and click OK.

Microsoft Project scrolls the view to display the Gantt bars for Task 6 and its adjacent tasks. Your screen should look similar to the illustration on the following page.

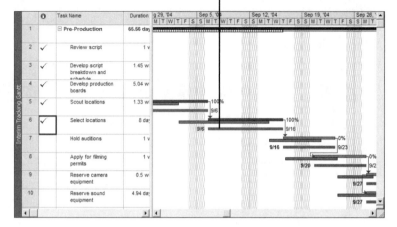

In this custom view, interim plans appear as green bars and the interim start and finish dates appear at either end of the interim bars.

Here you can see that the completed Task 6 (shown as a solid blue bar at the top of the task row) corresponds exactly to its interim plan bar (the green bar at the bottom of the task row), and both were scheduled later than the baseline (the patterned gray bar in the middle of the task row). That is because after the baseline was saved, changes to the schedule were made that pushed out the scheduled start date of the task. Later in the schedule (by task 14) additional changes in the schedule cause the scheduled tasks to differ from their interim start and finish dates as well.

To conclude this exercise, you'll display horizontal gridlines on the chart portion of the Interim Tracking Gantt view to better distinguish the rows of Gantt bars per task.

27 On the Format menu, click Gridlines.

The Gridlines dialog box appears.

28 In the Lines To Change box, make sure that Gantt Rows is selected, and then in the Type box, click the long dashed line, the last option in the list.

Your screen should look similar to the following illustration:

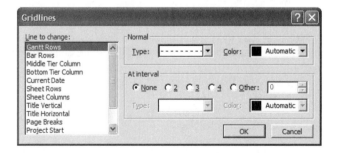

29 Click OK to close the Gridlines dialog box.

Microsoft Project draws gridlines between task rows in the chart. Your screen should look similar to the following illustration:

Horizontal gridlines help separate the sets of Gantt bars for each task from those of other tasks.

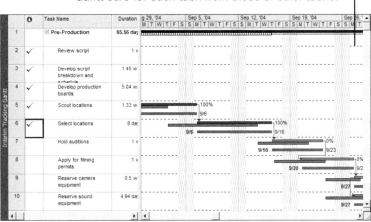

Displaying gridlines like this is a great idea when you print multiple Gantt bars for each task.

Displaying Task IDs and WBS Codes

Next we'll focus on a different type of formatting—using *task IDs* and *Work Breakdown Structure (WBS)* codes to uniquely identify tasks and their relationships to each other. Each task in a Microsoft Project schedule has a unique identifier, called the Task ID. As you enter tasks, Microsoft Project assigns them sequential ID numbers. When you insert, move, or delete a task, Microsoft Project updates the ID numbers so that the ID numbers always reflect the current task order. The Task ID column appears by default on the left side of most task tables in Microsoft Project. Resource IDs behave like Task IDs except that Resource IDs are assigned to resources.

Microsoft Project also keeps track of the order in which you enter tasks and resources. This order is stored in the *Unique ID* task and resource fields. If you want to see the order in which tasks or resources were entered after they've been reorganized, display the Unique ID field. If you want, you can then sort by this field.

Although Task IDs uniquely identify each task, they tell you nothing about a task's place in the hierarchy of a project plan—only where the task falls sequentially. For example, you cannot determine if the task is a *summary task* or a subtask just by looking at a Task ID. To better communicate the hierarchy of a project plan, you can display the *outline numbers* or WBS numbers of tasks. Both outline numbers and WBS numbers in Microsoft Project are numeric representations of the outline hierarchy of a project. The difference between the two is that you can change the appearance, or *mask*, of WBS codes to include any combination of letters and numbers you want, whereas outline codes are numeric only and generated by Microsoft Project. Initially the outline numbers and WBS numbers of tasks are identical.

Tip

To learn more about work breakdown structure codes, such as how to format a WBS code mask, type **All about WBS codes** into the Ask A Question box in the upper right corner of the Microsoft Project window.

In this exercise, you display both the Unique ID and WBS columns in the Task Sheet view and see how these and Task IDs are updated when you move tasks around:

1 On the View menu, click More Views.

2 In the More Views dialog box, click Task Sheet, and then click the Apply button.

The project appears in the Task Sheet view. Your screen should look similar to the following illustration:

	❶	Task Name	Duration	Start	Finish	Predecessors	Resource Names
1		⊟ Pre-Production	65.56 days	Mon 7/5/04	Mon 10/4/04		
2	✓	Review script	1 wk	Mon 7/5/04	Fri 7/9/04		Scott Cooper,Clair He
3	✓	Develop script breakdo	1.45 wks	Mon 7/12/04	Thu 7/22/04	2	Scott Cooper,John T
4	✓	Develop production boa	5.04 wks	Thu 7/22/04	Thu 8/26/04	3	Scott Cooper,John T
5	✓	Scout locations	1.33 wks	Thu 8/26/04	Mon 9/6/04	4	Jo Brown,Jan Mikso\
6	✓	Select locations	8 days	Mon 9/6/04	Thu 9/16/04	5	Scott Cooper,Clair He
7		Hold auditions	1 wk	Thu 9/16/04	Thu 9/23/04	6	Clair Hector,Scott Co
8		Apply for filming permit:	1 wk	Mon 9/20/04	Mon 9/27/04	7FS-50%	Kim Yoshida
9		Reserve camera equipr	0.5 days	Mon 9/27/04	Thu 9/30/04	8	Jan Miksovsky,Eric L
10		Reserve sound equipm	4.94 days	Mon 9/27/04	Mon 10/4/04	9SS	Peter Kelly,Eric Lang
11		Pre-Production complet	0 days	Mon 10/4/04	Mon 10/4/04	10	
12	📝	⊟ Production	34.13 days	Mon 10/4/04	Fri 11/19/04	1	
13		⊟ Scene 1	6.75 days	Mon 10/4/04	Wed 10/13/04		
14		Scene 1 setup	4 days	Mon 10/4/04	Fri 10/8/04		Jo Brown,Max Bens
15		Scene 1 rehearsal	1 day	Fri 10/8/04	Mon 10/11/04	14	Scott Cooper,Jo Bro\
16		Scene 1 shoot	6 hrs	Mon 10/11/04	Tue 10/12/04	15	Scott Cooper,Jo Bro\
17		Scene 1 teardown	1 day	Tue 10/12/04	Wed 10/13/04	16	Jo Brown,Max Bens
18		⊟ Scene 2	2.63 days	Wed 10/13/04	Fri 10/15/04	13	
19		Scene 2 setup	1 day	Wed 10/13/04	Thu 10/14/04		Jo Brown,Max Bens
20		Scene 2 rehearsal	6 hrs	Thu 10/14/04	Fri 10/15/04	19	Scott Cooper,Doug H
21		Scene 2 shoot	3 hrs	Fri 10/15/04	Fri 10/15/04	20	Scott Cooper,Doug H

3 Click the Task Name column heading.

4 On the Insert menu, click Column.

Tip

You can also right-click a column heading, and on the shortcut menu, click Insert Column.

The Column Definition dialog box appears.

5 In the Field Name drop-down list, click Unique ID, and then click OK.

Tip

Remember that you can type a letter in a list to go directly to items that begin with that letter. For example, you can type **U** to go to the items that begin with U.

Microsoft Project inserts the Unique ID column to the left of the Task Name column. Your screen should look similar to the following illustration:

The Unique ID column indicates the order in which tasks were entered into the project plan. Cutting and pasting a task causes its Unique ID value to change.

	🛈	Unique ID	Task Name	Duration	Start	Finish	Predecessors	Resource Names
1		10	⊟ Pre-Production	65.56 days	Mon 7/5/04	Mon 10/4/04		
2	✓	1	Review script	1 wk	Mon 7/5/04	Fri 7/9/04		Scott Cooper,Clair H
3	✓	2	Develop script breakdo	1.45 wks	Mon 7/12/04	Thu 7/22/04	2	Scott Cooper,John T
4	✓	3	Develop production boa	5.04 wks	Thu 7/22/04	Thu 8/26/04	3	Scott Cooper,John T
5	✓	4	Scout locations	1.33 wks	Thu 8/26/04	Mon 9/6/04	4	Jo Brown,Jan Mikso
6	✓	8	Select locations	8 days	Mon 9/6/04	Thu 9/16/04	5	Scott Cooper,Clair H
7		77	Hold auditions	1 wk	Thu 9/16/04	Thu 9/23/04	6	Clair Hector,Scott Co
8		9	Apply for filming permit	1 wk	Mon 9/20/04	Mon 9/27/04	7FS-50%	Kim Yoshida
9		6	Reserve camera equipr	0.5 wks	Mon 9/27/04	Thu 9/30/04	8	Jan Miksovsky,Eric L
10		7	Reserve sound equipm	4.94 days	Mon 9/27/04	Mon 10/4/04	9SS	Peter Kelly,Eric Lang
11		13	Pre-Production complet	0 days	Mon 10/4/04	Mon 10/4/04	10	
12	📝	14	⊟ Production	34.13 days	Mon 10/4/04	Fri 11/19/04	1	
13		15	⊟ Scene 1	6.75 days	Mon 10/4/04	Wed 10/13/04		
14		16	Scene 1 setup	4 days	Mon 10/4/04	Fri 10/8/04		Jo Brown,Max Bens
15		17	Scene 1 rehearsal	1 day	Fri 10/8/04	Mon 10/11/04	14	Scott Cooper,Jo Bro
16		18	Scene 1 shoot	6 hrs	Mon 10/11/04	Tue 10/12/04	15	Scott Cooper,Jo Bro
17		19	Scene 1 teardown	1 day	Tue 10/12/04	Wed 10/13/04	16	Jo Brown,Max Bens
18		21	⊟ Scene 2	2.63 days	Wed 10/13/04	Fri 10/15/04	13	
19		22	Scene 2 setup	1 day	Wed 10/13/04	Thu 10/14/04		Jo Brown,Max Bens
20		23	Scene 2 rehearsal	6 hrs	Thu 10/14/04	Fri 10/15/04	19	Scott Cooper,Doug H
21		24	Scene 2 shoot	3 hrs	Fri 10/15/04	Fri 10/15/04	20	Scott Cooper,Doug H

As you can see, the tasks in this project were entered in a different order than they are currently displayed. Should you ever want to reorder them to reflect the order in which they were entered, you could sort the Task Sheet by Unique ID.

Next you will display the WBS codes in the Task Sheet view.

6 Click the Task Name column heading.

7 On the Insert menu, click Column.

8 In the Field Name list, click WBS, and then click OK.

Microsoft Project inserts the WBS column to the left of the Task Name column. Your screen should look similar to the following illustration:

WBS codes represent the hierarchy of summary and subtasks in the project plan. This WBS numbering system is standard in project management.

	🛈	Unique ID	WBS	Task Name	Duration	Start	Finish	Predecessors	Resource Names
1		10	1	⊟ Pre-Production	65.56 days	Mon 7/5/04	Mon 10/4/04		
2	✓	1	1.1	Review script	1 wk	Mon 7/5/04	Fri 7/9/04		Scott Cooper,Clair H
3	✓	2	1.2	Develop script breakdo	1.45 wks	Mon 7/12/04	Thu 7/22/04	2	Scott Cooper,John T
4	✓	3	1.3	Develop production boa	5.04 wks	Thu 7/22/04	Thu 8/26/04	3	Scott Cooper,John T
5	✓	4	1.4	Scout locations	1.33 wks	Thu 8/26/04	Mon 9/6/04	4	Jo Brown,Jan Mikso
6	✓	8	1.5	Select locations	8 days	Mon 9/6/04	Thu 9/16/04	5	Scott Cooper,Clair H
7		77	1.6	Hold auditions	1 wk	Thu 9/16/04	Thu 9/23/04	6	Clair Hector,Scott Co
8		9	1.7	Apply for filming permit	1 wk	Mon 9/20/04	Mon 9/27/04	7FS-50%	Kim Yoshida
9		6	1.8	Reserve camera equipr	0.5 wks	Mon 9/27/04	Thu 9/30/04	8	Jan Miksovsky,Eric L
10		7	1.9	Reserve sound equipm	4.94 days	Mon 9/27/04	Mon 10/4/04	9SS	Peter Kelly,Eric Lang
11		13	1.10	Pre-Production complet	0 days	Mon 10/4/04	Mon 10/4/04	10	
12	📝	14	2	⊟ Production	34.13 days	Mon 10/4/04	Fri 11/19/04	1	
13		15	2.1	⊟ Scene 1	6.75 days	Mon 10/4/04	Wed 10/13/04		
14		16	2.1.1	Scene 1 setup	4 days	Mon 10/4/04	Fri 10/8/04		Jo Brown,Max Bens
15		17	2.1.2	Scene 1 rehearsal	1 day	Fri 10/8/04	Mon 10/11/04	14	Scott Cooper,Jo Bro
16		18	2.1.3	Scene 1 shoot	6 hrs	Mon 10/11/04	Tue 10/12/04	15	Scott Cooper,Jo Bro
17		19	2.1.4	Scene 1 teardown	1 day	Tue 10/12/04	Wed 10/13/04	16	Jo Brown,Max Bens
18		21	2.2	⊟ Scene 2	2.63 days	Wed 10/13/04	Fri 10/15/04	13	
19		22	2.2.1	Scene 2 setup	1 day	Wed 10/13/04	Thu 10/14/04		Jo Brown,Max Bens
20		23	2.2.2	Scene 2 rehearsal	6 hrs	Thu 10/14/04	Fri 10/15/04	19	Scott Cooper,Doug H
21		24	2.2.3	Scene 2 shoot	3 hrs	Fri 10/15/04	Fri 10/15/04	20	Scott Cooper,Doug H

In the WBS structure, you can see that the top-level summary tasks are sequentially numbered with a single digit, the second-level summary or subtasks append the first digit with a period and a second digit, and so on.

To conclude this exercise, you will see how the Task ID, Unique ID, and WBS numbers respond when tasks are reorganized.

9 In the Task ID column (the one on the far left), click 9 and 10. This selects the rows for the tasks *Reserve camera equipment* and *Reserve sound equipment*.

Indent

10 On the Formatting toolbar, click the Indent button.

Microsoft Project makes Tasks 9 and 10 subtasks of Task 8. The Task ID and Unique ID values for these tasks are not affected, but the WBS codes are. The WBS codes for Tasks 9 and 10 now indicate that they reside at the third level of the project hierarchy. In addition, Task 11, the only subsequent task in the 1.x branch of the WBS, is renumbered from 1.10 to 1.8. Also note that the link between Tasks 8 and 9 was broken when 9 became a subtask of 8.

Your screen should look similar to the following illustration:

Indenting these tasks changes the hierarchy of the project and the WBS codes. In this case, only the pre-production phase hierarchy was affected.

	ⓘ	Unique ID	WBS	Task Name	Duration	Start	Finish	Predecessors	Resource Names
1		10	1	⊟ Pre-Production	60.56 days	Mon 7/5/04	Mon 9/27/04		
2	✓	1	1.1	Review script	1 wk	Mon 7/5/04	Fri 7/9/04		Scott Cooper,Clair He
3	✓	2	1.2	Develop script breakdo	1.45 wks	Mon 7/12/04	Thu 7/22/04	2	Scott Cooper,John T
4	✓	3	1.3	Develop production bo:	5.04 wks	Thu 7/22/04	Thu 8/26/04	3	Scott Cooper,John T
5	✓	4	1.4	Scout locations	1.33 wks	Thu 8/26/04	Mon 9/6/04	4	Jo Brown,Jan Mikso'
6	✓	8	1.5	Select locations	8 days	Mon 9/6/04	Thu 9/16/04	5	Scott Cooper,Clair He
7		77	1.6	Hold auditions	1 wk	Thu 9/16/04	Thu 9/23/04	6	Clair Hector,Scott Co
8		9	1.7	⊟ Apply for filming per	4.94 days	Mon 9/20/04	Mon 9/27/04	7FS-50%	Kim Yoshida
9		6	1.7.1	Reserve camera equ	0.5 wks	Mon 9/20/04	Thu 9/23/04		Jan Miksovsky,Eric L
10		7	1.7.2	Reserve sound equi	4.94 days	Mon 9/20/04	Mon 9/27/04	9SS	Peter Kelly,Eric Lang
11		13	1.8	Pre-Production complet	0 days	Mon 9/27/04	Mon 9/27/04	10	
12	🖉	14	2	⊟ Production	34.13 days	Mon 9/27/04	Fri 11/12/04	1	
13		15	2.1	⊟ Scene 1	6.75 days	Mon 9/27/04	Wed 10/6/04		
14		16	2.1.1	Scene 1 setup	4 days	Mon 9/27/04	Fri 10/1/04		Jo Brown,Max Bens
15		17	2.1.2	Scene 1 rehearsal	1 day	Fri 10/1/04	Mon 10/4/04	14	Scott Cooper,Jo Bro
16		18	2.1.3	Scene 1 shoot	6 hrs	Mon 10/4/04	Tue 10/5/04	15	Scott Cooper,Jo Bro'
17		19	2.1.4	Scene 1 teardown	1 day	Tue 10/5/04	Wed 10/6/04	16	Jo Brown,Max Bens
18		21	2.2	⊟ Scene 2	2.63 days	Wed 10/6/04	Fri 10/8/04	13	
19		22	2.2.1	Scene 2 setup	1 day	Wed 10/6/04	Thu 10/7/04		Jo Brown,Max Bens
20		23	2.2.2	Scene 2 rehearsal	6 hrs	Thu 10/7/04	Fri 10/8/04	19	Scott Cooper,Doug H
21		24	2.2.3	Scene 2 shoot	3 hrs	Fri 10/8/04	Fri 10/8/04	20	Scott Cooper,Doug H

Outdent

11 On the Formatting toolbar, click the Outdent button.

Microsoft Project promotes Tasks 9 and 10 back to the second level of the project hierarchy and updates the WBS codes of the affected tasks.

Next you will see how Task IDs and WBS codes are affected by moving tasks.

12 With Tasks 9 and 10 still selected, on the Edit menu, click Cut Task.

Microsoft Project cuts the selected tasks to the Windows Clipboard. Your screen should look similar to the following illustration:

	❶	Unique ID	WBS	Task Name	Duration	Start	Finish	Predecessors	Resource Names
1		10	1	⊟ Pre-Production	60.56 days	Mon 7/5/04	Mon 9/27/04		
2	✓	1	1.1	Review script	1 wk	Mon 7/5/04	Fri 7/9/04		Scott Cooper,Clair H
3	✓	2	1.2	Develop script breakdo	1.45 wks	Mon 7/12/04	Thu 7/22/04	2	Scott Cooper,John T
4	✓	3	1.3	Develop production bo	5.04 wks	Thu 7/22/04	Thu 8/26/04	3	Scott Cooper,John T
5	✓	4	1.4	Scout locations	1.33 wks	Thu 8/26/04	Thu 9/6/04	4	Jo Brown,Jan Mikso
6	✓	8	1.5	Select locations	8 days	Mon 9/6/04	Thu 9/16/04	5	Scott Cooper,Clair H
7		77	1.6	Hold auditions	1 wk	Thu 9/16/04	Thu 9/23/04	6	Clair Hector,Scott Co
8		9	1.7	Apply for filming permi:	0.99 wks	Mon 9/20/04	Mon 9/27/04	7FS-50%	Kim Yoshida
9		13	1.8	Pre-Production complet	0 days	Mon 7/5/04	Mon 7/5/04		
10	◔	14	2	⊟ Production	34.13 days	Mon 9/27/04	Fri 11/12/04	1	
11		15	2.1	⊟ Scene 1	6.75 days	Mon 9/27/04	Wed 10/6/04		
12		16	2.1.1	Scene 1 setup	4 days	Mon 9/27/04	Fri 10/1/04		Jo Brown,Max Bens
13		17	2.1.2	Scene 1 rehearsal	1 day	Fri 10/1/04	Mon 10/4/04	12	Scott Cooper,Jo Bro
14		18	2.1.3	Scene 1 shoot	6 hrs	Mon 10/4/04	Tue 10/5/04	13	Scott Cooper,Jo Bro
15		19	2.1.4	Scene 1 teardown	1 day	Tue 10/5/04	Wed 10/6/04	14	Jo Brown,Max Bens
16		21	2.2	⊟ Scene 2	2.63 days	Wed 10/6/04	Fri 10/8/04	11	
17		22	2.2.1	Scene 2 setup	1 day	Wed 10/6/04	Thu 10/7/04		Jo Brown,Max Bens
18		23	2.2.2	Scene 2 rehearsal	6 hrs	Thu 10/7/04	Fri 10/8/04	17	Scott Cooper,Doug H
19		24	2.2.3	Scene 2 shoot	3 hrs	Fri 10/8/04	Fri 10/8/04	18	Scott Cooper,Doug H
20		25	2.2.4	Scene 2 teardown	0.5 days	Fri 10/8/04	Fri 10/8/04	19	Jo Brown,Max Bens
21		27	2.3	⊟ Scene 3	4 days	Fri 10/8/04	Thu 10/14/04	16	

Notice that the Task IDs are renumbered, the Unique IDs are unchanged, and only the WBS codes in the pre-production phase are renumbered. The WBS codes in other phases of the project are unaffected because that part of the project hierarchy did not change.

13 Click Task ID 5.

14 On the Edit menu, click Paste.

Microsoft Project pastes the previously cut tasks from the Windows Clipboard into the task list. Your screen should look similar to the following illustration:

After you paste tasks into the task list, the Unique ID values of these tasks change. After a task is moved by cutting and pasting, it is assigned the next sequential Unique ID number.

	❶	Unique ID	WBS	Task Name	Duration	Start	Finish	Predecessors	Resource Names
1		10	1	⊟ Pre-Production	60.56 days	Mon 7/5/04	Mon 9/27/04		
2	✓	1	1.1	Review script	1 wk	Mon 7/5/04	Fri 7/9/04		Scott Cooper,Clair H
3	✓	2	1.2	Develop script breakdo	1.45 wks	Mon 7/12/04	Thu 7/22/04	2	Scott Cooper,John T
4	✓	3	1.3	Develop production bo	5.04 wks	Thu 7/22/04	Thu 8/26/04	3	Scott Cooper,John T
5		78	1.4	Reserve camera equipn	0.5 wks	Thu 8/26/04	Mon 8/30/04	4	Jan Miksovsky,Eric L
6		79	1.5	Reserve sound equipm	4.94 days	Thu 8/26/04	Thu 9/2/04	5SS	Peter Kelly,Eric Lang
7	✓	4	1.6	Scout locations	1.33 wks	Thu 8/26/04	Thu 9/6/04	6	Jo Brown,Jan Mikso
8	✓	8	1.7	Select locations	8 days	Mon 9/6/04	Thu 9/16/04	7	Scott Cooper,Clair H
9		77	1.8	Hold auditions	1 wk	Thu 9/16/04	Thu 9/23/04	8	Clair Hector,Scott Co
10		9	1.9	Apply for filming permi:	0.99 wks	Mon 9/20/04	Mon 9/27/04	9FS-50%	Kim Yoshida
11		13	1.10	Pre-Production complet	0 days	Mon 7/5/04	Mon 7/5/04		
12	◔	14	2	⊟ Production	34.13 days	Mon 9/27/04	Fri 11/12/04	1	
13		15	2.1	⊟ Scene 1	6.75 days	Mon 9/27/04	Wed 10/6/04		
14		16	2.1.1	Scene 1 setup	4 days	Mon 9/27/04	Fri 10/1/04		Jo Brown,Max Bens
15		17	2.1.2	Scene 1 rehearsal	1 day	Fri 10/1/04	Mon 10/4/04	14	Scott Cooper,Jo Bro
16		18	2.1.3	Scene 1 shoot	6 hrs	Mon 10/4/04	Tue 10/5/04	15	Scott Cooper,Jo Bro
17		19	2.1.4	Scene 1 teardown	1 day	Tue 10/5/04	Wed 10/6/04	16	Jo Brown,Max Bens
18		21	2.2	⊟ Scene 2	2.63 days	Wed 10/6/04	Fri 10/8/04	13	
19		22	2.2.1	Scene 2 setup	1 day	Wed 10/6/04	Thu 10/7/04		Jo Brown,Max Bens
20		23	2.2.2	Scene 2 rehearsal	6 hrs	Thu 10/7/04	Fri 10/8/04	19	Scott Cooper,Doug H
21		24	2.2.3	Scene 2 shoot	3 hrs	Fri 10/8/04	Fri 10/8/04	20	Scott Cooper,Doug H

Again the Task IDs and the WBS codes in the pre-production phase are renumbered. The Unique IDs for the pasted tasks are updated with the next sequential numbers to indicate when they were added to the project.

15 On the Edit menu, click Undo Paste.

16 Click Task ID 9.

17 On the Edit menu, click Paste.

Microsoft Project restores the task list to its original order.

Again note that the Unique ID numbers of the tasks *Reserve camera equipment* and *Reserve sound equipment* are updated to reflect the order in which they were added to the task list.

Tip

To preserve Unique ID values when you rearrange tasks, drag tasks rather than cutting and pasting them.

If you were to sort, filter, or otherwise change the presentation of the task list, the WBS codes would still indicate the place in the project hierarchy of every task. In fact, it's common to use WBS codes instead of Task IDs or names when referencing specific tasks between team members on a project.

The final step to restoring the task list to its original state is to relink Tasks 8 and 9.

18 Click the Task IDs of Tasks 8 and 9.

Link Tasks

19 On the Standard toolbar, click the Link Tasks button.

Using Custom Outline Codes for More Sophisticated Needs

In complex projects, you might not find the work breakdown structure (WBS) or standard outline numbering schemes available in Microsoft Project adequate for your reporting or analysis needs. If this is the case, investigate Microsoft Project's capabilities to handle custom outline codes to identify a hierarchy within a project plan.

For example, you can define a custom outline code that associates different outline levels (or nested phases, subphases, and tasks) of a project plan with different levels of the organization's structure. The top level might be a division, the next lower level a business unit, and the third level a functional team. This would result in the more informative outline code of "Promotionals-Commercial-Film Crew," for example. Alternatively, you could use custom outline codes to associate different outline levels of a project plan with different internal accounting or job tracking codes. If you can represent a hierarchy of any type as strings of numbers and letters, you can represent that hierarchy in your project plan through custom outline codes.

After you've applied a custom outline code to your project plan, you can then group, sort, and filter tasks or resources by their outline codes. You can apply up to ten levels of a custom outline code for tasks and ten for resources in a single Microsoft Project plan.

To learn more about custom outline codes, type **Create an outline code** into the Ask A Question box in the upper right corner of the Microsoft Project window.

Formatting the Network Diagram View

In traditional project management, the Network Diagram is a standard way of representing project activities and their relationships. Tasks are represented as boxes, or nodes, and the relationships between tasks are drawn as lines connecting nodes. Unlike the Gantt Chart, which is a timescaled view, a network diagram enables you to see project activities in more of a flowchart format. This is useful if you'd like to focus more on the relationships between activities rather than on their durations.

Microsoft Project provides substantial formatting options for the Network Diagram. In this section, you will use just a few of these formatting options. If you're a heavy-duty Network Diagram user, you'll want to explore the formatting options in greater detail on your own.

In this exercise, you format items in the Network Diagram view:

1 On the View menu, click Network Diagram.

The Network Diagram view appears. In this view, each task is represented by a box or node, and each node contains several pieces of information about the task. Your screen should look similar to the following illustration:

The Network Diagram view focuses more on task relationships than on durations or sequence. Each task is represented as a box or node, and the relationships between tasks are represented as arrows.

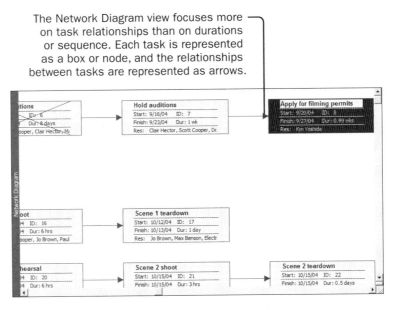

Tip

Nodes with an *X* drawn through them represent completed tasks.

Next you'll replace the task ID values with the WBS codes you worked with in the previous exercise in the task nodes.

2   On the Format menu, click Box Styles.

The Box Styles dialog box appears. Your screen should look similar to the following illustration:

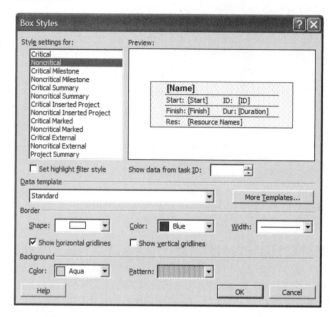

In the Style Settings For list, you can see all of the node box styles available in Microsoft Project. The Preview box shows you the specific labels and fields displayed in each box style.

3   Click the More Templates button.

The Data Templates dialog box appears.

4   In the Templates in Network Diagram list, make sure that Standard is selected, and then click the Copy button.

The Data Template Definition dialog box appears. You want to add the WBS code value to the upper right corner of the node.

5   In the Template Name box, type **Standard + WBS**.

6   Below Choose Cell(s), click the cell in the upper right corner; it currently contains "ID."

7   In the drop-down list of fields, click WBS, and then press the Enter key.

Pressing the Enter key causes Microsoft Project to update the preview in the dialog box. Your screen should look similar to the following illustration:

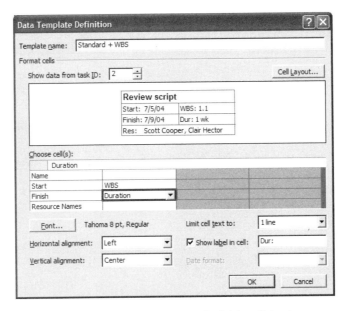

8 Click OK to close the Data Template Definition dialog box.

9 Click the Close button to close the Data Templates dialog box.

10 In the Box Styles dialog box, under Style Settings For, drag to select all the items in the box: Critical through Project Summary.

11 In the Data Template box, click Standard + WBS from the drop-down list box.

Your screen should look similar to the following illustration:

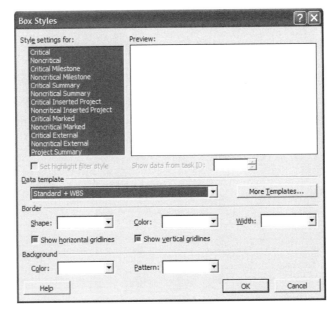

12 Click OK to close the Box Styles dialog box.

Microsoft Project applies the revised box style to nodes in the Network Diagram. Your screen should look similar to the following illustration:

After formatting the box style in the Network Diagram view, the WBS code has replaced the Task ID in each node.

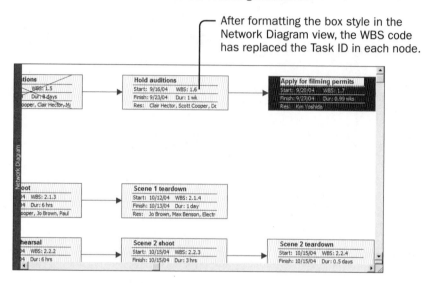

Formatting the Calendar View

The Calendar view is probably the simplest view available in Microsoft Project; however, even the Calendar view offers several formatting options. This view is especially useful for sharing schedule information with resources or other stakeholders who prefer a traditional "month-at-a-glance" format rather than a more detailed view, such as the Gantt Chart.

In this exercise, you reformat summary and critical tasks in the Calendar view.

1 On the View menu, click Calendar.

The Calendar view appears. It displays four weeks at a time, and it draws task bars on the days on which tasks are scheduled. Depending on your screen resolution, you might see additional task bars in the Calendar view.

The Calendar view resembles a traditional "month-at-a-glance" calendar and displays tasks as bars spanning the days on which they are scheduled to occur.

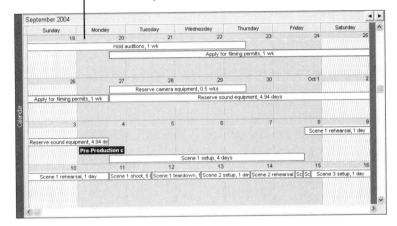

2 On the Format menu, click Bar Styles.

The Bar Styles dialog box appears. The additional item type you would like to show on the Calendar view is a summary bar.

3 In the Task Type box, click Summary.

4 In the Bar Type box, click Line in the drop-down list.

The next item type to reformat is critical tasks.

5 In the Task Type box, click Critical.

6 In the Pattern box, click the second option in the drop-down list: the solid black bar.

7 In the Color box, click Red in the drop-down list.

Your screen should look similar to the following illustration:

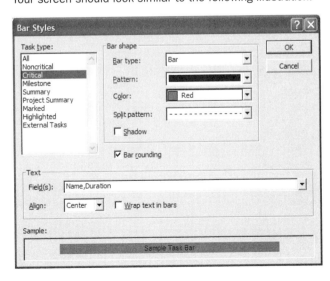

8 Click OK to close the Bar Styles dialog box.

9 On the Format menu, click Layout Now.

Microsoft Project applies the format options to the Calendar view. Rather than scrolling through the Calendar view, you can jump right to a specific date.

10 On the Edit menu, click Go To.

11 In the Date box (not the ID box), type or select **11/14/04**, and then click OK.

The Calendar view displays the first critical tasks. Your screen should look similar to the following illustration:

After formatting the Calendar view, critical tasks appear in red and summary tasks appear as lines.

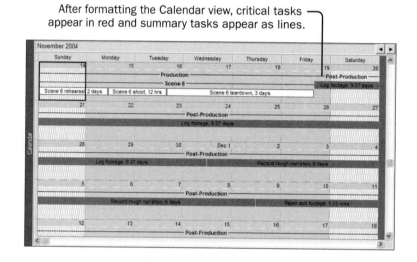

Chapter Wrap-Up

This chapter covered how to use some of the more advanced formatting features in Microsoft Project.

If you are going on to other chapters:

Save

1 On the Standard toolbar, click the Save button to save changes made to Parnell Film 17.

2 On the File menu, click Close to close the project plan.

If you aren't continuing to other chapters:

1 On the Standard toolbar, click the Save button to save changes made to Parnell Film 17.

2 To quit Microsoft Project for now, on the File menu, click Exit.

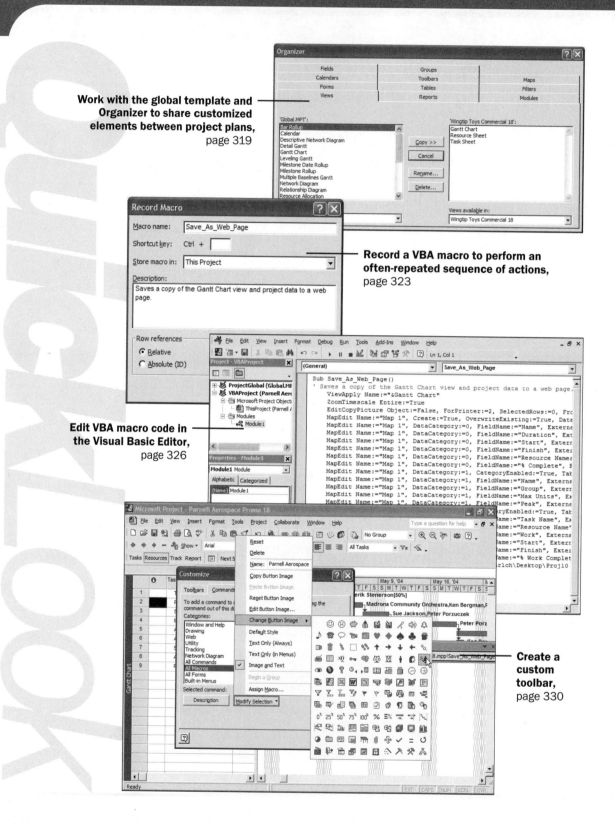

Work with the global template and Organizer to share customized elements between project plans, page 319

Record a VBA macro to perform an often-repeated sequence of actions, page 323

Edit VBA macro code in the Visual Basic Editor, page 326

Create a custom toolbar, page 330

Chapter 18
Customizing Microsoft Project

After completing this chapter, you will be able to:

✔ Copy a customized element, such as a table, from one Microsoft Project plan to another by using the Organizer.

✔ Record and play back a simple macro.

✔ Edit a macro in the Visual Basic Editor.

✔ Create a custom toolbar.

This chapter describes some of the ways you can customize Microsoft Project to fit your own preferences. Some of the customization options in Microsoft Project are similar to those you see in other Microsoft Office family applications like Microsoft Word or Microsoft Excel. Some customization options even apply to all Microsoft Office family applications regardless of the specific application in which you set them. Other options are unique to Microsoft Project.

Important

Some of the actions you perform in this chapter can affect your overall settings in Microsoft Project regardless of the specific project plan you are using. To keep your Microsoft Project environment unaffected or at the "factory settings," after you complete this chapter, we include steps to undo some actions.

Parnell Aerospace Promo 18a Wingtip Toys Commercial 18b

This chapter uses the practice files Parnell Aerospace Promo 18a and Wingtip Toys Commercial 18b. For details about installing the practice files, see "Using the Book's CD-ROM" at the beginning of this book.

Working with the Organizer

The *Organizer* is the feature you use to share customized elements among Microsoft Project plans. The complete list of elements you can copy between files with the Organizer is indicated by the names of the tabs in the Organizer dialog box, which you will see shortly.

One feature of Microsoft Project that you can work with through the Organizer is the *global template*. This is a Microsoft Project template named *Global.mpt*, and it is installed as part of Microsoft Project. The global template provides the default *views*, *tables*, and other elements in Microsoft Project. The list of elements provided by the global template includes the following:

- Calendars
- Filters
- Forms
- Groups
- Maps

- Reports
- Tables
- Menus and toolbars
- VBA modules (macros)
- Views

Initially, the specific definitions of all views, tables, and similar elements are contained in the global template. For example, the fact that the default usage table contains one set of fields and not others is determined by the global template. The very first time you display a view, table, or similar element in a Microsoft Project plan, it is automatically copied from the global template to that project plan. Thereafter, the element resides in the Microsoft Project plan. Any subsequent customization of that element in the Microsoft Project plan (for example, changing the fields displayed in a table) applies to only that one Microsoft Project plan and does not affect the global template.

You could use Microsoft Project extensively and never need to touch the global template. When you do work with the global template, you do so through the Organizer. There are two primary actions you can accomplish relating to the global template:

- Create a customized element, such as a custom view, and make it available in all project plans you work with by copying the custom view into the global template.
- Replace a customized element such as a view or table in a project plan by copying the original, unmodified element from the global template to the project plan in which you've customized the same element.

Important

In the Organizer, when you attempt to copy a view, table, or other element from a project plan to the global template, Microsoft Project alerts you if you will overwrite that same element in the global template. If you choose to overwrite it, that customized element (such as a customized view) will be available in all new project plans and any other project plans that do not already contain that element. If you choose to rename the customized element, it becomes available in all project plans but does not affect the existing elements already stored in the global template. It's generally a good idea to give your customized elements unique names, like *Custom Gantt Chart,* so you can keep the original element intact.

The settings in the global template apply to all project plans you work with in Microsoft Project. Because we don't want to alter the global template you use, in this exercise we'll focus on copying customized elements between two project plans. Keep in mind, though, that the general process of using the Organizer shown here is the same whether you are working with the global template and a project plan or two project plans. In fact, any custom element you copy into the global template becomes available in all the project plans you use.

In this exercise, you will copy a custom table from one project plan to another:

1 If Microsoft Project is not already open, start it now.

Open

2 On the Standard toolbar, click the Open button.

The Open dialog box appears.

3 Navigate to the Chapter 18 Customizing folder, and double-click the Parnell Aerospace Promo 18a file.

4 On the File menu, click Save As.

The Save As dialog box appears.

5 In the File Name box, type **Parnell Aerospace Promo 18**, and then click the Save button.

6 Repeat steps 3 through 5 to open Wingtip Toys Commercial 18b, and save it as **Wingtip Toys Commercial 18.**

The Wingtip Toys Commercial 18 project plan contains a custom table named *Custom Entry Table* that is currently displayed in the Task Sheet view. Your screen should look similar to the following illustration:

The table in this view has been customized by inserting and removing columns.

	ⓘ	Task Name	Resource Names	Duration	Start	Deadline	Finish
1		Log footage	Patricia Brooke[50%],Jon Ganio,Mary Anne Kol	1 wk	Mon 5/3/04	NA	Fri 5/7/04
2		Record rough narration	Ken Bergman,Matthew Dunn	4 days	Wed 5/5/04	NA	Mon 5/10/04
3		Paper edit footage	Ken Bergman,Jon Ganio,Mary Anne Kobylka	2 wks	Tue 5/11/04	NA	Mon 5/24/04
4		Rough cut edit	Ken Bergman,Lane Sacksteder	1 wk	Tue 5/25/04	NA	Mon 5/31/04
5		Fine cut edit	Patricia Brooke[50%],Sherri Hart	2 wks	Tue 6/1/04	NA	Mon 6/14/04
6		Hold formal approval show	Ken Bergman,Scott Fallon,Mary Anne Kobylka,	1 day	Tue 6/15/04	NA	Tue 6/15/04
7		Record final narration	Fabrikam Inc. Sound Studio,Jon Ganio	1 wk	Wed 6/16/04	NA	Tue 6/22/04
8		Add head and tail titles	Garrett R Vargas,Mary Anne Kobylka	1 wk	Wed 6/23/04	NA	Tue 6/29/04
9		Add final music	Ken Bergman,John Rodman,Lane Sacksteder	0.67 wks	Mon 6/28/04	NA	Thu 7/1/04
10		Print internegative of film	Lane Sacksteder	3 days	Thu 7/1/04	NA	Tue 7/6/04
11		Clone dubbing masters of	Suki White	4 days	Tue 7/6/04	NA	Mon 7/12/04
12		Archive master film and au	Suki White	1 day	Mon 7/12/04	NA	Tue 7/13/04
13		Hand off masters to distrib		0 days	Tue 7/13/04	NA	Tue 7/13/04

You'd like to copy this custom table to the Parnell Aerospace Promo 18 project plan.

7   On the Tools menu, click Organizer.

The Organizer dialog box appears. Your screen should look similar to the following illustration:

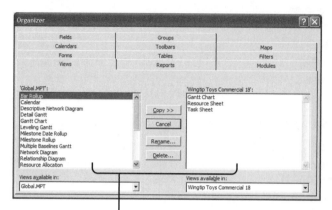

Every tab in the Organizer dialog box has a similar structure—the elements in the global template are on the left, and those in the active project plan are on the right.

8   Click several of the tabs in the dialog box, and then click the Tables tab.

As you can see, every tab of the Organizer dialog box has a similar structure.

Elements from the global template appear on the left side of the dialog box and the corresponding elements from the active project plan appear on the right. You might notice that the list of tables in the Wingtip plan, for example, is not the complete list of tables you can display. The list you see for the Wingtip plan in the Organizer includes only the tables that have actually been displayed already in the Wingtip plan. If you were to display another table, the Schedule table, for example, Microsoft Project would copy that table definition from the global template into the Wingtip plan.

Selecting an element on the left side of the dialog box and then clicking the Copy button will copy that element to the project plan listed on the right. Conversely, selecting an element on the right side of the dialog box and then clicking the Copy button will copy that element to the file listed on the left.

9   In the Tables Available In drop-down list on the left side of the Organizer dialog box, click Parnell Aerospace Promo 18.

This project plan appears in the list because it is open in Microsoft Project. Your screen should look similar to the following illustration:

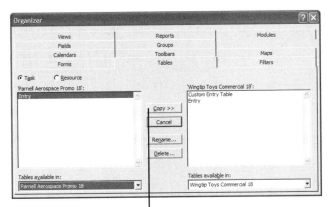

The side of the dialog box in which you've
selected an element determines the direction
in which you copy the element.

As you can see, the Parnell plan (on the left) does not have the Custom Entry Table,
and the Wingtip plan (on the right) does.

10 In the list of tables on the right side of the dialog box, click Custom Entry Table.

Tip

Notice that the two arrow symbols (>>) in the Copy button switch direction (<<) when
you select an element on the right side of the dialog box.

11 Click Copy.

Microsoft Project copies the Custom Entry Table from the Wingtip plan to the Parnell plan.
Your screen should look similar to the following illustration:

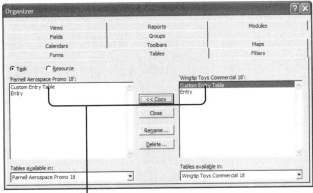

After clicking the Copy button, the Custom Entry Table
is copied from the Wingtip plan to the Parnell plan.

12 Click Close to close the Organizer dialog box.

To conclude this exercise, you will display the newly copied custom table.

13 On the Window menu, click Parnell Aerospace Promo 18.

Microsoft Project switches to the Parnell plan, the plan to which you just copied the custom table.

14 On the View menu, click More Views.

The More Views dialog box appears.

15 In the Views list, click Task Sheet, and then click Apply.

16 On the View menu, point to Table: Entry, and then click Custom Entry Table.

Microsoft Project displays the custom table in the Parnell plan. Your screen should look similar to the following illustration:

	❶	Task Name	Resource Names	Duration	Start	Deadline	Finish
1		Transfer soundtrack to m	Derk Stenerson[50%]	14 days	Mon 4/19/04	NA	Thu 5/6/04
2		Record music	Madrona Community Orchestra,Ken Bergman,F	7 days	Fri 4/30/04	NA	Mon 5/10/04
3		Sync sound	Sue Jackson,Peter Porzuczek	1.5 days	Tue 5/11/04	NA	Wed 5/12/04
4		Mix	Peter Porzuczek,Sue Jackson,Adam Barr	7 days	Wed 5/12/04	NA	Fri 5/21/04
5		Add effects	Ty Loren Carlson	3 days	Fri 5/21/04	NA	Wed 5/26/04
6		Add optical track	Ken Bergman,Joanna Fuller	1 day	Fri 5/21/04	NA	Mon 5/24/04
7		Split tracks	Stephanie Hooper	3 days	Wed 5/26/04	NA	Mon 5/31/04
8		Add dialog	Ken Bergman,Sue Jackson,Fabrikam Inc. Soun	1.33 days	Mon 5/31/04	NA	Tue 6/1/04
9		Release prints		0 days	Tue 6/1/04	NA	Tue 6/1/04

17 On the View menu, click Gantt Chart.

Important

In this exercise, you copied a table between project plans. When copying an entire view, however, keep in mind that it is comprised of tables, filters, and groups. When copying custom views between plans, you might also need to copy a custom table, filter, or group that is part of the custom view.

Recording Macros

Many activities you perform in Microsoft Project can be repetitive. To save time, you can record a *macro* that captures keystrokes and mouse actions. The macro is recorded in Microsoft Visual Basic for Applications (VBA), the built-in macro programming language of the Office family of desktop applications. You can do sophisticated things with VBA, but you can record and play back simple macros without ever directly seeing or working with VBA code.

The macros you create are stored in the global template by default, so they are available to you whenever Microsoft Project is running. (In fact, macros, toolbars, and maps are unique in that when you create or customize them, Microsoft Project will store them in the global template rather than the active project plan by default.) The project plan for which you originally created the macro need not be open to run the macro in other project plans. If you want, you can use the Organizer to copy the macro from the global template to another project plan to give it to a friend, for example.

Publishing a project plan in HTML format is a great way to share project details on an intranet or the World Wide Web. However, it's likely the details you initially publish will become obsolete quickly as the project plan is updated. Republishing is a repetitive task that is ideal for automation through a macro. In this exercise, you record and run a macro in the Parnell Aerospace Promo 18 project plan that publishes the project plan to HTML format:

1 On the Tools menu, point to Macro, and then click Record New Macro.

The Record Macro dialog box appears.

2 In the Macro Name box, type **Save_As_Web_Page**

Tip

Macro names must begin with a letter and cannot contain spaces. To improve the readability of your macro names, you can use an underscore (_) in place of a space. For example, rather than naming a macro *SaveAsWebPage*, you can name it *Save_As_Web_Page*.

For this macro, we will not use a shortcut key. When recording other macros, note that you cannot use a *Ctrl+* key combination already reserved by Microsoft Project, so combinations like Ctrl+F (the keyboard shortcut for Find) and Ctrl+G (Go To) are unavailable. When you click OK to close the dialog box, Microsoft Project alerts you if you need to choose a different key combination.

3 In the Store Macro In box, click This Project to store the macro in the active project plan.

When a macro is stored in a project plan, the macro can be used by any project plan when the project plan that contains the macro is open. The other option, *Global File*, refers to the global template. In this exercise, you will not customize your global template.

4 In the Description box, select the boilerplate text, and replace it by typing **Saves a copy of the Gantt Chart view and project data to a web page**.

Your screen should look similar to the following illustration:

The description is useful to help identify the actions the macro will perform.

5 Click OK.

Microsoft Project begins recording the new macro. Microsoft Project does not literally record and play back every mouse movement and passing second, but records only the results of the keystrokes and mouse actions you make. Do not feel rushed to complete the recording of the macro.

6 On the View menu, click Gantt Chart.

Even though the project plan is already showing the Gantt Chart view, including this step in the macro records the action so if the project plan were initially in a different view, the macro would switch to the Gantt Chart view.

7 On the View menu, click Zoom.

8 In the Zoom dialog box, select Entire Project, and then click OK.

Microsoft Project adjusts the timescale to display the entire project. Your screen should look similar to the following illustration:

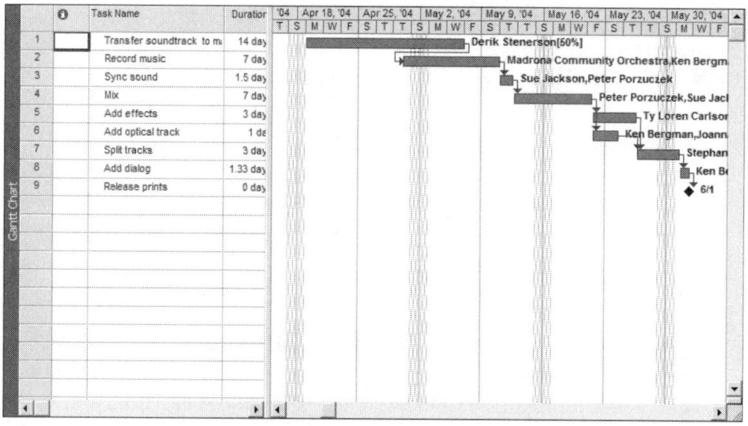

Copy Picture

9 On the Standard toolbar click the Copy Picture button.

The Copy Picture dialog box appears.

10 Under Render Image, click To GIF Image File, and then click OK.

The folder location and file name proposed for the GIF image are the same as those of the project plan, which is fine.

11 On the File menu, click Save As Web Page, and then click Save.

Again, the folder location and file name proposed for the HTML file are the same as those of the project plan, which is fine.

When you click Save, the Export Wizard appears.

12 In the Export Wizard, click the Next button.

The Map page of the Export Wizard appears.

13 Click Use Existing Map, and then click the Next button.

The Map Selection page of the Export Wizard appears.

14 Under Choose a Map For Your Data, click Export to HTML Using Standard Template, and then click the Next button.

The Map Options page of the Export Wizard appears.

15 Under HTML Options, click Include Image File in HTML Page, and then click Finish.

The Export Wizard saves the Web page as you've specified.

To wrap up the actions recorded in the macro, you will reset the timescale.

16 On the View menu, click Zoom, click Reset, and then click OK.

Now you are ready to stop recording.

17 On the Tools menu, point to Macro, and then click Stop Recorder.

Next you will run the macro to see it play back.

18 On the Tools menu, point to Macro, and then click Macros.

The Macros dialog box appears.

19 In the Macro Name box, click Parnell Aerospace Promo 18.mpp! Save_As_Web_Page, and then click the Run button.

The macro begins running but pauses as soon as Microsoft Project generates a confirmation message to replace the existing GIF image file.

20 Click Overwrite, and then click OK to overwrite the previously created Web page.

The macro republishes the project plan to HTML format. Next you'll see the results of the macro's actions.

21 In Windows Explorer, navigate to the Chapter 18 Customizing folder, and double-click the Parnell Aerospace Promo 18.html file to open it in your browser.

The Web page (consisting of the HTML file and related GIF image) appears in your browser. Your screen should look similar to the following illustration:

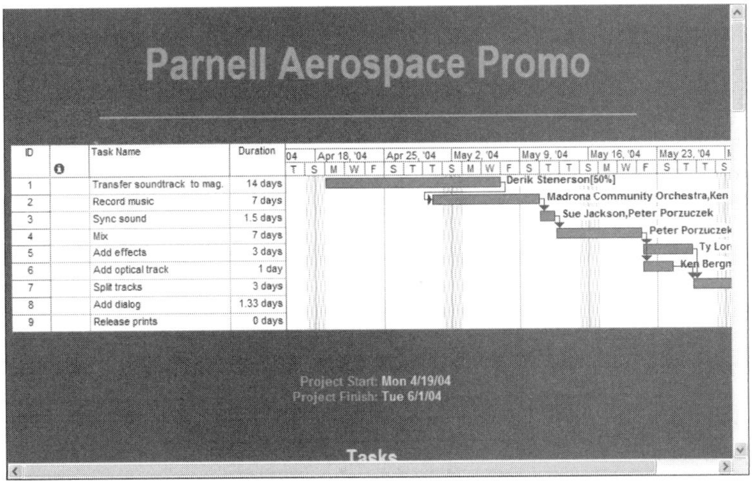

Leave the Web page open in your browser; you'll return to it in the next exercise.

22 Switch back to the Parnell Aerospace Promo 18 project plan in Microsoft Project.

This macro would be very useful if the Parnell project manager needed to republish the details of the project plan frequently. For example, the project manager could republish it at regular intervals during the planning stage when then details are being developed, and then again during the execution stage when the effects of actual progress change the remaining scheduled work.

Editing Macros

As handy as the Save_As_Web_Page macro is, it can be improved. Remember that when you ran it in the previous exercise, you had to confirm that Microsoft Project should overwrite the existing GIF image and HTML files. Because the intent of the macro is to publish the most current information, you would always want to overwrite the older information. You can change the macro code directly to accomplish this. The macro code resides in a VBA module, and you work with the code in the Visual Basic Environment.

Tip

The VBA language and Visual Basic Environment are standard in all the core Microsoft Office applications and many of the Office family applications (including Microsoft Project). Although the specific details of each application differ, the general way you use VBA in each is the same. VBA automation is a powerful tool you can master, and that knowledge can be used in many Microsoft applications.

In this exercise, you work in the Visual Basic Editor to fine-tune the macro you recorded in the previous exercise and then run it:

1   On the Tools menu, point to Macro, and then click Macros.

2   Under Macro Name, click Parnell Aerospace Promo 18.mpp!Save_As_Web_Page, and then click the Edit button.

Microsoft Project loads the module that contains the macro in the Visual Basic Editor. Your screen should look similar to the following illustration:

This is the VBA code that was generated by recording the actions you performed in Microsoft Project.

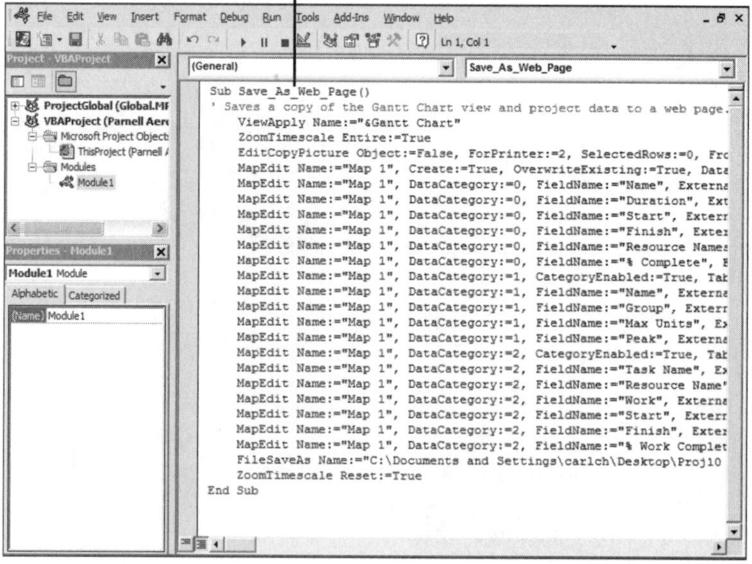

A full explanation of the VBA language is beyond the scope of this book, but we can walk you through some steps to change the behavior of the previously recorded macro. You might also recognize some of the actions that you recorded earlier by the names used in the VBA code.

3 Click at the beginning of the line ViewApply Name:="&Gantt Chart", and press Enter.

4 Click in the new line you just created, press Tab, and type **Application.Alerts False**

Your screen should look similar to the following illustration:

Here is the first line you typed.

```
Sub Save_As_Web_Page()
  ' Saves a copy of the Gantt Chart view and project data to a web page
    Application.Alerts False
    ViewApply Name:="&Gantt Chart"
    ZoomTimescale Entire:=True
    EditCopyPicture Object:=False, ForPrinter:=2, SelectedRows:=0, Fr
```

This will prevent the two prompts you received when running the macro and accept the default option of replacing the existing files with the same name.

Tip

Note that as you were typing, selection boxes and ScreenTips might have appeared. The Visual Basic Editor uses such tools and feedback to help you enter text in a module correctly.

5 In the line that begins with *EditCopyPicture*, select the test that follows *FromDate:=* text "4/15/04 12:00 AM" (including the quotation marks), and type **ActiveProject.Project-Start**

Note that the specific date you see might not be *4/15/04*.

This VBA code describes the project start date of the active project.

Your screen should look similar to the following illustration:

Here is the text you typed.

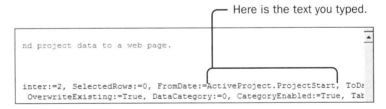

```
  nd project data to a web page.




    inter:=2, SelectedRows:=0, FromDate:=ActiveProject.ProjectStart, ToDa
     OverwriteExisting:=True, DataCategory:=0, CategoryEnabled:=True, Tab
```

This causes the macro to get the current start date of the active project for the GIF image the macro creates.

6 In the same row, select the text that follows *ToDate:=* text "6/5/04 12:00 PM" (including the quotation marks), and type **ActiveProject.ProjectFinish**

Again, note that the specific date you see might not be *6/5/04.*

Your screen should look similar to the following illustration:

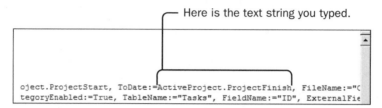

Here is the text string you typed.

```
oject.ProjectStart, ToDate:=ActiveProject.ProjectFinish, FileName:="C
tegoryEnabled:=True, TableName:="Tasks", FieldName:="ID", ExternalFie
```

This causes the macro to get the current finish date of the active project for the GIF image that the macro creates. Now if the project plan's start or finish date change, the date range for the GIF image will change as well.

7 On the File menu in the Visual Basic Editor, click Close And Return to Microsoft Project.

The Visual Basic Editor closes, and you return to the Parnell plan.

You could run the updated macro now, but to test if it really uses the most current project start and finish dates, you'll change the start date of the project plan.

8 On the Project menu, click Project Information.

The Project Information dialog box appears. Your screen should look similar to the following illustration:

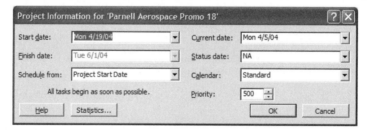

Note the current start and finish dates: 4/19/04 and 6/1/04.

9 In the Start Date box, type or click **4/26/04**, and then click OK to close the Project Information dialog box.

Microsoft Project reschedules the start (and all subsequent dates) of the project plan. Before you rerun the macro, however, you'll make one more major change to the plan. You'll change the duration of Task 1 from 14 days to 7.

10 In the Duration field for Task 1, *Transfer soundtrack to mag. stock,* type or select **7d**, and then press Enter.

Microsoft Project adjusts the duration for Task 1 and reschedules all successor tasks. Your screen should look similar to the following illustration:

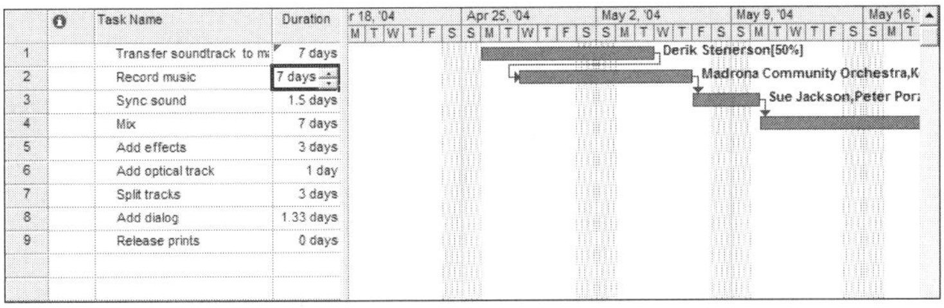

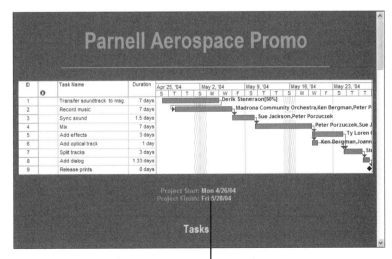

Now you are ready to rerun the macro.

11 On the Tools menu, point to Macro, and then select Macros.

The Macros dialog box appears.

12 In the Macro Name box, click Parnell Aerospace Promo 18.mpp!Save_As_Web_Page, and then click Run.

The macro runs, and this time you are not prompted to overwrite the previously saved files.

To verify that the macro ran correctly, you'll view the updated Web page in your browser.

13 Switch back to your browser. The previously viewed project plan should still be visible.

14 Click the Refresh button to reload the most recently saved HTML file and related GIF image.

The updated HTML file and related GIF image appear in your browser. Your screen should look similar to the following illustration:

The macro detected the updated project start and finish date, and adjusted the GIF image and other details on the Web page.

Now you can run the macro as frequently as needed to keep the most up-to-date information published.

Tip

VBA is a rich and well-documented programming language. If you would like to take a closer look at VBA in Microsoft Project, on the Tools menu, click Macro, and then click Visual Basic Editor. In the Microsoft Visual Basic window, on the Help menu, click Microsoft Visual Basic Help. To get help on specific items in a module such as objects, properties, and methods, click a word, and then press the F1 key. To return to Microsoft Project, on the File menu, click Close And Return To Microsoft Project.

Customizing a Toolbar

As with other Microsoft Office family applications, you have several choices about how to work with Microsoft Project. In fact, some of the preferences you set in Microsoft Project automatically apply in the other Microsoft Office family applications and vice versa. Some of the customization settings include:

■ Displaying or hiding the Office Assistant. (It's hidden by default in Microsoft Office XP and Microsoft Project 2002.) To display the Office Assistant, click Show The Office Assistant on the Help menu. To hide the Office Assistant, in the Assistant balloon, click Options, and then clear the Use The Office Assistant check box on the Options tab.

■ Setting up Microsoft Project to save the active file or all open files automatically at the time interval you specify. (On the Tools menu click Options, and on the Save tab of the Options dialog box, check Save Every and enter the time interval you want.)

■ Creating customized toolbars that include buttons for any commands you want. (You will do this in the following exercise.)

In this exercise, you create a custom toolbar and assign the macro you created previously in this chapter to a button on the custom toolbar:

1 Switch back to the Microsoft Project window that displays the Parnell project plan.

2 On the Tools menu, point to Customize, and then click Toolbars.

The Customize dialog box appears.

3 Click the Toolbars tab.

Your screen should look similar to the following illustration:

The toolbars that are currently displayed are checked; what you see might differ.

Tip

Toolbars are either docked or floating. When docked, a toolbar appears at one edge of the Microsoft Project window. Normally this is the top edge, but you can dock a toolbar at any edge of the window. When a toolbar is floating, it has a title bar that tells you the toolbar's name. To move a docked toolbar, point to the far left edge, and drag the toolbar either into the Microsoft Project window to make it float or to another edge of the window to redock it.

4 Click New.

The New Toolbar dialog box appears.

5 In the Toolbar Name box, type **My Custom Toolbar**, and then click OK.

The new toolbar appears in the list of toolbars and is displayed by default. (Initially it's a floating, empty toolbar.)

Your screen should look similar to the illustration on the following page.

Initially the new toolbar floats in the Microsoft Project window; it might not appear in this exact spot on your screen.

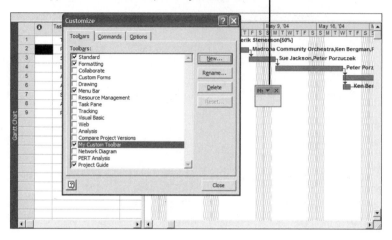

Next you'll add a command to the toolbar that runs the previously recorded macro.

6 Click the Commands tab.

In the Categories list, you can see several categories of commands. Many of these, such as *File* and *Edit*, correspond to menu names.

7 In the Categories list, click All Macros.

The commands in the All Macros category appear in the Commands list on the right. Your screen should look similar to the following illustration:

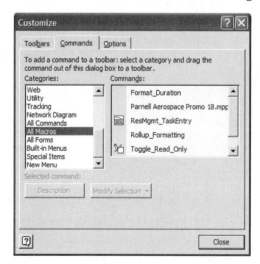

Most of the commands listed for the All Macros category relate to macros included with Microsoft Project, and what you see might differ. You should see the Parnell Aerospace Promo 18.mpp! Save_As_Web_Page macro listed, however, because it is stored in the active project plan.

8 Drag the Parnell Aerospace Promo 18.mpp!Save_As_Web_Page macro from the Customize dialog box onto the empty My Custom Toolbar.

The My Custom Toolbar widens to show the full title of the macro. If necessary, drag the toolbar so you can see all of it. Your screen should look similar to the following illustration:

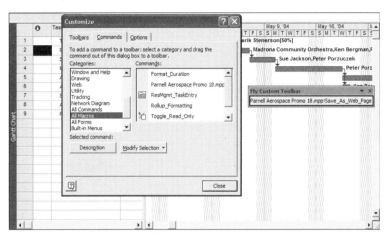

Next you'll change the text that appears on the button and add a graphic image.

9 In the Customize dialog box, click Modify Selection, and then click Image And Text.

This setting makes room on the button for an image as well as a text label.

10 Click Modify Selection, and then point to Change Button Image.

A submenu of button images appears. Your screen should look similar to the following illustration:

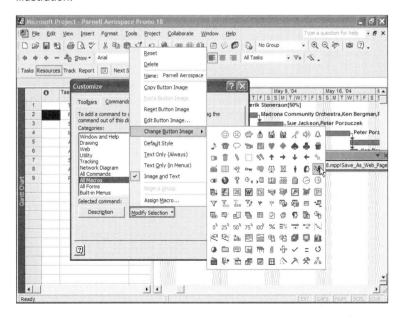

11 Click the last item on the fourth row, the running figure.

Microsoft Project adds the button image to the button. Next you will change the text label of the button.

12 Click Modify Selection, and then position your mouse pointer in the Name box. Drag the mouse pointer to the right to select the full name of the macro.

13 With the name of the macro selected, type **Publish To Web**, and then press Enter.

Microsoft Project changes the text label on the button. Your screen should look similar to the following illustration:

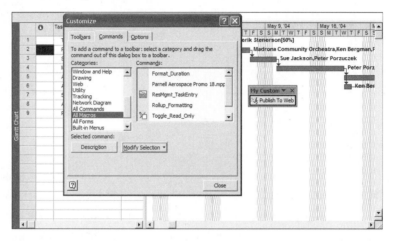

14 Click Close to close the Customize dialog box.

The custom toolbar remains floating in your Microsoft Project window.

15 On the My Custom Toolbar, click the Publish To Web button.

The Save_As_Web_Page macro runs. If you want, switch back to your browser and refresh it to see the results, and then switch back to Microsoft Project.

Custom toolbars and any other customizations made to built-in toolbars apply to all project plans you view in Microsoft Project. This is because toolbar settings must reside in the global template. To conclude this exercise, you'll delete the My Custom Toolbar and the map created by the Export Wizard from your global template so it doesn't affect your overall Microsoft Project environment.

16 On the Tools menu click Organizer.

The Organizer dialog box appears.

17 Click the Toolbars tab.

Your screen should look similar to the following illustration:

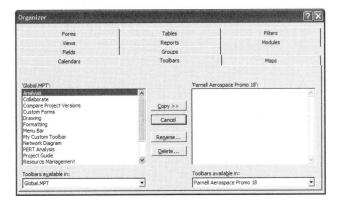

18 In the Global.MPT box, click My Custom Toolbar, and then click Delete.

19 Microsoft Project prompts you to confirm that you want to delete the toolbar; click Yes.

20 Click the Maps tab.

21 In the Global.MPT box, click Map 1, and then click Delete.

22 Microsoft Project prompts you to confirm that you want to delete the map; click Yes.

23 Click Close to close the Organizer dialog box.

Tip

You can also delete a toolbar on the Toolbars tab of the Customize dialog box (Tools menu).

Chapter Wrap-Up

This chapter introduced you to a variety of customization options in Microsoft Project.

If you are going on to other chapters:

● Save and close all open files.

If you aren't continuing to other chapters:

1 Save and close all open files.

2 To quit Microsoft Project for now, on the File menu, click Exit.

Set the status date, and see earned value schedule indicators to evaluate past schedule performance and forecast future performance, page 339

	Task Name	BCWS	BCWP	SV	SV%	SPI
0	⊟ Short Film Project	$44,618.50	$35,470.75	($9,147.75)	-20%	0.79
1	⊞ Pre-Production	$23,294.75	$21,821.75	($1,473.00)	-6%	0.94
26	⊟ Production	$20,259.00	$13,649.00	($6,610.00)	-32%	0.67
27	⊞ Scene 7	$3,702.50	$3,702.50	$0.00	0%	1
33	⊞ Scene 3	$4,170.00	$4,170.00	$0.00	0%	1
39	⊟ Scene 1	$5,950.00	$5,776.50	($173.50)	-2%	0.97
40	Scene 1 setup	$2,082.00	$2,082.00	$0.00	0%	1
41	Scene 1 rehears	$780.00	$780.00	$0.00	0%	1
42	Scene 1 shoot	$2,394.00	$2,394.00	$0.00	0%	1
43	Scene 1 teardow	$694.00	$520.50	($173.50)	-25%	0.75
44	Scene 1-process	$0.00	$0.00	$0.00	0%	0
45	⊟ Scene 2	$2,241.50	$0.00	($2,241.50)	-100%	0
46	Scene 2 setup	$518.00	$0.00	($518.00)	-100%	0
47	Scene 2 rehears	$507.00	$0.00	($507.00)	-100%	0
48	Scene 2 shoot	$957.50	$0.00	($957.50)	-100%	0
49	Scene 2 teardow	$259.00	$0.00	($259.00)	-100%	0
50	Scene 2-process	$0.00	$0.00	$0.00	0%	0
51	⊟ Scene 5	$4,195.00	$0.00	($4,195.00)	-100%	0
52	Scene 5 setup	$1,026.00	$0.00	($1,026.00)	-100%	0
53	Scene 5 rehears	$755.00	$0.00	($755.00)	-100%	0
54	Scene 5 shoot	$2,414.00	$0.00	($2,414.00)	-100%	0
55	Scene 5 teardow	$0.00	$0.00	$0.00	0%	0

	Task Name	BCWS	BCWP	CV	CV%	CPI	BAC	EAC	VAC
0	⊟ Short Film Project	$44,618.50	$35,470.75	$36.70	0%	CPI 61.55	$89,069.31	$92.24	
1	⊞ Pre-Production	$23,294.75	$21,821.75	($1,380.06)	-6%	Help on CPI 294.75	$24,767.97	($1,473.22)	
26	⊟ Production	$20,259.00	$13,649.00	$1,416.76	10%	1.12	$36,334.15	$32,562.69	$3,771.46
27	⊞ Scene 7	$3,702.50	$3,702.50	($333.13)	-8%	0.92	$3,702.50	$4,035.63	($333.13)
33	⊞ Scene 3	$4,170.00	$4,170.00	($1,460.15)	-35%	0.74	$4,170.00	$5,630.15	($1,460.15)
39	⊟ Scene 1	$5,950.00	$5,776.50	$3,210.03	55%	2.25	$5,950.00	$2,643.56	$3,306.44
40	Scene 1 setup	$2,082.00	$2,082.00	$342.00	16%	1.2	$2,082.00	$1,740.00	$342.00
41	Scene 1 rehears	$780.00	$780.00	$780.00	100%	0	$780.00	$1,760.00	($980.00)
42	Scene 1 shoot	$2,394.00	$2,394.00	$1,567.53	65%	2.9	$2,394.00	$826.47	$1,567.53
43	Scene 1 teardow	$694.00	$520.50	$520.50	100%	0	$694.00	$1,295.00	($601.00)
44	Scene 1-process	$0.00	$0.00	$0.00	0%	0	$0.00	$0.00	$0.00
45	⊟ Scene 2	$2,241.50	$0.00	$0.00	0%	0	$2,241.50	$2,077.10	$164.40
46	Scene 2 setup	$518.00	$0.00	$0.00	0%	0	$518.00	$406.00	$112.00
47	Scene 2 rehears	$507.00	$0.00	$0.00	0%	0	$507.00	$517.40	($10.40)
48	Scene 2 shoot	$957.50	$0.00	$0.00	0%	0	$957.50	$962.70	($5.20)
49	Scene 2 teardow	$259.00	$0.00	$0.00	0%	0	$259.00	$191.00	$68.00
50	Scene 2-process	$0.00	$0.00	$0.00	0%	0	$0.00	$0.00	$0.00
51	⊟ Scene 5	$4,195.00	$0.00	$0.00	0%	0	$4,537.00	$5,037.40	($500.40)
52	Scene 5 setup	$1,026.00	$0.00	$0.00	0%	0	$1,026.00	$1,388.00	($362.00)
53	Scene 5 rehears	$755.00	$0.00	$0.00	0%	0	$755.00	$755.00	$0.00
54	Scene 5 shoot	$2,414.00	$0.00	$0.00	0%	0	$2,414.00	$2,424.40	($10.40)
55	Scene 5 teardow	$0.00	$0.00	$0.00	0%	0	$342.00	$470.00	($128.00)

See earned value cost indicators to compare the project's performance to the baseline plan, page 341

Chapter 19
Measuring Performance with Earned Value Analysis

After completing this chapter, you will be able to:

✔ **Set a status date and see earned value indicators for schedule performance.**

✔ **See earned value cost performance indicators.**

Looking at task and resource *variance* throughout a project's duration is an essential project management activity, but it does not give you a complete picture of the project's long-term health. For example, a task might be over budget and ahead of schedule (possibly not good) or over budget and behind schedule (definitely not good). Viewing schedule or cost variance alone does not tell you much about performance trends that might continue for the duration of the project.

To get a more complete picture of overall project performance in terms of both time and cost, you can use *earned value analysis*. The purpose of earned value analysis is to measure the project's progress and help predict its outcome. Earned value analysis involves comparing thproject's progress to what you expected to achieve (as reflected in a baseline plan) by a specific point in the schedule or budget of a project plan, and forecasting future project performance.

The main differences between earned value analysis and simpler schedule and cost variance analysis can be summed up like this:

■ Simple variance analysis answers the question, "What current performance results are we getting?"

■ Earned value analysis addresses the question, "For the current performance results we are getting, are we getting our money's worth?"

The difference is subtle but important. Here is an example. Let's say a project has a baseline *duration* of 160 days and a budget of $82,000. After about half of the baseline duration has elapsed, the actual costs incurred are about $40,000. But what is the project's status? You cannot tell based on only this information. A simple distribution of cost over time would suggest that $40,000 spent by the midpoint of an $82,000 project is just about right.

But perhaps the project is running ahead of schedule—more work has been completed by midpoint than planned. That would be good news; the project might finish ahead of schedule. On the other hand, the project might be running behind schedule—less work has been accomplished than was planned. This would be bad news; the project will likely miss its planned finish date, exceed its budget, or both.

Earned value analysis enables you to look at project performance in a more sophisticated way. It helps you to determine two important things: the true cost of project results to date and the performance trend that is likely to continue for the remainder of the project.

Earned value analysis has its origins in large projects carried out for the U.S. government, and it remains an essential project status reporting tool for major government projects. However, because of the usefulness of earned value analysis in predicting future project performance, it is gaining popularity in the private sector and on smaller projects as well.

Tip

To learn more about earned value analysis, type **All about earned value** into the Ask A Question box in the upper right corner of the Microsoft Project window.

Short Film Project 19a

This chapter uses the practice file Short Film Project 19a. This file contains a baseline plan and actual work. For details about installing the practice files, see "Using the Book's CD-ROM" at the beginning of this book.

Viewing Earned Value Schedule Indicators

For Microsoft Project to calculate earned value amounts for a project plan, you must first do the following:

- Save a baseline plan so Microsoft Project can calculate the budgeted cost of the work scheduled before you start tracking actual work. (On the Tools menu, point to Tracking, and then click Save Baseline.)

- Record *actual* work on tasks or assignments.

- Set the *status date* so Microsoft Project can calculate actual project performance up to a certain point in time. (On the Project menu, click Project Information, and then select a status date.) If you do not specify a status date, Microsoft Project uses the current date.

Earned value analysis uses the following three key values to generate all other schedule indicator and cost indicator values:

- The budgeted cost of work scheduled, called *BCWS*. This is the value of the work scheduled to be completed as of the status date. Microsoft Project calculates this value by adding up all the timephased baseline values for tasks up to the status date.

- The actual cost of work performed, called ***ACWP***. This is the actual cost incurred to complete each task's actual work up to the status date.

- The budgeted cost of work performed, called ***BCWP*** or earned value. This is the portion of the budgeted cost that should have been spent to complete each task's actual work performed up to the status date. This value is called *earned value* because it is literally the value earned by the work performed.

Schedule and
Cost Earned
Value Tables
new in
Project
2002

- The earned value analysis schedule and the cost variance are directly related, but it's simpler to examine each independently. To accommodate this, Microsoft Project groups the earned value schedule indicator fields into one ***table***, and the earned value cost indicator fields into another table. A third table combines the key fields of both schedule and cost indicators.

In this exercise, you set the status date and view earned value schedule indicators for the project plan:

1 If Microsoft Project is not already open, start it now.

2 On the Standard toolbar, click the Open button.

Open

The Open dialog box appears.

3 Navigate to the Chapter 19 Earned Value folder, and double-click the Short Film Project 19a file.

4 On the File menu, click Save As.

The Save As dialog box appears.

5 In the File Name box, type **Short Film Project 19**, and then click the Save button.

Next you will set the project status date. Unless you specify a status date, Microsoft Project uses the current date when performing earned value calculations.

6 On the Project menu, click Project Information.

The Project Information dialog box appears.

7 In the Status Date box, type or select **June 22, 2004**, and click OK.

Now you will view the first earned value indicators table.

8 On the View menu, point to Table: Entry, and click More Tables.

The More Tables dialog box appears. In it, you see the three earned value tables.

9 In the Tables list, select Earned Value Schedule Indicators, and click the Apply button.

Microsoft Project displays the Earned Value Schedule Indicators table in the Task Sheet view.

10 Double-click between the column headings to widen any columns that display pound signs (##).

Your screen should look similar to the illustration on the following page.

Project-level earned value indicators.

Summary–task level earned value indicators.

Task-level earned value indicators.

	Task Name	BCWS	BCWP	SV	SV%	SPI
0	Short Film Project	$44,618.50	$35,470.75	($9,147.75)	-20%	0.79
1	Pre-Production	$23,294.75	$21,821.75	($1,473.00)	-6%	0.94
26	Production	$20,250.00	$13,640.00	($6,610.00)	-32%	0.67
27	Scene 7	$3,702.50	$3,702.50	$0.00	0%	1
33	Scene 3	$4,170.00	$4,170.00	$0.00	0%	1
39	Scene 1	$5,950.00	$5,776.50	($173.50)	-2%	0.97
40	Scene 1 setup	$2,082.00	$2,082.00	$0.00	0%	1
41	Scene 1 rehears	$780.00	$780.00	$0.00	0%	1
42	Scene 1 shoot	$2,394.00	$2,394.00	$0.00	0%	1
43	Scene 1 teardow	$694.00	$520.50	($173.50)	-25%	0.75
44	Scene 1-process	$0.00	$0.00	$0.00	0%	0
45	Scene 2	$2,241.50	$0.00	($2,241.50)	-100%	0
46	Scene 2 setup	$518.00	$0.00	($518.00)	-100%	0
47	Scene 2 rehears	$507.00	$0.00	($507.00)	-100%	0
48	Scene 2 shoot	$957.50	$0.00	($957.50)	-100%	0
49	Scene 2 teardow	$259.00	$0.00	($259.00)	-100%	0
50	Scene 2-process	$0.00	$0.00	$0.00	0%	0
51	Scene 5	$4,195.00	$0.00	($4,195.00)	-100%	0
52	Scene 5 setup	$1,026.00	$0.00	($1,026.00)	-100%	0
53	Scene 5 rehears	$755.00	$0.00	($755.00)	-100%	0
54	Scene 5 shoot	$2,414.00	$0.00	($2,414.00)	-100%	0
55	Scene 5 teardow	$0.00	$0.00	$0.00	0%	0

Here you can see the earned value schedule indicators for the project plan, summary tasks, and subtasks. All earned value numbers are reported either as dollars or as index ratios for easy comparison; negative cost values appear in parentheses. Note the information in the following columns:

New earned value schedule fields: SV%, SPI

new in
Project
2002

- **BCWS** is the budgeted cost of work scheduled, as described earlier. As of the status date, a total of $44,618.50 was scheduled to be spent on tasks. In the baseline plan, the short film project would have incurred this amount by the status date. Microsoft Project uses this value for comparison to the BCWP and to derive other values.

- **BCWP** is the budgeted cost of work performed. The value of the work performed as of status date in the short film project is just $35,470.75—quite a bit less than the BCWS value.

- **SV** is schedule variance, which is simply the difference between BCWP and BCWS. The short film project has negative schedule variance of $9,147.75.

- **SV%** is the ratio of schedule variance to BCWS, expressed as a percentage. This value tells you if the current level of completion on tasks is ahead of or behind the performance predicted in the baseline. The short film project is 20 percent behind or under baseline performance.

- **SPI** is the schedule performance index. This is the BCWP divided by BCWS, and it is the most common way to compare earned value schedule performance between tasks, summary tasks, or projects. For example, you can see that the pre-production phase of the short film project has a SPI of .94; the budgeted cost of work scheduled was very close to the budgeted cost of work performed. (If the two had matched exactly, SPI would have been 1.0.) However the second phase, Production, has a considerably worse SPI value: .67. The project summary task has a .79 SPI value. One way you can interpret this is that for every dollar's worth of work we had planned to accomplish by the status date, only 79 cents' worth was actually accomplished.

Tip

Here's a quick way to get help about an earned value field or any field in a table in Microsoft Project. Point to the column heading, and in the ScreenTip that appears, click the Help On <Field Name> link. Information about that field appears in the Help window.

You can use these schedule indicator values to address the question, "At the rate you're making progress, is there enough time left to complete the project?" In the case of the short film project, one area to investigate is the low SPI for the production work completed thus far—and whether the cause of that problem is likely to affect the remaining production work.

The values in the Earned Value Schedule Indicators table inform us about schedule performance, but they do not directly inform us about cost performance. You examine cost performance in the next section.

Viewing Earned Value Cost Indicators

The flip side of the question, "Is there enough time left to complete the project?" relates to cost: "Is there enough money available to complete the project?" Focusing on earned value cost indicators can help you answer this question. To calculate cost indicators, Microsoft Project uses the actual cost of work performed, or ACWP, as derived from the actual work values recorded in a project plan.

In this exercise, you display earned value cost indicators for the project plan:

1 On the View menu, point to Table: Earned Value Schedule Indicators, and click More Tables.

The More Tables dialog box appears.

2 In the Tables list, select Earned Value Cost Indicators, and click the Apply button.

Microsoft Project displays the Earned Value Cost Indicators table in the Task Sheet view.

3 Double-click between the column headings to widen any columns that display pound signs (##).

Your screen should look similar to the following illustration:

To get help about any field in a table, point to the column heading and in the ScreenTip that appears, click the Help link.

	Task Name	BCWS	BCWP	CV	CV%	CPI	BAC	EAC	VAC
0	Short Film Project	$44,618.50	$35,470.75	$36.70	0%	CPI 61.55	61.55	$89,069.31	$92.24
1	Pre-Production	$23,294.75	$21,821.75	($1,380.06)	-6%	Help on CPI 294.75		$24,767.97	($1,473.22)
26	Production	$20,259.00	$13,649.00	$1,416.76	10%	1.12	$36,334.15	$32,562.69	$3,771.46
27	Scene 7	$3,702.50	$3,702.50	($333.13)	-8%	0.92	$3,702.50	$4,035.63	($333.13)
33	Scene 3	$4,170.00	$4,170.00	($1,460.15)	-35%	0.74	$4,170.00	$5,630.15	($1,460.15)
39	Scene 1	$5,950.00	$5,776.50	$3,210.03	55%	2.25	$5,950.00	$2,643.56	$3,306.44
40	Scene 1 setup	$2,082.00	$2,082.00	$342.00	16%	1.2	$2,082.00	$1,740.00	$342.00
41	Scene 1 rehears	$780.00	$780.00	$780.00	100%	0	$780.00	$1,760.00	($980.00)
42	Scene 1 shoot	$2,394.00	$2,394.00	$1,567.53	65%	2.9	$2,394.00	$826.47	$1,567.53
43	Scene 1 teardow	$694.00	$520.50	$520.50	100%	0	$694.00	$1,295.00	($601.00)
44	Scene 1-process	$0.00	$0.00	$0.00	0%	0	$0.00	$0.00	$0.00
45	Scene 2	$2,241.50	$0.00	$0.00	0%	0	$2,241.50	$2,077.10	$164.40
46	Scene 2 setup	$518.00	$0.00	$0.00	0%	0	$518.00	$406.00	$112.00
47	Scene 2 rehears	$507.00	$0.00	$0.00	0%	0	$507.00	$517.40	($10.40)
48	Scene 2 shoot	$957.50	$0.00	$0.00	0%	0	$957.50	$962.70	($5.20)
49	Scene 2 teardow	$259.00	$0.00	$0.00	0%	0	$259.00	$191.00	$68.00
50	Scene 2-process	$0.00	$0.00	$0.00	0%	0	$0.00	$0.00	$0.00
51	Scene 5	$4,195.00	$0.00	$0.00	0%	0	$4,537.00	$5,037.40	($500.40)
52	Scene 5 setup	$1,026.00	$0.00	$0.00	0%	0	$1,026.00	$1,388.00	($362.00)
53	Scene 5 rehears	$755.00	$0.00	$0.00	0%	0	$755.00	$755.00	$0.00
54	Scene 5 shoot	$2,414.00	$0.00	$0.00	0%	0	$2,414.00	$2,424.40	($10.40)
55	Scene 5 teardow	$0.00	$0.00	$0.00	0%	0	$342.00	$470.00	($128.00)

Here you can see the earned value cost indicators for the project plan, summary tasks, and subtasks. Because BCWS and BCWP are key values for both schedule and cost indicators, they appear in both tables and were described in the previous section. (Note that the ACWP field does not appear on either the schedule indicators or cost indicators tables; it does appear on the Earned Value table, however.) Note the information in the following columns:

New earned
value cost
fields: CV%,
CPI, EAC, TCPI

new in
Project
2002

- **CV** is cost variance, the difference between BCWP and ACWP. The short film project has very low cost variance.

- **CV%** is the ratio of cost variance to BCWS, expressed as a percentage. This value tells you how close you are (under or over) to the budget plan per task. The short film project is essentially right on baseline cost performance.

- **CPI** the cost performance index. The short film project's CPI (as of the status date) is 1. One way you can interpret this is that for every dollar's worth of work we have paid for, a full dollar's worth of work was actually accomplished.

- **BAC** is budget at completion. This is simply the total baseline cost of a task, summary task, or the project. You evaluate this against EAC to derive VAC.

- **EAC** is estimate at completion. This value represents the forecasted cost to complete a task, summary task, or the project based on performance so far (up to the status date).

- **VAC** is variance at completion, or the difference between BAC and EAC. VAC represents the forecasted cost variance to complete a task, summary task, or the project based on performance so far (up to the status date). The short film project has very low variance at completion.

- **TCPI** is to complete performance index. This index value shows the ratio of remaining work to remaining budget, as of the status date. The short film project's TCPI value is 1, meaning remaining work and remaining budget are equal. Depending on your screen resolution, you might need to scroll right to see this column.

Tip

Although it might seem odd and even confusing to think of being ahead of or behind schedule in terms of dollars, remember that dollars buy work and work drives the completion of tasks.

From a pure cost variance analysis standpoint, the short film project appears to be in very good shape. Yet the schedule variance analysis suggests otherwise. The heart of the issue is that as of the status date, quite a bit of work has started later than planned but hasn't cost more than planned. The true health of the project is often not obvious and requires a comparison of both cost and schedule variance based on past performance, as well as forecasts of future performance.

Let's all take a deep breath. Earned value analysis is one of the more complicated things you can do in Microsoft Project but the information it provides on project status is invaluable. Earned value analysis also is a great example of one benefit of entering task and resource cost information in a project plan.

Tip

A quick way to view a task's earned value numbers in any task view is to display the Earned Value form. On the Tools menu, point to Customize, and then click Forms. In the Customize Forms dialog box, click Earned Value, and then click the Apply button.

Changing How Microsoft Project Calculates Earned Value Numbers

All the earned value calculations shown in the previous exercises use the default calculation options in Microsoft Project. However, you can change settings to give yourself more flexibility in how earned value is calculated. Some important settings you can change include:

Physical percent complete

new in **Project** 2002

■ Rather than using the percent complete of tasks that is based on actuals recorded in a project plan, you can tell Microsoft Project to use a percent complete value you enter—regardless of a task's calculated percent complete. The manual or override value is called physical percent complete.

■ Rather than using the initial baseline values stored in the default Baseline fields for earned value comparisons, you can tell Microsoft Project to use any baseline set you want—Baseline or Baseline1 through Baseline10.

You can set these options for an entire project plan or change just the calculation method for a specific task:

■ To change these options for an entire project plan, on the Tools menu click Options, and then in the Options dialog box, click the Calculation tab. Next click the Earned Value button. In the Earned Value dialog box, choose the calculation method and baseline options you want.

■ To change the earned value calculation method for a selected task, on the Project menu, click Task Information, and then in the Task Information dialog box, click the Advanced tab. In the Earned Value Method box, click the method you want.

If you choose to use the physical percent complete method for either an entire project plan or for a specific task, you must enter a percent complete value manually. This field is displayed in the Tracking table, and you can insert it into any other task table.

Chapter Wrap-Up

This chapter covered how to view schedule and cost variance analysis using earned analysis.

If you are going on to other chapters:

Save

1 On the Standard toolbar, click the Save button to save changes made to Short Film Project 19.

2 On the File menu, click Close to close the project plan.

If you aren't continuing to other chapters:

1 On the Standard toolbar, click the Save button to save changes made to Short Film Project 19.

2 To quit Microsoft Project for now, on the File menu, click Exit.

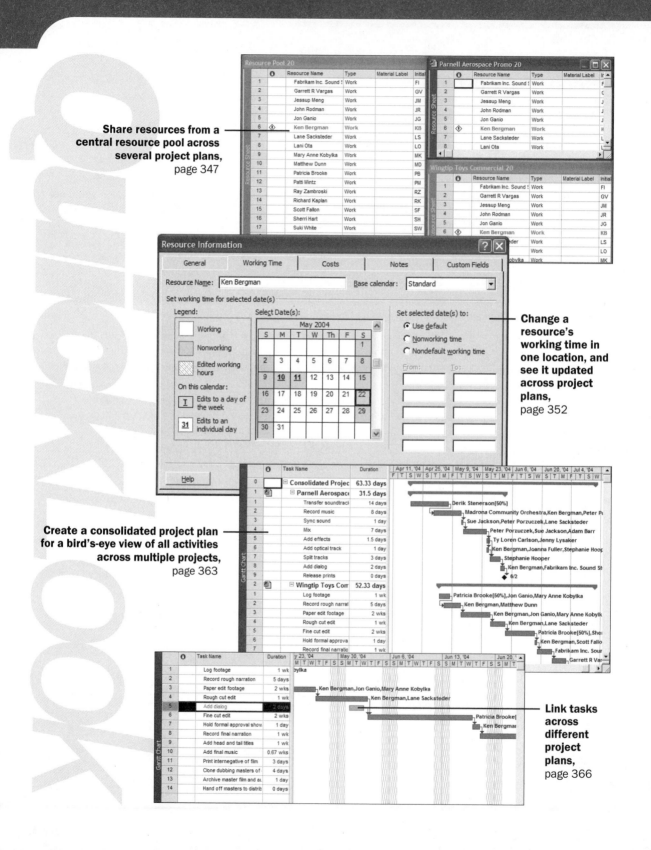

Share resources from a central resource pool across several project plans, page 347

Change a resource's working time in one location, and see it updated across project plans, page 352

Create a consolidated project plan for a bird's-eye view of all activities across multiple projects, page 363

Link tasks across different project plans, page 366

Chapter 20
Consolidating Projects and Resources

After completing this chapter, you will be able to:

✔ Create a resource pool to share resources across multiple projects.

✔ Look at resource allocation across multiple projects.

✔ Change resource assignments in a sharer plan, and see the effects in the resource pool.

✔ Change a resource's working time in the resource pool, and see the effects in the sharer plan.

✔ Make a specific date nonworking time in the resource pool, and see the effects in the sharer plans.

✔ Create a project plan, and make it a sharer plan for the resource pool.

✔ Manually update the resource pool from a sharer plan.

✔ Insert project plans to create a consolidated project.

Most project managers must juggle more than one project at a time. These projects often share resources and are worked on simultaneously. Microsoft Project has several features to make it easier to work with multiple projects. In this chapter, you share resource information between multiple project plans and join separate project plans as a single consolidated plan.

Important

This chapter describes various ways of sharing resources and managing multiple projects. This process is more generally called *portfolio management* or *enterprise project management*. Both Microsoft Project Standard and Professional editions, when used with Microsoft Project Server, offer much more sophisticated ways of managing a portfolio of projects and resources across an enterprise. To learn more about the portfolio management tools available with Microsoft Project Server, see Appendix A, "Introducing Microsoft Project Server."

Wingtip Toys Commercial 20a and Parnell Aerospace Promo 20b

This chapter uses two practice files, Wingtip Toys Commercial 20a and Parnell Aerospace Promo 20b. For details about installing the practice files, see "Using the Book's CD-ROM" at the beginning of this book.

Creating a Resource Pool

When managing multiple projects, it is common for *work resources* (people and equipment) to be assigned to more than one project at a time. It might become difficult to coordinate the resources' time among the multiple projects, especially if those projects are managed by different people. For example, a sound engineer in a film studio might have task assignments for a TV commercial, a promotional program, and a documentary film—three projects proceeding simultaneously. In each project, the engineer might be *fully allocated* or even *underallocated*. However, if you add together all her tasks from these projects, you might discover that she has been *overallocated*, or assigned to work on more tasks than she can handle at one time.

A *resource pool* can help you see how resources are utilized across multiple projects. The resource pool is a Microsoft Project plan from which other project plans draw their resource information. It contains information about all resources' task assignments from all the project plans linked to the resource pool. You can change resource information—such as maximum units, cost rates, and nonworking time—in the resource pool, and all linked project plans will use the updated information.

The project plans that are linked to the resource pool are called sharers. Here is one way of visualizing a resource pool and *sharer plans*:

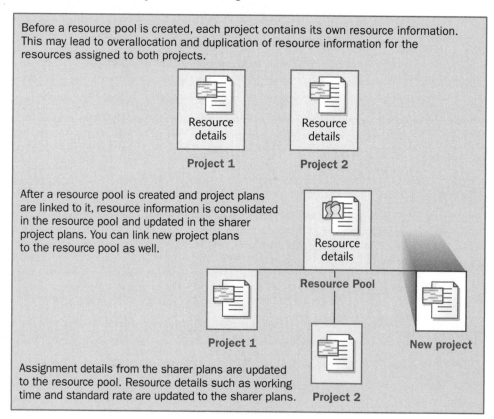

Before a resource pool is created, each project contains its own resource information. This may lead to overallocation and duplication of resource information for the resources assigned to both projects.

Resource details
Project 1

Resource details
Project 2

After a resource pool is created and project plans are linked to it, resource information is consolidated in the resource pool and updated in the sharer project plans. You can link new project plans to the resource pool as well.

Resource details
Resource Pool

Project 1

New project

Assignment details from the sharer plans are updated to the resource pool. Resource details such as working time and standard rate are updated to the sharer plans.

Project 2

If you manage just one project with resources that are not used in other projects, a resource pool provides you no benefit. However, if your organization plans to manage multiple projects, setting up a resource pool enables you to:

- Enter resource information once but use it in multiple project plans.
- View resources' assignment details from multiple projects in a single location.
- View assignment costs per resource across multiple projects.
- Find resources who are overallocated across multiple projects, even if those resources are underallocated in individual projects.
- Enter resource information, such as nonworking time, in any of the sharer plans or in the resource pool so that it is instantly available in the other sharer plans.

A resource pool is especially beneficial when working with other Microsoft Project users across a network. In those cases, the resource pool is stored in a central location, such as a network server, and the individual owners of the sharer plans (that might be stored locally or on a network server) share the common resource pool.

In this exercise, you arrange the windows of two project plans that will become sharer plans; this helps you see the effects of creating a resource pool. You then create a project plan that will become a resource pool and you link the two sharer plans to it:

1 If Microsoft Project is not already open, start it now.

2 If Microsoft Project created a new, blank project plan when you started it, close the blank project plan as well as the New Project task pane.

Open

3 On the Standard toolbar, click the Open button.

The Open dialog box appears.

4 Navigate to the Chapter 20 Consolidating folder, and double-click the Wingtip Toys Commercial 20a file.

5 On the File menu, click Save As.

The Save As dialog box appears.

6 In the File Name box, type **Wingtip Toys Commercial 20**, and then click the Save button.

7 On the Standard toolbar, click the Open button.

The Open dialog box appears.

8 Double-click the Parnell Aerospace Promo 20b file.

9 On the File menu, click Save As.

The Save As dialog box appears.

10 In the File Name box, type **Parnell Aerospace Promo 20**, and then click the Save button.

These two project plans were previously created, and both contain resource information. Next you will create a new project plan that will become a resource pool.

New

11 On the Standard toolbar, click the New button.

12 If the Project Guide Tasks pane appears, click the Close button in the upper right corner of the Project Guide pane to close it.

13 On the File menu, click Save As.

14 In the File Name box, type **Resource Pool 20**, and then click the Save button.

Tip

You can name a resource pool anything you want, but it is a good idea to indicate that it is a resource pool in the file name.

15 On the Window menu, click Arrange All.

Microsoft Project arranges the three project plan windows within the Microsoft Project window. You do not need to arrange the project windows in this way to create a resource pool, but it is helpful to see the results as they occur in this chapter.

Next you will switch the resource pool to the Resource Sheet view.

16 On the View menu, click Resource Sheet. Your screen should look similar to the following illustration:

Title bar

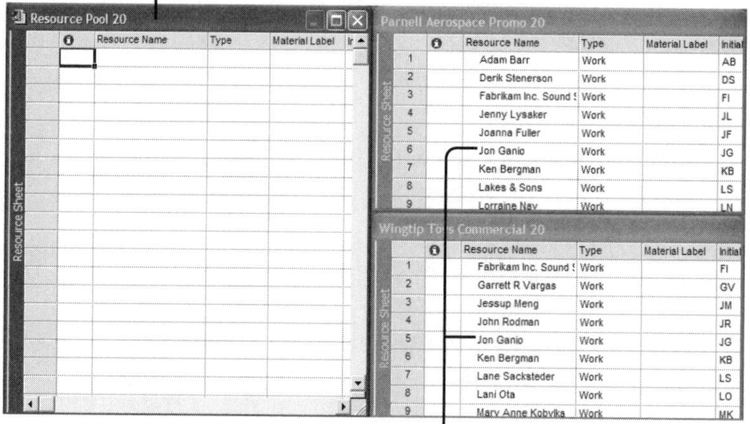

Prior to being linked to a resource pool, some resource names and other details are duplicated in these project plans.

Looking at the resource names in the two project plans (*Parnell Aerospace Promo 20* and *Wingtip Toys Commercial 20*), you can see that several of the same resources appear in both project plans. These include Fabrikam Inc. Sound Studio, Jon Ganio, Ken Bergman, and others. None of these resources are overallocated in either project.

17 Click the title bar of the Wingtip Toys Commercial 20 window.

18 On the Tools menu, point to Resource Sharing, and click Share Resources.

The Share Resources dialog box appears.

19 Under Resources For 'Wingtip Toys Commercial 20', select the Use Resources option.

The Use Resources list contains the open project plans that can be used as a resource pool.

20 In the From list, click Resource Pool 20 in the drop-down list.

Your screen should look similar to the following illustration:

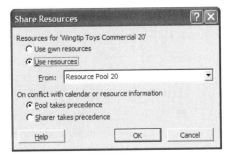

21 Click OK to close the Share Resources dialog box.

Tip

If you decide you do not want to use a resource pool with a project plan, you can break the link. On the Tools menu, point to Resources Sharing, and click Share Resources. Under Resources For <Current Project Name>, select the Use Own Resources option.

You see the resource information from the Wingtip Toys Commercial 20 project plan appear in the Resource Pool 20 plan. Next you will set up the Parnell Aerospace Promo 20 project plan as a sharer plan with the same resource pool.

22 Click the title bar of the Parnell Aerospace Promo 20 window.

23 On the Tools menu, point to Resource Sharing, and then click Share Resources.

24 Under Resources For 'Parnell Aerospace Promo 20', click the Use Resources option.

25 In the From list, make sure that Resource Pool 20 is selected.

26 Under the On Conflict With Calendar Or Resource Information label, make sure that Pool Takes Precedence option is selected.

Selecting this option causes Microsoft Project to use resource information (such as cost rates) in the resource pool rather than in the sharer plan should it find any differences between the two project plans.

27 Click OK to close the Share Resources dialog box.

You see the resource information from the Wingtip Toys Commercial 20 project plan appear in the resource pool. Your screen should look similar to the following illustration:

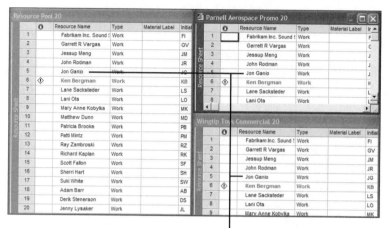

After these two sharer plans have been linked to the resource pool, the combined resource information appears in all three files.

The resource pool contains the resource information from both sharer plans. Microsoft Project will consolidate information from the sharer plans based on the name of the resource. Jon Ganio, for example, is listed only once in the resource pool, no matter how many sharer plans list him as a resource. However, Microsoft Project cannot match variations of a resource's name—for example, Jon Ganio from one sharer plan and J. Ganio from another. For this reason, it is a good idea to develop a convention for naming resources and stick with it.

Again, you do not have to arrange the project windows as you did in this exercise to link the sharer plans to the resource pool. But it is helpful in this chapter to see the results as they occur.

Creating a Dedicated Resource Pool

Any Microsoft Project plan, with or without tasks, can serve as a resource pool. However, it is a good idea to designate a project plan that does not contain tasks as the resource pool. This is because any project with tasks will almost certainly conclude at some point, and you might not want assignments for those tasks (with their associated costs and other details) to be included indefinitely in the resource pool.

Moreover, a dedicated resource pool without tasks can enable people such as *line managers* or *resource managers* to maintain some information about their resources, such as nonworking time, in the resource pool. These people might not have a role in project management, and they will not need to deal with task-specific details in the resource pool.

Viewing Assignment Details in a Resource Pool

One of the most important benefits of using a resource pool is that it allows you to see how resources are allocated across projects. For example, you can identify resources that are overallocated across the multiple projects to which they are assigned.

For example, as you might have noticed in the previous section, the resource Ken Bergman, who was not overallocated in either of the individual project plans, did appear overallocated after Microsoft Project accounted for all his assignments across the two project plans. This is because when Ken's assignments from the two sharer plans were combined, they exceeded his capacity to work on at least one day. Although Ken most likely was well aware of this problem, the project manager may not have known about it without setting up a resource pool (or hearing about the problem directly from Ken).

In this exercise, you look at the information in the resource pool:

1 Double-click the title bar of the Resource Pool 20 window.

The resource pool window is maximized to fill the Microsoft Project window. In the resource pool, you can see all of the resources from the two sharer plans. To get a better view of resource usage, you will change views.

2 On the View menu, click Resource Usage.

The Resource Usage view appears.

3 In the Resource Name column, click the name of Resource 6, Ken Bergman, and then scroll the Resource Usage view to display all of Ken's assignments below his name.

Go To
Selected Task

4 On the Standard toolbar, click the Go To Selected Task button.

The timescale details on the right side of the Microsoft Project window scroll horizontally to show Ken Bergman's earliest task assignments.

5 Scroll the timescale details to the right to see more of Ken's assignments during the week of May 2 if they are not already visible.

The red numbers (for example, 16 hours on Wednesday through Friday, May 5 through 8) indicate days on which Ken is *overallocated*.

Next you will display the Resource Form to get more detail about Ken's assignments.

6 On the Window menu, click Split.

Your screen should look similar to the illustration shown on the following page.

In this combination view, you can see both the resource's
assigned task and details about each assignment.

In this combination view, you can see all resources in the resource pool and their assignments (in the upper pane), as well as each resource's details (in the lower pane) from all sharer plans. You can see, for example, that the *Record rough narration* task to which Ken is assigned is from the Wingtip Toys Commercial 20 project, and the *Record music* task is from the Parnell Aerospace Promo 20 project. Ken was not overallocated in either project, but he is overallocated when you see his assignments across projects in this way.

If you want, click different resource names in the Resource Usage View to see their assignment details in the Resource Form.

7 On the Window menu, click Remove Split.

Tip

In a resource pool, the Resource Form is just one way to see the details of specific assignments from sharer files. Other ways include inserting the Project or Task Summary columns into the table portion of the Resource Usage view. (On the Insert menu, click Column.)

Updating Assignments in a Sharer Plan

You might recall that an assignment is the matching of a resource to a task. Because a resource's assignment details originate in sharer plans, Microsoft Project updates the resource pool with assignment details as you make them in the sharer plan.

In this exercise, you change resource assignments in a sharer plan, and you see the changes posted to the resource pool:

1 In the Resource Usage view, scroll down until you see Resource 20, Jenny Lysaker, in the Resource Name column, and then click her name.

You can see that Jenny Lysaker has no task assignments in either sharer plan. (The value of her Work field is zero.) Next you will assign Jenny to a task in one of the sharer plans, and you will see the result in the resource pool as well as in the project.

2 On the Window menu, click Parnell Aerospace Promo 20.

3 On the View menu, click Gantt Chart.

Assign
Resources

4 On the Standard toolbar, click the Assign Resources button.

5 In the Task Name column, click the name of Task 5, Add Effects.

6 In the Resource Name column in the Assign Resources dialog box, click Jenny Lysaker, and click the Assign button.

7 Click the Close button to close the Assign Resources dialog box.

8 On the Window menu, click Resource Pool 20 to switch back to the resource pool.

Go To
Selected Task

9 On the Standard toolbar, click the Go To Selected Task button.

Your screen should look similar to the following illustration:

	ⓘ	Resource Name	Work	Details					May 23, '04			
					W	T	F	S	S	M	T	W	T
20		⊟ Jenny Lysaker	12 hrs	Work			4h			8h			
		Add effects	12 hrs	Work			4h			8h			
21		⊟ Joanna Fuller	8 hrs	Work			4h			4h			
		Add optical track	8 hrs	Work			4h			4h			

As expected, Jenny Lysaker's new task assignment appears in the resource pool.

When the resource pool is open in Microsoft Project, any changes you make to resource assignments or other resource information in any sharer immediately show up in all other open sharers and the resource pool. You don't need to switch between sharers and the resource pool, as you did in this chapter, to verify the updated resource assignments.

Updating a Resource's Information in a Resource Pool

Another important benefit of using a resource pool is that it gives you a central location in which to enter resource details, such as cost rates and working time. When a resource's information is updated in the resource pool, the new information is available in all the sharer plans. This can be especially useful in organizations with a large number of resources working on multiple projects. In larger organizations, people such as line managers, resource managers, or staff in a *program office* are often responsible for keeping general resource information up to date.

Ken Bergman has told you that he will be unavailable to work on May 10 and 11. In this exercise, you update a resource's working time in the resource pool, and you see changes in the sharer plans:

1 In the Resource Name column, click the name of Resource 6, Ken Bergman.

Resource
Information

2 On the Standard toolbar, click the Resource Information button.

The Resource Information dialog box appears.

3 Click the Working Time tab.

4 In the calendar below the Select Date(s) label, drag the vertical scroll bar or click the up or down arrow button until May 2004 appears.

5 Select the dates May 10 and 11.

Tip

To select this date range with the mouse, drag from 10 to 11.

6 Under Set Selected Date(s) To, select the Nonworking Time option, and then click OK to close the Resource Information dialog box.

Tip

When making such changes in the resource pool, you should have it open as read-write (as you do now). Whenever you open a resource pool, Microsoft Project asks if you want to open it as read-only (the default) or read-write.

7 Scroll the timescale details to see that on May 10 and 11 Ken has no work scheduled. (Previously he did.) Your screen should look similar to the following illustration:

Because May 10 and 11 have been marked as nonworking days for this resource, no work is scheduled on these days.

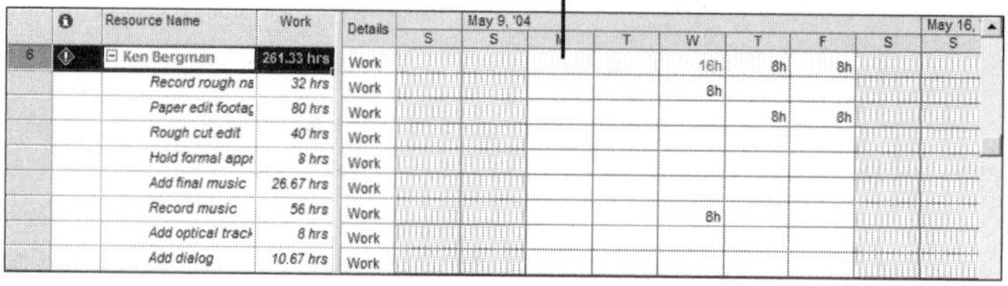

To verify that Ken's nonworking time setting was updated in the sharer plans, you will look at his working time in one of those project plans.

8 On the Window menu, click Parnell Aerospace Promo 20.

Assign Resources

9 On the Standard toolbar, click the Assign Resources button.

10 In the Assign Resource dialog box, double-click Ken Bergman.

The Resource Information dialog box appears.

11 Click the Working Time tab.

12 In the calendar below the Select Date(s) label, drag the vertical scroll bar or click the up or down arrow button until May 2004 appears.

May 10 and 11 are flagged as nonworking days for Ken; the change to this resource's working time in the resource pool has been updated in the sharer plans.

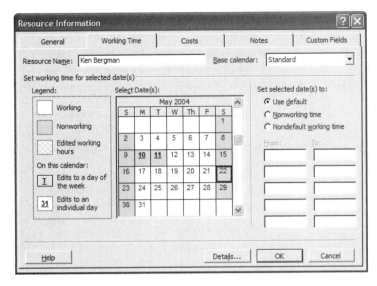

13 Click Cancel to close the Resource Information dialog box, and then click the Close button to close the Assign Resources dialog box.

Updating All Projects' Working Times in a Resource Pool

In the previous exercise, you changed an individual resource's working time in the resource pool, and you saw the change posted to the sharer plans. Another powerful capability of a resource pool is to enable you to change working times for a *base calendar* and to see the changes updated to all sharer plans that use that calendar. For example, if you specify that certain days (such as holidays) are to be nonworking days in the resource pool, that change is posted to all sharer plans.

Tip

By default, all sharer plans share the same base calendars, and any changes you make to a base calendar in one sharer plan are reflected in all other sharer plans through the resource pool. If you have a specific sharer plan for which you want to use different base calendar working times, change the base calendar that sharer plan uses.

In this exercise, you set nonworking time in a base calendar in the resource pool, and you see this change in all sharer plans:

1 On the Window menu, click Resource Pool 20.

The entire company will be attending a local film festival on May 10, and you want this to be a nonworking day for all sharer projects.

2 On the Tools menu, click Change Working Time.

3 In the For box, click Standard (Project Calendar) in the drop-down list.

4 In the calendar below the Select Date(s) label, drag the vertical scroll bar or click the up or down arrow buttons until May 2004 appears, and then click May 10.

5 Under Set Selected Date(s) To, select the Nonworking Time option.

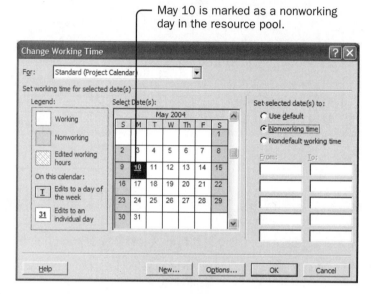

May 10 is marked as a nonworking day in the resource pool.

6 Click OK to close the Change Working Time dialog box.

To verify that this change to the resource pool's Standard base calendar was updated in the sharer plans, you will look at working time in one of the sharer plans.

7 On the Window menu, click Wingtip Toys Commercial 20.

8 On the Tools menu, click Change Working Time.

The Change Working Time dialog box appears.

9 In the For box, click Standard (Project Calendar) in the drop-down list.

10 In the calendar below the Select Date(s) label, drag the vertical scroll bar or click the up or down arrow button until May 2004 appears.

May 10 is flagged as a nonworking day. All project plans that are sharer plans of the same resource pool will see this change in this base calendar.

In the sharer plans linked to the resource pool, May 10 appears as a nonworking day in the Standard base calendar.

11 Click Cancel to close the Change Working Time dialog box.

If you want, you can switch to the Parnell Aerospace Promo 20 project plan and verify that May 10 is also a nonworking day for that project.

12 Close and save changes to all open project plans, including the resource pool.

When working with sharer plans and a resource pool, it is important to understand that when you open a sharer plan, you must also open the resource pool if you want the sharer plan to be updated with the most recent changes to the resource pool. For example, if you change the project calendar's working time in the resource pool, save and close it, and then later open a sharer plan but don't also open the resource pool, that sharer plan will not reflect the updated project calendar's working time.

Linking New Project Plans to a Resource Pool

You can make a project plan a sharer plan for a resource pool at any time: when initially entering the project plan's tasks, after you have assigned resources to tasks, or even after work has begun. After you have set up a resource pool, you might find it helpful to make sharer plans of not only projects already under way but also all new projects. That way, you get used to relying on the resource pool for resource information.

Tip

A big timesaving advantage of making new project plans sharers of a resource pool is that your resource information is instantly available. You don't have to reenter any resource data.

In this exercise, you create a project plan and make it a sharer plan for the resource pool:

Open

1 On the Standard toolbar, click the Open button.

The Open dialog box appears.

2 Navigate to the Chapter 20 Consolidating folder, and double-click Resource Pool 20.

Microsoft Project prompts you to select how you want to open the resource pool.

Important

The default option is to open the resource pool as read-only. You might want to choose this option if you and other Microsoft Project users are sharing a resource pool across a network. If you store the resource pool locally, however, you should open it as read-write. To read more about how to open a resource pool, click the Help button in the Open Resource Pool dialog box.

3 Click the second option to open the project plan as read-write, and then click OK.

4 On the View menu, click Resource Sheet.

The Resource Sheet view appears.

New

5 On the Standard toolbar, click the New button.

6 If the Project Guide Tasks pane appears, click the Close button in the upper right corner of the Project Guide pane to close it.

7 On the File menu, click Save As.

The Save As dialog box appears.

8 In the File Name box, type **Hanson Brothers Project 20**, and then click the Save button.

Assign
Resources

9 On the Standard toolbar, click the Assign Resources button.

The Assign Resources dialog box is initially empty because you have not yet entered any resource information in this project plan.

10 On the Tools menu, point to Resource Sharing, and then click Share Resources.

The Share Resources dialog box appears.

11 Under Resources For 'Hanson Brothers Project 20', select the Use Resources option.

12 In the From list, make sure that Resource Pool 20 is selected in the drop-down list, and then click OK to close the Share Resources dialog box.

In the Assign Resources dialog box, you see all of the resources from the resource pool appear.

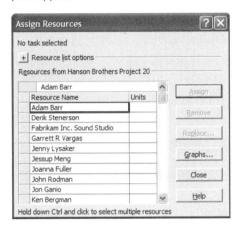

Now these resources are ready for assignments to tasks in this project.

13 Click the Close button to close the Assign Resources dialog box.

14 On the File menu, click Close. When prompted, click the Yes button to save your changes.

The Hanson Brothers Project 20 project plan closes, and the Resource Pool 20 plan remains open.

15 On the File menu, click Close. When prompted, click the Yes button to save your changes to Resource Pool 20.

You save changes to the resource pool because it records the names and locations of its sharer plans.

Tip

To learn more about sharing resources with Microsoft Project, type **All about sharing resources** into the Ask A Question box in the upper right corner of the Microsoft Project window.

Opening a Sharer Plan and Updating a Resource Pool

If you are sharing a resource pool with other Microsoft Project users across a network, whoever has the resource pool open as read-write prevents others from updating resource information such as standard cost rates or making other project plans sharers of that resource pool. For this reason, it is a good idea to open the resource pool as read-only and to use the Update Resource Pool command only when you need to update the resource pool with assignment information. You can click the Update Resource Pool command from the Resource Sharing submenu of the Tools menu. This command updates the resource pool with new assignment information; once that is done, anyone else who opens the resource pool will see the latest assignment information.

In this chapter, you are working with the resource pool and sharer plans locally. If you are going to use a resource pool over a network, it is a good idea to understand the updating process. This exercise introduces you to that process.

In this exercise, you change assignments in a sharer plan, and then you manually update the assignment information in the resource pool:

Open

1 On the Standard toolbar, click the Open button.

The Open dialog box appears.

2 Navigate to the Chapter 20 Consolidating folder, and double-click the Parnell Aerospace Promo 20 file.

Because this project plan is a sharer plan linked to a resource pool, Microsoft Project gives you the following options:

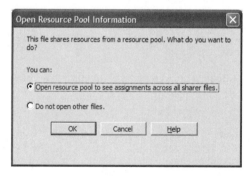

3 Click the Open Resource Pool To See Assignments Across All Sharer Files option, and then click OK.

Choosing the second option, Do Not Open Other Files, enables you to see assignments only in the one sharer.

The resource pool opens as read-only in the background. (If you want to verify this, look at the items on the Window menu.) Next you will change some assignments in the sharer plan.

Assign
Resources

4   On the Standard toolbar, click the Assign Resources button. The Assign Resources dialog box appears.

5   In the Task Name column, click the name of Task 6, Add Optical Tracks.

6   In the Resource Name column in the Assign Resources dialog box, click Stephanie Hooper, and click the Assign button.

7   In the Task Name column, click the name of Task 8, Add Dialog.

8   In the Resource Name column in the Assign Resources dialog box, click Sue Jackson (located at the top of the Resource Name column), and then click the Remove button.

You have made two assignment changes in the sharer plan. Because the resource pool is opened as read-only, those changes have not been permanently saved in the resource pool. Next you will update the resource pool.

9   On the Tools menu, point to Resource Sharing, and then click Update Resource Pool.

Microsoft Project updates the assignment information in the resource pool with the new details from the sharer plan. Anybody else who opens or refreshes the resource pool now will see the updated assignment information.

Tip

Only assignment information is saved to the resource pool from the sharer plan. Any changes you make to resource details, such as maximum units, in the sharer plan are not saved in the resource pool when you update. When you want to change the resource details, open the resource pool as read-write. After it is open as read-write, you can change resource details in either the resource pool or the sharer plan, and the other project plans will be updated.

Next you will change an assignment in the sharer plan, close the project plan, and then update the resource pool.

10   In the Task Name column, click the name of Task 3, Sync Sound.

11   In the Resource Name column in the Assign Resources dialog box, click Lane Sacksteder, and then click the Assign button.

12   Click the Close button to close the Assign Resources dialog box.

13   On the File menu, click Close.

14   When prompted to save changes, click the Yes button.

Microsoft Project determines that because the resource pool was open as read-only, the latest assignment changes from the sharer plans have not been updated in the resource pool. You are offered the choices shown in the illustration on the following page.

15 Click OK.

Microsoft Project updates the assignment information with the new details from the sharer plan. The resource pool remains open as read-only.

16 On the File menu, click Close.

Because the resource pool was opened as read-only, Microsoft Project closes it without prompting you to save changes.

What to Do When a Sharer Plan Is Deleted

If a sharer plan is deleted, assignment information from that sharer is still stored in the resource pool. To clear this assignment information from the resource pool, you must break the link to the sharer plan. Open the resource pool as read-write. On the Tools menu, click Resource Sharing, and then click Share Resources. In the Share Resources dialog box, click the name of the now-deleted sharer, and click the Break Link button.

Working With Consolidated Projects

Most projects often involve several people working on tasks at different times, sometimes in different locations, and frequently for different supervisors. Although a resource pool can help you manage resource details across projects, it might not give you the level of control that you want over tasks and relationships between projects.

A good way to pull together far-flung project information is to use a *consolidated project*. This is a project plan that contains other project plans, called *inserted projects*. The inserted projects do not reside within the consolidated project plan, but they are linked to it in such a way that they can be viewed and edited from it. If an inserted project plan is edited outside of the consolidated project, the updated information appears in the consolidated project plan the next time it is opened.

Tip

Consolidated project plans are also known as master projects, and inserted project plans are also known as subprojects. This chapter uses the terms *consolidated* and *inserted*.

To learn more about consolidated project plans, type **All about master and subprojects** into the Ask A Question box in the upper right corner of the Microsoft Project window.

Using consolidated project plans enables you to:

■ See all tasks from your organization's project plans in a single view.

■ "Roll up" project information to higher levels of management. For example, one team's project plan might be an inserted project plan for the department's consolidated project plan, which in turn might be an inserted project plan for the organization's consolidated project plan.

■ Divide your project data into different project plans to match the nature of your project, for example, by phase, component, or location. Then you can pull the information back together in a consolidated project plan for a comprehensive look at the whole.

■ See all your projects' information in one location, so you can filter, sort, and group the data.

Consolidated project plans use Microsoft Project's outlining features. An inserted project plan appears as a summary task in the consolidated project plan, except that its summary Gantt bar is gray and an inserted project icon appears in the Indicators column. When you save a consolidated project plan, you are also prompted to save any changes you have made to inserted project plans as well.

Tip

If you have a set of project plans that you normally work on, but you don't want to combine them into one consolidated project plan, consider saving them as part of a *workspace* instead. A workspace simply records the names and window sizes of the open project plans into one file that you can later open. On the File menu, click Save Workspace.

In this exercise, you create a new consolidated project plan and view the two inserted project plans:

Open

1 On the Standard toolbar, click the Open button.

The Open dialog box appears.

2 Navigate to the Chapter 20 Consolidating folder, and double-click the Parnell Aerospace Promo 20 file.

Tip

You can also click the file name at the bottom of the File menu.

3 Microsoft Project asks if you want to open the Resource Pool. Click Do Not Open Other Files option, and then click OK.

4 On the Standard toolbar, click the Open button.

The Open dialog box appears.

5 Navigate to the Chapter 20 Consolidating folder, and double-click the Wingtip Toys Commercial 20 file.

6 Microsoft Project asks if you want to open the Resource Pool. Select the Do Not Open Other Files option, and then click OK.

Next you will use a handy shortcut to insert both open project plans into a new plan, creating a consolidated project plan.

7 On the Window menu, click New Window.

The New Window dialog box appears.

8 Under Projects, hold down the Ctrl key while clicking or drag to select the names of both open project plans, and then click OK.

Microsoft Project creates a new project plan that will become the consolidated project, and then inserts the two projects into the consolidated project as expanded summary tasks.

Tip

To add project plans to a consolidated project, on the Insert menu, click Project.

9 If the Project Guide Tasks pane appears, click the Close button in its upper right corner to close it.

10 On the View menu, click Zoom.

11 In the Zoom dialog box, click the Entire Project option, and then click OK.

Microsoft Project adjusts the timescale in the Gantt chart so that the full duration of the two projects is visible. If necessary, double-click the right edge of any columns that display pound signs (###). Your screen should look similar to the following illustration:

Inserted objects appear as expanded summary tasks in the consolidated project plan. Note the Inserted Project icon in the Indicators column and the gray project summary task bars.

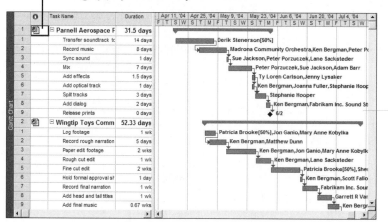

Tip

If you point to the Inserted Project icon in the Indicators column, Microsoft Project displays the full path to the inserted project plan.

To conclude this exercise, you will save the consolidated project plan and display its project summary task.

12 On the File menu, click Save As.

13 In the File Name box, type **Consolidated Projects 20**, and then click the Save button.

14 When prompted to save changes to the inserted projects, click the Yes To All button.

Next you will display the project summary task for the consolidated project.

15 On the Tools menu, click Options.

16 In the Options dialog box, click the View tab.

17 Under Outline Options, select the Show Project Summary Task box, and then click OK.

Microsoft Project displays the *Consolidated Projects 20* summary task. Your screen should look similar to the following illustration:

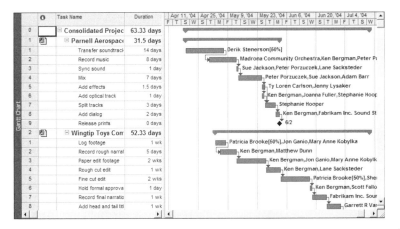

The values of this summary task, such as duration and work, represent the rolled-up values of both inserted projects. As Southridge Video takes on more projects, inserting them into the consolidated project plan in this way gives you a single location in which to view all activities of the organization.

Creating Dependencies Between Projects

Other than the International Space Station, most projects do not exist in a vacuum. Tasks or phases in one project might depend on tasks in other projects. You can show such dependencies by linking tasks between projects.

Reasons that you might need to create dependencies between projects include the following:

■ The completion of one task in a project might enable the start of a task in another project. For example, another project manager might need to complete an environmental impact statement before you can start to construct a building. Even if these two tasks are managed in separate project plans (perhaps because separate departments of a development company are completing them), one project has a logical dependency on the other.

■ A person or a piece of equipment might be assigned to a task in one project, and you need to delay the start of a task in another project until that resource completes the first task. The two tasks might have nothing in common other than that the same resource is required for both.

Task relationships between project plans look similar to links between tasks within a project plan, except that external predecessor and successor tasks have gray task names and Gantt bars. Such tasks are sometimes referred to as *ghost tasks*, because they are not linked to tasks within the project plan, only to tasks in other project plans.

In this exercise, you link tasks in two project plans, and you see the results in the two project plans, as well as in a consolidated project plan:

1 On the Window menu, click Parnell Aerospace Promo 20.

2 In the Task Name column, click the name of Task 8, Add Dialog.

Go To
Selected Task

3 On the Standard toolbar, click the Go To Selected Task button.

To the right of the task's Gantt bar, one of the resources assigned to this task is named Fabrikam Inc. Sound Studio. You want to use this studio for work on the Wingtip Toys project after this task is completed. Next you will link Task 8 to a task in the Wingtip Toys Commercial 20 project plan.

4 On the Window menu, click Wingtip Toys Commercial 20.

5 On the View menu, click Gantt Chart.

6 Click the name of Task 5, Fine Cut Edit.

Task
Information

7 On the Standard toolbar, click the Task Information button.

The Task Information dialog box appears. In the next two steps you will enter the filename and task ID of the predecessor task in this format: File Name\Task ID.

8 Click the Predecessors tab.

9 In the ID column, click the next empty cell below Task 4, and type **Parnell Aerospace Promo 20\8**

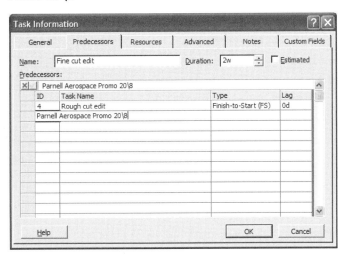

10 Press the Enter key, and then click OK to close the Task Information dialog box.

Microsoft Project inserts the ghost task named *Add dialog* in the project. The ghost task represents Task 8 from the Parnell project.

11 On the Standard toolbar, click the Go To Selected Task button.

The ghost task appears in the project to which it is linked with a gray task name.

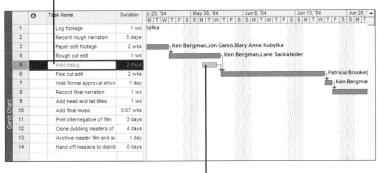

The ghost task's Gantt bar is gray.

Tip

If you point to the ghost task's Gantt bar, Microsoft Project displays a ScreenTip that contains details about the ghost task, including the full path to the external project plan where the external predecessor task (the ghost task) resides.

Next you'll look at the ghost task in the Parnell project.

12 On the Window menu, click Parnell Aerospace Promo 20.

Here you can see that ghost Task 9, Fine cut edit, is a successor for Task 8, Add dialog. Because Task 9 is a successor task with no other links to this project, it has no effect on other tasks here.

The link between these two project plans will remain until you break it. Deleting a task in the source plan or the ghost task in the destination plan deletes the corresponding task or ghost task in the other plan.

Tip

If you do not want to see cross-project links, on the Tools menu, click Options. On the View tab, clear the Show External Successors or Show External Predecessors check boxes.

Link Tasks

When viewing a consolidated project, you can quickly create cross-project links by clicking the Link Tasks button on the Standard toolbar. Dragging the mouse between two task bars will do the same thing.

To conclude this exercise, you will display the link between these two projects in the consolidated project plan.

13 On the Window menu, click Consolidated Projects 20.

You can see the link line between the task *Add dialog* in the first inserted project and the task *Fine cut edit* in the second inserted project.

Your screen should look similar to the following illustration:

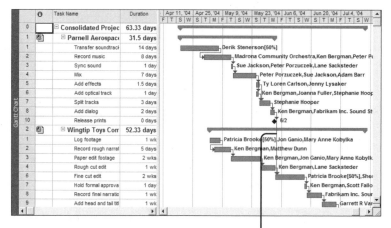

In the consolidated project plan, the cross-project link appears as a normal task link.

Because you are looking at a consolidated project plan that shows the tasks from both project plans, the cross-project link does not appear as a ghost task.

Tip

Each time you open a project plan with cross-project links, Microsoft Project will prompt you to update the cross-project links. You can suppress this prompt if you would rather not be reminded, or you can tell Microsoft Project to automatically accept updated data from the linked project plan. On the Tools menu, click Options, and then click the View tab. Under Cross-Project Linking Options For <File Name>, select the options you want.

Chapter Wrap-Up

This chapter covered how to create a resource pool and consolidated project plan. You also learned how to link tasks between projects.

If you are going on to other chapters:

● Save and close all open files.

If you aren't continuing to other chapters:

1 Save and close all open files

2 To quit Microsoft Project for now, on the File menu, click Exit.

Appendices

4

Appendix A
Introducing
Microsoft Project Server

For many project managers, communicating project details is one of the most important, time-consuming tasks they perform. Many project teams enjoy computer-based collaboration systems such as local area networks (LANs), e-mail, and access to intranets and the World Wide Web, but critical project information might seem "locked up" in Microsoft Project plans under the control of the project manager. With Microsoft Project, you can publish project details in HTML format for viewing on an intranet or on the Web. In addition to publishing Microsoft Project information, you can also use collaboration features to collect information from resources. Taking full advantage of the collaboration features of Microsoft Project enables the entire project team and other stakeholders to communicate online when performing essential tasks such as building project plans, tracking progress, reporting status, and viewing a wide range of project details.

This appendix introduces the two major ways of communicating project information among the project manager, resources, and other stakeholders. They are:

- Using intranet-based collaboration with Microsoft Project Standard or Professional edition and Microsoft Project Server. This combination offers a broad range of collaborative planning and tracking capabilities for all stakeholders in a project. Microsoft Project Server is a separate product that has system requirements in addition to those of Microsoft Project, as well as licensing requirements for Microsoft Project Web Access, the browser-based interface through which you work with Microsoft Project Server.

- Using Microsoft Project Standard or Professional edition with the Workgroup Message Handler. This enables e-mail–based communication using a MAPI-compliant e-mail system such as Microsoft Outlook, Microsoft Outlook Express, or Lotus Notes. This approach is limited to reporting task assignments, status, and updates. The Workgroup Message Handler is included with Microsoft Project and has no additional licensing requirements.

Important

This appendix illustrates some common activities supported by Microsoft Project Server. You don't need a practice file to complete these exercises. If you have access to Microsoft Project Server, you can explore some of these features at your leisure.

The specific collaboration solution that's best for you depends on your project team's network infrastructure, technical resources, and information needs. E-mail-based collaboration has relatively few setup requirements but it is limited in what it can do for the project manager and resources. Microsoft Project Server requires more setup but offers far more capabilities and benefits.

Tip

To learn more about Microsoft Project Server, type **All about Microsoft Project Server** into the Ask A Question box in the upper right corner of the Microsoft Project window.

The one thing both collaboration solutions have in common is that they let the project manager maintain control over the project plan in Microsoft Project. You control what information flows into and out of the project plan.

Tip

Because the Workgroup Message Handler is included with Microsoft Project and has no licensing requirements, you can try it out to see how online collaboration on project plans (especially collecting actuals from resources) fits within your organization. If it fits well, you might want to move up to the substantially richer capabilities of Microsoft Project Server.

Setting Up Collaboration Features in Microsoft Project

Both the Microsoft Project Server-based and e-mail-based communication solutions have their own system requirements and setup processes. For more information, see the following online documents:

- For Microsoft Project Server-based communication, see the online help file Pjsvr10.chm included with Microsoft Project Server.

- For e-mail-based communication, see the section titled "Workgroup Message Handler" in the online document C:\Program Files\Microsoft Office\Office10\1033 \Prjsetup.htm (assuming you installed Microsoft Project to the default location).

After you have deployed Microsoft Project Server or the Workgroup Message Handler, you must configure Microsoft Project:

1   Open the Microsoft Project plan for which you want to enable collaboration.

2   On the Collaborate menu, click Collaboration Options.

The Options dialog box appears with the Collaborate tab selected.

3 In the Collaborate Using box, either click Microsoft Project Server and then enter the URL for the Microsoft Project Server, or click Email Only for e-mail-based communication.

The URL of your Microsoft Project Server needs to be determined (by setting up and configuring Microsoft Project Server) before you can enable collaboration here.

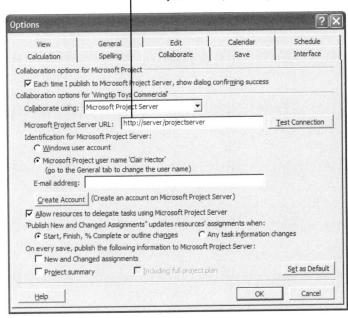

4 Click OK to close the Options dialog box.

The option you choose will be the default collaboration method used for the resources who have assignments in the open Microsoft Project plan, though different resources working on the same projects can use different workgroup communication methods. For example, you might have some resources with intranet access who use Microsoft Project Server and others who use e-mail-based communication.

Using Microsoft Project Server at the Workgroup Level

Microsoft Project Server is a companion product that works with Microsoft Project Standard or Professional edition. Microsoft Project Server enables a broad range of collaboration among stakeholders and provides a central data store for project details and supporting information such as documents and issues. Microsoft Project Server uses a role-based system in which every user is assigned to a specific group, and the group defines the capabilities each user has within Microsoft Project Server. Microsoft Project Server is very flexible and scalable; it can be used by a small team for a single project, by a department and a collection of related projects, or by an entire organization and a portfolio of projects.

When using Microsoft Project Professional with Microsoft Project Server, you can move from workgroup-level capabilities to enterprise-level capabilities; these are described in the next section.

Microsoft Project Server consists of two major components:

■ Microsoft Project Server runs on a Windows 2000 Server with Service Pack 1 or later or a Windows 2000 Advanced Server with Service Pack 1 or later. It utilizes Microsoft SQL Server as the data store and Microsoft Internet Information Server (IIS) 5.0 or later for the Web-based services.

■ The client component, Microsoft Project Web Access, runs in Microsoft Internet Explorer on the desktops of the project manager, resources, and other stakeholders you've enabled to connect to Microsoft Project Server.

Together, Microsoft Project and Microsoft Project Server provide a complete Web-based communication and collaboration tool for project teams and stakeholders. Some of the most important activities that Microsoft Project Server facilitates include the following:

■ Project managers can publish project and portfolio (multiproject) status and other details in one central location.

■ Resources can view personal task assignments and Gantt Charts, report actual work and other status, and, if enabled by the project manager, create new tasks and delegate tasks to other resources.

■ Stakeholders such as resource managers, upper management, and customers can view whatever project details they are most interested in (if the project manager has made them available).

■ Everyone involved in a project or portfolio of projects can use one standard tool to communicate project information.

Working in the Planning Phase

The following sequence of actions describes some of the most useful capabilities afforded by Microsoft Project Server: publishing project plans, collecting actuals from resources, and updating the project plan. These actions are organized by project life cycle phase, and they are in the order in which the project manager and the resources would most likely accomplish these activities.

Publishing the Plan and Assignments to Project Server

The first step in Microsoft Project Server-based collaboration is for the project manager to publish information from a project plan to Microsoft Project Server. After initially publishing a project plan to Microsoft Project Server, the project manager should republish updated information to keep the data others see in Microsoft Project Server fresh.

In this section, the project manager Clair Hector publishes a project plan to Microsoft Project Server.

1 In Microsoft Project, open the project plan that you are ready to publish.

2 On the Collaborate menu, point to Publish.

3 When initially publishing a project plan, click All Information.

This action will publish both assignments and the project plan to Microsoft Project Server. A confirmation dialog box appears:

4 Click OK.

Another confirmation dialog box appears after you have published information to Microsoft Project Server:

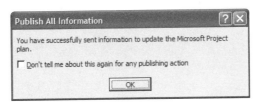

5 Click OK again.

After initially publishing a project plan to Microsoft Project Server, Clair will republish updated information to keep the assignments in Microsoft Project Server accurate.

6 On the Collaborate menu, point to Publish, and then click New And Changed Assignments.

A confirmation dialog box appears, and then the Publish New And Changed Assignments dialog box appears:

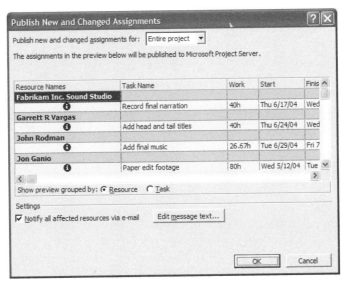

7   Click OK to close the Publish New and Changed Assignements dialog box.

The project plan is available for you and others to view in the Project Center in Microsoft Project Web Access. You can also display the Project Center right in Microsoft Project by clicking Project Center on the Collaborate menu.

Reviewing Assignments and Creating New Tasks

After the project manager has published a project plan to Microsoft Project Server, resources can review their assignments in Microsoft Project Web Access.

In this section, the resource Ken Bergman logs onto Microsoft Project Server to view his assignments in the Microsoft Project Web Access interface:

1   Log on to Microsoft Project Server through the Microsoft Project Web Access interface running in Internet Explorer:

The links on the left side of the logon screen give you some introductory information about Microsoft Project Web Access and setting up user accounts.

Microsoft Project
Web Access

What is Microsoft Project Web Access?

Setting up a Microsoft Project Server account

Log on using a different Microsoft Windows user account

Log on using your Microsoft Windows user account

Welcome to Microsoft Project Web Access

Please log on.

User name: Ken Bergman

Password: [   ]   Go

Type in your user name and password. If you do not have a user account yet, read Instructions on how to get an account set up on the Microsoft Project Server.

Copyright © 1990-2002 Microsoft Corporation. All rights reserved. License Agreement.

Tip

If you set up a user account that uses a Microsoft Windows User Account logon, you won't see this screen.

After logging on, you will see a personalized Home page that lists any new tasks or other items that affect you:

The links at the top of the screen enable you to navigate to different pages, or centers, in Microsoft Project Web Acess.

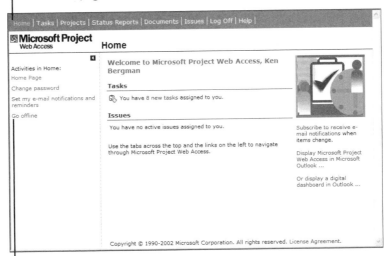

The links in the pane on the left side of the Microsoft Project Web Access screen enable you to perform common activities just for the active page or center.

The resource in the example, Ken Bergman, has new tasks assigned to him.

2 To view assigned tasks, click Tasks at the top of the screen.

The Tasks page appears:

On the Tasks page, a resource sees all tasks to which he or she has been assigned in all projects published to Microsoft Project Server. The resource can view this information in a Gantt Chart format or as a timesheet.

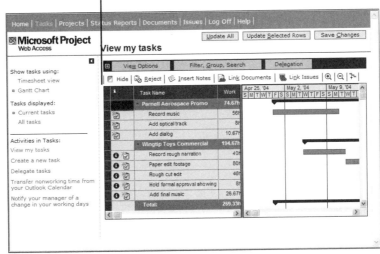

Here Ken can see his assignments for multiple projects.

To fine-tune how you see tasks here, you can change options on the View Options: Filter, Group, Search: and Delegation tabs:

Click here to expand or collapse the tabs that enable you to change what assignment information you see and how it's organized.

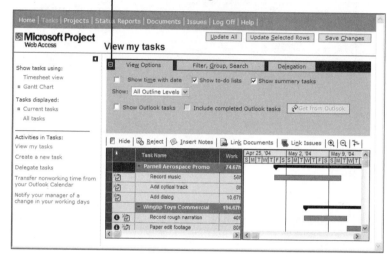

By default, resources accept all their assignments, and no reply to the project manager is required. However, a resource can reject these assignments or, depending on how his or her Project Server user account has been set up, delegate some of their assignments to other resources.

Resources can also create new tasks and make them subtasks of summary tasks in the project plan. This is useful for bottom-up planning, in which the project manager might specify a summary task but not develop all of the required subtasks. In Microsoft Project Web Access, the resources who perform the work can create additional subtasks of the summary task.

3 On the Tasks page, click the Create A New Task link in the pane on the left.

The Create A New Task page appears:

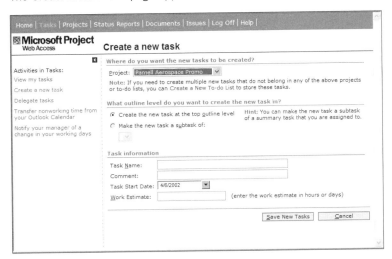

Here a resource can specify the project to which he or she wants to add the task and information about the task, such as a work estimate. Before the new task is created in the Microsoft Project plan, however, the project manager must approve it.

4   To log out of Microsoft Project Web Access, click Log Off at the top of the screen.

Reviewing Project Plans

The Project Server administrator can give a variety of stakeholders permission to view project plans in Microsoft Project Server. These stakeholders might be executives, customers, and other project managers as well as resources. Every Microsoft Project Server user is assigned to a predefined group that determines what type of data he or she sees, and how it is presented.

In this section, the executive Kathryn Wilson will view the portfolio of projects in her organization:

1   Log on to Microsoft Project Server through the Microsoft Project Web Access interface running in Internet Explorer. The interface is shown on the next page.

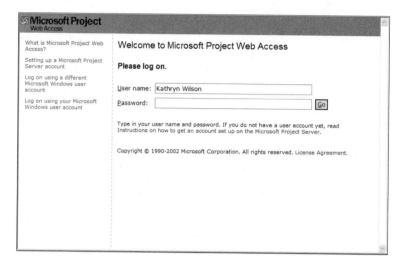

Because this Microsoft Project Server user is in the executive group, the welcome screen and other parts of the Microsoft Project Web Access interface that an executive sees differ from what resources see:

> When a Microsoft Project Web Access user in an executive group logs on, what that person sees differs from what a resource or someone in a different group would see. For example, an executive does not have tasks assigned, so the Tasks line is removed from the interface.

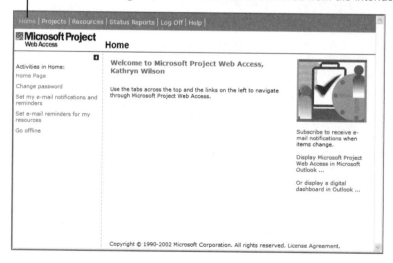

As an executive, Kathryn is most interested in a top-level view of all project work going on in the organization. To see this, she'll view the Projects page.

2 Click Projects at the top of the screen.

The Project Center appears.

Here Kathryn can see a top-level portfolio view of all projects in this Microsoft Project Server. Initially the projects are collapsed:

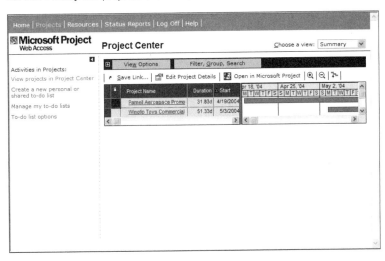

3 To expand a project, click the project's name in the Project Name column.

The expanded project appears in the View A Project page.

To look deeper into specific aspects of the portfolio, Kathryn can click another view in the Choose A View drop-down list:

When a project is fully expanded in Microsoft Project Web Access, you can change the view here.

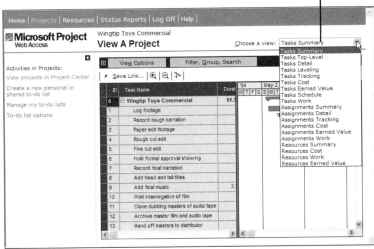

4 To log out of Microsoft Project Web Access, click Log Off at the top of the screen.

Working in the Tracking Phase

As noted earlier, one of the beneficial capabilities of Microsoft Project Server is collecting actual work on assignments from resources and updating that information in a project plan. The interface to do this is a timesheet in Microsoft Project Web Access.

Reporting Actual Work and Nonworking Time

In this section, the resource Ken Bergman reports actual work on one of his tasks:

1 Log on to Microsoft Project Server through the Microsoft Project Web Access interface running in Internet Explorer.

2 To report actual work on tasks, click Tasks at the top of the screen.

The Tasks page appears.

3 On the Tasks page, click the Timesheet View link in the pane on the left.

The Timesheet view appears.

To see his scheduled work for his first task, Ken adjusts the settings on the View Options tab:

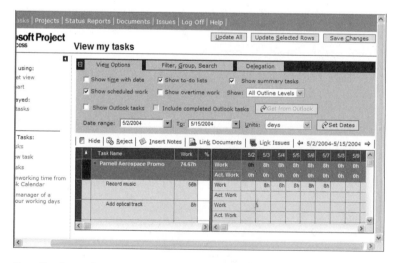

Now Ken is ready to report his actual work on the task Record Music for the week of May 3rd.

Tip

In addition to tracking work done by time period, you can also track work as percent of work complete, actual work, and remaining work.

4   In the Act. Work row for the task you want to report work on, enter the daily work values you want:

In the timesheet, the resource's scheduled work appears in the Work row. The resource can then enter actual work in the Act. Work row.

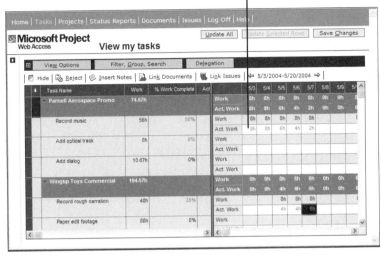

5   To report the actual work values to the project manager now, click the Update All or Update Selected Rows buttons.

To save the updates in Microsoft Project Server without reporting them to the project manager yet, click the Save Changes button.

Resources can also report their personal nonworking time through Microsoft Project Web Access. They can enter this information directly into Microsoft Project Web Access or import it from Microsoft Outlook into Microsoft Project Web Access. For example, a resource can import any Outlook calendar appointments or events longer than four hours and marked as *Busy* or *Out of Office* as nonworking time. The project manager then reviews these submissions and can post them to the individual resource calendar in a project plan. This is a great way to simplify the task of keeping resource calendars accurate and avoid scheduling work for a resource when he or she will not be available to work.

Ken needs to let Clair Hector, the project manager, know that he will be unavailable to work Friday, May 7. Ken does not use Microsoft Outlook, so he'll report the nonworking time directly in Microsoft Project Web Access.

6 On the Tasks page, click the Notify Your Manager Of A Change In Your Working Days link in the pane on the left.

Step 1 of 3 of the Notify Your Manager Of A Change In Your Working Days wizard appears.

Ken enters his nonworking time:

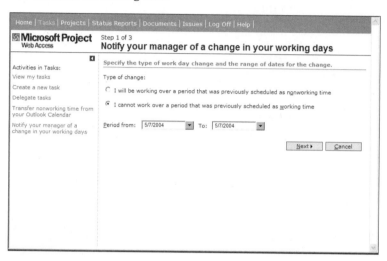

7 Click the Next button.

Page 2 of the Notify Your Manager Of A Change In Your Working Days Wizard appears.

Ken chooses the project manager to whom he wants to submit his nonworking time:

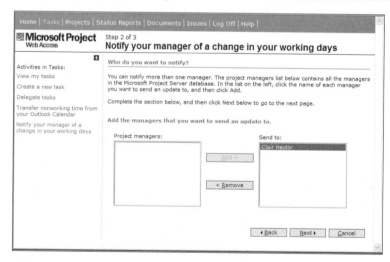

8 Click the Next button.

Page 3 of the Notify Your Manager Of A Change In Your Working Days Wizard appears. This is a confirmation of the information to be sent to the project manager.

9 Click the Send button.

Microsoft Project Server confirms that the calendar updates have been sent to the project manager.

10 To log out of Microsoft Project Web Access, click Log Off at the top of the screen.

Reviewing Actuals and Updating the Project Plan

When the project manger logs onto Microsoft Project Server, he or she sees immediately if resources have submitted new actual work. The project manager can then review the submissions and have them posted to the project plan. After they are in the project plan, Microsoft Project responds to the actuals by recalculating task durations and rescheduling remaining work as needed.

In this section, the project manager Clair Hector logs onto Microsoft Project Server, reviews and accepts actual work submitted by Ken Bergman, and updates the project plan with the actuals:

1 Log on to Microsoft Project Server through the Microsoft Project Web Access interface running in Internet Explorer.

Tip

You can also display the task changes submitted by resources by clicking Update Project Progress on the Collaborate menu in Microsoft Project.

The Home page appears.

Because the resource Ken Bergman has submitted actual work and a working time update to Clair Hector, notifications of these transactions appear on Clair's Home page:

When a project manager logs on to Microsoft Project Web Access, he or she can see any new work submissions or other updates from resources.

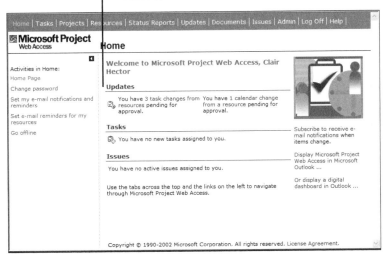

First Clair reviews and accepts the task updates.

2 Click Updates at the top of the screen.

The Updates page appears with the specific task and project updates displayed:

When approving actual work submissions, the project manager can quickly approve all submissions, all submissions for a specific project, all assignments on a task, or just a specific resource's submissions.

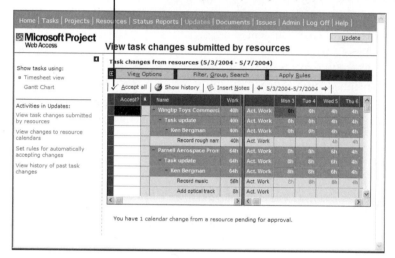

Tip

A project manager can define rules to automatically process updates from resources. On the Updates page, click the Apply Rules tab.

Clair reviews the actual work values submitted by the resource Ken Bergman and approves them.

3 Click the Accept All button.

4 Click the Update button at the top right corner of the screen.

The actual work is updated to the project plan in Microsoft Project.

Clair reviews the actual work after it's updated in the project plan in Microsoft Project (the other resources assigned to the same task as Ken in this project have already reported their work on the task):

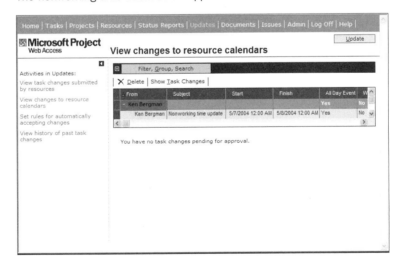

After the project manager approves the resource's actual work in Microsoft Project Web Access and updates the project plan, those actuals appear in Microsoft Project just as if they'd been entered there directly.

Next, the project manager accepts the change in working time submitted by the resource.

5 Click the View Changes To Resource Calendars link in the pane on the left.

The nonworking time submission appears:

Clair reviews the nonworking time submitted by Ken Bergman and approves it.

6 Click the Update button at the top right corner of the screen.

The nonworking time is updated to the project plan in Microsoft Project.

Clair reviews Ken Bergman's working time settings in the project plan in Microsoft Project and verifies that he is no longer scheduled to do any work on May 7:

After the project manager approves the resource's nonworking time submission in Microsoft Project Web Access and updates the project plan, the nonworking time appears in Microsoft Project.

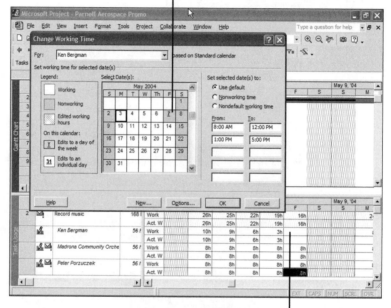

No work is scheduled for the resource during nonworking time.

All the actual work and resource working time settings recorded in the project plan have come directly from the resources; the project manager has not had to reenter this information into the project plan. However, the project manager can always maintain control over what gets updated in the project plan from Microsoft Project Web Access.

7 To log out of Microsoft Project Web Access, click Log Off at the top of the screen.

Using Microsoft Project Server at the Enterprise Level

When you use Microsoft Project Server in conjunction with Microsoft Project Professional, you gain enterprise-level project management functionality. This combination of products can do everything described earlier and more. The combination of these two products offers a scalable solution for large organizations in search of a powerful project and resource management solution. With Microsoft Project Server and Microsoft Project Professional, you can:

■ Develop enterprise-wide standards with an enterprise global template, enterprise codes, custom fields, and templates for all project plans.

■ Gain enterprise resource management through a central enterprise resource pool. If you have a catalog of each resource's skills, you can use the Resource Substitution Wizard to define the skills required by a new project and then staff your project with generic resources. Later, you can locate the resources within your organization who have matching skills and availability.

■ Specify if a resource should be requested or demanded from the enterprise resource pool; the relative priority of resources for assignments is set in the Resource Substitution Wizard.

■ Use the Portfolio Analyzer (based on an OLAP cube generated by Microsoft SQL Server 2000 Analysis Service) for enterprise-wide analysis of project and resource data.

■ Save versions of project plans to Microsoft Project Server so you can do full comparisons between projects, look at trends, and do what-if analysis.

■ Use logon accounts to create connections to Microsoft Project Server and open projects and enterprise global files stored there. Authenticate users against Microsoft Project Server security.

The full feature set of Microsoft Project Professional with Microsoft Project Server is described elsewhere (for example, the Microsoft Web site), and a full evaluation of this powerful solution is no small task. Here we've described just some of the features this combination offers.

Using E-Mail Based Collaboration

Both Microsoft Project Standard and Professional editions support e-mail-based collaboration right out of the box; you do not need Microsoft Project Server to use e-mail-based collaboration. The name of this feature is the Workgroup Message Handler.

The Workgroup Message Handler is designed primarily to enable the following two activities:

■ The project manager can send task assignments, updates, and status requests to assigned resources.

■ The assigned resources can accept task assignments and send status on tasks to the project manager.

For the project manager, the primary benefit of using e-mail-based communication is that the resources themselves supply the actual work details that are saved in the Microsoft Project plan. This is extremely useful for two reasons. First, it gives the project manager a detailed and presumably accurate status of tasks in progress. Second, it captures detailed actuals in the Microsoft Project plan that you can use later to analyze work patterns, develop standard task duration metrics, and more.

This section describes common activities that both the project manager and the assigned resources can accomplish using the Workgroup Message Handler for e-mail-based collaboration. These activities are organized in the order in which the project manager and the resources would likely accomplish these activities.

Important

Before performing the following actions, you and the project's resources must first install the Workgroup Message Handler, and then you must configure Microsoft Project to use it, as described earlier.

Notifying Resources of Task Assignments

After assigning resources to tasks in Microsoft Project, the project manager notifies the resource of the assignment:

1   In Microsoft Project, assign resources to tasks.
2   Select the task or tasks for which you want to send assignment notifications.
3   On the Collaborate menu, point to Publish, and then click New And Changed Assignments.

Tip

If you display the Collaborate toolbar, you can also click the Publish New And Changed Assignments button.

Microsoft Project displays a Publish New And Changed Assignments dialog box.

4   Click OK.

Microsoft Project sends an e-mail message with the assignment details to the assigned resources.

Accepting a Task Assignment Request

The resource reviews the assignment details, accepts or rejects the assignments, and returns his or her response to the project manager:

1   In your e-mail application, open the message from the project manager.
2   In the message form, click the Reply button.
3   In the Message box, type any message you want the project manager to see.
4   To accept the assignment, click the Send button. To reject the assignment, in the Accept? column, click No, and then click the Send button.

Tip

If you are running Microsoft Outlook, tasks you accept are added to your Outlook Task list. Information about these tasks' percent complete is recorded in status reports you send to the project manager.

Requesting the Resource's Assignment Status

The project manager can request status from resources at any time:

1 Select the task or tasks for which you want to request the status.

2 On the Collaborate menu, click Request Progress Information.

Tip

If you display the Collaborate toolbar, you can also click the Request Progress Information button.

Microsoft Project displays the Request Progress Information dialog box.

3 Select the progress options you want, and then click OK.

Microsoft Project sends an e-mail message to the assigned resources with the progress request attached.

Sending Assignment Status to the Project Manager

The resources reply to the status request:

1 In your e-mail application, open the message from the project manager.

2 In the message form, click the Reply button.

3 Enter the remaining work, daily actual work, and comments you want to make for the tasks listed.

4 Click the Send button.

Your status is sent to the project manager.

Updating the Microsoft Project Plan with the Resource's Progress Response

The project manager reviews the resources' status, and then posts this information in the project plan:

1 In your e-mail application, open the response message from the resource.

2 Review the actual values reported by the resource. If they meet with your approval, click the Update Project button.

Microsoft Project updates the plan with the actuals from the resource. Any comments from the resource appear as task notes.

Appendix B
A Short Course in Project Management

Throughout this book, we've included advice on how best to use Microsoft Project while following sound project management practices. This appendix focuses on the basics of project management, regardless of any software tools you may use to help you manage projects. Although project management is a broad subject, this appendix uses the "project triangle" model. In this model, you consider projects in terms of time, cost, and scope.

Understanding What Defines a Project

Succeeding as a project manager requires that you complete your projects on time, finish within budget, and make sure your customers are happy with what you deliver. That sounds simple enough, but how many projects have you heard of (or worked on) that were completed late, or cost too much, or didn't meet the needs of their customers?

A Guide to the Project Management Body of Knowledge (published by the Project Management Institute, 2000)—referred to as the PMBOK, pronounced "pimbok"—defines a ***project*** as "a temporary endeavor undertaken to create a unique product or service." Let's walk through this definition to clarify what a project is and is not.

Tip

For more information about the Project Management Institute and the PMBOK, see Appendix C, "What's Next?"

First, a project is *temporary*. A project's duration might be just a week, or it might go on for years, but every project has an end date. You might not know that end date when the project starts, but it's out there somewhere in the future. Projects are not the same as ***ongoing operations***, although the two have a lot in common. Ongoing operations, as the name suggests, go on indefinitely; you don't establish an end date. Examples include most activities of accounting and human resources departments. People who run ongoing operations might also manage projects; for example, a manager of a human resources department for a large organization might plan a college recruiting fair. But projects are distinguished from ongoing operations by an expected end date, such as the date of the recruiting fair.

Next, a project is an *endeavor*. **Resources**, such as people and equipment, need to do work. The endeavor is undertaken by a team or an organization, so projects have a sense of being intentional, planned events. Successful projects don't happen spontaneously; some amount of preparation and planning happens first.

Finally, every project *creates a unique product or service*. This is the **deliverable** for the project, the reason that the project was undertaken. A refinery that produces gasoline does not produce a unique product. The whole idea, in this case, is to produce a standardized commodity; you usually don't want to buy gas from one station that is significantly different from gas at another station. On the other hand, commercial airplanes are unique products. Although all Boeing 777 airplanes might look about the same to most of us, each is, in fact, highly customized for the needs of its purchaser.

By now, you may be getting the idea that a lot of the work that goes on in the world is project work. If you schedule, track, or manage any of this work, then congratulations are in order: you are already doing some project management work!

Project management has been a recognized profession since about the 1950s, but project management work in some form has been going on as long as people have been doing complex work. When the Great Pyramids in Egypt were built, somebody somewhere was tracking resources, schedule, and the specifications for the final deliverable.

Tip

Project management is now a well-recognized job in most industries. To learn more about organizations that train project managers and advance project management as a profession, see Appendix C, "What's Next?"

The Project Triangle:
Seeing Projects in Terms of Time, Cost, and Scope

You can visualize project work in many ways, but our favorite is what's sometimes called the *project triangle*:

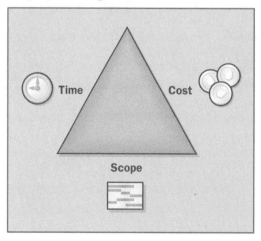

This theme has many variations, but the basic idea is that every project has some element of a time constraint, has some type of budget, and requires some amount of work to complete. (In other words, it has a defined scope.) The term *constraint* has a specific meaning in Microsoft Project, but here we're using the more general meaning of a limiting factor. Let's consider these constraints one at a time.

Time

Have you ever worked on a project that had a deadline? (Maybe we should ask whether you've ever worked on a project that did not have a deadline.) Limited time is the one constraint of any project with which we are all probably most familiar. If you're working on a project right now, ask your team members what the project deadline is. They might not know the project budget or the scope of work in great detail, but chances are they all know the project deadline.

Here are some examples of time constraints:

- You're building a house and you must finish the roof before the rainy season arrives.
- You are assembling a large display booth for a trade show that starts in two months.
- You are developing a new inventory tracking system that must be tested and running by the start of the next fiscal year.

Most of us have been trained to understand time since we were children, and we carry wristwatches, paper and electronic organizers, and other tools to help us manage time. For many projects that create a product or result in an event, time is the most important constraint to manage.

Cost

You might think of cost just as dollars, but project cost has a broader meaning: costs include all the resources required to carry out the project. Costs include the people and equipment who do the work, the materials they use, and all the other events and issues that require money or someone's attention in a project.

Here are some examples of cost constraints:

- You have signed a fixed-price contract to deliver an inventory-tracking software system to a client. If your costs exceed the agreed-upon price, your customer might be sympathetic but probably won't be willing to renegotiate the contract.
- The president of your organization has directed you to carry out a customer-research project using only the staff and equipment in your department.
- You have received a $5,000 grant to create a public art installation. You have no other funds.

For virtually all projects, cost is ultimately a limiting constraint; few projects could go over budget without eventually requiring corrective action.

Scope

You should consider two aspects of *scope*: product scope and project scope. Every successful project produces a unique product: a tangible item or a service. You might develop some products for one customer you know by name. You might develop other products for millions of potential customers waiting to buy them (you hope). Customers usually have some expectations about the features and functions of products they consider purchasing. *Product scope* describes the intended quality, features, and functions of the product—often in minute detail. Documents that outline this information are sometimes called product specifications. A service or an event usually has some expected features as well. We all have expectations about what we'll do or see at a party, a concert, or a sporting event.

Project scope, on the other hand, describes the work required to deliver a product or a service with the intended product scope. Whereas product scope focuses on the customer or the user of the product, project scope is mainly the concern of the people who will carry out the project. Project scope is usually measured in tasks and phases.

Here are some examples of scope constraints:

- Your organization won a contract to develop an automotive product that has exact requirements—for example, physical dimensions measured to 0.01 mm. This is a product scope constraint that will influence project scope plans.

- You are constructing a building on a lot that has a height restriction of 50 feet.

- You can use only internal services to develop part of your product, and those services follow a product development methodology that is different from what you had planned.

Product scope and project scope are closely related. The project manager who manages project scope well must also understand product scope or must know how to communicate with those who do.

Time, Cost, and Scope: Managing Project Constraints

Project management gets most interesting when you have to balance the time, cost, and scope constraints of your projects—"balance" as on a high wire. You could also think of juggling these constraints, or juggling them while on a high wire...well, you get the idea. Let's return to the project triangle model. The project triangle illustrates the process of balancing constraints because the three sides of the triangle are connected, and changing one side of a triangle affects at least one other side. Here are some examples of constraint balance:

- If the duration (*time*) of your project schedule decreases, you might need to increase budget (*cost*) because you must hire more resources to do the same work in less time. If you can't increase the budget, you might need to reduce the *scope* because the resources you have can't do all of the planned work in less time.

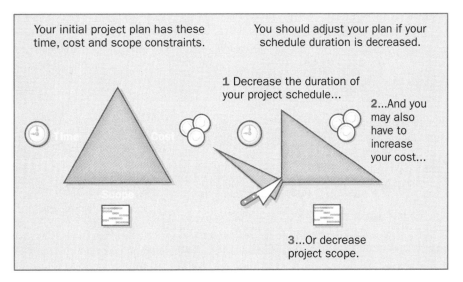

If you must decrease a project's duration, make sure that overall project quality is not unintentionally lowered. For example, testing and quality control often occur last in a software development project; if the project duration is decreased late in the project, those tasks might be the ones cut back. You must weigh the benefits of decreasing the project duration against the potential downside of a deliverable with poorer quality.

■ If the budget (cost) of your project decreases, you might need more time because you can't pay for as many resources or for resources of the same efficiency. If you can't increase the time, you might need to reduce project scope because fewer resources can't do all of the planned work in the time you have.

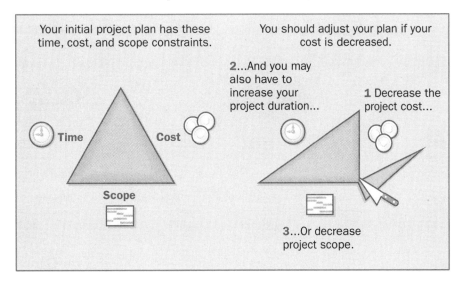

If you must decrease a project's budget, you could look at the *grades* of material resources for which you had budgeted. For example, did you plan to shoot a film in 35 mm when cheaper 16 mm film would do? A lower-grade material is not necessarily a lower-quality material. As long as the grade of material is appropriate for its intended use, it might still be of high quality. Another example: fast food and gourmet are two grades of restaurant food, but you may find high-quality and low-quality examples of each.

You should also look at the costs of the human and equipment resources you have planned to use. Can you hire less experienced people for less money to carry out simpler tasks? Reducing project costs can lead to a poorer-quality deliverable, however. As a project manager, you must consider (or more likely, communicate to the decision makers) the benefits versus the risks of reducing costs.

■ If your project scope increases, you might need more time or more resources (cost) to do the additional work. If the project scope increases after the project has started, it's called *scope creep*. Changing project scope midway through a project is not necessarily a bad thing; for example, your intended customer might have changed and you need to deliver a different product to the new customer. Changing project scope is a bad thing only if the project manager doesn't recognize and plan for the new requirements—that is, when other constraints (cost, time) are not correspondingly examined and, if necessary, adjusted.

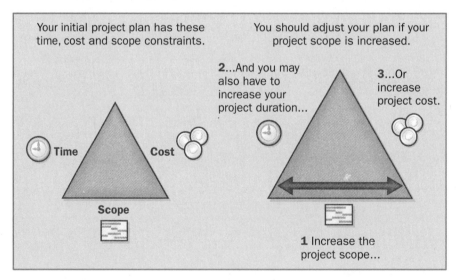

Time, cost, and scope are the three essential elements of any project. To succeed as a project manager, you'll have to know quite a bit about how all three of these constraints apply to your projects. You need a tool to help manage them.

Managing Your Projects with Microsoft Project

The best project management tool in the world can never replace your good judgment. However, the right tool can and should help you accomplish the following while looking and feeling like other productivity programs you might use frequently:

- Track all the information you gather about the work, duration, and resource requirements for your project.
- Visualize your project plan in standard, well-defined formats.
- Schedule tasks and resources consistently and effectively.
- Exchange project information with all *stakeholders* over an intranet or the Internet.
- Communicate with resources and other stakeholders, while leaving ultimate control in the hands of the project manager.

In the chapters of this book, you were introduced to the rich functionality of Microsoft Project in a realistic context: managing a project from conception to completion.

Not everything in this book might have applied to your needs, and you probably have needs that this book didn't address. But, after completing this tutorial, you're off to a great start with Microsoft Project.

Appendix C
What's Next?

If you've completed most or all the chapters in this book, you're well on your way to mastering Microsoft Project. However, one book can only get you so far. To help further your Microsoft Project and project management knowledge, here are a few sources available to you.

Joining a Microsoft Project Learning Community

If there's one thing we can say about Microsoft Project users, it's that they love to talk about the program and their work with it and to share ideas with others. Whether you work in a large organization or independently, you're likely to find a community of Microsoft Project users nearby.

If you're in a large organization, especially one with a strong project management focus, you might find an internal Microsoft Project user group or support group there. Such groups often meet informally to provide peer training and support, to critique project plans, and to share best practices. If there isn't such a group in your organization, you might well start one.

In the public realm, there are many Microsoft Project user groups around the world. These groups typically meet on a regular basis to share tips and tricks about Microsoft Project. For example, in the Puget Sound area in the northwest United States, where the authors live and work, there's an active Microsoft Project user group that meets most months for informal idea sharing and for formal presentations by industry experts. Joining a user group is a great way to broaden your exposure to Microsoft Project usage; it also can be a great source for informal product support, training, and career networking.

Here are a few places where you can investigate Microsoft Project user groups and related resources:

- The Microsoft Project Users Group (MPUG) offers both free and subscription-based information about a variety of Microsoft Project and project management resources, as well as a directory of Microsoft Project user groups around the world. Find it on the Web at *www.mpug.org*

- Msproject.com is an independent clearinghouse of information about Microsoft Project. The Web site contains links to a variety of resources that would interest any Microsoft Project user. Find it on the Web at *www.msproject.com*

- The official Microsoft Project Web site at microsoft.com includes a variety of tools to help you manage your projects, product specifications, and links to other resources. Find it on the Web at *www.microsoft.com/office/project/*

- The official Microsoft Project newsgroup offers help and discussions with other users of Microsoft Project, including Microsoft Most Valuable Professionals (MVPs). You can use any newsreader software to access this newsgroup. To view or subscribe to this newsgroup, point your newsreader to *news://msnews.microsoft.com /microsoft.public.project*

- For help with Visual Basic for Applications (VBA) in Microsoft Project, point your newsreader to *news://msnews.microsoft.com/microsoft.public.project.vba*

Joining a Project Management Learning Community

Probably more than most other desktop programs, Microsoft Project requires you to be involved in a specific formal activity: project management. Project management can be an exciting mix of technical, organizational, and social challenges. The Project Management Institute (PMI) is the leading organization of professional project management. PMI focuses on setting project management standards, developing and offering educational programs, and certifying Project Management Professionals (PMPs).

PMI's *A Guide to the Project Management Body of Knowledge* (PMBOK Guide 2000 Edition) describes generally accepted project management practices, knowledge areas, and terminology. In addition, PMI publishes the journals *Project Management Journal* and *PM Network*. You can learn more about PMI on the Web at *www.pmi.org*.

Two Web sites or "portals" that might interest you are Project Connections and GanttHead. You can find these subscription-based sites at the following Web addresses:

- *www.projectconnections.com/*
- *www.gantthead.com/*

Both sites offer a wide variety of training, discussion forums, and industry-specific metrics and best practices for project management.

Final Words

There are, of course, many worthwhile commercial and nonprofit organizations dedicated to Microsoft Project and project management besides those we've described here. Microsoft Project enjoys a leading position in the diverse, sometimes contentious, but always interesting world of project management. Wherever you are in your own Microsoft Project and project management knowledge and career development, you can find a great variety of supporting organizations and peers today. Good luck!

Quick Reference

47 **To set up people and equipment resources**

1 On the View menu, click Resource Sheet.

2 In the Resource Name field, enter the resource's name.

3 In the Type field, click Work.

4 In the Max. Units field, type or click the maximum capacity of this resource to accomplish any task.

5 Enter whatever other resource information would be useful to your project.

6 Repeat steps 2 through 5 for each resource.

50 **To set up material resources**

1 On the View menu, click Resource Sheet.

2 In the Resource Name field, enter the material resource's name.

3 In the Type field, click Material.

4 In the Material Label field, enter the unit of measure you want to use for this resource. For example, you might measure cement in pounds or tons.

5 In the Std. Rate field, enter the cost per unit of measure for this material resource.

6 Enter whatever other resource information would be useful for your project.

7 Repeat steps 2 through 6 for each resource.

50 **To enter resource pay rates**

1 On the View menu, click Resource Sheet.

2 In the Std. Rate field, enter the resource's pay rate, including the duration of a pay period.

3 If the resource should accrue overtime pay, enter his or her overtime pay rate in the Ovt. Rate field.

4 If the resource accrues a per-use cost, enter that amount in the Cost/Use field.

5 In the Accrue At field, click the method by which the resource accrues cost.

6 Repeat steps 2 through 5 for each resource.

53 **To adjust working time for individual resources**

1 On the Tools menu, click Change Working Time.

2 In the For box, click the name of the resource whose working time you want to change.

3 In the calendar below the Select Date(s) label, click the date range or day(s) of the week for which you want to adjust working time.

4 Under Set Selected Date(s) To, click the options you want.

55 **To document resources with resource notes**

1 Switch to a resource view such as the Resource Sheet view.

2 Click the name of the resource for which you want to create a note.

Notes

3 On the Standard toolbar, click the Resource Notes button.

4 In the Resource Information dialog box, type the note you want associated with this resource.

Chapter   4   Assigning Resources to Tasks

Page   58   **To assign resources using the Project Guide**

1   On the Project Guide toolbar, click the Resources button.

2   In the Resources pane, click the Assign People And Equipment To Tasks link, and then follow the instructions that appear on your screen.

58   **To assign resources using the Assign Resources dialog box**

Assign
Resources

1   On the Standard toolbar, click Assign Resources.

2   In the Gantt Chart view, click the name of the task to which you want to assign a resource.

3   In the Resource Name column of the Assign Resources dialog box, click a resource, and then click the Assign button.

64   **To control how Microsoft Project schedules the work on a task after assigning an additional resource**

Smart Tag
Actions

1   Assign an additional resource to a task.

2   Click the Smart Tag Actions button, and choose the action you want.

67   **To assign material resources to tasks**

Assign
Resources

1   On the Standard toolbar, click Assign Resources.

2   In the Gantt Chart view, click the name of the task to which you want to assign a resource.

3   In the Resource Name column of the Assign Resources dialog box, click a resource, and in the Units column, enter the number of units of the material resource you want to assign.

4   Click the Assign button.

Chapter   5   Formatting and Printing Your Plan

Page   72   **To create a custom view**

1   On the View menu, click More Views.

2   In the More Views dialog box, do one of the following:

■   To create a view, click the New button. Click Single View or Combination View in the Define New View dialog box, and then click OK.

■   To redefine a view, click the view's name, and then click the Edit button.

■   To create a new view based on another view, click the view's name, and then click the Copy button.

3   In the View Definition dialog box, choose the options you want.

74   **To format Gantt bars with the Gantt Chart Wizard**

1   On the Format menu, click Gantt Chart Wizard.

2   Follow the instructions that appear on your screen.

77 **To draw a text box on a Gantt chart**

  1 On the View menu, point to Toolbars, and then click Drawing.

Text Box

  2 On the Drawing toolbar, click the Text Box button, and then drag a small square anywhere on the chart portion of a Gantt Chart view.

  3 In the square you just drew, type the text you want.

79 **To format a category of text in a view**

  1 On the Format menu, click Text Styles.

  2 In the Items To Change list, click the type of text you want to format.

  3 Select the f and other formatting options you want.

81 **To format selected text in a view**

  1 Click the cell that contains the text you want to format.

  2 On the Format menu, click Font.

  3 Select the font and other formatting options you want.

85 **To edit a report's header**

  1 On the View menu, click Reports.

  2 Click a report category, or to see all reports, click Custom, and then click the Select button.

  3 Select the report you want, and then click the Select or Preview button.

  4 On the Print Preview toolbar, click the Page Setup button.

  5 In the Page Setup dialog box, click the Header tab, and select the options you want.

Chapter 6 **Tracking Progress on Tasks**

Page 91 **To save a baseline using the Project Guide**

  1 On the Project Guide toolbar, click the Track button.

  2 In the Track pane, click the Save A Baseline Plan To Compare With Later Versions link, and then follow the instructions that appear on your screen.

92 **To display the Variance table in the Task Sheet view**

  1 On the View menu, click More Views to display the More Views dialog box.

  2 In the Views box, click Task Sheet, and click the Apply button.

  3 On the View menu, point to Table:Entry, and click Variance.

93 **To track a project as scheduled**

  1 On the Tools menu, point to Tracking, and click Update Project.

  2 In the Update Project dialog box, make sure the Update Work As Complete Through option is selected. In the adjacent date list, type or click the date you want, and click OK.

94 **To enter a task's percent complete using the Project Guide**

1 On the Project Guide toolbar, click the Track button.

2 In the Track pane, click the Prepare To Track The Progress Of Your Project link.

3 Click the Save And Go To Step 2 link.

4 Click Always Track By Entering The Percent Of Work Complete, and then click the Save And Finish link at the bottom of the Setup Tracking pane.

5 In the Track pane, click the Incorporate Progress Information Into The Project link.

6 In the % Work Complete field for a task, type or click the percent complete value you want, and then press Enter.

96 **To enter actual values for tasks using the Project Guide**

1 On the Project Guide toolbar, click the Track button.

2 In the Track pane, click the Prepare To Track The Progress Of Your Project link.

3 Click the Save And Go To Step 2 link.

4 Click Always Track By Entering The Actual Work Done And Work Remaining, and then click Save And Finish.

5 In the Track pane, click the Incorporate Progress Information Into The Project link.

6 In the Actual Work field for a task, type or click the actual work value you want, and then press Enter.

97 **To enter actual start dates and durations of tasks**

1 Click the task for which you want to enter actual values.

2 On the Tools menu point to Tracking, and then click Update Tasks.

3 In the Start field in the Actual box on the left side of the Update Tasks dialog box, type or click the start date you want.

4 In the Actual Dur field, type or click the duration value you want, and then click OK.

Chapter 7 Fine-Tuning Task Details

Page **105** **To change task relationships**

1 Click the successor task whose predecessor relationship you want to change.

Task Information

2 On the Standard toolbar, click the Task Information button.

3 In the Task Information dialog box, click the Predecessors tab, and then select the options you want.

106 **To enter lead and lag time between predecessor and successor tasks**

1 Click the successor task whose lead or lag time with a predecessor you want to change.

Task Information

2 On the Standard toolbar, click the Task Information button.

3 In the Task Information dialog box, click the Predecessors tab.

4 In the Lag field for a predecessor task, enter the value you want (enter a positive value for lag time, or a negative value for lead time).

107 **To change the task relationship between tasks**

Task
Information

🗔

1 Click the successor task whose relationship with a predecessor you want to change.

2 On the Standard toolbar, click the Task Information button.

3 In the Task Information dialog box, click the Predecessors tab.

4 Click in the Type column for predecessor task, and click the type of task relationship you want.

110 **To apply a constraint to a task using the Project Guide**

1 On the Project Guide toolbar, click the Tasks button.

2 Click the Set Deadlines And Constrain Tasks link, and then follow the instructions that appear on your screen.

113 **To view a project's critical path**

1 On the View menu, click More Views.

2 In the More Views dialog box, click Detail Gantt, and then click the Apply button.

114 **To interrupt work on a task**

Split Task

🗔

1 On the Standard toolbar, click the Split Task button.

2 Move the mouse pointer over the task's Gantt bar where you want to start the split, click, and then drag to the right.

117 **To create a new base calendar**

1 On the Tools menu, click Change Working Time.

2 In the Change Working Time dialog box, click the New button.

3 In the Name box, type a name for the base calendar.

4 Click Create A New Base Calendar, or click Make A Copy Of and then choose the base calendar on which you want to base the new calendar.

5 Click OK.

6 In the Selected Date(s) box, click the days of the week for which you want to change working and nonworking time.

7 Under Set Selected Date(s) To, click Nonworking Time for those days you want to mark as nonworking time.

8 For working days, in the From and To boxes, enter the working time you want.

118 **To apply a task calendar to a task**

Task
Information

🗔

1 In the Gantt Chart view, click a task.

2 On the Standard toolbar, click the Task Information button.

3 In the Task Information dialog box, click the Advanced tab.

4 In the Calendar box, choose the task calendar you want to apply.

5 If you want the task calendar to override resource calendar settings, click the Scheduling Ignores Resource Calendars box.

120 **To change a task type**

Task
Information

1 In the Gantt Chart view, click a task.

2 On the Standard toolbar, click the Task Information button.

3 In the Task Information dialog box, click the Advanced tab.

4 In the Task Type box, click the task type you want.

123 **To enter a deadline date using the Project Guide**

1 On the Project Guide toolbar, click the Tasks button.

2 In the Tasks pane, click the Set Deadlines And Constrain Tasks link, and then follow the instructions that appear on your screen.

125 **To enter a fixed cost**

1 On the View menu, point to Table: Entry, and then click Cost.

2 In the Fixed Cost field for the task you want, type or click an amount, and press Tab.

3 In the Fixed Cost Accrual field, choose a method, and then press Enter.

126 **To create a recurring task**

1 In the Gantt Chart view, click the task above which you want to insert a recurring task.

2 On the Insert menu, click Recurring Task.

3 In the Recurring Task Information dialog box, select the options you want.

Chapter 8 Fine-Tuning Resource and Assignment Details

Page 132 **To create multiple pay rates for a resource**

1 Switch to a resource view such as the Resource Sheet view.

2 Click the name of the resource for whom you want to create an additional pay rate.

3 On the Project menu, click Resource Information.

4 In the Resource Information dialog box, click the Costs tab.

5 Under Cost Rate Tables, the resource's initial pay rate information appears on tab A. Click one of the other tabs, and then enter the rate information you want.

6 To apply different cost rate tables, pick the one you want in the Cost Rate Tables field when you are in a usage view.

134 **To create multiple pay rates that apply at different times**

1 Switch to a resource view such as the Resource Sheet view.

2 Click the name of the resource for whom you want to create an additional pay rate.

3 On the Project menu, click Resource Information.

4 In the Resource Information dialog box, click the Costs tab.

5 Click the tab of the rate you want to edit.

6 In the second or later row of the Effective Date column, enter the date the new pay rate is to take effect.

7 In the Standard Rate column (and, if applicable, the Overtime Rate or Per Use Cost columns), enter either a dollar amount or a positive or negative percentage of the existing pay rate. If you enter a percentage value, Microsoft Project will calculate the new pay rate amount.

135 **To customize a resource's availability over time**

1 Switch to a resource view such as the Resource Sheet view.

2 Click the name of the resource whose availability you want to change.

3 On the Project menu, click Resource Information.

4 In the Resource Information dialog box, click the General tab.

5 In the Resource Availability grid, enter the date ranges and unit values you want.

137 **To delay the start of an assignment**

1 On the View menu, click Task Usage or Resource Usage.

2 Click the assignment you want to delay.

Assignment
Information

3 On the Standard toolbar, click the Assignment Information button.

4 In the Assignment Information dialog box, click the General tab.

5 In the Start box, type or click the date on which you want the selected resource to start work on the assignment, and then click OK.

138 **To apply a contour to an assignment**

1 On the View menu, click Task Usage or Resource Usage.

2 Click the assignment for which you want to contour to an assignment.

Assignment
Information

3 On the Standard toolbar, click the Assignment Information button.

4 In the Assignment Information dialog box, click the General tab.

5 In the Work Contour box, click the contour you want, and then click OK.

141 **To apply a different cost rate to an assignment**

1 On the View menu, click Task Usage or Resource Usage.

2 Click the assignment for which you want to apply a different cost rate table.

Assignment
Information

3 On the Standard toolbar, click the Assignment Information button.

4 In the Assignment Information dialog box, click the General tab.

5 In the Cost Rate Table box, type or click the rate table you want to apply to this assignment, and then click OK.

143 **To enter a material resource consumption rate on an assignment**

1 In the Gantt Chart view, click the name of the task to which you want to assign a material resource.

Assign
Resources

2 On the Standard toolbar, click the Assign Resources button.

3 In the Assign Resources dialog box, in the Units field for the material resource, type the consumption rate you want in the format quantity/time period. For example, to specify 20 feet per hour, type 20/hr.

4 Click the Assign button.

Chapter 9 Fine-Tuning the Project Plan

Page 148 **To view resource allocations over time using the Project Guide**

1 On the Project Guide toolbar, click the Report button.

2 In the Report pane, click the See How Resources' Time Is Allocated link, and then follow the instructions that appear on your screen.

154 **To manually resolve resource overallocations by changing assignment units**

1 On the View menu, click More Views, click Resource Allocation, and then click the Apply button

2 In the Resource Name column, click the name of an assignment for the resource you want to work with.

Assignment
Information

3 On the Standard toolbar, click the Assignment Information button.

4 In the Assignment Information dialog box, click the General tab.

5 In the Units box, enter the unit value you want, and then click OK.

158 **To level overallocated resources**

1 On the Tools menu, click Level Resources, and then choose the leveling options you want.

2 Click Level Now.

164 **To examine project costs and display the project summary task**

1 On the View menu, click More Views, click Task Sheet, and then click the Apply button.

2 On the Tools menu, click Options.

3 In the Options dialog box, click the View tab.

4 Under the Outline Options For label, select the Show Project Summary Task check box, and then click the OK button.

5 On the View menu, point to Table: Entry, and click Cost.

165 **To check a project's finish date**

1 On the Project menu, click Project Information.

2 In the Project Information dialog box, click the Statistics button.

Chapter 10   Organizing and Formatting Project Details

170   **To sort data in a view**

1   Switch to the view or table you want to sort.

2   On the Project menu, point to Sort, and then click the field by which you want to sort the view. To specify a custom sort, click Sort By, and in the Sort dialog box, choose the options you want.

172   **To group data in a view**

1   Switch to the view or table you want to group.

2   On the Project menu, point to Group By: No Group, and then choose the criteria by which you want to group the view. To specify different grouping options, click Customize Group By, and then choose the options you want in the Customize Group By dialog box.

178   **To turn AutoFilter on or off**

Auto Filter

●   On the Formatting toolbar, click the AutoFilter button.

178   **To filter data in a view**

1   Switch to the view you want to filter.

2   On the Project menu, point to Filtered For, and click More Filters.

3   In the More Filters dialog box, choose the filter you want, and then click the Apply button.

179   **To create a custom filter**

1   On the Project menu, point to Filtered For: All Tasks (for task views) or All Resources (for resource views), and then click More Filters.

2   In the More Filters dialog box, click the New button.

3   In the Filter Definition dialog box, select the options you want.

180   **To remove a filter**

●   On the Project menu, point to Filtered For:<filter name>, and then click All Tasks (for task views) or All Resources (for resource views).

181   **To create a custom table**

1   On the View menu, point to Table: Entry, and then click More Tables.

2   In the More Tables dialog box, do one of the following:

■   To create a new table, click the New button.

■   To redefine a table, click the table's name, and then click the Edit button.

■   To create a new table based on another table, click the table's name, and then click the Copy button.

3   In the Table Definition dialog box, choose the options you want.

202 **To print a predefined report**

1 On the View menu, click Reports.

2 In the Reports dialog box, click the category of report you want, and then click the Select button.

3 In the dialog box that appears next, click the specific report you want to print, and click the Select button.

4 In the Print Preview window, click Print.

203 **To edit a predefined report**

1 On the View menu, click Reports.

2 In the Reports dialog box, click the category of report you want, and then click the Select button (or for custom reports, click the Preview button).

3 In the dialog box that appears next, click the specific report you want to edit, and then click the Edit button.

4 In the dialog box that appears next, choose the options you want.

Chapter 12 **Publishing Project Information Online**

Page 208 **To save a snapshot of a view as a GIF image**

1 Set up the view with the specific details (such as the table, filter, or group) you want.

Copy Picture

2 On the Standard toolbar, click the Copy Picture button.

3 Under the Render Image label, click To GIF Image File, and then specify the file name and location you want.

4 Select whatever other options you want, and click OK.

211 **To customize how Microsoft Project saves a Web page**

1 On the File menu, click Save As Web Page.

2 Specify the file name and location you want, and click the Save button.

3 In the Export Wizard, select the options you want.

Chapter 13 **Sharing Project Information with Other Programs**

Page 220 **To copy text from a Microsoft Project table to the Windows Clipboard**

1 Set up the table to display only the data you want to copy—for example, apply a filter or insert or hide columns.

2 Select the range of data you want to copy.

3 On the Edit menu, click Copy Cell, Copy Task, or Copy Resource.

221 **To copy a snapshot of a view to the Windows Clipboard**

1 Set up the view with the specific details (such as tables, filters, or groups) you want.

Copy Picture

2 On the Standard toolbar, click Copy Picture.

3 In the Copy Picture dialog box, click either For Screen, to optimize the snapshot for online viewing, or For Printer, to optimize it for printing.

4 Select whatever other options you want, and then click OK.

417

287 **To replace one resource with another**

1 On the View menu, click Task Usage.

2 Click the Task Name column heading.

Assign
Resources

3 On the Standard toolbar, click the Assign Resources button.

4 In the Assign Resources dialog box, in the Resource Name column, click the name of the resource you want to replace, and then click the Replace button.

5 In the Replace Resource dialog box, click the name of the replacement resource, and click OK.

290 **To filter for critical tasks**

● On the Project menu, point to Filtered For: All Tasks, and then click Critical.

290 **To enter overtime work values in the Task Form**

1 On the View menu, click Gantt Chart.

2 On the Window menu, click Split.

3 Click anywhere in the Task Form, on the Format menu, point to Details, and then click Resource Work.

4 In the Ovt. Work column for the resource to which you want to assign overtime work, enter the number of hours of overtime work you want.

Chapter 17 Applying Advanced Formatting

Page 298 **To format bar styles in a Gantt chart view**

1 On the Format menu, click Bar Styles.

2 In the Bar Styles dialog box, select the options you want.

302 **To display horizontal gridlines on the chart portion of a Gantt chart view**

1 On the Format menu, click Gridlines.

2 In the Lines To Change box, make sure that Gantt Rows is selected, and then in the Type box, click the type of line you want.

304 **To display the Unique ID value of each task in the Task Sheet**

1 On the View menu, click More Views.

2 In the More Views dialog box, click Task Sheet, and then click the Apply button.

3 Click the Task Name column heading.

4 On the Insert menu, click Column.

5 In the Field Name drop-down list, click Unique ID, and then click OK.

305 **To display the WBS code of each task in the Task Sheet**

1 On the View menu, click More Views.

2 In the More Views dialog box, click Task Sheet, and then click the Apply button.

3 Click the Task Name column heading.

4 On the Insert menu, click Column.

5 In the Field Name list, click WBS, and then click OK.

309 **To format boxes in the Network Diagram view**

1 On the View menu, click Network Diagram.

2 On the Format menu, click Box Styles.

3 In the Box Styles dialog box, select the options you want.

312 **To format bars in the Calendar view**

1 On the View menu, click Calendar.

2 On the Format menu, click Bar Styles.

3 In the Bar Styles dialog box, select the options you want.

Chapter 18 **Customizing Microsoft Project**

Page 319 **To copy a custom element from one project plan to another through the Organizer**

1 First open the project plan that contains the custom element (such as a custom table), and then open the project plan to which you want to copy the custom element.

2 On the Tools menu, click Organizer.

3 Click the tab name that corresponds to the type of custom element you want to copy.

4 In the <Custom Elements> Available In drop-down list on the left side of the Organizer dialog box, click the name of the project plan that contains the custom element.

5 Click the Copy button.

323 **To record a macro**

1 On the Tools menu, point to Macro, and then click Record New Macro.

2 In the Macro Name box, enter a name for the macro (no spaces allowed).

3 In the Store Macro In box, click This Project to store the macro in the active project plan, or Global File to store it in the global template.

4 Click OK.

5 Perform the actions you want recorded in the macro.

6 On the Tools menu, point to Macro, and then click Stop Recorder.

325 **To run a macro**

1 On the Tools menu, point to Macro, and then click Macros.

2 In the Macro Name box, click the name of the macro you want to run, and then click the Run button.

330   To edit a macro in the Visual Basic Editor

1   On the Tools menu, point to Macro, and then click Macros.

2   In the Macro Name box, click the name of the macro you want to edit, and then click the Edit button.

3   In the Visual Basic Editor, edit the macro.

4   On the File menu in the Visual Basic Editor, click Close And Return To Microsoft Project.

330   To create a custom toolbar

1   On the Tools menu, point to Customize, and then click Toolbars.

2   Click the Toolbars tab.

3   Click the New button.

4   In the Toolbar Name box, type the toolbar name you want, and then click OK.

332   To add a command to a custom toolbar

1   On the Tools menu, point to Customize, and then click Toolbars.

2   Click the Commands tab.

3   In the Categories list, click the category you want.

4   Drag the command you want from the Commands list to the custom toolbar.

333   To edit the graphic image and text that appears on a custom toolbar button

1   On the Tools menu, point to Customize, and then click Toolbars.

2   Click the Commands tab.

3   Click the custom button you want to modify in the custom toolbar.

4   Click the Modify Selection button, and then point to Change Button Image.

5   In the list of images that appears, click the image you want.

6   Click Modify Selection, and in the Name box, type the text you want for the custom button name.

Chapter 19   Measuring Performance with Earned Value Analysis

Page   **339   To set the project status date**

1   On the Project menu, click Project Information.

2   In the Project Information dialog box, in the Status Date box, type or click the status date you want, and click OK.

339   To view earned value schedule indicators

1   On the View menu, click More Views.

2   In the More Views dialog box, click Task Sheet and then click Apply.

3   On the View menu, point to Table: Entry, and click More Tables.

4   In the More Tables dialog box, click Earned Value Schedule Indicators, and click the Apply button.

341 **To view earned value cost indicators**

1 On the View menu, click More Views.

2 In the More Views dialog box, click Task Sheet and then click Apply.

3 On the View menu, point to Table: Entry, and click More Tables.

4 In the More Tables dialog box, click Earned Value Cost Indicators, and click the Apply button.

Chapter 20 **Consolidating Projects and Resources**

Page **347** **To create a resource pool**

1 Create a new project plan.

2 Save the new project plan that will become a resource pool.

3 Open one of the Microsoft Project plans you want to make a sharer plan.

4 On the Tools menu, point to Resource Sharing, and click Share Resources.

5 Under Resources For <Sharer Plan Name>, click Use Resources.

6 In the From list, click the name of your resource pool, and click OK to close the Share Resources dialog box.

7 If you have more than one sharer plan, open another sharer plan.

8 Repeat steps 3–7 for the other sharer plans.

351 **To view assignment details in the resource pool**

1 On the View menu, click Resource Usage.

2 In the Resource Name column, click the name of a resource.

3 On the Window menu, click Split to display the Resource Form.

353 **To update a resource's working time in the resource pool**

1 Open the resource pool as read-write.

2 On the View menu, click Resource Usage.

Resource
Information

3 In the Resource Name column of the Resource Usage view, click the name of the resource whose working time you want to change, and click the Resource Information button.

4 In the Resource Information dialog box, click the Working Time tab.

5 In the calendar below the Select Date(s) label, drag the vertical scroll bar or click the up or down arrow buttons until the month and year you want appears.

6 Click the dates you want to designate as nonworking time.

7 Under Set Selected Date(s) To, click Nonworking Time, and click OK to close the Resource Information dialog box.

255 **To update working time for all sharer plans from the resource pool**

1 Open the resource pool as read/write.

2 On the Tools menu, click Change Working Time.

3 In the Change Working Time dialog box, in the For box, click the base calendar you want to change, for example Standard (Project Calendar).

4 In the calendar below the Select Date(s) label, drag the vertical scroll bar or click the up or down arrow buttons until the month and year you want appears, and then click the specific days you want to make nonworking time.

5 Under Set Selected Date(s) To, click Nonworking Time.

6 Click OK to close the Change Working Time dialog box.

358 **To link new project files to the resource pool**

1 Open the resource pool as read/write.

New

2 On the Standard toolbar, click the New button.

3 On the Tools menu, point to Resource Sharing, and click Share Resources.

4 In the Share Resources dialog box, under Resources For <File Name>, click Use Resources.

5 In the From list, click the name of the resource pool, and click OK to close the Share Resources dialog box.

6 Save the sharer plan and resource pool.

360 **To edit a sharer plan and update the resource pool**

1 Open a sharer plan.

2 When prompted, open the resource pool.

3 In the sharer plan, make changes to assignments.

4 On the Tools menu, point to Resource Sharing, and click Update Resource Pool.

363 **To create a consolidated project plan**

New

1 On the Standard toolbar, click the New button.

2 Save the new project plan.

3 On the Insert menu, click Project.

4 In the Insert Projects dialog box, locate and click the Microsoft Project plan you want to insert into the consolidated project plan. To select multiple plans, hold down the Ctrl key while you click the name of each plan.

5 Click the Insert button.

366 **To create task dependencies between projects**

1 Open the two project plans between which you want to create a task dependency.

2 Switch to the project plan that contains the task you want to make the successor task.

3 On the View menu, click Gantt Chart.

4 Click the name of the task you want to make the successor task.

Task Information

5 On the Standard toolbar, click the Task Information button.

6 Click the Predecessors tab.

7 In the ID column, click the next empty cell below any other predecessor tasks, and enter the name of the predecessor task from the other project file in this format: Filename

8 Press Enter, and click OK to close the Task Information dialog box.

Glossary

accrual The method by which a project incurs the cost of a task or a resource. The three types of accrual are start, prorated, and end.

actuals The details about task completion recorded in a Microsoft Project plan. Prior to recording actuals, the project plan contains scheduled or planned information. Comparing planned project information to actuals helps the project manager better control project execution.

ACWP An earned value indicator; the acronym stands for Actual Cost of Work Performed. In earned value analysis, this is the actual costs of tasks that have been completed (or the portion completed of each) by the status date.

allocation The portion of the capacity of a resource devoted to work on a specific task.

assignment The matching of a work resource (a person or a piece of equipment) to a task. You can also assign a material resource to a task, but those resources have no effect on work or duration.

AutoFilter A quick way to view in a table only the task or resource information that meets the criteria you choose. To turn on AutoFilter, on the Project menu, point to Filtered For <filter name>, and then click AutoFilter. To filter a table with AutoFilter, click the arrow next to a column heading, and choose the criteria you want.

BAC An earned value indicator; the acronym stands for Budget At Completion. This is the same as baseline cost.

base calendar A calendar that can serve as the project calendar or a task calendar. A base calendar defines the default working times for resources. Microsoft Project includes three base calendars, named Standard, 24 Hours, and Night Shift. You can customize these, or you can use them as a basis for your own base calendar.

baseline The original project plan, saved for later comparison. The baseline includes the planned start and finish dates of tasks and assignments, as well as their planned costs. Microsoft Project plans can have up to 11 baselines.

BCWP An earned value indicator; the acronym stands for Budgeted Cost of Work Performed. In earned value analysis, this is the budgeted cost of tasks that have been completed (or the portion completed of each) by the status date. BCWP also is called earned value, because it represents the value earned in the project by the status date.

BCWS An earned value indicator; the acronym stands for Budgeted Cost of Work Scheduled. In earned value analysis, this is the portion of the project's budget that is scheduled to be spent by the status date.

bottom-up planning A method of developing a project plan that starts with the lowest-level tasks and organizes them into broad phases.

burdened labor rate   A resource cost rate that reflects not only the resource's direct pay-roll cost, but also some portion of the organization's costs not directly related to the resource's assignments on a project. Note that Microsoft Project doesn't support a bur-dened labor rate directly; if you want to use one, just enter it as a resource's standard or overtime cost rate.

calendar   The settings that define the working days and time for a project, resources, and tasks.

consolidated project   A Microsoft Project plan that contains one or more inserted project plans. The inserted projects are linked to the consolidated project so that any changes to the inserted projects are reflected in the consolidated plan, and vice versa. A con-solidated project plan is also known as a master project plan.

constraint   A restriction, such as Must Start On (MSO) or Finish No Later Than (FNLT), that you can place on the start or finish date of a task.

contour   The manner in which a resource's work on a task is scheduled over time. Microsoft Project includes several predefined work contours that you can apply to an assignment. For example, a back-loaded contour schedules a small amount of work at the beginning of an assignment, and then schedules increasing amounts of work as time progresses. You can also manually contour an assignment by editing work val-ues in a usage view, such as the Resource Usage. Applying a predefined contour or manually contouring an assignment causes Microsoft Project to display a work con-tour icon in the Indicators column.

Copy Picture   The feature that enables you to copy images and create snapshots of a view.

cost   The resources required to carry out a project, including the people who do the work, the equipment used, and the materials consumed as the work is completed. Cost is one side of the project triangle model.

cost rate table   The resource pay rates that are stored on the Costs tab of the Resource Information dialog box. You can have up to five separate cost rate tables per resource.

CPI   An earned value indicator; the acronym stands for Cost Performance Index. In earned value analysis, this is the ratio of budgeted to actual cost (CPI = BCWP/ACWP).

critical path   A series of tasks that, if delayed, will push out the end date of a project.

CV   An earned value indicator; the acronym stands for Cost Variance. In earned value analysis, this is the difference between budgeted and actual cost (CV = BCWP − ACWP).

CV%   The ratio of cost variance to BCWS, expressed as a percentage (CV% = [(BCWP − ACWP)/BCWP] x 100). This is an earned value indicator.

deadline   A date value you can enter for a task that indicates the latest date by which you want the task to be completed. Should the scheduled completion date of a task exceed its deadline, you are notified. The benefit of entering deadline dates is that they do not constrain tasks.

deliverable   The final product, service, or event a project is intended to create.

dependency   A link between a predecessor task and a successor task. A dependency controls the start or finish of one task relative to the start or finish of the other task. The most common dependency is finish-to-start, in which the finish date of the predecessor task determines the start date of the successor task.

destination program   The program you placed data into when exchanging data between Microsoft Project and another program.

duration   The span of working time you expect it will take to complete a task.

EAC   An earned value indicator; the acronym stands for Estimate At Completion. In earned value analysis, this is the forecasted cost to complete a task based on performance up to the status date (EAC = ACWP + (BAC − BCWP)/CPI).

earned value analysis   A sophisticated form of project performance analysis that focuses on schedule and budget performance as compared to baseline plans. Earned value uses your original baseline estimates and progress to date to show if you're ahead or behind schedule as compared with the actual costs incurred.

effort-driven scheduling   A scheduling method in which the work of a task remains constant regardless of the number of resources assigned to it. As resources are added to a task, the duration decreases, but the work remains the same and is distributed among the assigned resources. Effort-driven scheduling is the default scheduling method in Microsoft Project, but it can be turned off for any task.

elapsed duration   The amount of time it will take to finish a task, based on a 24-hour day and a 7-day week.

Entry table   The grid on the left side of the default Gantt Chart view.

export map   The specifications for exporting fields from Microsoft Project to other file formats, such as HTML. Microsoft Project includes several export maps, which you can use as they are or modify.

field   The lowest-level information about a task, resource, or assignment.

filtering   A way to see or highlight in a view only the task or resource information that meets the criteria you choose.

fixed consumption rate   A fixed quantity of a material resource to be consumed in the completion of an assignment.

fixed cost   A set amount of money budgeted for a task. This amount is independent of resource costs and task duration.

Fixed Duration   A task type in which the duration value is fixed. If you change the amount of work you expect a task to require, Microsoft Project recalculates units for each resource. If you change duration or units, Microsoft Project recalculates work.

Fixed Units   A task type in which the units value is fixed. If you change the duration of a task, Microsoft Project recalculates the amount of work scheduled for the task. If you change units or work, Microsoft Project recalculates duration.

Fixed Work   A task type in which the work value is fixed. If you change the duration of the task, Microsoft Project recalculates units for each resource. If you change units or work, Microsoft Project recalculates duration.

flexible constraint   A constraint type that gives Microsoft Project the flexibility to change the start and finish dates (but not the duration) of a task. As Soon As Possible (ASAP) and As Late As Possible (ALAP) are both flexible constraints.

free slack   The amount of time that a task can be delayed without delaying the start date of another task.

fully allocated   The condition of a resource when the total work of his or her task assignments is exactly equal to the work capacity of that resource.

Gantt Chart view   A predefined view in Microsoft Project consisting of a table (the Entry table by default) on the left and a graphical bar chart on the right that shows the project plan over time.

ghost task   A task that represents a link from one Microsoft Project plan to another. Ghost tasks appear as gray bars.

Global template   A Microsoft Project template named Global.mpt that contains the default views, tables, filters, and other items that Microsoft Project uses.

group   A way to reorder task or resource information in a table and display summary values for each group. You can specify several levels of groups. (The term group is also used to refer to the Resource Group field, which is unrelated.)

Group field   A field in which you can specify a group name (such as a department) with which you want to associate a resource. If you organize resources into groups, you can sort, filter, or group resources by group.

HTML template   A set of HTML tags and codes applied to Microsoft Project data as it's exported through a map. Microsoft Project includes several HTML templates, which you can use as they are or modify.

hyperlink   A link to another file, a specific location in a file, a page on the World Wide Web, or a page on an intranet.

import/export map   A set of specifications for importing specific data to or from Microsoft Project fields. Microsoft Project includes several built-in maps, which you can use as they are or modify. Import and export maps are sometimes referred to as data maps.

inflexible constraint   A constraint type that forces a task to begin or end on a certain date. Must Start On (MSO) and Must Finish On (MFO) are both inflexible constraints.

inserted project   A Microsoft Project plan that is inserted into another Microsoft Project plan, called a consolidated plan. An inserted project is also known as a subproject.

interim plan   A task's start and finish values, saved for later comparison. Each Microsoft Project plan can have, at most, 10 interim plans.

lag time   A delay between tasks that have a task relationship. For example, lag time causes the successor task in a finish-to-start relationship to begin some time after its predecessor task concludes.

lead time   An overlap between tasks that have a task relationship. For example, lead time causes the successor task in a finish-to-start relationship to begin before its predecessor task concludes. In the Microsoft Project interface, you enter lead time as negative lag time.

line manager   A manager of a group of resources; also called a functional manager. A line manager might also have project management skills and responsibilities, depending on the organization's structure.

link   A logical relationship between tasks that controls sequence and dependency. In the Gantt Chart and Network Diagram views, links appear as lines between tasks.

macro   A recorded or programmed set of instructions that carry out a specific action when initiated. Macros in Microsoft Project use Visual Basic for Applications.

mask   A tool used when working with outline codes or WBS codes to define the format of the code. Masks define the order and number of alphabetic, numeric, and alphanumeric strings in a code and the separators between them.

material resources   The consumables that are used up as a project progresses. As with work resources, you assign material resources to tasks. Unlike work resources, material resources have no effect on the total amount of work scheduled on a task.

maximum units   The maximum capacity (as entered into the Max Units field) of a resource to accomplish tasks. If you allocate the resource beyond capacity, Microsoft Project alerts you that the resource is overallocated.

milestone   A significant event that is reached within the project or imposed upon the project. In Microsoft Project, milestones are normally represented as tasks with zero duration.

negative slack   The amount of time that tasks overlap due to a conflict between task relationships and constraints.

Night Shift   A base calendar included with Microsoft Project designed to accommodate an 11:00 P.M.–8:00 A.M. "graveyard" work shift.

noncritical tasks   The tasks that have slack. Noncritical tasks can finish within their slack time without affecting the project completion date.

note   The information (including linked or embedded files) that you want to associate with a task, resource, or assignment.

OLE   A protocol that enables you to transfer information, such as a chart or text (called an object), to documents in different programs.

ongoing operation   An activity that has no planned end date and is repetitive in nature. Examples include accounting, managing human resources, and some manufacturing.

Organizer   A dialog box with which you can copy views, tables, filters, and other items between the Global.mpt template and other Microsoft Project plans, or between two different Microsoft Project plans.

outline   A hierarchy of summary tasks and subtasks within Microsoft Project, usually corresponding to major phases of work.

outline number   Numbers that indicate the position of a task in the project's hierarchy. For example, a task with an outline number of 4.2 indicates that it's the second subtask under the fourth top-level task.

overallocated   The condition of a resource when he or she is assigned to do more work than can be within the normal work capacity.

phase   A sequence of tasks that represent a major portion of the project's work. In Microsoft Project, phases are represented by summary tasks.

planning   The first major phase of project management work. Planning includes all the work in developing a project schedule up to the point where the tracking of actual work begins.

predecessor   A task whose start or end date determines the start or finish of another task or tasks, called successor tasks.

product scope   The quality, features, and functions (often called specifications) of the deliverable of the project.

program office   A department within an organization that oversees a collection of projects (such as producing wings and producing engines), each of which contributes to a complete deliverable (such as an airplane) and the organization's strategic objectives.

progress bar   A graphical representation on a bar in the Gantt Chart view that shows how much of a task has been completed.

project   A temporary endeavor undertaken to create a unique product or service.

project calendar   The base calendar that is used by the entire project. The project calendar defines normal working and nonworking days and times.

project scope   The work required to produce a deliverable with agreed-upon quality, features, and functions.

project summary task   A summary task that contains top-level information such as duration, work, and costs for the entire project. The Project summary task has a task ID of 0 and is displayed through the View tab of the Options dialog box, which is available by clicking the Options command on the Tools menu.

project triangle   A popular model of project management in which time, cost, and scope are represented as the three sides of a triangle. A change to one side will affect at least one of the other two sides. There are many variations on this model.

recurring task   A task that repeats at established intervals. You can create a recurring task that repeats for a fixed number of times or that ends by a specific date.

relationship   The type of dependency between two tasks, visually indicated by a link line. The types of relationships include finish-to-start, start-to-start, finish-to-finish, and start-to-finish. Also known as a link, a logical relationship, a task dependency, or a precedence relationship.

report   A format designed for printing. Microsoft Project includes several predefined reports, each focusing on specific aspects of your project data. You can also define your own reports.

resources   People, equipment, and material (and the associated costs of each) needed to complete the work on a project.

resource calendar   The working and nonworking days and times of an individual work resource.

resource leveling   A method of resolving resource overallocation by delaying the start date of an assignment or an entire task or splitting up the work on a task. Microsoft Project can level resources automatically or you can do it manually.

resource manager   A person who oversees resource usage in project activities specifically to manage the time and costs of resources. A resource manager might also have project management skills and responsibilities, depending on the organization's structure.

resource pool   A Microsoft Project plan that other projects use for their resource information. Resource pools contain information about resources' task assignments from all project plans (called sharer plans) linked to the resource pool.

risk   An event that decreases the likelihood of completing the project on time, within budget, and to specification.

scheduling formula   A representation of how Microsoft Project calculates work, based on the duration and resource units of an assignment. The scheduling formula is Duration × Units = Work.

scope   The products or services to be provided by a project, and the work required to deliver it. For project planning, it's useful to distinguish between product scope and project scope. Scope is one side of the project triangle model.

ScreenTip   A short description of an item on the screen, such as a toolbar, button, or bar. To see a ScreenTip, briefly point to an item.

semi-flexible constraint   A constraint type that gives Microsoft Project the flexibility to change the start and finish dates of a task within one date boundary. Start No Earlier Than (SNET), Start No Later Than (SNLT), Finish No Earlier Than (FNET), and Finish No Later Than (FNLT) are all semi-flexible constraints.

sequence   The chronological order in which tasks occur. A sequence is ordered from left to right in most views that include a timescale, for example, the Gantt Chart view.

sharer plan   A project plan that is linked to a resource pool. Sharer plans use resources from a resource pool.

shortcut menu   A menu you display by pointing to an item on the screen and then right-clicking. Shortcut menus contain only the commands that apply to the item to which you are pointing.

slack   The amount of time that a task can be delayed without delaying a successor task (free slack) or the project end date (total slack). Slack is also known as float.

sorting   A way of ordering task or resource information in a view by the criteria you choose.

source program   When exchanging data between Microsoft Project and another program, the program in which the data resided originally.

SPI   An earned value indicator; the acronym stands for Schedule Performance Index. In earned value analysis, this is the ratio of performed to scheduled work (SPI = BCWP/BCWS).

split   An interruption in a task, represented in the Gantt bar as a dotted line between segments of a task. You can split a task multiple times.

sponsor   An individual or organization that both provides financial support and champions the project team within the larger organization.

stakeholders   The people or organizations that might be affected by project activities (those who "have a stake" in its success). These also include those resources working on the project, as well as others (such as customers) external to the project work.

Standard base calendar   A base calendar included with Microsoft Project designed to accommodate an 8:00 A.M.–5:00 P.M. Monday through Friday work shift.

status date   The date you specify (not necessarily the current date) that determines how Microsoft Project calculates earned value indicators.

successor   A task whose start or finish is driven by another task or tasks, called predecessor tasks.

summary task   A task that is made up of and summarizes the subtasks below it. In Microsoft Project, phases of project work are represented by summary tasks.

SV   An earned value indicator; the acronym stands for Schedule Variance. In earned value analysis, this is the difference between current progress and the baseline plan (SV = BCWP – BCWS).

SV%   The ratio of schedule variance to BCWS, expressed as a percentage (SV% = SV/BCWS) x 100). This is an earned value indicator.

table   A spreadsheet-like presentation of project data, organized in vertical columns and horizontal rows. Each column represents one of the many fields in Microsoft Project, and each row represents a single task or resource. In a usage view, additional rows represent assignments.

task   A project activity that has a starting and finishing point. A task is the basic building block of a project.

task calendar   The base calendar that is used by a single task. A task calendar defines working and nonworking times for a task, regardless of settings in the project calendar.

task ID   A unique number that Microsoft Project assigns to each task in a project. In the Entry table, the task ID appears in the far left column.

task priority   A numeric ranking between 0 and 1000 of a task's importance and appropriateness for leveling. Tasks with the lowest priority are delayed or split first. The default value is 500.

task type A setting applied to a task that determines how Microsoft Project schedules the task, based on which of the three scheduling formula values is fixed. The three task types are fixed units, fixed duration, and fixed work.

TCPI An earned value indicator; the acronym stands for To Complete Performance Index. In earned value analysis, this is the ratio of remaining work to remaining budget, as of the status date (TCPI = (BAC-BCWP/(BAC-ACWP)).

template A Microsoft Project file format that enables you to reuse existing project plans as the basis for new project plans. Microsoft Project includes several templates that relate to a variety of industries, and you can create your own templates.

time The scheduled durations of individual tasks and the overall project. Time is one side of the project triangle model.

timephased field The task, resource, or assignment values that are distributed over time. The values of timephased fields appear in the timescale grid on the right side of views such as the Task Usage or Resource Usage.

timescale The timescale appears in views such as Gantt Chart and Resource Usage as a band across the top of the grid and denotes units of time. You can customize the timescale in the Timescale dialog box, which you can open from the Format menu.

top-down planning A method of developing a project plan by identifying the highest-level phases or summary tasks before breaking them into lower-level components or subtasks.

total slack The amount of time that a task can be delayed without delaying the project's end date.

tracking The second major phase of project management work. Tracking includes all the collecting, entering, and analyzing of actual project performance values such as work on tasks and actual durations.

underallocated The condition of a resource when he or she is assigned to do less work than can be within the normal work capacity. For example, a full-time resource who has only 25 hours of work assigned in a 40-hour workweek is underallocated.

Unique ID A permanent, sequential number that Microsoft Project generates each time a task, resource, or assignment is added to the project. Each Unique ID number is used only once.

units A standard way of measuring the capacity of a resource to work when you assign the resource to a task in Microsoft Project. Units are one variable in the scheduling formula: Duration × Units = Work.

variable consumption rate A quantity of a material resource to be consumed that will change if the duration of the task to which it is assigned changes.

VAC An earned value indicator; the acronym stands for Variance At Completion. In earned value analysis, this is the forecasted cost variance to complete a task based on performance up to the status date (VAC = BAC − EAC).

variance A deviation from the schedule or budget established by the baseline plan.

view A visual representation of the tasks or resources in your project. The three categories of views are charts, sheets, and forms. Views enable you to enter, organize, and examine information in a variety of formats.

work The total scheduled effort for a task, resource, resource assignment, or entire project. Work is measured in person-hours and might not match the duration of the task. Work is one variable in the scheduling formula: Duration × Units = Work.

Work Breakdown Structure (WBS) The identification of every task in a project that reflects that task's location in the hierarchy of the project.

work resources The people and equipment that do the work of the project.

workspace A set of project plans and settings that you can save and reopen by opening a single workspace file. Workspace files have the .mpw extension.

Index

A

abbreviations, time unit, 28
actual costs, manually entering, 247
actuals, 89
  collecting from resources, 252
  entering, 95–98
  reporting, with status dates, 255
  tracking, 93, 235
actual values. *See* tasks, actual values
actual work, 4
  timephased, tracking, 248
actual work values, entering for assignments, 251
adding. *See* entering, creating
adjusting. *See* changing
allocation
  adjusting, 158
  defined, 147
  maximum units, 148
  measuring, 155
  reducing, 154, 156
Analyze Timescaled Data Wizard, 232
applying
  constraints, 110
  contours to assignments, 138
  multiple cost rates, 141
Ask A Question box, 7
As Late As Possible constraint, 108
Assign Resources dialog box, 68
assigning base calendar to task, 117
assignment notes, 38
assignments
  accepting or rejecting, 392
  actual work values, entering, 251
  applying contours, 138
  changing in sharer plan, 352, 360
  creating, 58–60
  defined, 57
  delaying, 136
  deleting, 61
  deleting from resource pool, 362
  notes, 141
  notifying resources of, 392
  resource, and duration, 66–67

  resource, contouring, 49
  start times, default, 138
  start times, specifying, 138
  and tasks, breaking relationship, 252
  viewing, in resource pool, 351
  work values, entering, 245
As Soon As Possible constraint, 108
availability, resource, 43

B

base calendars, 20
  24 Hours, 20
  assigning, to task, 117
  changing, 54
  changing in resource pool, 355
  Night Shift, 20
  Standard, 20, 52
baselines, 90, 237, 257
  defined, 90
  vs. interim plans, 240
  multiple, saving, 91
  saving, 91, 237, 239
  task values, viewing, 92
  updating, 237
  updating, for selected tasks only, 239
  variance from, 258
bottom-up planning, 32
budget, decreasing, 389
burdened labor rates, 271

C

calculating
  costs, automatically, 247
  critical path, 112
  duration, 62
  project duration, 28
  units, 62
  work, 62
calendars, 19
  base (*see* base calendars)
  date, selecting, 18

  project (*see* project calendars)
  resource (*see* resources calendars)
Calendar view, 12–13
  formatting, 318
changing
  base calendars, 54
  default view, 72
  footers, 86
  headers, 86
  maximum units, 135
  nonworking time, 53–54
  pay rates, 133
  project scope, 16
  relationships, 105
  scheduling formula values, 120
  start dates, 17
  time units, 21
  working times, 20, 53–54
charts, 232
check boxes, selecting and clearing, 160
closing
  Project Guide, 14
  project plans, 16
collaboration. *See also* Microsoft Project Server
  choosing a solution for, 374
  enabling, 374
collapsing tasks, 249
column headings, selecting, 54
columns, inserting, 310
combination views, 13
communication, importance of, 257
completion percentage, 93–94
  evaluating, 99
  updating, 93–94
  viewing, 95
consolidated project plans
  benefits of, 363
  creating, 363
consolidated projects, adding project plan to, 364
constraints
  applying, 110
  driving, 279
  flexible, 108–9
  inflexible, 108, 110
  negative slack, 112
  semi-flexible, 108, 110

About the Authors

Carl S. Chatfield

Carl is the manager of the Project User Assistance team at Microsoft. Prior to working on Microsoft Project, Carl had worked on Microsoft Office applications since 1991. Carl is also a technical communication instructor at the University of Washington. He is a graduate of the Masters program in Technical Communication at the University of Washington and has been certified as a Project Management Professional (PMP) by the Project Management Institute. He lives in Kirkland, Washington.

Timothy D. Johnson

Tim is a technical editor in the Project User Assistance team at Microsoft. Prior to joining the Project User Assistance team in 2000, he was a Microsoft Project support professional for six years (going all the way back to Microsoft Project 3.0—if you called Microsoft Product Support Services with a Microsoft Project question, there's a good chance you talked to Tim). Tim lives in Issaquah, Washington.

Acknowledgments

The authors wish to thank their families for their patience while we developed this book. For Carl: thank you Rebecca, Alden, Lathan, and Mona. For Tim: thank you Ratsamy (Mimi), Brian, and Brenda.

The authors also wish to acknowledge the members of the Project Business Unit at Microsoft who provided valuable and timely answers to our technical questions—Adrian Jenkins in particular.

The manuscript for this book was prepared and galleyed using Microsoft Word 2000. Pages were composed by Online Training Solutions, Inc. (OTSI) using Adobe FrameMaker+SGML 6.0, with text in Garamond and display type in ITC Franklin Gothic. Composed pages were delivered to the printer as electronic prepress files.

Cover Designer

GIRVIN/Strategic Branding & Design

Interior Graphic Designer

James D. Kramer

OTSI Team

R.J. Cadranell

Liz Clark

Joyce Cox

Nancy Depper

Aaron L'Heureux

Martin Stillion

Lisa Van Every

Nealy White

Self-paced
training that works
as hard as you do!

Information-packed STEP BY STEP courses are the most effective way to teach yourself how to complete tasks with the Microsoft Windows operating system and Microsoft Office applications. Numbered steps and scenario-based lessons with practice files on CD-ROM make it easy to find your way while learning tasks and procedures. Work through every lesson or choose your own starting point—with STEP BY STEP'S modular design and straightforward writing style, *you* drive the instruction. And the books are constructed with lay-flat binding so you can follow the text with both hands at the keyboard. Select STEP BY STEP titles also prepare you for the Microsoft Office User Specialist (MOUS) credential. It's an excellent way for you or your organization to take a giant step toward workplace productivity.

Microsoft Press also has STEP BY STEP titles to help you use earlier versions of Microsoft software.

- **Home Networking with Microsoft® Windows® XP Step by Step**
  ISBN 0-7356-1435-0

- **Microsoft Windows XP Step by Step**
  ISBN 0-7356-1383-4

- **Microsoft Office XP Step by Step**
  ISBN 0-7356-1294-3

- **Microsoft Word Version 2002 Step by Step**
  ISBN 0-7356-1295-1

- **Microsoft Project Version 2002 Step by Step**
  ISBN 0-7356-1301-X

- **Microsoft Excel Version 2002 Step by Step**
  ISBN 0-7356-1296-X

- **Microsoft PowerPoint® Version 2002 Step by Step**
  ISBN 0-7356-1297-8

- **Microsoft Outlook® Version 2002 Step by Step**
  ISBN 0-7356-1298-6

- **Microsoft FrontPage® Version 2002 Step by Step**
  ISBN 0-7356-1300-1

- **Microsoft Access Version 2002 Step by Step**
  ISBN 0-7356-1299-4

- **Microsoft Visio® Version 2002 Step by Step**
  ISBN 0-7356-1302-8

microsoft.com/mspress

Work smarter—
conquer your
software *from the inside out!*

Hey, you know your way around a desktop. Now dig into Office XP applications and the Windows XP operating system and *really* put your PC to work! These supremely organized software reference titles pack hundreds of timesaving solutions, troubleshooting tips and tricks, and handy workarounds in a concise, fast-answer format. They're all muscle and no fluff. All this comprehensive information goes deep into the nooks and crannies of each Office application and Windows XP feature. INSIDE OUT titles also include a CD-ROM full of handy tools and utilities, sample files, an eBook links to related sites, and other help. Discover the best and fastest ways to perform everyday tasks, and challenge yourself to new levels of software mastery!

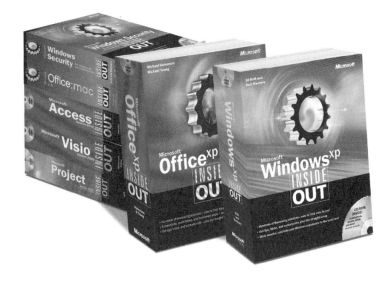

MICROSOFT® WINDOWS® XP INSIDE OUT
ISBN 0-7356-1382-6

MICROSOFT WINDOWS SECURITY INSIDE OUT FOR WINDOWS XP AND WINDOWS 2000
ISBN 0-7356-1632-9

MICROSOFT OFFICE XP INSIDE OUT
ISBN 0-7356-1277-3

MICROSOFT OFFICE V. X FOR MAC INSIDE OUT
ISBN 0-7356-1628-0

MICROSOFT WORD VERSION 2002 INSIDE OUT
ISBN 0-7356-1278-1

MICROSOFT EXCEL VERSION 2002 INSIDE OUT
ISBN 0-7356-1281-1

MICROSOFT OUTLOOK® VERSION 2002 INSIDE OUT
ISBN 0-7356-1282-X

MICROSOFT ACCESS VERSION 2002 INSIDE OUT
ISBN 0-7356-1283-8

MICROSOFT FRONTPAGE® VERSION 2002 INSIDE OUT
ISBN 0-7356-1284-6

MICROSOFT VISIO® VERSION 2002 INSIDE OUT
ISBN 0-7356-1285-4

MICROSOFT PROJECT VERSION 2002 INSIDE OUT
ISBN 0-7356-1124-6

microsoft.com/mspress

Target your problem and
fix it yourself—
fast!

When you're stuck with a computer problem, you need answers right now. TROUBLESHOOTING books can help. They'll guide you to the source of the problem and show you how to solve it right away. Get ready solutions with clear, step-by-step instructions. Go to quick-access charts with *Top 20 Problems* and *Prevention Tips*. Find even more solutions with *Quick Fixes* and handy *Tips*. Walk through the remedy with plenty of screen shots. Find what you need with the extensive, easy-reference index. Get the answers you need to get back to business fast with TROUBLESHOOTING books.

Microsoft®
microsoft.com/mspress

Work anywhere, anytime

with the Microsoft® guide to mobile technology

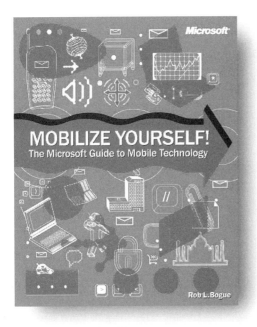

U.S.A. **$29.99**
Canada $43.99
ISBN: 0-7356-1502-0

Okay. You're at the airport but your flight has been delayed. For four hours. No worries—you've got your laptop so you're ready to work. Or are you? Can you connect to the Internet? What about reliable battery power? Here's the answer: MOBILIZE YOURSELF! THE MICROSOFT GUIDE TO MOBILE TECHNOLOGY. This comprehensive guide explains how to maximize the mobility of the technology you have today. And it provides smart answers about the mobile technologies and services you might be considering. From PDAs to the wireless Web, this book packs the insights and solutions that keep you—and your technology—up and running when you're out and about.

microsoft.com/mspress

Get a **Free**
e-mail newsletter, updates,
special offers, links to related books,
and more when you

register on line!

Register your Microsoft Press® title on our Web site and you'll get
a FREE subscription to our e-mail newsletter, *Microsoft Press
Book Connections.* You'll find out about newly released and upcoming
books and learning tools, online events, software downloads, special
offers and coupons for Microsoft Press customers, and information
about major Microsoft® product releases. You can also read useful
additional information about all the titles we publish, such as detailed book descriptions, tables of contents and indexes, sample
chapters, links to related books and book series, author biographies,
and reviews by other customers.

Registration is easy. Just visit this Web page and fill in your information:

http://www.microsoft.com/mspress/register

Microsoft®

Proof of Purchase

Use this page as proof of purchase if participating in a promotion or rebate offer on
this title. Proof of purchase must be used in conjunction with other proof(s) of
payment such as your dated sales receipt—see offer details.

Microsoft® Project Version 2002 Step by Step
0-7356-1301-X

CUSTOMER NAME

Microsoft Press, PO Box 97017, Redmond, WA 98073-9830

MICROSOFT LICENSE AGREEMENT
Book Companion CD

IMPORTANT—READ CAREFULLY: This Microsoft End-User License Agreement ("EULA") is a legal agreement between you (either an individual or an entity) and Microsoft Corporation for the Microsoft product identified above, which includes computer software and may include associated media, printed materials, and "online" or electronic documentation ("SOFTWARE PRODUCT"). Any component included within the SOFTWARE PRODUCT that is accompanied by a separate End-User License Agreement shall be governed by such agreement and not the terms set forth below. By installing, copying, or otherwise using the SOFTWARE PRODUCT, you agree to be bound by the terms of this EULA. If you do not agree to the terms of this EULA, you are not authorized to install, copy, or otherwise use the SOFTWARE PRODUCT; you may, however, return the SOFTWARE PRODUCT, along with all printed materials and other items that form a part of the Microsoft product that includes the SOFTWARE PRODUCT, to the place you obtained them for a full refund.

SOFTWARE PRODUCT LICENSE

The SOFTWARE PRODUCT is protected by United States copyright laws and international copyright treaties, as well as other intellectual property laws and treaties. The SOFTWARE PRODUCT is licensed, not sold.

1. **GRANT OF LICENSE.** This EULA grants you the following rights:

    a. **Software Product.** You may install and use one copy of the SOFTWARE PRODUCT on a single computer. The primary user of the computer on which the SOFTWARE PRODUCT is installed may make a second copy for his or her exclusive use on a portable computer.

    b. **Storage/Network Use.** You may also store or install a copy of the SOFTWARE PRODUCT on a storage device, such as a network server, used only to install or run the SOFTWARE PRODUCT on your other computers over an internal network; however, you must acquire and dedicate a license for each separate computer on which the SOFTWARE PRODUCT is installed or run from the storage device. A license for the SOFTWARE PRODUCT may not be shared or used concurrently on different computers.

    c. **License Pak.** If you have acquired this EULA in a Microsoft License Pak, you may make the number of additional copies of the computer software portion of the SOFTWARE PRODUCT authorized on the printed copy of this EULA, and you may use each copy in the manner specified above. You are also entitled to make a corresponding number of secondary copies for portable computer use as specified above.

    d. **Sample Code.** Solely with respect to portions, if any, of the SOFTWARE PRODUCT that are identified within the SOFTWARE PRODUCT as sample code (the "SAMPLE CODE"):

        i. **Use and Modification.** Microsoft grants you the right to use and modify the source code version of the SAMPLE CODE, *provided* you comply with subsection (d)(iii) below. You may not distribute the SAMPLE CODE, or any modified version of the SAMPLE CODE, in source code form.

        ii. **Redistributable Files.** Provided you comply with subsection (d)(iii) below, Microsoft grants you a nonexclusive, royalty-free right to reproduce and distribute the object code version of the SAMPLE CODE and of any modified SAMPLE CODE, other than SAMPLE CODE, or any modified version thereof, designated as not redistributable in the Readme file that forms a part of the SOFTWARE PRODUCT (the "Non-Redistributable Sample Code"). All SAMPLE CODE other than the Non-Redistributable Sample Code is collectively referred to as the "REDISTRIBUTABLES."

        iii. **Redistribution Requirements.** If you redistribute the REDISTRIBUTABLES, you agree to: (i) distribute the REDISTRIBUTABLES in object code form only in conjunction with and as a part of your software application product; (ii) not use Microsoft's name, logo, or trademarks to market your software application product; (iii) include a valid copyright notice on your software application product; (iv) indemnify, hold harmless, and defend Microsoft from and against any claims or lawsuits, including attorney's fees, that arise or result from the use or distribution of your software application product; and (v) not permit further distribution of the REDISTRIBUTABLES by your end user. Contact Microsoft for the applicable royalties due and other licensing terms for all other uses and/or distribution of the REDISTRIBUTABLES.

2. **DESCRIPTION OF OTHER RIGHTS AND LIMITATIONS.**

    - **Limitations on Reverse Engineering, Decompilation, and Disassembly.** You may not reverse engineer, decompile, or disassemble the SOFTWARE PRODUCT, except and only to the extent that such activity is expressly permitted by applicable law notwithstanding this limitation.

    - **Separation of Components.** The SOFTWARE PRODUCT is licensed as a single product. Its component parts may not be separated for use on more than one computer.

    - **Rental.** You may not rent, lease, or lend the SOFTWARE PRODUCT.

    - **Support Services.** Microsoft may, but is not obligated to, provide you with support services related to the SOFTWARE PRODUCT ("Support Services"). Use of Support Services is governed by the Microsoft policies and programs described in the user manual, in "online" documentation, and/or in other Microsoft-provided materials. Any supplemental software code provided to you as part of the Support Services shall be considered part of the SOFTWARE PRODUCT and subject to the terms and conditions of this EULA. With respect to technical information you provide to Microsoft as part of the Support Services, Microsoft may use such information for its business purposes, including for product support and development. Microsoft will not utilize such technical information in a form that personally identifies you.

- **Software Transfer.** You may permanently transfer all of your rights under this EULA, provided you retain no copies, you transfer all of the SOFTWARE PRODUCT (including all component parts, the media and printed materials, any upgrades, this EULA, and, if applicable, the Certificate of Authenticity), **and** the recipient agrees to the terms of this EULA.

- **Termination.** Without prejudice to any other rights, Microsoft may terminate this EULA if you fail to comply with the terms and conditions of this EULA. In such event, you must destroy all copies of the SOFTWARE PRODUCT and all of its component parts.

3. **COPYRIGHT.** All title and copyrights in and to the SOFTWARE PRODUCT (including but not limited to any images, photographs, animations, video, audio, music, text, SAMPLE CODE, REDISTRIBUTABLES, and "applets" incorporated into the SOFTWARE PRODUCT) and any copies of the SOFTWARE PRODUCT are owned by Microsoft or its suppliers. The SOFTWARE PRODUCT is protected by copyright laws and international treaty provisions. Therefore, you must treat the SOFTWARE PRODUCT like any other copyrighted material **except** that you may install the SOFTWARE PRODUCT on a single computer provided you keep the original solely for backup or archival purposes. You may not copy the printed materials accompanying the SOFTWARE PRODUCT.

4. **U.S. GOVERNMENT RESTRICTED RIGHTS.** The SOFTWARE PRODUCT and documentation are provided with RESTRICTED RIGHTS. Use, duplication, or disclosure by the Government is subject to restrictions as set forth in subparagraph (c)(1)(ii) of the Rights in Technical Data and Computer Software clause at DFARS 252.227-7013 or subparagraphs (c)(1) and (2) of the Commercial Computer Software—Restricted Rights at 48 CFR 52.227-19, as applicable. Manufacturer is Microsoft Corporation/One Microsoft Way/Redmond, WA 98052-6399.

5. **EXPORT RESTRICTIONS.** You agree that you will not export or re-export the SOFTWARE PRODUCT, any part thereof, or any process or service that is the direct product of the SOFTWARE PRODUCT (the foregoing collectively referred to as the "Restricted Components"), to any country, person, entity, or end user subject to U.S. export restrictions. You specifically agree not to export or re-export any of the Restricted Components (i) to any country to which the U.S. has embargoed or restricted the export of goods or services, which currently include, but are not necessarily limited to, Cuba, Iran, Iraq, Libya, North Korea, Sudan, and Syria, or to any national of any such country, wherever located, who intends to transmit or transport the Restricted Components back to such country; (ii) to any end user who you know or have reason to know will utilize the Restricted Components in the design, development, or production of nuclear, chemical, or biological weapons; or (iii) to any end user who has been prohibited from participating in U.S. export transactions by any federal agency of the U.S. government. You warrant and represent that neither the BXA nor any other U.S. federal agency has suspended, revoked, or denied your export privileges.

DISCLAIMER OF WARRANTY

NO WARRANTIES OR CONDITIONS. MICROSOFT EXPRESSLY DISCLAIMS ANY WARRANTY OR CONDITION FOR THE SOFTWARE PRODUCT. THE SOFTWARE PRODUCT AND ANY RELATED DOCUMENTATION ARE PROVIDED "AS IS" WITHOUT WARRANTY OR CONDITION OF ANY KIND, EITHER EXPRESS OR IMPLIED, INCLUDING, WITHOUT LIMITATION, THE IMPLIED WARRANTIES OF MERCHANTABILITY, FITNESS FOR A PARTICULAR PURPOSE, OR NONINFRINGEMENT. THE ENTIRE RISK ARISING OUT OF USE OR PERFORMANCE OF THE SOFTWARE PRODUCT REMAINS WITH YOU.

LIMITATION OF LIABILITY. TO THE MAXIMUM EXTENT PERMITTED BY APPLICABLE LAW, IN NO EVENT SHALL MICROSOFT OR ITS SUPPLIERS BE LIABLE FOR ANY SPECIAL, INCIDENTAL, INDIRECT, OR CONSEQUENTIAL DAMAGES WHATSOEVER (INCLUDING, WITHOUT LIMITATION, DAMAGES FOR LOSS OF BUSINESS PROFITS, BUSINESS INTERRUPTION, LOSS OF BUSINESS INFORMATION, OR ANY OTHER PECUNIARY LOSS) ARISING OUT OF THE USE OF OR INABILITY TO USE THE SOFTWARE PRODUCT OR THE PROVISION OF OR FAILURE TO PROVIDE SUPPORT SERVICES, EVEN IF MICROSOFT HAS BEEN ADVISED OF THE POSSIBILITY OF SUCH DAMAGES. IN ANY CASE, MICROSOFT'S ENTIRE LIABILITY UNDER ANY PROVISION OF THIS EULA SHALL BE LIMITED TO THE GREATER OF THE AMOUNT ACTUALLY PAID BY YOU FOR THE SOFTWARE PRODUCT OR US$5.00; PROVIDED, HOWEVER, IF YOU HAVE ENTERED INTO A MICROSOFT SUPPORT SERVICES AGREEMENT, MICROSOFT'S ENTIRE LIABILITY REGARDING SUPPORT SERVICES SHALL BE GOVERNED BY THE TERMS OF THAT AGREEMENT. BECAUSE SOME STATES AND JURISDICTIONS DO NOT ALLOW THE EXCLUSION OR LIMITATION OF LIABILITY, THE ABOVE LIMITATION MAY NOT APPLY TO YOU.

MISCELLANEOUS

This EULA is governed by the laws of the State of Washington USA, except and only to the extent that applicable law mandates governing law of a different jurisdiction.

Should you have any questions concerning this EULA, or if you desire to contact Microsoft for any reason, please contact the Microsoft subsidiary serving your country, or write: Microsoft Sales Information Center/One Microsoft Way/Redmond, WA 98052-6399.